Orientalische Religionen in der Antike

Ägypten, Israel, Alter Orient

Oriental Religions in Antiquity

Egypt, Israel, Ancient Near East

(ORA)

Herausgegeben von / Edited by

Angelika Berlejung (Leipzig)
Nils P. Heeßel (Marburg)
Joachim Friedrich Quack (Heidelberg)

Beirat / Advisory Board

Uri Gabbay (Jerusalem)
Michael Blömer (Aarhus)
Christopher Rollston (Washington, D.C.)
Rita Lucarelli (Berkeley)

49

Assaf Kleiman

Beyond Israel and Aram

The Archaeology and History of Iron Age
Communities in the Central Levant

Research on Israel and Aram in Biblical Times VI

Mohr Siebeck

Assaf Kleiman, born 1985; 2019 PhD; 2019–22 post-doctoral fellow of the Minerva Stiftung at Leipzig University; since 2022 Senior Lecturer at the Department of Archaeology, Ben-Gurion University of the Negev, Israel.
orcid.org/0000-0001-5267-7011

ISBN 978-3-16-161543-6 / eISBN 978-3-16-162012-6
DOI 10.1628/978-3-16-162012-6

ISSN 1869-0513 / eISSN 2568-7492 (Orientalische Religionen in der Antike)

The Deutsche Nationalbibliothek lists this publication in the Deutsche Nationalbibliographie; detailed bibliographic data are available at *http://dnb.dnb.de*.

© 2022 Mohr Siebeck Tübingen, Germany. www.mohrsiebeck.com

This book may not be reproduced, in whole or in part, in any form (beyond that permitted by copyright law) without the publisher's written permission. This applies particularly to reproductions, translations and storage and processing in electronic systems.

The book was printed on non-aging paper by Gulde Druck in Tübingen, and bound by Buchbinderei Spinner in Ottersweier.

Printed in Germany.

for Sabine and Irmi

Preface

This monograph is based on my Ph.D. dissertation written at Tel Aviv University under the guidance of Prof. Israel Finkelstein and Prof. Benjamin Sass. I wish to thank both of them for countless hours of fascinating conversations on archaeology, history, and modern life, and for making so many insightful comments on earlier drafts of my dissertation. Additional research, especially concerning the northern sectors of the Levant, was conducted during my postdoctoral studies at Leipzig University in 2020–2021. During these years, Prof. Angelika Berlejung, my host, was a source of tremendous support and constant encouragement in an ever-changing world.

It would not have been possible to accomplish the research without the help of my colleagues and friends (in alphabetic order): Prof. Erez Ben-Yosef (Tel Aviv University), Ms. Liora Bouzaglou (Tel Aviv University), Dr. Karen Covello-Paran (IAA), Prof. Alexander Fantalkin (Tel Aviv University), Dr. Liora Freud (Tel Aviv University), Dr. Ortal Harush (Hebrew University), Dr. Elon D. Heymans (Utrecht University), Dr. Ido Koch (Tel Aviv University), Prof. Aren M. Maeir (Bar-Ilan University), Ms. Myrna Pollak, Dr. Abra Spiciarich (Tel Aviv University), Ms. Juliane Stein (Leipzig University), Prof. Gunnar Lehmann (Ben-Gurion University of the Negev), and Prof. Jakob Wöhrle (University of Tübingen). Special thanks go to Dr. Eran Arie (Haifa University), Dr. Zachary C. Dunseth (Brown University), and Dr. Omer Sergi (Tel Aviv University) for showing good friendship all along the way. The following colleagues also graciously provided me with published and unpublished data: Ms. Deborah Ben-Ami (IAA), Prof. Amnon Ben-Tor (Hebrew University), Dr. Ron Beeri (IAA), Dr. Moshe Hartal (IAA), Dr. Jérôme Rohmer (CNRS), Ms. Debora Sandhaus (Tel Aviv University), Mr. Yosef Stepansky (IAA), Prof. Stefan Münger (University of Bern), Dr. Yifat Thareani (Hebrew Union College), Mr. Barak Tzin (IAA), and Dr. Šárka Velhartická (Ankara University). Prof. Oded Lipschits and Prof. Yuval Gadot (Tel Aviv University), in particular, offered much help and advice during my Ph.D. studies and afterward. Many of the ideas expressed in this book were presented in events of the Minerva Center for the Relations between Israel and Aram in Biblical Times (directed by Prof. Angelika Berlejung and Prof. Aren M. Maeir). The center has provided an excellent atmosphere for discussions on the archaeology and history of the Levant in the Bronze and Iron Ages. In the last decade, I benefited significantly from my work at Tel Megiddo. Although situated outside of the research area, the time in the field and the lab helped me to shape my understanding of the material culture of northern Israel in a considerable way. Apart from the people already mentioned above, I would like to thank Dr. Matthew J. Adams, Dr. Margaret C. Cohen (W.F. Albright Institute of Archaeological Research), Dr. Melissa Cradic

(University of Pennsylvania), Dr. Robert S. Homsher (University College London), Ms. Yana Kirilov, Dr. Mario A.S. Martin, and Ms. Naʻama Walzer (Tel Aviv University).

Financial support for the research was provided by the project, "The History of the Pentateuch: Combining Literary and Archaeological Approaches," funded by the Swiss National Science Foundation (Sinergia project CRSII1 160785/1). The project was directed by Konrad Schmid (University Zurich), Christophe Nihan, and Thomas Römer (University of Lausanne), and Israel Finkelstein and Oded Lipschits (Tel Aviv University). Additional funding was provided by a stipend from the School of Jewish Studies and Archaeology and the Minerva Stiftung, which generously supported my stay at Leipzig University. Special thanks go to Ms. Julia Lechler for helping with many administrative issues.

Finally, my most sincere thanks go to Sabine and Irmi, my beloved wife and daughter, *meine Liebe des Lebens*, without whom not a single word would have been written. Both made the present enjoyable and at least as mysterious as the past.

Assaf Kleiman
Tübingen, April 2022

Table of Contents

Preface VII

1. Introduction 1
    1.1. On the Formation of the Territorial Kingdoms 3
    1.2. In the Shadow of the Deuteronomistic History 4
    1.3. Between Israel and Aram-Damascus 6
        1.3.1. The 10th Century BCE 6
        1.3.2. The Early 9th Century BCE 8
        1.3.3. The Late 9th Century BCE 9
        1.3.4. The 8th Century BCE 9
        1.3.5. The Contribution of the Archaeological Research 10
    1.4. Geographical and Chronological Frameworks 11
        1.4.1. Defining the Central Levant 11
        1.4.2. The Chronology of the Iron Age 11
    1.5. Research Organization 16

Part I. The Settlement History 17

2. The Lebanese Beqaa 19
    2.1. Introduction 19
    2.2. Key Sites 20
        2.2.1. Tell Sugha 21
        2.2.2. Tell Qasr Labwa 21
        2.2.3. Baalbek 22
        2.2.4. Tell Hizzin 23
        2.2.5. Tell Hashbe 25
        2.2.6. Tell el-Ghassil 25
        2.2.7. Tell Barr Elyas 29

2.2.8.	Tell Dayr Zanun	29
2.2.9.	Tell Kamid el-Loz	30
2.2.10.	Tell Dibbin	32

2.3. Regional Synthesis 33

3. The Hula Valley 39

3.1. Introduction 39

3.2. Key Sites 40

3.2.1.	Tel Abel Beth-Maacah	42
3.2.2.	Tel Dan	43
3.2.3.	Tel Tannim	48
3.2.4.	Kiryat Shmona South	49
3.2.5.	Tel Anafa	49
3.2.6.	Tel Hazor	49
3.2.7.	Tel Ya'af	56
3.2.8.	Tel Ya'af South	57
3.2.9.	Rosh Pinna	57
3.2.10.	Tel Nes	57

3.3. Regional Synthesis 58

4. The Sea of Galilee 63

4.1. Introduction 63

4.2. Key Sites 64

4.2.1.	et-Tell/Bethsaida	65
4.2.2.	Tel Kinrot	67
4.2.3.	Tel Hadar	69
4.2.4.	Tel Soreg	72
4.2.5.	Tel Dover	73
4.2.6.	Tel 'Ein Gev	74

4.3. Regional Synthesis 77

5. The Golan Heights 82

5.1. Introduction 82

5.2. Key Sites 84

5.2.1.	Horvat Sa'ar	84

5.2.2. Mitzpe Golani	84
5.2.3. Bab el-Hawa	84
5.2.4. Metzad Yonathan	85
5.2.5. Rujm el-Hiri	85
5.2.6. Tell Shuqayyif	86
5.2.7. Tell Abu ez-Zeitun	87
5.2.8. Tel Nov	87
5.2.9. Khirbet 'Ain et-Taruq	88
5.3. Regional Synthesis	89
Excursus A: The Cities of the Land of Garu and the Golan Heights	94

6. The Nuqra Plain 96

6.1. Introduction	96
6.2. Key Sites	97
6.2.1. Tell ed-Dunayba	98
6.2.2. Qarrasa South	98
6.2.3. Sheikh Sa'ad	98
6.2.4. Tell ed-Dabba	100
6.2.5. Tell 'Ashtara	101
6.2.6. Tell el-Ash'ari	106
6.2.7. Sahem el-Jawlan	107
6.2.8. Tell esh-Shihab	107
6.2.9. Dar'a	108
6.2.10. Tayyiba	108
6.2.11. Busra esh-Sham	109
6.3. Regional Synthesis	109
Excursus B: In Search of the Archaeology of the Damascus Oasis	114

7. The Irbid Plateau 116

7.1. Introduction	116
7.2. Key Sites	117
7.2.1. Qwayliba	118
7.2.2. et-Turra	118
7.2.3. Tell el-Fukhar	118
7.2.4. Tell Irbid	119
7.2.5. Tell er-Rumeith	122
7.2.6. Tell Johfiyeh	125

	7.2.7. Tell el-Husn	127
7.3.	Regional Synthesis	127

Part II. The Material Culture ... 133

8. Architectural Styles ... 135

8.1. Introduction ... 135

8.2. Monumental Structures ... 135

    8.2.1. Bamah B at Tel Dan ... 137
    8.2.2. Building 8158 at Tel Hazor ... 137
    8.2.3. Citadel 3090 at Tel Hazor ... 138
    8.2.4. The Bit-Hilani at et-Tell/Bethsaida ... 138

8.3. Other Building Types ... 139

    8.3.1. Pillared Buildings ... 139
    8.3.2. Four-Room Houses ... 141

8.4. Residential Quarters ... 144

    8.4.1. Tell Kamid el-Loz ... 144
    8.4.2. Tel Dan ... 145
    8.4.3. Tel Hazor ... 145
    8.4.4. Tel Kinrot ... 146
    8.4.5. Tel Hadar ... 146

8.5. Summary ... 148

9. Ceramic Traditions ... 150

9.1. Introduction ... 150

9.2. Local Wares ... 151

    9.2.1. Serving Vessels ... 151
    9.2.2. Cooking Vessels ... 154
    9.2.3. Small Containers ... 156
    9.2.4. Storage Vessels ... 158
    9.2.5. Cult-Related Vessels ... 163

9.3. Imported Wares ... 165

    9.3.1. Phoenician Wares ... 165
    9.3.2. Philistine Wares ... 167

9.3.3. Cypriot Wares	167
9.3.4. Aegean Wares	168
9.4. Decoration Techniques	169
9.5. Summary	171

10. Monumental Art 173

10.1. Introduction 173

10.2. Architectural Elements 173

    10.2.1. Capitals 173
    10.2.2. Pillars 176
    10.2.3. Bases 177

10.3. Figurative Orthostats 177

    10.3.1. The Ruler Orthostat from Tell es-Salahiyeh 178
    10.3.2. Winged-Sphinx Orthostat from Damascus 179
    10.3.3. Lion Orthostat from Sheikh Sa'ad 179

10.4. Moon/Storm-God Steles 180

10.5. Summary 182

11. Mortuary Practices 183

11.1. Introduction 183

11.2. Intramural Burials 185

    11.2.1. Tell Hizzin 185
    11.2.2. Kiryat Shmona South 185
    11.2.3. Tel Kinrot 185
    11.2.4. Horvat Menorim 186
    11.2.5. Tel Soreg 186
    11.2.6. Tel Dover 186
    11.2.7. Tell 'Ashtara 187
    11.2.8. Tell Irbid 187

11.3. Burials Sites 188

    11.3.1. Tell es-Safa 188
    11.3.2. Jaz'ir 189
    11.3.3. Kir'ad el-Baqq'ara South 189
    11.3.4. Khirbet el-Lawziyeh 189
    11.3.5. Sahem el-Jawlan 190

11.4. Summary 190

12. Writing and Literacy 191

12.1. Introduction 191

12.2. Inscribed Objects 192

12.2.1. Distribution, Quantity, and Dating 192
12.2.2. The Function of the Inscribed Objects 193
12.2.3. The Content of the Inscriptions 195

12.3. Royal Inscriptions 198

12.3.1. Egyptian Inscriptions 198
12.3.2. The Tel Dan Inscription 199

12.4. Summary 200

Part III. Synthesis 203

13. Between Local and Foreign Rulers 205

13.1. Introduction 205

13.2. From Crisis to Collapse 206

13.2.1. The Crisis Days at the End of the Late Bronze Age 206
13.2.2. New Canaan in the Central Levant? 207
13.2.3. The Collapse of the Urban Societies in Canaan 209

13.3. Foreign Invasions and their Consequences 211

13.3.1. An Early Bird? Shoshenq I's Campaign(s) to Canaan 211
13.3.2. Political Statements in the Landscape 211
13.3.3. The Archaeology of the Days of Hazael 212

13.4. Shifting Alliances 216

13.4.1. The Rise and Fall of the Kingdom of Geshur 216
13.4.2. The Days of Joash and Jeroboam II 217
13.4.3. What Happened after 732 BCE? 221

13.5. The Long-Term Perspective 222

13.5.1. Demographic Changes 222
13.5.2. Economic Aspects 224
13.5.3. Dissemination of Writing 227
13.5.4. Cult-Related Activity 228

13.5.5. A Central Levantine Cultural Sphere?...229

14. Conclusions..231

Appendices...233

Appendix A: Iron Age Sites 235
A.1. The Lebanese Beqaa..236
A.2. The Hula Valley..239
A.3. The Sea of Galilee 242
A.4. The Golan Heights...243
A.5. The Nuqra Plain 249
A.6. The Irbid Plateau..251

Appendix B: Inscriptions and Inscribed Items..256

Appendix C: Short-Lived Radiocarbon Samples 262

Bibliography..265

Index of References 295

Index of Ancient Names and Places 297

Index of Modern Authors..304

1. Introduction

At the end of the second millennium BCE, far-reaching changes occurred in the cultural and political landscapes of the Levant. After several centuries of Hittite and Egyptian imperial domination, clan leaders expanded their political control far beyond the immediate vicinity of their hometowns, gradually creating large-scale entities often described in research as the territorial kingdoms of the Iron Age.[1] Historical sources, especially those from Syria and Anatolia, inform us that some of these rulers were descendants of royal families who survived the crisis at the end of the Late Bronze Age, while other kingdoms and royal dynasties were seemingly new on the stage of history.[2] Most of them maintained their political independence for several centuries until the Neo-Assyrian Empire completed its expansion to the west in the 8th–7th centuries BCE.

From a long-term perspective, the territorial kingdoms, especially those of the southern Levant, had a lasting impact on the culture and history of the Ancient Near East. In less than three centuries, they established relatively stable royal dynasties, initiated building projects, including sophisticated architecture and monumental art, constructed administrative centers and harbors, and even participated in long-distance trade of raw materials and prestige objects.[3] However, the cultural and economic prosperity of the territorial kingdoms also led to competition and rivalry. Military conflicts between neighboring polities were common and usually related to disputes over lands located at the edge of their political control.[4] At other times, primarily as the military pressure of the Assyrians increased, cross-regional coalitions were formed, although participation in these alliances was not always voluntary.[5] It was after nearly two centuries of more or less independent existence that the new policy of the Neo-Assyrian Empire led to the

---

[1] The political history of the territorial kingdoms has been discussed extensively. For studies that deal with the Neo-Hittite/Aramaean kingdoms of Syria and Anatolia, see Sader 1987; idem 2014a; Lipiński 2000; Younger 2016; Osborne 2021; for the Kingdom of Israel, see Finkelstein 1999a; idem 2013. Note that I refrain from using the term "state" in relation to the Levantine Iron Age kingdoms in order to differentiate them from the concept of "nation-states" of the modern era (Pfoh 2008, 111–112).

[2] For studies that discuss the end of the Bronze Age, see Ward/Joukowsky 1992; Cline 2014; Millek 2020; Knapp 2021 with a recent review of the literature. For the political continuity in the northern Levant in the early stages of the Iron Age, see Bryce 2012, 83–98; Weeden 2013, 6–10.

[3] In recent years, there has been a widespread agreement that copper was one of the most important raw materials originating in the Levant during the Iron Age. For the excavations carried out at the copper production sites in the Aravah Valley, see Levy/Najjar/Ben-Yosef 2014; Ben-Yosef 2016.

[4] Na'aman 1997, 125–126; Sader 2014a, 26; Sergi/de Hulster 2016.

[5] On forced participation in local alliances in the Ancient Near East, see Na'aman 1991.

collapse of many of the territorial kingdoms[6] and thus also to the conclusion of an important chapter in the history of the Levant.

In this book, I discuss the archaeology and history of the Iron Age communities located in the territories between the core regions of Israel and Aram-Damascus, two of the most influential kingdoms that emerged across the Levant (Figure 1). While the names of most of these communities remain unknown, a bottom-up approach to their settlement history and material culture reveals a distinct narrative that only at times intersected with the story of Israel and Aram-Damascus.[7] It produces, thus, a more complex understanding of the historical upheavals and power relations in the central Levant.

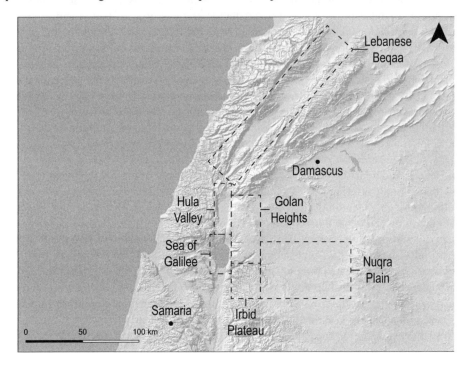

Figure 1: The central Levant with regions included in this study marked in dashed line (created with QGIS 3.16 and World Shaded Relief of Esri 2014)

---

[6] For overviews of the Assyrian policy in the west, see Berlejung 2012; Aster/Faust 2018.

[7] In the last years, it became evident that the attempts to reconstruct large-scale identities based on material culture (e.g., "Israelites" or "Aramaeans") ultimately lead to dead ends and generate frustration (see especially Bonatz 2019 in relation to the so-called material culture of the Aramaeans; see also Frevel 2018a, 217). Against this background, A.M. Maeir (2021, 143) has recently suggested abandoning what he calls "grand narratives" in favor of bottom-up archaeological reconstructions.

1.1 On the Formation of the Territorial Kingdoms

Conventionally, the formation of territorial kingdoms in the Levant has been understood in neo-evolutionary terms as the development of rural kin-based populations into urban societies, which together formed a highly centralized political entity.[8] Some scholars emphasized the role of environmental conditions, while others highlighted the ethnic or social ties of the local populations,[9] but the basic theory remained the same.

In the last few decades, the traditional approaches to Ancient Near East state-formation processes have been challenged. It has been argued that ancient polities, the Iron Age kingdoms of the Levant among them, should not be viewed as a reflection of modern national states but rather be understood in social terms that fit past societies.[10] Following Max Weber, several scholars proposed that the social and political structures of Ancient Near Eastern societies were always kin-based and that the understanding of authority did not depend on their socio-economic mode.[11] Others, who discussed the nature of the relationship between rulers and the populations living in their domain, argue that the political hierarchy in ancient kingdoms should be seen as patronage relations.[12] According to this view, the king, who stood at the top of the political hierarchy, and various local clan leaders were bonded in a patron-client relationship that imposed reciprocity on both sides, usually in the form of political or economic exchange.[13]

All of these new concepts, well-received and gradually adopted by many historians and archaeologists,[14] force us to rethink the formation of Israel and Aram-Damascus, and particularly, the meaning of the territorial expansion of these kingdoms into the central Levant. The Israelite and Damascene monarchs apparently established their authority over this region by forming (or enforcing) alliances with numerous clan leaders with whom they did not necessarily have previous contacts.[15] With these thoughts in mind, it is apparent why the history and archaeology of the Iron Age communities in the

---

[8] For the history of the conventional paradigm, see Master 2001, 123–128; more broadly, VanValkenburgh/Osborne 2013, 3–7. See also Osborne 2021, 9–11.

[9] E.g., Finkelstein 1988; Knauf 1992; Joffe 2002; Faust 2006.

[10] Stager 1985, 25; idem 2003; Master 2001; Schloen 2001; most recently, Thomas 2021.

[11] Master 2001, 128–130; Schloen 2001, *passim*.

[12] E.g., Pfoh 2009; Sergi/de Hulster 2016. Based on an analysis of the Mesha Stele, it has been argued that the entities involved usually formed from the integration of earlier and smaller in size political associations (Routledge 1997; idem 2004; see also Sergi/de Hulster 2016, 2).

[13] Niemann 2008; Nam 2012 (both based on the Samaria Ostraca). See also Master 2014, 83–85.

[14] In light of these new advances, A.M. Maeir and I. Shai (2016) argued that the Kingdom of Judah was established on alliances between the royal dynasty in Jerusalem and strong clans in the south, including ones that formerly prospered under Philistine Gath's shadow (see also Shai/Maeir 2018 with some updates). For a similar argument regarding the Kingdom of Geshur, see Sergi/Kleiman 2018.

[15] A particularly relevant historical example of such a process is the case of Dahir al-'Umar, a local leader that was active in the Lower Galilee in the late 17th and 18th centuries CE. At that time, the imperial control of the Ottoman Empire over Palestine weakened, and through a series of alliances with local tribes, he succeeded in imposing his political authority over the Galilee, the coast, and even parts of the highlands (Niemann 1997, 265–267; Joudah 1987). For similar case studies from the Ottoman period, see Marfoe 1979a, 25 (on the rise of Fakhar ed-Din II); Arie 2011, 71–72 (on the rise of Aqil Agha); Thareani 2019a, 193–196 (on the rise of the el-Fa'our family).

central Levant should not be reconstructed through the lens of the elite groups who subjugated them, i.e., the Hebrew Bible, but rather on finds from the central Levant itself.

1.2 In the Shadow of the Deuteronomistic History

The Hebrew Bible, and more specifically, the parts associated by scholars with the Deuteronomistic History, had and still has an overwhelming lingering influence on the interpretation of the history and archaeology of Iron Age communities in the central Levant. By adhering to the biblical narratives, it has often been assumed that at the end of the second millennium BCE, territories such as the Hula Valley and Golan Heights were repopulated by foreign people, sometimes designated Proto-Israelites.[16] As the Hebrew Bible mentions the presence of Canaanite populations in the central Levant, as well as local allegedly Aramaean kingdoms (e.g., Jos 13:13), scholars have been forced to acknowledge the existence of local enclaves in this region. However, they have downplayed their socio-cultural and political impact to the minimum.[17] It is also frequently assumed that with the establishment of David and Solomon's United Monarchy, the settled populations, who until then lived in kin-based rural settlements, underwent rapid urbanization and constructed elaborate cities and cultic centers. And for the most part, these settlements developed without much disturbance until the late 8th century BCE.

Fieldwork carried out at prominent sites in the central Levant, especially Tel Hazor and Tel Dan, revealed detailed stratigraphic sequences and many finds,[18] generally interpreted to line up with the main stages in the biblical history of Ancient Israel. First, the decline of the Canaanite city-states in the 13th century BCE and the destruction of Stratum XIII at Tel Hazor were correlated to the conquest narrative (e.g., Jos 11). Second, the appearance of many rural settlements in the 12th–11th centuries BCE and the so-called Israelite material culture in some sites (e.g., Strata VI–IVB at Tel Dan and Strata XII–XI at Tel Hazor) was evidence of the settlement of the tribes (e.g., Judg 18). Third, monumental architecture at Tel Hazor (Strata X–IX) represented the establishment of David and Solomon's kingdom (e.g., 1 Kgs 9:15) and the development of the northern cities (e.g., Strata VIII–V at Tel Hazor or Strata IVA–II at Tel Dan) reflected the prosperity of the Northern Kingdom in the 9th–8th centuries BCE (e.g., 2 Kgs 14:25). Fourth, the destruction of northern cities (e.g., Stratum V at Tel Hazor and Stratum II at Tel Dan) was correlated to the Assyrian conquests of 732 BCE (e.g., 2 Kgs 15:29).

Biblical scholars today agree that most of the relevant biblical accounts, specifically those originating from the Deuteronomistic school, were committed to writing many years after the fall of the Northern Kingdom (and sometimes even centuries after the

---

[16] Dever 2003, 194–200. For problems with the term Proto-Israelites, see Kletter 2006.

[17] E.g., Mazar *et al.* 1964; Kochavi 1989; Lemaire 2019, 249–250.

[18] For the most up-to-date information regarding the Iron Age at Hazor, see Ben-Tor/Ben-Ami/Sandhaus 2012; Ben-Tor 2016, 118–166. The Iron Age I finds revealed in the old excavations at Tel Dan were recently published (Ilan 2019a), and the Iron Age II remains are currently being prepared for final publication by Y. Thareani (for preliminary reports on the finds, see idem 2016a; idem 2016b).

periods they allegedly described).¹⁹ Consequently, these texts reflect a combination of the theological ideology of the authors and the historical reality of their days and not of earlier periods. Moreover, the authors never intended to write a political history of Israel and Judah in the modern sense, nor did they plan to sketch a social history of Canaan or systematically describe the different identities that existed in the region or beyond (and this is without even delving into the hermeneutical issues relating to the meaning of identity in ancient societies).²⁰ The biblical authors selectively reworked ancient sources that were available to them in order to promote their theological ideas. Detailed descriptions of non-Judahite identities (and histories) were, therefore, of little importance to the authors, especially groups that prospered many years before their time or those located far to the north, on which they knew very little.²¹

Archaeological research has also contributed significantly to the collapse of this conventional paradigm. Most scholars agree that the Late Bronze Age city-states declined over several decades²² and especially that this process was a broad Eastern Mediterranean phenomenon.²³ The appearance of the new villages in the central hill country and beyond is regarded nowadays as the result of a complex and cyclical set of socio-economic processes resulting in the archaeological visibility of local groups already there (and such developments were neither unique to the highlands nor to the Iron Age I).²⁴ Changes in the absolute dates of Iron Age ceramic horizons, many of which are enjoying widespread consensus, called for parting from the traditional interpretation of David and Solomon's kingdom, leaving little material evidence supporting a large-scale polity centered in Jerusalem.²⁵ Nothing in the excavations carried out in the city or its countryside justify the reconstruction of the early monarchy as depicted in the Hebrew Bible.²⁶ Even the impressive finds from Samaria, which by far surpass those found in the extensively-excavated Jerusalem, do not facilitate the reconstruction of a large-scale entity without

---

[19] E.g., Na'aman 1994; idem 2007, 387–388; Finkelstein/Silberman 2002; Mazar 2014, 347–349.

[20] Maeir 2019; idem 2021 with detailed discussion and updated literature.

[21] Na'aman 2002a; idem 2016a, 131.

[22] E.g., Finkelstein 1988, 295–302; Dever 2003, 37–74; Faust 2006, 176; Mazar 2014, 349.

[23] Ward/Joukowsky 1992; Cline 2014; Knapp 2021 with an extensive list of earlier studies.

[24] Finkelstein 1988. For a similar phenomenon in the northern Levant, see Schwartz 1989. Recently, Y. Gadot (2017) proposed that the settlement of rural settlements in the highlands could also be linked to the expansion of the urban sector of the Iron Age cities (e.g., the city-state of Shechem).

[25] E.g., Wightman 1990; Finkelstein 2010a; idem 2019; Herzog/Singer-Avitz 2004. For other viewpoints on Jerusalem (and its monuments) in the 10th century BCE, see Sergi 2017; Mazar 2020a.

[26] Herzog/Singer-Avitz 2004; Lehmann 2004; Finkelstein 2011a; Maeir 2012; Sergi 2013; Na'aman 2013; Lehmann/Niemann 2014; and see, in particular, Gadot/Uziel 2017 for the few pre-late 8th century BCE monuments that were found in the city. In the past few years, several archaeologists working in lowland sites (Beth-Shemesh, Khirbet Qeiyafa, and Tel 'Eitun) argued that there is sufficient evidence for reconstructing a large-scale kingdom centered in Jerusalem as early as the 10th century BCE (Bunimovitz/Lederman 2001; Garfinkel *et al.* 2016; Faust/Sapir 2018). However, the dating of some of the finds to the 10th century BCE (e.g., Building 101 at Tel 'Eitun) is highly problematic (Shai/Maeir 2018, n. 6; Finkelstein 2020). In other cases, with more secure dating (e.g., Khirbet Qeiyafa), the connection of the finds to the highlands, rather than to a local polity, is unproven (Na'aman 2010a; idem 2017a; Koch 2012, 54–56; idem 2021, n. 10; Lehmann/Niemann 2014, 86; Niemann 2017; for the alternative reconstructions, see Garfinkel *et al.* 2016; Fantalkin/Finkelstein 2017; Faust 2020).

the evidence from the lowlands (e.g., Tel Hazor, Tel Megiddo, and Tel Gezer).[27] After all, it is the political influence and impact over territories located beyond its immediate vicinity that differentiate a territorial kingdom from a city-state.[28]

Altogether, a reconstruction of the settlement history of Iron Age communities in the central Levant based solely on biblical evidence is methodologically unsound and, in essence, subjugates the local narratives to those of the ruling elites. Here, I intended to reproduce a narrative based on the material remains found in those communities while not ignoring the historical fact that for an extended period, they were indeed ruled by the elites who emerged in the Samaria Highlands and the Damascus Oasis. While it is clear that the interpretation of the archaeological record is not problem-free,[29] it still provides discrete evidence collected from the investigated societies themselves.

1.3 Between Israel and Aram-Damascus

Biblical and extra-biblical texts suggest that Israel and Aram-Damascus competed over the political control of the territories and communities located between them for most of their existence. Interpreting these textual sources is not always easy, especially in the case of biblical narratives that allegedly describe 10th and early 9th centuries BCE realities. Nevertheless, from the mid-9th century BCE, there is more or less a consensus among scholars on the sequences of events and the frequent changes in the power balance between the two kingdoms (Figure 2).[30]

1.3.1 The 10th Century BCE

Biblical references to early events in the history of Israel and Aram-Damascus are surprisingly plentiful, especially compared to the limited information on the first half of the 8th century BCE.[31] Having said that, most scholars also agree that these accounts are colored by the ideologies of the biblical authors in the late monarchic period, as well as conflated by the passage of many generations before they were written, as mainly expressed in the depiction of David and Solomon's kingdom. Consequently, the historical reliability and chronological setting of nearly every event that refers to the time before the mid-9th century BCE have been questioned and depend entirely on one's approach to the biblical materials. Scholars who support the existence of a large-scale territorial entity ruled from Jerusalem in the early 10th century BCE usually accept the description of David's wars against the kingdoms of Beth-Rehob and Aram-Damascus (2 Sam 8:3;

---

[27] On the excavations, see Tappy 1992; Franklin 2004; Finkelstein 2011b; Sergi/Gadot 2017.

[28] For a comparison between the case of Labayu, almost certainly the ruler of Shechem in the 14th century BCE, and the territorial expansion of the Northern Kingdom, see Finkelstein/Na'aman 2005.

[29] Na'aman 2010b, and especially, Pioske 2019 with detailed discussion.

[30] The literature on the relations between Israel and Aram, especially during Hazael's reign, is particularly extensive. For historical reevaluations from the last decades, see Pitard 1987; Lemaire 1991; idem 2019; Lipiński 2000, 367–470; Hafthorsson 2006; Niehr 2011; Hasegawa 2012; Ghantous 2013; Berlejung 2014; Younger 2016, 564–652; Frevel 2018, 213–221; idem 2019a; Zwickel 2019.

[31] See summaries in Hafthorsson 2006, 137–184; Lemaire 2019; Zwickel 2019.

1 Kgs 11:23–24) as reflecting historical reality, and only minor details in some of the narratives are questioned.³² According to this line of interpretation, more clues for the United Monarchy's territorial extent during the 10th century BCE can be gleaned from the following accounts: 1) David's marriage to the daughter of the king of Geshur (2 Sam 3:3), 2) the list of the cities built by Solomon (1 Kgs 9:15), and 3) the description of Sheba's revolt and his flight to Abel Beth-Maacah (2 Sam 20). Based on these sources, it has been assumed that in the 10th century BCE, the Hula Valley and nearby regions were included within the extent of the United Monarchy and that these territories were inherited by the north-Israelite kings (see, e.g., 1 Kgs 12:26–33; 1 Kgs 15:20).³³

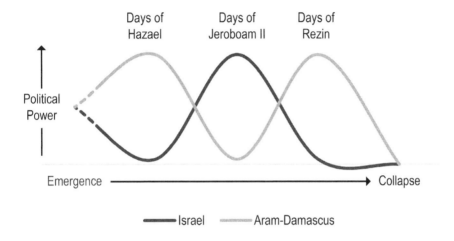

Figure 2: Schematic illustration of the shifting power balance between Israel and Aram

An utterly different picture is drawn by scholars who do not accept the historicity of the United Monarchy and question the reliability of at least some of the events associated with the 10th and early 9th centuries BCE.³⁴ I. Finkelstein, for instance, has contested the traditional view presented above in a series of articles and books, arguing that the Northern Kingdom expanded its political influence to the far north only after the rise of the Omride Dynasty in Samaria.³⁵ Furthermore, he asserted that these regions were previously ruled by local city-states, similar to those encountered in the Jezreel Valley (e.g., Stratum VIA at Megiddo or Stratum XVII at Tel Yoqneʻam).³⁶ In addition, most of the critical scholars dismiss today the accounts of 1 Kgs 12:26–33 (the construction of the

---

³² Younger 2016, 565–571; Lemaire 2019, 246–250; Zwickel 2019, 272–274.
³³ See, e.g., Ben-Tor 2000, 11; Lipiński 2000, 372; Hafthorsson 2006, 143–144; Younger 2016, 571–580; Lemaire 2019, 250–251; Zwickel 2019, 274–275; Yahalom-Mack et al. 2021.
³⁴ See, e.g., Finkelstein 2011c; idem 2013; idem 2016a; Naʼaman 2002b; idem 2007; idem 2012; idem 2017b; Arie 2008; Hasegawa 2012; Berlejung 2009; idem 2014; Sergi 2015, 60–62.
³⁵ Finkelstein 2011c, 230–231; idem 2013, 74–76; idem 2016a. See also Arie 2008.
³⁶ Finkelstein 1999b, 59–60; idem 2017 (see also Kleiman 2019a; idem 2019b). For a comprehensive discussion of the archaeology and history of the Jezreel Valley in the Iron Age I, see Arie 2011.

cult centers in Bethel and Dan) and 1 Kgs 15:20 (Ben-Hadad I's campaign) as reliable sources for reconstructing events in the late 10th/early 9th centuries BCE.[37]

1.3.2 The Early 9th Century BCE

As already stated above, more agreement exists in regard to the reliability of events that occurred in the first half of the 9th century BCE, many of which are also mentioned in extra-biblical sources. For instance, there is a wide consensus that the military campaigns of the Assyrians to the west in the days of Shalmaneser III forced some cooperation between the local kingdoms. The Kurkh Monolith particularly provides a unique snapshot of these local alliances, revealing, *inter alia*, an interesting collaboration between Israel and Aram-Damascus.[38] Both kingdoms fought side by side against the Assyrians in the Orontes Valley in 853 BCE. However, the cooperation between them did not last long. A decade later, around 842/841 BCE, Joram and Ahaziah attacked Ramoth-Gilead (1 Kgs 22), a Damascene stronghold in the Irbid Plateau.[39] From a historical perspective, the battle was disastrous for the Israelite monarchy. Besides the probable death of Joram and Ahaziah,[40] the remaining heirs of the Omride Dynasty fell victim to a rebellion led by Jehu (2 Kgs 9), a military official and a member of an influential clan named Nimshi, which most likely resided in the Beth-Shean Valley.[41]

---

[37] Note that while the construction of the cult centers in Bethel and Dan by Jeroboam I can hardly be taken as representing 10th century BCE reality (for the biblical materials, see Berlejung 2009; for the archaeological remains from Tel Dan and Bethel, see Arie 2008; Finkelstein/Singer-Avitz 2009, respectively), the description of the cities conquered by Ben-Hadad I (1 Kgs 15:20) could be understood as an older, fragmentary source that was compiled using later materials, such as the list of towns conquered by Tiglath-Pileser III in 2 Kgs 15:29 (Na'aman 2007, 406; Sergi 2015, 60–62).

[38] Grayson 1996, 11, 24. This alliance must have been a temporary arrangement, as in the following years, the Northern Kingdom did not fight against the Assyrians (Lipiński 1977, 273–274).

[39] During the 838/837 BCE military campaigns of the Assyrians against Aram-Damascus, Israel's northeastern border was located to the west of the Hauran (and probably also to the west of the Jordan River as was the case in the late 8th century BCE). In the royal annals of Shalmaneser III, he mentions two main Damascene cities in addition to the capital: Danabu and Malaha (Grayson 1996, 79; Yamada 2000, 205–209). The exact location of these cities is disputed, but most scholars place them in the Nuqra Plain, east of the Ruqqad River (for discussions, see Lipiński 2000, 350–354; Hasegawa 2012, 55–58; Na'aman 2012, 92–93; Younger 2016, 558–564; Lemaire 2019, 255; Zwickel 2019, 277–278). As of today, the easternmost identification for Malaha is in Malah es-Sarrar, a small village in the eastern part of Jabal ed-Druz (Sader 1987, 266). No mound was reported in the village itself, but scholars, who visited the Hauran at the beginning of the 20th century CE, mentioned that about 1.6 km to the northeast, there is a 60 m high hill with ancient architectural remains that is called Tell el-Mujedda (Butler/Norris/Stoever 1930, 29). Another archaeological site in the vicinity of Malah es-Sarrar exists *ca.* 7 km to the north of the village and is called Hebike. It was surveyed by F. Braemer (1993, 144), who reported the existence of Iron Age sherds and a 'cyclopean' wall which he dates to the Middle Bronze Age. Danabu should most likely be identified with Tell ed-Dunayba near Izraa (e.g., Lemaire 2019, 255) or with Tell ed-Dabba, *ca.* 30 km to the east (e.g., Rohmer 2020, 235).

[40] Lipiński 1977, 274–275; Na'aman 2000, 104; Sergi 2016 with earlier references.

[41] For a reevaluation of the relations between Israel and Aram during the time of the Nimshide kings, see Hasegawa 2012. For the possible background of Jehu, see Mazar 2016, 110. Interestingly, the events associated with this *coup d'état* seem to be remembered in the north for many years (Hos 1:4).

1.3.3 The Late 9th Century BCE

The dominance of Aram-Damascus in the second half of the 9th century BCE, during the reign of Hazael, is attested by many biblical and extra-biblical sources (especially the Tel Dan Stele, but also by Hazael's Booty Inscriptions) and is accepted by many scholars.[42] During the years, scholars even characterized Aram-Damascus of Hazael's reign as a mini-empire, a description that may be justified bearing in mind the inconsistent use of the term in the current historical and archaeological literature.[43] References to the political supremacy of Aram-Damascus during the reign of Hazael are also common in the biblical sources (e.g., 2 Kgs 12:18; 13:3, 22; Amos 1:3; 6:2). All of this means that during most of the reigns of Jehu and Jehoahaz, the political control of Israel was perhaps limited to the Samaria Highlands and its immediate vicinity.

1.3.4 The 8th Century BCE

Our historical information regarding the relations between Israel and Aram-Damascus in the 8th century BCE is surprisingly low.[44] However, it is clear that the superiority of Aram-Damascus obviously did not last long, and towards the end of the 9th century BCE, the Kingdom of Israel struck back, probably exploiting Hazael's death (*ca.* 805) and the renewal of the military campaigns of the Assyrians to the west in the days of Adad-Nirari III (810–783 BCE).[45] If the biblical accounts of Israel's territorial expansion into the Lebanese Beqaa in the days of Jeroboam II (2 Kgs 14:25) and the Transjordan (Amos

---

[42] Pitard 1987, 145–159; Na'aman 1997; Hafthorsson 2006; Niehr 2011; Hasegawa 2012, 52–83, 105; Finkelstein 2013, 119–128; Ghantous 2013; Younger 2016, 591–630; Frevel 2018a, 220–221.

[43] E.g., Mazar 1962; Younger 2016, 591–632, and see detailed discussion in Frevel 2018b. Archaeologically speaking, the evidence for Hazael's expansion to the northern Levant remains unclear. Destruction layers dating to the Iron Age IIA have not been detected in mounds located in Syria or southeastern Turkey. At most of the local settlements (e.g., the Hama Citadel, Tell Qarqur, and Tell Afis), the timeframe of the 9th–8th centuries BCE is understood as an uninterrupted sequence, with an apparent traumatic event occurring only with the Assyrian campaigns to the west in the 8th century BCE; this is probably one of the reasons for the difficulties in determining the ceramic profile of the Iron IIA in inland Syria (Mazzoni 2014, 694–697). Of course, relying too much on negative evidence is always risky, especially when dealing with the fragmentary nature of many of the Iron Age remains exposed in the northern Levant. However, the fact that events dated to the Iron Age IIB have been found (e.g., Period E1 at Hama Citadel) should facilitate a case against assumed and undetected Iron Age IIA destructions. Our knowledge regarding the involvement of Aram-Damascus in the Lebanese Beqaa in the 10th and 9th centuries BCE is similarly limited, but there are still some clues. N. Na'aman (1995a, 388–390; see also Ghantous 2013) proposed that the 'mq mentioned in Hazael's Booty Inscriptions alludes to the Lebanese Beqaa, known in the Late Bronze Age as the Land of 'Amqi (Aharoni 1953; Na'aman 1999; Rainey 2015, 21–22) and that Hazael's hometown was in this area. If Na'aman's proposal is correct, then there are good reasons to assume that this region was also controlled by Aram-Damascus, at least in the 9th century BCE (but for an alternative view, see Younger 2016, 602, n. 193).

[44] Only a few bits of historical information illuminate the days of Jeroboam II (Finkelstein/Schmid 2017 with additional articles in the same issue; see also Na'aman 2019), and nearly nothing is known about the reign of Hadyan of Damascus (Grayson 1996, 239–240; Younger 2016, 356, 640–642).

[45] For a historical reevaluation of Adad-Nirari III's reign, see Siddall 2013. Note that Joash is mentioned among the kings that paid tribute to the Assyrians (Grayson 1996, 209–212).

6:13–14) are accurate, then in the early 8th century BCE, the southwestern border of Aram-Damascus was pushed back to the Laja, or even to the Damascus Oasis.[46]

But a few decades later, around the mid-8th century BCE, the political balance shifted once again. Biblical and extra-biblical sources inform us that during the reign of Rezin (*ca.* 738–732 BCE), the last king of Aram-Damascus, the borders of the Aramaean kingdom expanded at the expense of its southern neighbor. Details on this period derive from short remarks in the Hebrew Bible (2 Kgs 15:36; 16:1–6; Isa 7:1). These comments indicate the superiority of Aram-Damascus over Israel (and Judah) at that time. Lastly, additional data on the relations between the two kingdoms are supplied by two summary inscriptions from the time of Tiglath-Pileser III, which delineate the border between Aram-Damascus and Israel along the Jordan River.[47] These inscriptions indicate that Aram-Damascus's political control reached Abel Shittim, at that time, a town located in the Jordan Valley (possibly to be located in Tell el-Kefrein or Tell el-Hammam).[48]

1.3.5 The Contribution of the Archaeological Research

Archaeology has played only a minor role in the reconstruction of the history of the relations between Israel and Aram-Damascus and, in general, in determining the role played by the local populations of the central Levant. In most cases, the data from the field were brought in to support or reject the identification of ancient sites or to reinforce some aspects of the texts.[49] More recent works have indeed attempted to integrate the material evidence into historical reconstructions in a more comprehensive fashion, although usually, this remains secondary to the texts.[50] Only in three cases has archaeological research played a major role: 1) the attribution of Iron Age IIA destructions to the military campaigns of Aram-Damascus against Israel[51] and nearby polities,[52] 2) the correlation of the settlement system emerged around the Sea of Galilee with a small Aramaean polity known in the biblical sources as Geshur,[53] and 3) the association of the construction of two royal cities in the Hula Valley, Tel Dan and Tel Hazor, with Aram-Damascus.[54] While these suggestions have gained much support in research, many scholars have also argued against their viability and suggested more conventional interpretations.[55] Accordingly, one of the goals of the current study is also to re-evaluate these issues, especially those pertaining to Iron Age communities in the central Levant.

---

[46] For the possibility that some of David's wars against the Arameans reflect the territorial expansion of the Northern Kingdom in the days of Jeroboam II, see Na'aman 2017b, 313–315.

[47] Na'aman 1995b; Tadmor/Yamada 2011, 105–107 (for H. Tadmor's old view, see idem 1962).

[48] For the identification of Abel Shittim, see Finkelstein/Koch/Lipschits 2012, 138.

[49] E.g., Mazar 1962; Pitard 1987, n. 79.

[50] Lipiński 2000, 347–407; Hasegawa 2012, 65–68; Ghantous 2013, 16–17.

[51] Na'aman 1997, 126–127; Finkelstein 2009, 118, 121–122; Kleiman 2016.

[52] Maeir 2012, 26–49 (for Tell es-Safi/Gath); Lehmann 2019 (for other settlements in the south).

[53] Kochavi 1989; Na'aman 2012; Arav 2013; Sergi/Kleiman 2018.

[54] Finkelstein 1999b; Lipiński 2000, 351; Arie 2008, 36–37.

[55] E.g., Herr 2013, 240; Zwickel 2019, 278 (on the attribution of the destruction of Philistine Gath to Hazael of Damascus); Ben-Tor 2000 (on the association of Stratum VIII at Tel Hazor with the Aramaeans); Thareani 2016a; idem 2019a; idem 2019b (on the dating of Stratum IVA at Tel Dan); Pakkala 2010; idem 2013 (on the identification of the Kingdom of Geshur in the archaeological record).

1.4 Geographical and Chronological Frameworks

1.4.1 Defining the Central Levant

Since my goal in this study is to provide a distinct narrative for the Iron Age communities that prospered under the shadow of Israel and Aram-Damascus, it makes sense to focus on their mutual borderlands rather than on regions located in the heartlands of these polities (e.g., the Samaria Highlands or the Damascus Oasis).[56] However, and as is the case with the territories of other kingdoms in the Ancient Near East, the political border between Israel and Aram-Damascus was loosely defined, and its exact extent was a matter of ongoing dispute.[57] In this light, it is clear why determining the location of their borderlands, and thereby the geographical scope of this study, is a challenging endeavor. To overcome this obstacle, I decided to limit my discussion to several well-defined regions mentioned in biblical and extra-biblical sources in conjunction with territorial disputes, military conflicts, or political achievements, and located outside the heartlands[58] of either Israel and Aram-Damascus: the Lebanese Beqaa (including Marj 'Ayyun), the Hula Valley (including the Korazim Plateau), the Sea of Galilee, the Golan Heights, the Nuqra Plain (down to Busra esh-Sham), and the Irbid Plateau. In contrast to the Jezreel and Beth-shean Valleys and the Laja, which probably comprised the core territories of Israel and Aram-Damascus from the beginning, the regions listed above changed hands several times during the 9th and 8th centuries BCE. Echoes of these territorial shifts can be found in the Hebrew Bible (e.g., Judg 18:27; 2 Kgs 13:14–19; 14:25; Amos 1:3; 6:13–14), in a single royal inscription (i.e., the Tel Dan Stele), and indirectly, also in the Assyrian texts (e.g., the royal annals of Shalmaneser III).

It is difficult to find a term that encapsulates these regions, which are located today within four modern states[59] and cover various geographical niches and environments. For convenience, I will use the term "central Levant" in this book, although, in theory, it may include areas that are not discussed here (e.g., the Galilee Mountains).[60]

1.4.2 The Chronology of the Iron Age

The chronological framework of this study ranges from the collapse of the Late Bronze Age city-states to the beginning of Assyrian conquests against Israel and Aram-

---

[56] According to the Oxford English Dictionary, the term "borderland" means "a land or district on or near the border between two countries or districts." B.J. Parker (2006, 80) expressed his uneasiness regarding the term, arguing that the word "border" may increase confusion regarding its definition. In my view, the opposite is true. The inclusion of the word "land" in this term prevents any confusion regarding its spatial definition as an area rather than a line (e.g., boundary or border).

[57] Sader 2014a, 26; Finkelstein 2016; Sergi/de Hulster 2016. For the territories held by the Aramaean Kingdoms, see Dušek/Mynářová 2019, with several case studies from the Ancient Near East.

[58] R. Kletter (1999, 27–28), for instance, employed the term "heartland" as a reference to territories that were always under the political control of the Judean Kingdom.

[59] While the inclusion of territories located in different modern states in this research resulted in some challenges (e.g., accessibility), it also yields a few advantages, especially the elimination of modern borders as a guiding principle for the geographical framework (see also Osborne 2021, 1–4).

[60] For recent works dealing with the Galilee Mountains in the Iron Age, see Katz 2020; idem 2021.

Damascus in the second half of the 8th century BCE (*ca.* 1150–750 BCE). As chronological issues are at the center of many of the historical problems concerning this period, a few words must be dedicated to the topic.

It is a well-known fact that the relative and absolute chronology of the Iron Age has been the subject of intensive debate for several decades, particularly since the introduction of the Low Chronology in the mid-1990s.[61] In recent years, however, several publications, mainly from the long-term excavation projects of Tel Megiddo, Tel Rehov, and Tel Dor, added important data to the discussion and forced all the participants in the debate to modify their initial views on various chronological issues such as the absolute date of the Iron Age I/II transition. In the following sections, I specify my view on three relevant chronological problems (for the relative and absolute dates, see Table 1).[62]

Table 1: Comparative table of radiocarbon-dated stratigraphic sequences in the southern Levant

NEAEHL	T. Megiddo	T. Rehov	T. Dor	This Study
Iron Age IB (*ca.* 1200–1150 BCE)	VIIB	D-7 D-6	LB|Ir1	Late Bronze Age III (*ca.* 1200–1150 BCE)[63]
Iron Age IA (*ca.* 1150–1000 BCE)	VIIA VIB	VII	Ir1a	Early Iron Age I (*ca.* 1150–1100 BCE)
	VIA		Ir1a|b Ir1b	Late Iron Age I (*ca.* 1100–950 BCE)
Iron Age IIA (*ca.* 1000–900 BCE)	VB	VI	Ir1|2	Early Iron Age IIA (*ca.* 950–900 BCE)
	Level Q-5[64] VA-IVB	V IV	Ir2a	Late Iron Age IIA (*ca.* 900–830 BCE)
	Gap	(IV cont.?)	Ir2a|b	Final Iron Age IIA (*ca.* 830–800 BCE)
Iron Age IIB (*ca.* 900–700 BCE)	IVA	IIIB IIIA	Ir2b	Early Iron Age IIB (*ca.* 800–730/720 BCE)

Note: Based on the dates and correlations given in Stern 1993; Gilboa *et al.* 2018; Mazar 2020b; Finkelstein *et al.* 2022.

---

[61] Finkelstein 1996. For recent and relevant studies concerning the debate over the chronology of the Iron Age, see Finkelstein/Piasetzky 2011; Mazar 2011; Lee/Bronk Ramsey/Mazar 2013; Toffolo *et al.* 2014; Fantalkin/Finkelstein/Piasetzky 2015; Kleiman *et al.* 2019.

[62] For accounts of these excavations, see Gilboa *et al.* 2018 (Tel Dor); Mazar/Panitz-Cohen 2020 (Tel Rehov); Finkelstein/Ussishkin/Cline 2013; Finkelstein *et al.* 2022 (Tel Megiddo). The date of the transition between the early and late parts of the Iron Age I, which is of less importance to our subject, is not entirely clear. According to M.B. Toffolo *et al.* (idem 2014, 241; see also Finkelstein *et al.* 2017, 274–275), it occurred around the mid-11th century BCE.

[63] Based on his work at Tel Lachish, D. Ussishkin (2004, 72–75) proposed that the timeframe of the 12th century BCE should be nicknamed "Late Bronze Age III," a designation that has been adopted by some (e.g., Finkelstein *et al.* 2017, 262) but rejected by others (e.g., Mazar 2009a, 24).

[64] Level Q-5 is a unique stratigraphic phase that was identified in the southeastern sector of Tel Megiddo (Area Q). It represents the early days of the late Iron Age IIA, parallel to Stratum V at Tel Rehov (see, e.g., Finkelstein/Kleiman 2019). For the stratigraphy, ceramic data, and radiocarbon dates of this phase, see Homsher/Kleiman 2022; Kleiman 2022a; Boaretto 2022, respectively.

a. The End of the Iron Age I

According to A. Mazar, the destruction of the late Iron Age I cities in the northern valleys (e.g., Stratum VIA at Tel Megiddo) and the coast (e.g., Stratum X at Tell Qasile) represents the shift between the ceramic traditions of the Iron Age I and those of the Iron Age IIA.[65] He sets, then, the transition between these periods a little bit lower than the traditional date, around 980 BCE. I. Finkelstein, in contrast, assumes that a short period of transformation between the ceramic assemblages is unlikely and that the destruction of the Canaanite cities was a gradual process.[66] In my view, a lower date for the Iron Age I/II transition around the mid-10th century BCE should be preferred for the following reasons. First, squatter activity on the ruins of several Iron Age I settlements (e.g., Stratum IV at Tel Kinrot and Stratum XVI at Tel Yoqne'am) includes ceramic assemblages still exhibiting Iron Age I traditions[67] and strengthening the idea that the Iron Age I/IIA transition was a slow process during the first half of the 10th century BCE.[68] Second, considering that the early Iron Age IIA strata in the north (e.g., Stratum VB at Tel Megiddo; for the sub-division of the period, see below) are relatively poor in finds, it is doubtful if this period should be allocated with more than half-century; this is to differ from the subsequent period, the late Iron Age IIA, which includes two phases with substantial building activity, e.g., Strata X–IX at Hazor, Strata V–IV and Tel Rehov, Levels Q-5 and Q-4 at Tel Megiddo, and Strata VIII and VII at Tel Gezer.[69]

b. The Division of the Iron Age IIA

The Iron Age IIA was conventionally perceived as a monolithic period and dated by scholars to the 10th century BCE.[70] A. Zarzecki-Peleg's research on the ceramic traditions of Tel Hazor, Tel Yoqne'am, and Tel Megiddo was among the first attempts to develop a more nuanced framework for the Iron Age II ceramic industry in the northern valleys, but ultimately this work did not define clear sub-stages within the period.[71] A. Gilboa and I. Sharon's study was more comprehensive and even included references to archaeological evidence from Israel, Greece, Cyprus, and Phoenicia, as well as to radiocarbon-dated strata, especially from the excavations of Tel Dor.[72] Gilboa and Sharon defined two clear horizons within the "classical" Iron Age IIA: "Ir1|2" and "Ir2a." Although they were the first to identify indicative ceramic forms characterizing these

---

[65] Mazar 2005, 21, Table 2.1; idem 2011, 107, Table 2; idem 2020b, 85, Tables 4.2–4.3.

[66] Based on radiocarbon dates from sites in the northern valleys, I. Finkelstein and E. Piasetzky (2007a) proposed that the destruction of the Iron Age I cities was gradual. In their view, sites located in the Jezreel Valley were destroyed in the first half of the 10th century (maximum range of 985–935 for the destruction of Stratum VIA at Tel Megiddo in Toffolo *et al.* 2014), while sites located in the east (e.g., Stratum IV at Tel Hadar) were destroyed a few decades later (*ca.* 950 BCE).

[67] Münger/Zangenberg/Pakkala 2011, 87 (on Tel Kinrot); Arie 2011, 275 (on Tel Yoqne'am).

[68] Radiocarbon dates of short-lived samples from arid zones (Routledge *et al.* 2014; Ben-Yosef 2016; Kleiman/Kleiman/Ben-Yosef 2017) support lower dates for the Iron Age I/II transition.

[69] On the early days of the late Iron Age IIA, see Kleiman 2018; Finkelstein/Kleiman 2019.

[70] Amiran 1969, 191; Mazar 1990, 372–373, Table 6; Stern 1993, 1529.

[71] Zarzecki-Peleg 1997; Zarzecki-Peleg/Cohen-Anidjar/Ben-Tor 2005.

[72] Gilboa/Sharon 2003. See also Gilboa/Sharon/Bloch-Smith 2015; Gilboa *et al.* 2018.

phases (e.g., the absence of Black-on-Red imports in the early horizon),[73] their terminology was not adopted by archaeologists working in the southern Levant.[74]

Immediately after the publication of Gilboa and Sharon's study, Z. Herzog and L. Singer-Avitz introduced their own chronological scheme for the Iron Age IIA in the south, attempting to reconcile the problems arising from both the conventional dates and the Low Chronology, mainly based on the stratified ceramic sequences of Tel Sheva (also known as Beersheba).[75] In a nutshell, Herzog and Singer-Avitz argued for the longevity of Iron Age IIA strata in the southern Levant[76] and asserted that clear early and late ceramic phases could be discerned within it.[77] Two years later, they published another article that dealt explicitly with the northern valleys.[78] Relying on D. Ussishkin and J. Woodhead's excavation at Tel Jezreel,[79] they defined three phases within the Iron Age IIA in northern Israel: "pre-Jezreel Compound" ("early Iron Age IIA"), "Jezreel Compound" ("late Iron Age IIA") and "post-Jezreel Compound" ("the final phase of the late Iron Age IIA").[80] However, the attempts to identify *fossil directeurs* for the early Iron Age IIA were not successful, and it was dated by the appearance of new types not produced in the Iron Age I, as well as by the absence of other ceramic forms indicative of the late Iron Age IIA horizon.[81] Eventually, Herzog and Singer-Avitz's terminology, and to a certain degree their dating, was adopted by many scholars.[82]

Dating the absolute date of the transition between the early and late phases of the Iron Age IIA can be established today using the high-resolution archaeological data derived from two well-preserved "intermediate" Iron Age IIA phases, Level Q-5 at Tel Megiddo[83] and Stratum V at Tel Rehov.[84] These layers include clear remains and are accompanied by rich ceramic assemblages assigned to the cultural horizon of the late Iron Age IIA. Short-lived radiocarbon dates and Bayesian models from both sites limit the existence of these layers to the late 10th or early 9th century BCE. Important as well is

---

[73] For the convoluted history of research of the Black-on-Red Ware, see Schreiber 2003.

[74] For an updated discussion on the chronology of Phoenicia, see Sader 2019, 15–23, Table 1.1.

[75] Note that the essence of Z. Herzog and L. Singer-Avitz's study was the question of state-formation in Judah. In contrast to the common view, they argued that social complexity developed first in the periphery of the kingdom (e.g., the Judean Shephelah) and not in Jerusalem. Despite its originality, this idea has not been accepted in research (e.g., Na'aman 2013; Sergi 2013; Lehmann/Niemann 2014).

[76] For a similar argument based on the excavations of Tel Hazor, see Aharoni/Amiran 1958.

[77] See also Ben-Shlomo/Shai/Maeir 2004, who also employed the term "Early Iron Age IIA."

[78] Herzog/Singer-Avitz 2006, 166–167.

[79] For the results of the excavations at Tel Jezreel, see Ussishkin/Woodhead 1997.

[80] Herzog/Singer-Avitz 2006, 187. In this study and elsewhere, I refer to the last stage simply as "final Iron Age IIA" (Kleiman 2015, 199–200; idem 2021; Finkelstein/Kleiman 2019). Other scholars suggested different terminologies for this period, but all of them referred, more or less, to the same timeframe (Finkelstein/Sass 2013, 152; Katz/Faust 2014, 105–106; Shochat/Gilboa 2019, 380).

[81] See, in particular, E. Arie's (2013a, 738) detailed study of the pottery of Stratum V at Megiddo.

[82] Fantalkin/Finkelstein 2006, 18–19; Maeir *et al.* 2008; Mazar/Bronk Ramsey 2008, 172; Mazar 2014, 357; idem 2020b; Arie 2013a; Na'aman 2013; idem 2016b, and many others. A somewhat similar sub-division of the late Iron Age IIA was suggested by I. Finkelstein and B. Sass (2013, 152) in an article that dealt with the development of alphabetic writing in the southern Levant.

[83] Kleiman *et al.* 2017, 26–27; Homsher/Kleiman 2022; Kleiman 2022a; Boaretto 2022.

[84] Mazar 2016; idem 2020b; Mazar *et al.* 2005.

the fact that these layers do not signify the end of the Iron Age IIA at these sites; their (partial) destruction (or abandonment) is followed by successive phases (Level Q-4 at Tel Megiddo and Stratum IV at Tel Rehov), radiocarbon dated to the second half of the 9th century BCE.[85] According to these data, the ceramic traditions of the late Iron Age IIA emerged at the end of the 10th century BCE or slightly later (*ca.* 900 BCE).

c. The Iron Age IIA/B Transition

Notwithstanding the impressive results of Z. Herzog and L. Singer-Avitz's research, their "final phase of the Iron Age IIA" was ill-defined and too reliant on the Jezreel Valley for stratigraphic and historical observations. A few years ago, I added to the discussion by suggesting that the appearance of ceramic forms heralding the beginning of the Iron Age IIB (e.g., shallow bowls, cooking pots with inverted stances and grooved rims, lamps with a flat base) may indicate that sites in the Coastal Plain (e.g., Stratum A7 at Tel Aphek) and the Judean Shephelah (e.g., Stratum A3 at Tell es-Safi/Gath) were destroyed at the end of the 9th century BCE, in the very end of the Iron Age IIA (i.e., the final phase of the Iron IIA);[86] this scenario is supported by several radiocarbon dates.[87]

Regarding the transition between the Iron Age IIA and IIB, A. Mazar sets the end of the Iron Age IIA at *ca.* 830 BCE based on the radiocarbon dates from the destruction of Stratum IV at Tel Rehov. Consequently, in his view, the last third of the 9th century BCE should be considered the beginning of the Iron Age IIB.[88] However, the (partial) destructions of Iron Age IIA cities in the southern Levant –attributed to the wars between Israel and Aram-Damascus – did not necessarily lead to radical changes in ceramic traditions (as was the case of the Iron Age I/II transition).[89] On the contrary, new data from excavated sites in the southern Levant[90] suggest that both the Iron Age IIA/IIB transition and the destruction of the Iron Age IIA cities were gradual.[91] In this light, I prefer to date the beginning of the Iron Age IIB to the early 8th century BCE with the construction of many new sites in the northern valleys (e.g., Stratum IVA at Tel Megiddo), the Judean Shephelah (e.g., Level 3 at Beth-Shemesh), and the desert (Kuntillet 'Ajrud).

Indeed, the ceramic assemblages of Stratum IVA at Tel Megiddo, Level 3 at Tel Beth-Shemesh,[92] and Kuntillet 'Ajrud roughly belong to the same chronological horizon, the

---

[85] For the absolute dates from Tel Megiddo, see Toffolo *et al.* 2014; Boaretto 2022; for those from Tel Rehov, see Mazar *et al.* 2005; Lee/Bronk Ramsey/Mazar 2013; Mazar 2016, 105–112.

[86] Kleiman 2015, 198–200.

[87] E.g., Finkelstein/Piasetzky 2009; Garfinkel *et al.* 2019, Table 4.

[88] See also Arie 2008; Singer-Avitz 2018. In a few places, however, A. Mazar seems to acknowledge the possible continuation of the Iron Age IIA until *ca.* 800 BCE, especially concerning the destruction of Stratum IX at Tell Deir 'Alla and Stratum IX at Tel Dothan (idem 2020b, 115; see also p. 127).

[89] For the destructions, see Na'aman 1997, 126–127; Finkelstein 2009, 121–122; Kleiman 2016.

[90] Arie 2008 (for Tel Dan); Ben-Tor/Ben-Ami/Sandhaus 2012 (for Tel Hazor); Shai/Maeir 2012 (for Tell es-Safi); Kleiman 2015 (for Tel Aphek); Shochat 2017 (for Tel Dor).

[91] See details in Kleiman 2015 (for the Sharon Plain); idem 2016 (for the southern Levant).

[92] Note that the excavators of Tel Beth-Shemesh (Bunimovitz/Lederman 2009, 136) do not accept a mid-8th century date for the destruction of Level 3. In their view, the destruction of the city should be understood as the result of the war between Joash and Amaziah (2 Kgs 14:11–13).

first half of the 8th century BCE.[93] All of them represent, in my view, the early Iron Age IIB ceramic horizon (i.e., one stage before the cultural horizon associated with Stratum III at Tel Lachish). Having said that, the only places in the north that exhibit dense stratigraphic sequences within this period are Tel Dan (Strata III–II) and Tel Hazor (Strata VII–V). The former remains largely unpublished, and quantitative analyses of ceramic assemblages, so crucial in any attempt for high-resolution relative dating schemes, were not conducted for the latter.[94] Activity in southern sites, such as Stratum III at Tel Lachish or Stratum II at Beer-Sheba, was maintained until Sennacherib's campaign of 701 BCE, about 30 years after the destruction of the northern sites.

1.5 Research Organization

The book is divided into three parts: 1) settlement history, 2) material culture, and 3) synthesis. Due to the low level of scholarly acquaintance with the settlement history of various sites in the central Levant, and especially in order to allow the development of regional narratives, I decided to present in Chapters 2–7 a critical review of the archaeology of the discussed regions: from the Lebanese Beqaa to the Irbid Plateau. Each of these chapters consists of a brief description of the historical and geographical context, a presentation of several key sites, and a regional synthesis.[95] I specifically did not divide the examined settlements between excavated and surveyed sites, as it was clear to me that the settlement trends in certain regions are not always accurately represented by the state of research; this was especially evident in the cases of the Lebanese Beqaa and the Irbid Plateau. Altogether, this part of the monograph can be seen as a guide for the less familiar (and discussed) sectors of the Levant in the Iron Age.

Chapters 8–12 focus, then, on several cross-regional themes, such as architectural styles, ceramic traditions, and mortuary practices, and thus bring us one step closer to the synthesis. Choosing the discussed categories was not easy, of course, but I tried to select features representing different aspects of the local societies rather than limiting the study to one type of material culture (e.g., architecture or pottery). Chapters 13 and 14 summarize, then, the results of the research and provide an archaeological-historical narrative for the Iron Age communities of the central Levant, as well as comments on selected long-term processes and issues (e.g., demographic changes, cult-related activity, and the question of whether a cohesive central Levantine cultural sphere exists). In addition, I also bring here three appendices with essential information on the discussed archaeological sites (Appendix A), a catalog of all the inscriptions and other inscribed items discovered throughout the years in the central Levant (Appendix B), and a list of all the published radiocarbon results of short-lived samples (Appendix C).

---

[93] Tel Beth-Shemesh until *ca.* 760 BCE (Finkelstein/Piasetzky 2009, 270–271), the northern sites (e.g., Stratum V at Tel Hazor) and Kuntillet 'Ajrud, until the second half of the 8th century BCE.

[94] For an analysis of the published ceramic data from Stratum II at Tel Dan, see Arie 2008. The Iron Age II remains from the old excavations are the subject of ongoing research by Y. Thareani.

[95] References to the data in the website of the Israel Archaeological Survey (IAS) are based on the map numbers (e.g., IAS 36/1, no. 89). For the website, see https://survey.antiquities.org.il.

Part I. The Settlement History

2. The Lebanese Beqaa

2.1 Introduction

During the Late Bronze Age (*ca.* 1450–1150 BCE), the political control in the northern and central districts of the Lebanese Beqaa was divided among the Kingdom of Kadesh and several smaller city-states known in historical sources as the cities of the Land of 'Amqi.[1] In the southern Beqaa, the most prominent settlement was Kumidi, which enjoyed close relations with the Egyptian Empire.[2] However, during the 11th–9th centuries BCE, the local political institutions were significantly weakened, and the region as a whole gradually transformed into the borderlands of several polities: Hamath to the north, Aram-Damascus to the east, Israel to the south, and perhaps the Phoenician city-states to the west. This change obviously did not occur overnight, nor did it signify the disappearance of local and independent polities in the valley. After all, even the biblical authors note that a small kingdom named Beth-Rehob thrived in this region in the Early Iron Age (e.g., Judg 18:25; 2 Sam 10:6, 8).[3] The historical background for this transformation is not entirely clear, resulting from a lack of excavated stratified sites or any comprehensive publication of archaeological data. Still, in contrast to the less-investigated neighboring regions, this area has been fully covered by field surveys which supply a sufficient database for discussing the settlement history of this important territory. Moreover, the data retrieved from the few excavated sites in the valley that were published (or partially published) have not been reexamined in decades and provide additional information on the Lebanese Beqaa during the Iron Age.

From a geographical perspective, the Lebanese Beqaa stretches between the southern margin of the Homs Plain in the north and the Marj 'Ayyun in the south (Figure 3). Its boundaries in the west and the east are demarcated by the slopes of the Lebanon and Anti-Lebanon Mountains (total area of *ca.* 1900 sq km). The environmental conditions in the Lebanese Beqaa are more than suitable for human activity, as this region receives between 200–400 mm annual rainfall, and local water sources are quite abundant. In addition, two major rivers with small tributaries flow through the valley. The first is the

---

[1] The city-states of the Land of 'Amqi are mentioned in several Amarna Letters and Hittite texts dating to the 14th century BCE (Aharoni 1953; Sader/van Ess 1998; Rainey 2015, 21–22; Na'aman 1995a, 384). The main cities mentioned in these texts are Hasi, Hashabu, and Enishasi. Archaeological data, combined with the survival of local toponyms, suggest that these cities should be identified with the large mounds of Tell Hizzin (Hasi), Tell Hashbe (Hashabu), Tell el-Ghassil, and the unexcavated Tell 'Ain Sharif (the latter two sites were proposed to be the location of Enishasi).

[2] Marfoe 1995, 121–128; Heinz 2010, 25–28; idem 2016, 129–183.

[3] Lipiński 2000, 319–345; Na'aman 2002b, 204–205; Younger 2016, 192–204.

Orontes River (Nahr el-'Asi) which originates near Labwa and flows north through the Homs Plain (*ca.* 570 km in length). The second is Nahr el-Litani which originates near Baalbek and flows through Marj 'Ayyun, where it turns west to the coast (*ca.* 140 km in length). Many of the settlements in the valley were located along these rivers, which also delineate the major ancient overland routes of the region.[4]

Figure 3: Agricultural fields in the Beqaa Valley with the Lebanon Mountains in the background (photographed by F. Molle / CC BY 2.0)

2.2 Key Sites

As mentioned above, most of the archaeological data from the Lebanese Beqaa in the Iron Age derive from field surveys as only a few sites were excavated (Figure 4).[5] Hitherto, the most detailed attempt to delineate the settlement history of the valley was carried out by L. Marfoe, who surveyed several sites in the region and integrated the results of earlier field projects into his work.[6] His publications represent the state of research at the end of the 1970s, but apart from the excavations of Tell Kamid el-Loz, not much fieldwork has been conducted since in this region.[7] To date, the only excavated sites with Iron Age remains are Baalbek, Tell Hizzin, Tell el-Ghassil, and Tell Kamid el-Loz. Stratified information is available only for Tell el-Ghassil and Tell Kamid el-Loz, while Iron Age activity at Baalbek and Tell Hizzin is discerned based on ceramic grounds.[8] Due to their possible historical importance, I also include in this chapter an extended

---

[4] More details on the geographical setting of the Lebanese Beqaa in Marfoe 1979a, 12–13.

[5] Copeland/Wescombe 1966; Marfoe 1995; idem 1998; Sader/van Ess 1998, 259–260.

[6] Marfoe 1979b; idem 1995; idem 1998.

[7] Sader 2014b. Field research in the Anti-Lebanon Mountains revealed only four Iron Age sites from the end of this period or even the beginning of the Persian period (Bonatz 2002, 299). Work in Baalbek's hinterland has not reported even a single Iron Age site (Fischer-Genz/Ehrig 2005).

[8] Sader/van Ess 1998, 262–265; Genz/Sader 2008.

description of several under-explored sites: Tell Sugha, Tell Qasr Labwa, Tell Barr El-yas, Tell Dayr Zanun, Tell Bir Dhakwa, and Tell Dibbin.

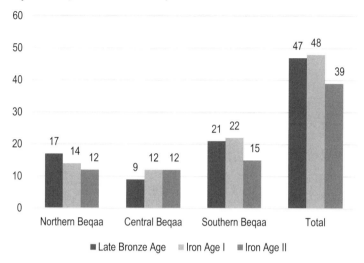

Figure 4: Settlement oscillations in the Lebanese Beqaa

2.2.1   Tell Sugha

Little information is available on Tell Sugha. It is a small mound located near the Orontes River, approximately 4.5 km northwest of modern Labwa.[9] Based on its proximity to the villages of Sbuba and Zabbud, G. Abousamra recently considered Tell Sugha as a possible candidate for the location of Subat/Soba together with the unexplored Tell el-Bellan.[10] Perhaps the main objections to this proposal are the small size of the archaeological site (55 × 25 × 4 m), suggesting that it was no more than a village, and more substantially, the absence of Iron Age II sherds in the field surveys.

2.2.2   Tell Qasr Labwa

Tell Qasr Labwa (Tell el-Husn) is a large site *ca.* 1 km west of Labwa.[11] It is commonly identified with Lebo.[12] During the Late Bronze Age, this site marked the border between the Land of 'Amqi and the Kingdom of Kadesh, and thus, also the boundary between the influence spheres of the Egyptian and Hittite Empires.[13] In the Hebrew Bible, Labwa

---

[9] Marfoe 1995, 270–271; Lehmann 2002, 542; Goren/Finkelstein/Na'aman 2004, 336.

[10] Abousamra 2019, 232–236 with the necessary reservations regarding his proposal.

[11] Marfoe 1995, 271–272; Lehmann 2002, 316; Goren/Finkelstein/Na'aman 2004, 336. It is not as small as it is sometimes described in the literature (e.g., Na'aman 1999, 421). L. Marfoe (1995, 271), for instance, estimated its size as 290 × 210 m (*ca.* 6 hectares). L. Copeland and P.J. Wescombe (1966, 71–72) mention that D. Kirkbride carried out excavations at the site in 1966.

[12] Copeland/Wescombe 1966, 71–72; Marfoe 1995, 271; Younger 2016, 444.

[13] Na'aman 1999, 421.

(Lebo-Hamath) is mentioned 11 times as the northernmost extent of Canaan and as the northernmost point of Israel in the days of Jeroboam II (e.g., 2 Kgs 14:25; Amos 6:14).[14] Beyond the survey data, nothing is known archaeologically about this site, but it probably had an important role in the Lebanese Beqaa during the Bronze and Iron Ages.

Figure 5: Jupiter's Temple courtyard at Baalbek (photographed by E. Hermans / CC BY 2.0)

2.2.3   Baalbek

Baalbek, Hellenistic Heliopolis, is located less than 1 km west of the modern city bearing the same name.[15] It was previously suggested that the site could be identified with several toponyms appearing in the Hebrew Bible, although none of these proposals gained broad consensus, and some were unanimously rejected (e.g., Baal-Gad). Scholars proposed identifying the early settlement with various toponyms (e.g., Tushultu, Tubuhi, or even Sobah) but again without much evidence.[16] It can be concluded that while the name Baalbek probably has pre-Hellenistic roots, its exact meaning remains ambiguous.[17] From an archaeological perspective, it has long been assumed that the early remains at the site are buried under the remnants of the Jupiter Temple (Figure 5). Soundings carried out in the courtyard of the temple during the 1960s by J. Hajjar (1961–1962) and by I. Kaoukabani (1967–1968) confirmed this assumption.[18] Aside

---

[14] Based on an analysis of the historical references to Labwa and Subat, N. Na'aman (1999) concluded that the term "Lebo-Hamath" is anachronistic and derives from political changes brought by the Assyrians in the late 8th century BCE, after the fall of Israel and Aram-Damascus. In his view, the use of this expression in earlier contexts (e.g., 2 Kgs 14:25) results from later redactions.

[15] Smith 1992; Marfoe 1995, 255–256; Lehmann 2002, 65–71.

[16] See a summary of the different proposals in Sader/van Ess 1998, 250–251.

[17] For a discussion on the etymology of the name Baalbek, see Steiner 2009.

[18] Copeland/Wescombe 1966, 25; Genz 2006, 127 with earlier references.

from unstratified sherds from the Chalcolithic and Early Bronze Age, *in situ* remains of Middle Bronze Age tombs and several domestic structures possibly dated to the Iron Age were exposed.[19] H. Sader and M. van Ess, who discussed the results of the excavations, were careful to state that there is any historical or archaeological evidence to suggest that the earlier settlement was ever an important cult place or a powerful city. In other words, we can conclude that the later importance of the site should not necessarily be projected back into the Bronze and Iron Ages.[20]

Figure 6: Satellite view of Tell Hizzin (created with QGIS 3.16 and Google Satellite)

2.2.4   Tell Hizzin

Tell Hizzin is commonly identified by scholars as Hasi, a prominent city-state known from the Late Bronze Age[21] due to its name, its relatively large size (*ca.* 3.5–5 hectare; Figure 6), and the finds exposed during the excavations.[22] In 1949–1950, the site was excavated by M. Chehab, but for a long time, only limited data from these excavations were published. A few years ago, H. Genz and H. Sader[23] restudied the old excavations and proposed that the Iron Age occupation at Tell Hizzin is represented chiefly by unstratified material and one tomb (for selected vessels from the Iron Age settlement, see

---

[19] Sader/van Ess 1998, 262–265.
[20] Sader/van Ess 1998, 259.
[21] Aharoni 1953; Sader/van Ess 1998, 251–252; Rainey 2015, 21–22. A collection of distinct Egyptian items found during the excavations of the site (e.g., inscribed statues) reinforces this identification (Ahrens 2010). For the provenance of the three letters from the Amarna Correspondence mentioning Hasi (EA 175, 185, and 186), see Goren/Finkelstein/Na'aman 2004, 127–128, 130.
[22] Copeland/Wescombe 1966, 66–67; Marfoe 1995, 241; Lehmann 2002, 287–288.
[23] Genz/Sader 2008.

Figure 7). According to the surviving records, the latest occupational phase of the site was destroyed by fire,[24] although its extent and exact date remain unknown.

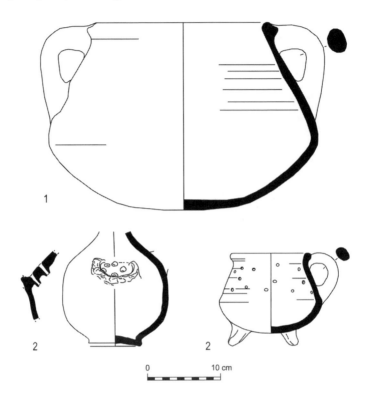

Figure 7: Selected Iron Age vessels from M. Chehab's excavation at Tell Hizzin (redrawn by the author based on Genz/Sader 2008, pl. 5: 1, 4–5)

Among the published finds are several complete Iron Age I vessels: two cooking pots with inverted and pinched rims (e.g., Figure 7, 1), two tripod cups (e.g., Figure 7, 3), and one undecorated strainer jug (e.g., Figure 7, 2).[25] Similar vessels are known from nearby Iron Age I sites in the Lebanese Beqaa (e.g., Tell Kamid el-Loz and Tell el-Ghassil) and found at sites located further to the south (e.g., Tel Dan and Tel Hadar). The ceramic material belonging to the Iron Age II occupation likewise comprises only several vessels. Among the published items are two shallow decorated bowls, one plain jug with a flaring rim and ridged neck, one bichrome flask, and one bichrome jug.[26] All of these items are inspired by the ceramic traditions prevailing in Phoenicia at the time and, in fact, could have been imported from there. In contrast, the pottery found in the tomb mentioned above includes items likely imported from Cyprus: two Black-on-Red

---

[24] Genz/Sader 2008, 184–185.
[25] Genz/Sader 2008, pl. 5.
[26] Genz/Sader 2008, pl. 6, 5–9

juglets (e.g., Figure 91) and a White-Painted barrel juglet.[27] Most, if not all, of these vessels, should be dated to the Iron Age IIA. Nothing in the published ceramic assemblages of Tell Hizzin indicates activity in the Iron Age IIB, but the limited material kept by the excavator forces caution against any conclusions based on negative evidence. From the available data, one can also conclude that the Iron Age I ceramic traditions of the site were quite similar to those of other inland sites located along the Rift Valley (e.g., Tell el-Ghassil, Tel Dan, and Tel Hadar), while the published Iron Age II items have apparent affinities with the Phoenicia and Cyprus.

2.2.5 Tell Hashbe

No excavations were carried out at Tell Hashbe, a prominent mound located about 20 km to the southwest of Baalbek (Figure 8).[28] However, based on its name, size (*ca.* 5–7 hectares), and commanding view over the valley, it is usually identified with Hashabu, an important city-state from the Late Bronze Age.[29] No references to the city exist in later texts, but Iron Age I and II sherds were found at the site.

Figure 8: Satellite view of Tell Hashbe (created with QGIS 3.16 and Google Satellite)

2.2.6 Tell el-Ghassil

Located *ca.* 11.5 km northeast of modern Riyaq, Tell el-Ghassil is the second most investigated site in the Lebanese Beqaa, with remains from the Bronze and Iron Ages

---

[27] Genz/Sader 2008, pl. 6, 1–4
[28] Copeland/Wescombe 1966, 64–65; Marfoe 1995, 240–241.
[29] E.g., Sader/van Ess 1998, 252; Na'aman 1999, 420; Lipiński 2000, 329.

(Figure 9). It is a large site (*ca.* 3–5 hectares)[30] and commonly identified with Enishasi, one of the city-states of the Land of 'Amqi (but without any certainty).[31]

Excavations at Tell el-Ghassil commenced in the late 1950s by D.C. Baramki on behalf of the American University of Beirut (1956–1963, 1968–1969, 1972–1974). During these excavations, substantial Iron Age remains were found in three adjacent areas at the northeastern sector of the mound (Areas I–III),[32] along with exceptionally rich ceramic assemblages.[33] The pottery from these investigations was meticulously analyzed by M.S. Joukowsky.[34] Baramki's careful documentation of the excavation and coherent preliminary publications were exceptional for the time and established Tell el-Ghassil as a key site for the Iron Age (for a proposed stratigraphic correlation, see Table 2).

Figure 9: Satellite view of Tell el-Ghassil with the main area excavated during D.C. Baramki's project and the so-called Iron Age temple (created with QGIS 3.16 and Google Satellite)

According to the preliminary reports, five strata were identified in Area I/II (the southern part of the main excavated area in Tell el-Ghassil). The uppermost stratum, encountered about a meter below the modern surface, consisted of isolated walls built of

---

[30] Copeland/Wescombe 1966, 64; Marfoe 1995, 241–242; Lehmann 2002, 235–236.

[31] Sader/van Ess 1998, 253. On this toponym, see Na'aman 1988, 188–190. For the provenance of the letters that mentioned the city, see Goren/Finkelstein/Na'aman 2004, 126–127, 130.

[32] Due to the proximity between Areas I and II, I decided to discuss them together.

[33] Baramki 1961; idem 1964; idem 1966. For the Bronze Age finds, see Doumet-Serhal 1996.

[34] Joukowsky 1972. Note that many of the sherds that were drawn are too small for exact identification, and the inclusion of many non-indicative parts (e.g., bases) in the statistics made M.S. Joukowsky's tabulations essentially unusable. In some cases, deep intrusions from later strata are also evident among the published assemblages (e.g., a large fragment of a Phoenician Bichrome flask presented in Joukowsky 1972, pl. XXX, 4; see also Lehmann 1996, 141).

roughly-cut stone (Level 1). Below it, more robust architecture was revealed, mainly a rectangular building sub-divided into three rooms (Level 2; see the reconstruction in Figure 10). Many complete and restorable vessels were found in this layer.[35]

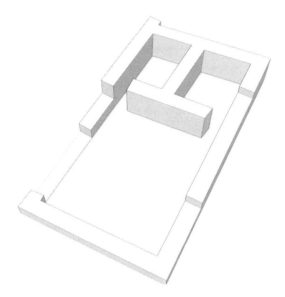

Figure 10: Possible reconstruction of the main Iron Age structure revealed at Tell el-Ghassil (drawn with Trimble Sketchup Pro 2021 and based on Baramki 1966, plan 1)

Excavations below the rectangular structure exposed the remains of two additional superimposed buildings, which most likely represent earlier sub-phases of the rectangular structure of Level 2 but with slightly different internal divisions (Levels 3 and 4).[36] Based on several cult-related objects found in this area, the excavator suggested that the three structures functioned as temples.[37] In addition to the main structure, two silos were attributed to Level 4.[38] The floor of one of them was paved with mudbricks,[39] but this sort of investment in the floor of a small silo is odd. It is much more likely that during the construction of the silo, the inhabitants of the site simply encountered the remains of a substantial, earlier mudbrick wall, maybe a fortification line, and reused it as a floor. Support for this conclusion comes from the exposure of sherds and items from the Late Bronze Age at the silo's bottom. In any case, the lowest stratum identified here was found below the silos, including wall remnants, sherds, and cylinder seals (Level 5).[40]

---

[35] Joukowsky 1972, pls. II–IV.
[36] Note that the earliest phase was covered by burnt debris (Baramki 1964, 48, 52–55).
[37] Baramki 1961, 95.
[38] Baramki 1964, 49.
[39] See photo in Baramki 1964, pl. VIII, 1.
[40] Baramki 1966, 31.

Excavations carried out in Area III, located only a few meters to the north of Area I/II, revealed a somewhat different stratigraphic picture, only encountering two distinct strata.[41] In the upper phase, the excavations revealed the remains of two structures with a passage between them (Level 1). The published architectural plans suggest the contemporaneity of these structures with the temples of Levels 2–4 in Area I/II. Many complete and restorable vessels were found in this layer as well, and indicated that the settlement was rapidly abandoned (or destroyed).[42] Below the structures, a significantly larger building with 1 m high mudbricks walls was exposed (Level 2).[43]

Despite its immense importance, dating the stratigraphic sequences of Tell el-Ghassil is a challenging task.[44] This partly results from the nature of the old excavation (despite its relatively high quality) and partly from the lack of stratigraphic sequences with secure Iron Age ceramic assemblages elsewhere in the Lebanese Beqaa. However, the published pottery allows some chronological conclusions. In Area I/II, for instance, there are no significant differences between the ceramic assemblages of Levels 5–1 (for some exceptions, see below). Considering the conspicuous presence of painted ware, amphorae with two handles, storage jars with elongated bodies and carinated shoulders, wavy-band pithoi or closely related forms, Phoenician Bichrome Ware and the paucity of red-slipped vessels,[45] assigning them to the Iron Age I is very reasonable. And yet, some items in the ceramic repertoire published by D.C. Baramki and M.S. Joukowsky are certainly later than the rest. I refer to 1) a red-slipped bowl and a decanter found in Level 2 in Area I/II[46] that are unlikely to appear in Iron Age I strata and are more typical to the ceramic traditions of the Iron Age II,[47] 2) a nearly jar found in Level 2 in Area I, is probably a torpedo jar,[48] and ceramic studies on stratified materials from various sites showed that these jars did not appear before the beginning of the Iron Age IIB,[49] and 3) fragments of probable Cypriot Black-on-Red juglets and bowls were found in Level 1 in Area I/II.[50] These imports were not produced before the Cypro-Geometric III.[51]

H. Sader, who summarized the Iron Age I remains in Lebanon, noted that Levels 5–4 in Area I/II and Levels 6–3 in Area III represent the ceramic horizon of the Iron Age I.[52] Implicitly, she assumed that the later levels in both areas – Levels 3–1 in Area I/II

---

[41] Baramki 1964, 55–58.

[42] Joukowsky 1972, pls. XV–XVI.

[43] For restorable vessels from this building, see Joukowsky 1972, pls. XVII–XXIII.

[44] Lehmann 1996, 141.

[45] E.g., Joukowsky 1972, pls. I, 14, 18; II, 12, 35; III, 3; IV, 2; V, 15; VI, 10–11; IX, 18, 24; X, 3–11; XI, 4, 29; XIV, 1. Some of the pithoi that appear at Tell el-Ghassil are similar to wavy-band pithoi but seem to reflect a local version (e.g., Joukowsky 1972, pl. XXII). For the chronology, distribution, and function of the wavy-band pithoi (also known as "Tyrian Pithoi"), see Gilboa 2001.

[46] Joukowsky 1972, pl. II, 9, 30.

[47] See also Lehmann 1996, 141.

[48] Joukowsky 1972, pl. III, 14.

[49] Finkelstein/Zimhoni/Kafri 2000, 319; Singer-Avitz 2014, 132; Kleiman 2022a. Note that the shape of this vessel differs from storage jars with carinated shoulders and an elongated body found in Level 3 in Area I/II (Joukowsky 1972, pl. VI, 9–11).

[50] Baramki 1964, fig. 36, 1; Joukowsky 1972, pl. I, 1–2 (pl. XI, 34?); Lehmann 1996, 141.

[51] Gilboa/Sharon 2003; Georgiadou 2014, 383–384; and more recently, Kleiman et al. 2019.

[52] Sader 2014b.

and Levels 2–1 in Area III – are later, i.e., belong to the Iron Age II. However, and as explained above, only a few items in the ceramic assemblages of these phases suggest an Iron Age II date, and most of the vessels belong to the ceramic horizon of the previous period (e.g., the wavy-band pithos or derived form found in Level 1 in Area I/II). Consequently, the only way, in my view, to explain this phenomenon is to acknowledge the presence of later intrusions from a poorly preserved Iron Age II layer at the site. An Iron Age II Phoenician jug, found in Level 3 in Area III with what seems to be wavy-band pithoi and amphorae with a biconical body, strengthens this proposal.[53]

It can be concluded that Tell el-Ghassil features a dense stratigraphic sequence throughout the Iron Age I. During this timeframe, the site experienced at least two, if not three, traumatic events. With the evidence at hand, it is difficult to say when exactly activity resumed at the site, but considering the intrusive elements within Levels 5–1, any date between the Iron Age IIA and Iron Age IIB is reasonable.

Table 2: The stratigraphy of Tell el-Ghassil

Period	Area I/II (Squares E–I/10–15)	Area III (Squares D–G/16–19)
Iron Age II	Unstratified (intrusive vessels in earlier layers)	
Iron Age I	Level 1 (isolated walls)	–
	Levels 4–2 (mainly the temple)	Level 1 (Houses A and B)
	Level 5 (isolated walls)	Level 2 (large structure)

2.2.7   Tell Barr Elyas

According to L. Marfoe, Tell Barr Elyas constitutes an important landmark in the valley.[54] It is indeed a large mound in Barelias, about 7.5 km to the south of Zahlah. In the past, scholars proposed identifying this site with Tubuhi, mentioned in EA 179 as a Late Bronze Age city-state.[55] Its history in the Iron Age is unclear, but like Tell Dayr Zanun, the site was considered the possible location of Shazana (see below).

2.2.8   Tell Dayr Zanun

Tell Dayr Zanun, a large tell site with a flat hilltop,[56] is often considered one of the leading candidates for the identification of Shazana.[57] This toponym is known from two different historical sources: the cuneiform tablets discovered during the excavations of Tell Kamid el-Loz, and a Neo-Assyrian text dated to the late 8th century BCE.[58]

---

[53] Joukowsky 1972, pls. XXV, 9; XXIV, 33. For a newly published jug, see Núñez 2009.
[54] Marfoe 1995, 227.
[55] Sader/van Ess 1998, 250; Lipiński 2000, 323. It is possible that the city is mentioned in 2 Sam 8:8 (Betah) and 1 Chr 18:8 (Tibhath) (both described David's war against Hadad-Idri/Ezer).
[56] Copeland/Wescombe 1966, 63; Marfoe 1995, 225–226.
[57] Lipiński 2000, 328.
[58] Eph'al 1971, 157.

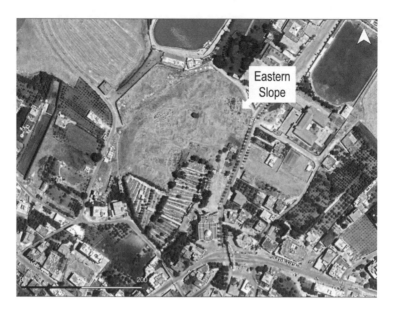

Figure 11: Satellite view of Tell Kamid el-Loz with the main area excavated during the University of Freiburg project (created with QGIS 3.16 and Google Satellite)

2.2.9   Tell Kamid el-Loz

Rising to a height of *ca.* 25 m above the plain surrounding it, Tell Kamid el-Loz (or Tell Abu Yun) is a distinct and visible feature in the landscape of the Lebanese Beqaa. It is situated in the northern sector of the city bearing the same and is undoubtedly the location of ancient Kumidi, one of the most important Bronze Age city-states in southern Syria, especially under the rule of the Egyptian Empire (Figure 11).[59] Previous explorations of the site, conducted by the Saarland University (1963–1981), focused mainly on the exposure of the impressive Bronze Age city, although remains dated from the beginning of the Iron Age were also uncovered.[60] The excavations of the site were resumed by the University of Freiburg and intended to illuminate the lesser-known periods at the site, including the Iron Age.[61] Both expeditions demonstrated that following the partial destruction of the Late Bronze Age IIB city, and perhaps a short squatters' phase, its layout underwent a significant transformation.[62]

In contrast to the Bronze Age city, the Iron Age settlement was rural in nature and included three major building periods (Building Periods 3–1) with eight sub-divisions (Building Levels 8–1). It mostly consists of domestic units of various sizes (for a proposed stratigraphic correlation, see Table 3).[63] Despite the settlement's modest nature, some disturbances in the occupational history of the site were traceable. Burnt debris

---

[59] Hachmann 1983, 28–32; Heinz 2010, 24–28; idem 2016, 129–183.
[60] Marfoe 1995, 159–165; Heinz 2016, 186.
[61] Heinz 2010; idem 2016; Wagner-Durand 2020.
[62] Marfoe 1995, 160–151; Wagner-Durand 2020, 75, 77.
[63] Echt 1984, 42–49, pl. 13.

covered the remains of Building Level 3, in some places reaching half a meter. A similar event also characterized the end of Building Period 1.[64]

During the University of Freiburg excavations,[65] a domestic quarter with Iron Age I remains was uncovered below the Persian period cemetery on the eastern slope of the site; it provided another opportunity to understand the Iron Age sequences at Tell Kamid el-Loz. In some places, the excavators noted evidence of reused Late Bronze walls, alluding to a short interval between the destruction of the Late Bronze Age city and its resettlement.[66] Moreover, some areas in the new town suffered at least two destruction events during the period: one at the end of Building Level 4 and another at the end of Building Level 3.[67] The first destruction included traces of fire and burnt debris that, in some places, reached *ca.* 75 cm.[68] Nevertheless, this event did not lead to the abandonment of the domestic quarter, which was rebuilt according to almost the same plan.[69] The second destruction was also intense and led to an occupational gap until the Persian period, when this sector of the site was transformed into a burial ground.[70]

In terms of material culture, the excavations of Tell Kamid el-Loz revealed modest yet significant ceramic assemblages from the Iron Age I settlements which supply important data on the pottery traditions of the Lebanese Beqaa in this period (in addition to the information from the excavations carried out in Tell Hizzin and Tell el-Ghassil). Published vessels from domestic structures include cooking pots, jugs, juglets, tripod cups, amphorae, wavy-line pithoi (only in Building Period 3), incense burners (only in Building Period 3), and Phoenician Bichrome vessels (see, e.g., Figure 12).[71] As was the case of the pottery revealed at Tell Hizzin (see above), some of these forms represent traditions known at other sites located along the Rift Valley (e.g., Tell el-Ghassil, Tel Dan, and Tel Hadar), while others reflect cultural connections with the Phoenician coast.

---

[64] Marfoe 1995, 160.

[65] Heinz 2010, 28–30, 33–74; Heinz *et al.* 2004, 102–105, 113–114; idem 2006, 88–90. Later Iron Age deposits (Iron Age IIB?) were also found in only one place (Heinz *et al.* 2004, 103).

[66] In several places, the excavators alluded to the continuous use of the domestic structures during the early days of the Iron Age II (Heinz 2010, 15–16, 29). This idea may have come from the exposure of a group of Phoenician Bichrome vessels in House no. 1 on the eastern slope (Heinz 2010, pl. 5), which were distributed in the southern Levant as early as the late Iron Age I (Arie 2006, 222). S. Kulemann-Ossen (2010, 61), who analyzed the pottery from the renewed excavations at Tell Kamid el-Loz, concluded that there is not much evidence to support the idea that settlement activity at the site continued into the Iron Age II. Still, Phoenician Bichrome jugs with horizontal bands are usually more typical of post-Iron Age I contexts (e.g., Gilboa 1999, 12; idem 2018, 128) and may suggest that the settlement activity in Tell Kamid el-Loz indeed lingered into the early days of the Iron Age IIA.

[67] Heinz *et al.* 2004, 103–105; idem 2006, 88–90; idem 2010, 37–41.

[68] Heinz *et al.* 2004, 41.

[69] Compare figs. 24 and 26 in Heinz *et al.* 2010.

[70] Heinz 2010, 8.

[71] Marfoe 1995, figs. 103–106; Heinz *et al.* 2010, fig. 11, a–g.

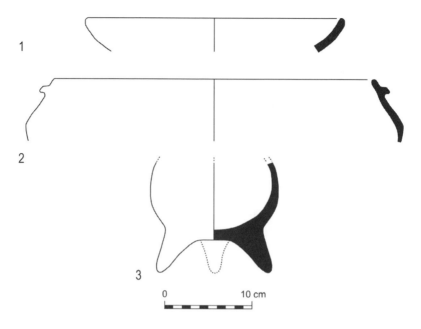

Figure 12: Selected Iron Age vessels from Saarland University's excavations at Tell Kamid el-Loz (redrawn by the author based on Marfoe 1995, fig. 105, 1, 5, 9)

Table 3: The stratigraphy of Tell Kamid el-Loz

Period	Saarland University		University of Freiburg	Comments
Iron Age II	-		Pottery? -	Iron Age II deposit in Area II-e-5/6 (the eastern slope)?
Iron Age I	Period 1	Level 1 Level 2 Level 3	Level 3	Reuse of House 1 and destruction in Area II-e-5/6 (the eastern slope)
	Period 2	Level 4 Level 5 Level 6	Level 4	Reuse of House 2 and construction of House 1 in Area II-e-5/6 (the eastern slope)
	Period 3	Level 7 Level 8		

2.2.10 Tell Dibbin

Tell Dibbin is situated next to a major highway leading from Sidon to Damascus (Figure 13).[72] Besides its common identification with biblical Ijon, this mound reaches an impressive size of *ca.* 8–10 hectares, which consequently makes it one of the largest tell sites in the central Levant. In the Hebrew Bible, it is mentioned in the description of Ben-Hadad I's campaign in the days of Baasha in the early 9th century BCE (1 Kgs

---

[72] Copeland/Wescombe 1966, 63; Mullins 1992; Marfoe 1995, 185.

15:20; 2 Chr 16:4) and in the description of Tiglath-Pileser III's attack in the days of Pekah, in the late 8th century BCE (2 Kgs 15:29). In both contexts, the author seems to affiliate the city with the Northern Kingdom rather than with an Aramaean entity (but these verses are certainly open to interpretation). No excavations were conducted at the site, but a research team visited there in the early 1980s observed sherds dating to the Late Bronze Age II, Iron Age I, and Iron Age II on the surface.[73]

Figure 13: Satellite view of Tell Dibbin (created with QGIS 3.16 and Google Satellite)

2.3 Regional Synthesis

At the end of the Bronze Age, most of the settlements in the Lebanese Beqaa were located north of Tell Kamid el-Loz, with only two sites to its south (Tell Dibbin and Tell ez-Zeitun). A closer examination of the data reveals three main clusters along the valley: near the sources of the Orontes River (the largest mounds in this group are Tell Qasr Labwa and Tell el-'Ayyun), near the sources of Nahr el-Litani (the largest mounds in this group are Tell Hizzin, Tell Hashbe, Tell el-Ghassil, and Tell 'Ain Sharif), and near Tell Kamid el-Loz (the largest mounds in this group, apart from the latter, are Tell Dalhamiya, Tell es-Sirhan, Tell Barr Elyas, Tell Dayr Zanun, and Tell ed-Dar).

Our knowledge of the first group is minimal, but based on the impressive size of Tell Qasr Labwa, as well as its identification as the location of an important city (at least in the Iron Age II), we may conjecture that during the Late Bronze Age this was the

---

[73] I. Finkelstein, personal communication. Note that in some of the satellite photos, possible remains of a moat can be observed on the southern margin of the settlement (see also Section 6.2.5).

regional center of the northern sector of the Beqaa. More extensive but still somewhat limited fieldwork was conducted in the area of the second group (near the sources of Nahr el-Litani). Due to the preservation of some of the ancient names, there is a consensus among scholars on the identification of Tell Hashbe with Hashabu of EA 174 and of Tell Hizzin with Hasi of EA 175. In contrast, the identification of the two other large sites in this cluster, Tell 'Ain Sharif and Tell el-Ghassil, is uncertain (but both have been proposed as the location of Enishasi mentioned in EA 363).[74] In regard to the third group, here it is clear that during the Late Bronze Age, the central site in the region was Tell Kamid el-Loz. Practically no sites existed to its south, and thus this city probably dominated the territory to its north, where several large-size mounds were documented (e.g., Tell Dalhamiya, Tell Barr Elyas, and Tell Dayr Zanun).[75]

Interestingly, the survey data show that the destruction of Tell Kamid el-Loz at the end of the Late Bronze Age IIB did not lead to dramatic changes in the Lebanese Beqaa as the distribution of settlements in the Iron Age I remained, more or less, the same (Figures 14–15).[76] Near the sources of the Orontes River, only two small-scale sites were abandoned, and no new sites were settled. In the center of the Beqaa, two sites were deserted, but eight new sites were established, including four medium-sized settlements; these sites existed alongside the large mounds from the previous periods. A similar process also characterizes the area to the north of Tell Kamid el-Loz, where only four sites were abandoned. Of these, the only significant site is the unexplored Tell ed-Dar (*ca.* 8 km to the northwest of Tell Kamid el-Loz). Excavations at Tell el-Ghassil (in the central Beqaa) and Tell Kamid el-Loz (in the southern Beqaa) strengthen the impression of settlement and cultural continuity and suggest that the Iron Age I in Lebanese Beqaa should be perceived as a continuation of the social order of the Late Bronze Age, even if some of the old political institutions collapsed (a phenomenon refer to in region located to the south of the Lebanese Beqaa as New Canaan).[77] Due to the insufficient datasets, the location of the central settlements of the Iron Age I in the Lebanese Beqaa remains at this point uncertain but Tell el-Ghassil, where a series of superimposed public buildings was revealed, might be one of them. Moreover, if the identification of Tell el-Ghassil as Enishasi, one of the city-states of the Land of 'Amqi, is correct, then we have some clues for the survival of some of the Late Bronze Age local polities into the Iron Age I.[78] Nevertheless, the recurring destructions identified during the excavations of Tell Kamid el-Loz and Tell el-Ghassil (and perhaps also at Tell Hizzin) also allude to a situation where the local institutions of the Iron Age I did not fully control their surroundings and were often the subject for violent attacks.

---

[74] One of these sites may have been the origin of EA 176, a broken tablet that was sent from a city in the Land of 'Amqi and whose name has not been preserved (Rainey 2015, 22).

[75] The identifications of Tell Barr Elyas as Tubuhi (Lipiński 2000, 323) and of Tell Jita as Gudashuna (Sader/van Ess 1998, 253) are possible but remain uncertain.

[76] In some cases, one can even observe the resettlement of a large site (e.g., Tell Ghazze) following the abandonment of a nearby one of comparable size (e.g., Tell ed-Dar).

[77] See also Wagner-Durand 2020, 77–79. For Phoenicia, see Sader 2019, 4, 33, 48–49.

[78] Note N. Na'aman's (1995a, 384) suggestion to identify the 'mq mentioned in two inscribed ivories found in Samos and Eretria with Hazael's hometown.

2.3 Regional Synthesis

While the survey data suggest that the transition to the Iron Age II did not lead to a major change in the Lebanese Beqaa (especially in the northern and central sectors of the region), settlement activity certainly decreased near the now-deserted Tell Kamid el-Loz (Figure 16). Eight medium settlements were abandoned in this region (e.g., Tell Satiya South, Tell Ghazza, and Tell el-Jisr), and only two small sites were established (Tell 'Aqaibi and Siret ed-Diyab). New regional centers possibly emerged in this period, but most of the prominent Iron Age II archaeological sites in the Lebanese Beqaa remain unexcavated. I refer, in particular, to Tell Qasr Labwa (Labwa) in the north, Tell Dayr Zanun (Shazana?) in the south, and Tell Dibbin (Ijon) in the Marj 'Ayyun.

On the whole, the archaeological data reveal a remarkable survival in the settlement patterns in the Lebanese Beqaa throughout the Late Bronze and the Iron Ages. Abandonment of settlements usually followed the foundation of new sites of about the same size or, alternatively, several smaller sites. Most of the changes occurred in the southern sector of the Beqaa, almost certainly the result of the abandonment of Tell Kamid el-Loz towards the end of the Iron Age I (or slightly later). A new regional center must have emerged afterward, but its location remains uncertain (for a comparative stratigraphy of the excavated sites in the Lebanese Beqaa, see Table 4).

Table 4: Comparative stratigraphy of excavated sites in the Lebanese Beqaa

Site	Late Bronze Age	Iron Age I	Iron Age II
Baalbek	Sherds	Sherds	Sherds
T. Hizzin	Tomb 8A and sherds	Sherds	Tomb 7B and sherds
T. el-Ghassil	13–6	5–1	Unstratified vessels
T. Kamid el-Loz	7 6	4 3	Sherds?

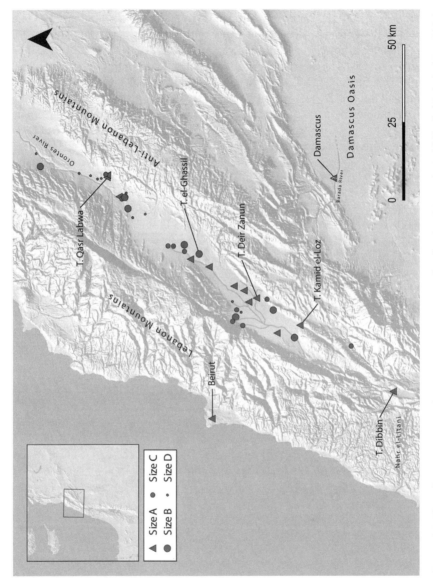

Figure 14: The Lebanese Beqaa in the Late Bronze Age (created with QGIS 3.16 and World Shaded Relief of Esri 2014)

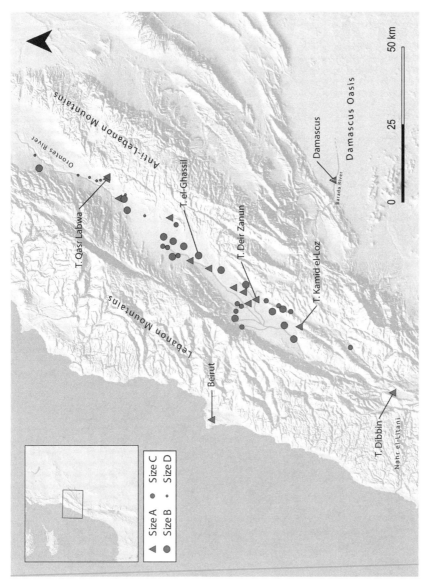

Figure 15: *The Lebanese Beqaa in the Iron Age I (created with QGIS 3.16 and World Shaded Relief of Esri 2014)*

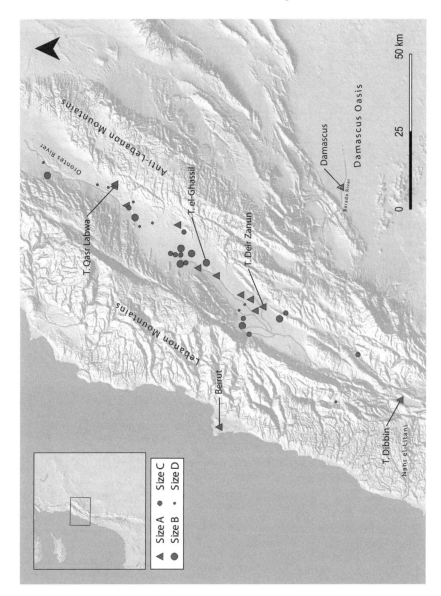

Figure 16: The Lebanese Beqaa in the Iron Age II (created with QGIS 3.16 and World Shaded Relief of Esri 2014)

3. The Hula Valley

3.1 Introduction

With abundant water sources and fertile land suitable for agriculture, the Hula Valley is among the most attractive territories for human settlement in the central Levant. During the Bronze and Iron Ages, the region was home to some of the largest urban centers in Canaan. Tel Hazor, the most well-known of these cities, grew to an enormous *ca.* 80 hectares during the second millennium BCE and was engaged in international relations with distant cities in the Ancient Near East, such as Mari.[1] While the destruction of Canaanite Hazor towards the end of the 13th century BCE substantially impacted the political structure of the region, the emergence of several new fortified cities such as Tel Hazor (the so-called Israelite city), Tel Dan, and probably also Abel Beth-Maacah indicates its recovery during the Iron Age II. Interestingly, the distance of the local cities from Jerusalem (*ca.* 150 km) did not diminish their importance to the biblical author(s), who embedded many narratives in the Hebrew Bible related to them (e.g., Jos 11:10; 2 Sam 20:14–22; 1 Kgs 12:29). Perhaps the most celebrated archaeological find from the Hula Valley is a royal Aramaic inscription found at Tel Dan. It describes the victory of Hazael over the kings of Israel and Judah and stimulated a long and interesting debate regarding the political authority over the region during the 9th–8th centuries BCE.[2]

The Hula Valley is a fertile plain that enjoys 400–600 mm annual rainfall, situated between the mountains of the Upper Galilee to the west and the Golan Heights and the Hermon Ridge to the east (Figure 17). The northern and southern boundaries of the valley are more loosely defined. In the south, the valley gradually shifts into the Korazim Plateau. In the north, near Metula, low hills separate the Hula Valley from Marj 'Ayyun. The valley covers approximately 200 sq km, at its longest *ca.* 22 km and *ca.* 10 km wide. In geographical literature, it is common to divide the area of the Hula Valley into four different units: 1) a series of topographic steps, which are known as the "northern threshold," 2) the northern plain, the most fertile territory of the valley, 3) the Hula Lake itself (now drained), and 4) the alluvial lands to the south of the lake, on the border of the Korazim Plateau. The largest ancient settlements in the valley are located along its edges: Tel Dan and Tel Abel Beth-Maacah in the north and Tel Hazor in the south.

---

[1] For the Bronze Age remains revealed at Tel Hazor, see Yadin 1972; Ben-Tor 2016.
[2] Finkelstein 2000a, 241; Arie 2008, 36; Frevel 2018a, 217.

Figure 17: The fertaile plain of the Hula Valley with the Hermon mountain ridge in the background (photographed by N. Frankel / CC BY 2.5)

3.2 Key Sites

In contrast to other regions discussed in this study, archaeological research in the Hula Valley is plentiful, and several sub-areas in this region have been surveyed intensively (Figure 18). However, this was not always done sufficiently. For instance, Y. Dayan dated many sites to the Bronze and Iron Ages based on surface collection, but his identification of some of the collected pottery was undoubtedly incorrect.[3] An excellent example of this is the survey of Tel Dan, which yielded only a few sherds dating to the Iron Age, although later excavations revealed significant Iron Age activity at the site. Additional Iron Age sites were identified during I. Shaked yet-unpublished field surveys.[4] To date, the most comprehensive fieldwork related to the periods discussed here was carried out by Y. Stepansky, who focused on the area around Tel Hazor and the Korazim Plateau.[5] Further data are from the IAA surveys, which primarily focused on the Golan Heights but included some sites located on the eastern margins of the Hula Valley.[6] Over the years, there have also been several intensive research projects at tell sites in the Hula Valley, especially Tel Hazor and Tel Dan. Tel Abel Beth-Maacah, a place where excavations began only recently, holds promise to contribute to our

---

[3] Dayan 1962.

[4] Nevertheless, references to Iron Age sites, included in IAS Maps Nos. 10 and 14, appear in several dissertations (Ilan 1999, 162–163, Table 5.1; Ben-Ami 2003, 232–236; Zuckerman 2003, 339–346). R. Frankel *et al.*'s (2001) survey focused on the mountainous region of the Upper Galilee, with a small segment on the western edge of the Hula Valley, the eastern boundary of their fieldwork.

[5] Stepansky 1999; idem 2014; IAS 18.

[6] IAS Maps Nos. 11, 15, and 18/1.

knowledge of the region in the future. Salvage excavations at smaller sites (e.g., Rosh Pinna) also provide additional perspectives on the settlement history of the region.

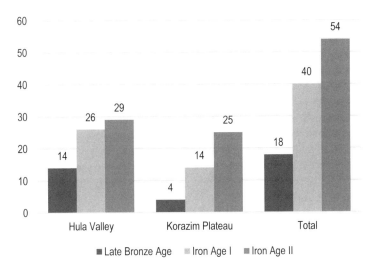

Figure 18: Settlement oscillations in the Hula Valley

Figure 19: Satellite view of Tel Abel Beth-Maacah with the main areas excavated during the Hebrew University of Jerusalem project (created with QGIS 3.16 and Google Satellite)

3.2.1 Tel Abel Beth-Maacah

Tell Abil el-Qamh is identified with Abel mentioned in various second millennium BCE texts and with biblical Abel Beth-Maacah (e.g., 2 Sam 20:14–22; 1 Kgs 15:20; 2 Kgs 15:29).[7] It is one of the largest tell sites in the central Levant (*ca.* 10 hectares) and is located on the ancient highway leading into the Marj 'Ayyun Valley, about 7 km to the west of Tel Dan (Figure 19). At the beginning of the 1970s, the site was surveyed by W.G. Dever, who found evidence of activity during the Late Bronze Age I–II, Iron Age I, and Iron Age II, as well as other periods. In his view, Tel Abel Beth-Maacah was not important during the Iron Age I and reached prosperity only during the Iron Age II, and specifically, not until the 8th century BCE, when a citadel was built at the top of the mound.[8] Excavations at the site by a team from the Hebrew University of Jerusalem commenced in 2013 and focused primarily on three areas: Area A (on the eastern slope), Area B (at the top of the mound), and Area F (on the southern slope).[9] As the excavations are still new, the information concerning the chronology and material culture of the Iron Age settlement is understandably incomplete.

According to the preliminary publications, the settlement at Tel Abel Beth-Maacah reached its maximum size during the Iron Age I. Excavations on the eastern slope (Area A) of the settlement discerned a remarkable stratigraphic sequence dated to this period (Strata A-2 to A-6). According to the excavators, the earliest phase, Phase A-6, may even be dated to the 12th century BCE, which would suggest a certain continuity between the Late Bronze and Iron Ages at the site.[10] During the Iron Age I, the settlement suffered two destruction events: one at the end of Stratum A-4 and another at the end of Stratum A-2.[11] Although the exposure of Iron Age IIA and IIB remains at the site is more limited at the moment, the settlement was probably not as populated as the previous city. In Area A, architectural remains dating to the Iron Age IIA were found above the destruction debris of the Iron Age I settlement (Stratum A-1), but the exact dating of this phase within the Iron Age IIA sequence is currently unclear. Recently, a storage room full of jars, including an inscribed item, was revealed in Area K. Radiocarbon dating and preliminary ceramic observations suggest that it dates to the Iron Age IIA.[12]

More substantial finds from the Iron Age IIA were found at the top of the mound, in Area B, where the remains of casemate rooms belonging to a citadel were found below a Persian-period structure and above the destruction debris of the Iron Age I

---

[7] Dever 1986, 207–217; Panitz-Cohen/Mullins/Bonfil 2013, 27–34.

[8] Dever 1986, 220–221.

[9] For preliminary reports, see Panitz-Cohen/Mullins/Bonfil 2013; idem 2015; Panitz-Cohen/Mullins 2016; Yahalom-Mack/Panitz-Cohen/Mullins 2018. For the few Late Bronze Age remains found at the site, see David/Mullins/Panitz-Cohen 2016. A salvage excavation was carried out on the southeastern slope of the site in 2000 and revealed a few MB II vessels (Stepansky 2005).

[10] Panitz-Cohen/Mullins/Bonfil 2015, 56; Yahalom-Mack/Panitz-Cohen/Mullins 2018, 150. For cult-related activity at the site during this timeframe, see idem 2019.

[11] Radiocarbon dates from these layers have not been fully published, but they seem to put the destruction of both layers between the end of the 11th century and the 10th century BCE (N. Yahalom-Mack in a lecture at the Hebrew University of Jerusalem, 26/4/2018).

[12] Yahalom-Mack *et al.* 2021.

settlement.[13] Based on a small ceramic assemblage found within the casemate rooms that included red-slipped and hand-burnished items, the excavators dated the structure to the Iron Age IIA comparable with other palatial structures, such as Palace 6000 at Tel Megiddo, Citadel 3090 at Tel Hazor, and the Bit-Hilani structures at Zincirli Hoyuk (ancient Sam'al).[14] Additional finds from Area B include the bearded head of a faience figurine, a decorated Phoenician jar, and an inscribed sherd.[15]

3.2.2   Tel Dan

Tel Dan (Tell el-Qadi) is also among the largest sites in the central Levant, reaching an enormous size of *ca.* 20–25 hectares (Figure 20). It is identified with Laish, mentioned in Bronze Age texts, and with biblical Dan. Excavations from 1966 to 1998 by A. Biran on behalf of the Hebrew Union College revealed significant Iron Age remains. Despite the extensive investigation of the site, most of the information on the Iron Age II settlement derives only from preliminary publications.[16]

a. Strata VII–IVB

During the Late Bronze Age, Tel Dan was most likely part of the territory of the Kingdom of Hazor.[17] However, unlike Tel Hazor, the Late Bronze Age IIB settlement at Tel Dan (Stratum VII) did not experience a massive, traumatic end. Yet, even though it was not destroyed, its material culture reflects a change.[18] Most conspicuous was the appearance of multiple pits and silos, found in all excavated areas but particularly in the southern sector of the site. D. Ilan, who analyzed the archaeological remains from the old excavations, encountered difficulties in defining the exact character of the site during the Iron Age I, a result of the problematic documentation of the old excavations.[19] Nevertheless, he defined a dense stratigraphic sequence of four general strata covering the partial destruction of the Late Bronze Age IIB city (Stratum VII) through the massive destruction at the end of the Iron Age I (Stratum IVB).[20] In some areas, such as Areas B and M, several distinct local phases were associated with this timeframe. In Ilan's view, the Iron Age I settlement at Tel Dan developed gradually into a town, demonstrating over time increasing signs of specialization, centralization, and development of social hierarchy.[21] Evidence of this process can also be seen in the pottery and faunal assemblages, as well as in the metallurgical remains.[22] Ultimately, the Iron Age I settlement

---

[13] Yahalom-Mack/Panitz-Cohen/Mullins 2018, 152–153.
[14] Yahalom-Mack/Panitz-Cohen/Mullins 2018, 152. For the distinction between palatial structures across the Levant, see Sharon/Zarzecki-Peleg 2006; Lehmann/Killebrew 2010.
[15] Yahalom-Mack/Panitz-Cohen/Mullins 2018, 152–154.
[16] Biran 1994; Ilan 1999; idem 2019a; Thareani 2016a; idem 2019a; idem 2019b.
[17] Goren/Finkelstein/Na'aman 2004, 226. For the Late Bronze Age, see Ben-Dov 2011.
[18] Biran 1994, 126.
[19] Ilan 1999, 27–28; idem 2019a, 17.
[20] Ilan 1999, 26–67; idem 2019a, 18–19, Table 2.2.
[21] Ilan 1999, 146–147; idem 2019a, 617–619.
[22] His proposal that the digging of so many pits at the site reflects regional insecurity is intriguing, especially in light of the destructions of Strata V and IVB (Ilan 2008; idem 2019a, 597–598).

was destroyed in a fierce conflagration (Stratum IVB). No radiocarbon dates from the event are available, but considering that all the ceramic assemblages originating in this destruction layer belong to the ceramic horizon of the late Iron Age I, dating it to somewhere in the first half of the 10th century BCE (or slightly later) is reasonable.

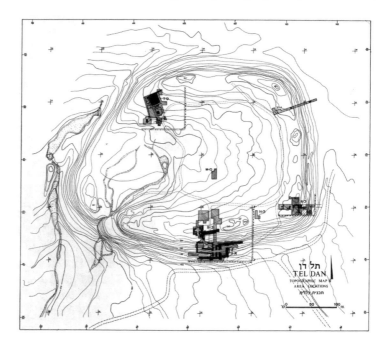

Figure 20: General plan of Tel Dan with the main areas excavated during the Hebrew Union College project (Biran 1982, fig. 1)

b. *Strata IVB–III*

It is not entirely clear what happened at the site after the destruction of Stratum IVB. Architectural remains associated with the next phase, Stratum IVA, were found primarily in Area A ("the gate area") and Area T ("the cultic area"), but their exact dating is disputed in research (see below). Based on the preliminary publications, the remains exposed in Area A can be divided into two places of interest: 1) the eastern sector (nicknamed Hussot by the excavator), which includes a stratigraphic sequence of four building phases, and 2) the western sector, which includes, in essence, two building episodes in the gate complex, the later one sealed by thick destruction debris containing Iron Age IIB restorable vessels. A sounding below the gate area revealed a thick fill that yielded sherds from the Bronze and Iron Ages, the latest of which were dated by A. Biran to the "first half of the 9th century BCE" (for a schematic plan of the gate area, see Figure 21).[23] Considering the relative chronology at that time, this means the Iron Age IIB. This means that the ceramic assemblages found above the floors of the entrance compound,

---

[23] Biran 1994, 246.

and the latest sherds found in its fills, are dated roughly to the same time. Unfortunately, no sherds from the aforementioned fills have been published, so any firm conclusions regarding the construction date of the gate complex are premature. However, considering the overall transformation of the site in the transition between Strata IVB and IVA and the general continuity observed in the remains of Strata IVA–II, it is reasonable to assume that the gate complex was built at the same time with Stratum IVA, and stayed in use until the destruction of the city.

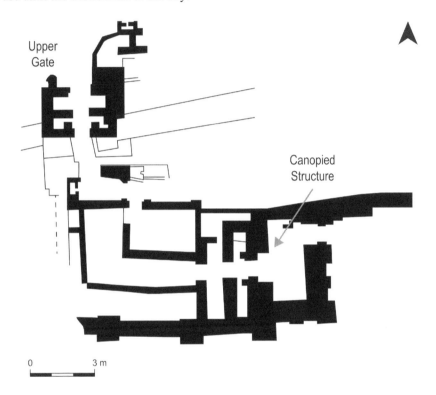

Figure 21: Plan of the gate complex at Tel Dan (redrawn by the author based on Arie 2008: fig. 8)

In Area T, the stratigraphic sequence is a bit different. First, probes dug in this area revealed several phases dating to the Iron Age I, including two successive destruction episodes.[24] Above the destruction of the latest Iron Age I phase (Stratum IVB), the remains of domestic/industrial buildings, an olive press installation,[25] and what seems like a small altar were found. To the north of these features, a large rectangular stone monument (Bamah A) was exposed. All of the domestic/industrial remains were sealed below a thick layer of crushed travertine.[26] In the next building phase, a large altar was

---

[24] Ilan 1999, 60.
[25] Stager/Wolff 1981; Arie 2008, 28.
[26] Biran 1994, 165.

constructed above the smaller one and a massive building (Bamah B) was built above the monument of the previous layer (Figure 76, 1). In this stage, an enclosure wall surrounded these features.

More than a decade ago, I. Sharon and A. Zarzecki-Peleg[27] contested the conventional interpretation of the stratigraphy of Area T. In their view, the first elements built after the destruction of Stratum IVB were the olive oil installation and the irregular rooms (designated above as domestic/industrial buildings). In the next stage, the earlier small altar was built together with Bamah A. In Sharon and Zarzecki-Peleg's opinion, these elements were constructed in an intermediate stage between Strata IVA and III. Afterward, Bamah B was built above Bamah A, and the large altar replaced the small one. The casemate enclosure was built around these features, together with the "travertine floor," i.e., in Stratum III. All of these elements remained in use until the destruction of the site (Stratum II). In my view, there is no stratigraphic reason to separate the small altar from the domestic remains; this feature, if indeed an altar, can also signify a small neighborhood shrine. More importantly, while Bamah A has often been interpreted as a distinct feature that must precede the construction of Bamah B, it makes sense to understand it as a support system for the monument built above it. Evidence for similar support features was exposed below other monumental buildings, for instance, Buildings 338 and 1616 at Tel Megiddo.[28] With these points in mind, I reconstruct only three stages in Area T, in fact, as suggested originally by A. Biran (see summary in Table 5).

Table 5: Different views on the stratigraphy of Tel Dan in Area A

Feature	Biran 1994	Sharon/Zarzecki-Peleg 2006	This Study
Domestic remains	Stratum IVA	Stratum IVA	Stratum IVA
Olive-oil installation	Stratum IVA		
Small altar	Stratum IVA	Post-Stratum IVA/Pre-Stratum III	
Large altar	Strata III–II	Strata III–II	Strata III–II
Bamah B	Stratum III–II		
Casemates	Strata IVA–II		
Bamah A	Stratum IVA	Post-Stratum IVA/Pre-Stratum III	Part of Bamah A

It is impossible to continue without a few words on the chronological debate surrounding the Iron Age II strata of Tel Dan (for a proposed stratigraphic correlation, see Table 6). According to the traditional view, supported by the excavators, the activity at Tel Dan quickly resumed after the destruction of Stratum IVB. Most of the scholars supporting this view date the construction of Stratum IVA to the late 10th century BCE.[29] About a decade ago, E. Arie reexamined the pottery figures published by A. Biran (see, e.g., Figure 22) and concluded that Stratum IV contained many ceramic forms that are

---

[27] Sharon/Zarzecki-Peleg 2006.

[28] Lamon/Shipton 1939, fig. 122 (Square S/9); Franklin 2006, 102; Kleiman/Kaplan/Finkelstein 2016, 170–171. For a similar proposal, see already Davis 2013, n. 3.

[29] E.g., Biran 1994, 165; Ilan 1999, Table 3.11. Others pushed the date of this stratum slightly later, to the days of the Omrides, specifically Omri and Ahab (e.g., Finkelstein 1999b, 61).

typical to Iron Age IIB contexts.[30] Since Stratum IVB dates to the late Iron Age I, he argued for an extended gap or insignificant activity at the site during the Iron Age IIA.

Figure 22: Selected complete vessels from Stratum IVA at Tel Dan (adapted from Biran 1982: pl. 8: 1)

In the following years, E. Arie's proposal gained both supporters[31] and critics.[32] The latter group has emphasized an apparent weakness – that Arie's conclusions were based only on the (incompletely) published data.[33] Other arguments are more difficult to comprehend. D.T. Sugimoto,[34] for instance, argued that Arie ignored the radiocarbon results from Stratum IVB and that since the remains of Stratum IVA were found directly above those of Stratum IVB, the two layers must have been close in time. Such arguments cannot be accepted. First, only one sample from the Iron Age I settlement is short-lived (and it originated from Stratum V, see Appendix C). Second, the remains of Stratum IVA were built above the destruction debris of Stratum IVB but with no evidence of architectural continuity between the two layers. Y. Thareani, on the other hand, criticized Arie from a different angle.[35] In her view, Arie's theory is hampered by the nature of the material culture exposed in Strata IVA–II, which reflects a mixture of different traditions ("Israelite" and "Phoenician"). However, the relevance of the cultural argument to the chronological debate is unclear, as the ceramic traditions of the late Iron Age IIA are well-represented in Strata X–IX at Tel Hazor, located only a few kilometers to the south of Tel Dan.

---

[30] Arie 2008.
[31] E.g., Finkelstein 2011c; Na'aman 2012; Hasegawa 2012; Ghantous 2013, 23–30.
[32] E.g., Davis 2013; Thareani 2016a; Younger 2016, 576–578; Greer 2017.
[33] Davis 2013, n. 2; Greer 2017, n. 20.
[34] Sugimoto 2015a, n. 10.
[35] Thareani 2016b; idem 2019a; idem 2019b.

So far, more than a decade after the publication, the critics of E. Arie's theory have not presented any ceramic assemblage from a secure context dated to the early or late Iron Age IIA at Tel Dan.[36] His conclusions, then, are sound and safe to follow. I would only propose associating Stratum IVA with the end of the Iron Age IIA (i.e., in parallel to Stratum VIII at Tel Hazor or Stratum III at Tel Hadar) rather than with an early phase of the Iron Age IIB (e.g., Stratum VII at Tel Hazor or Stratum IVA at Tel Megiddo). The reason behind this assertation is that, on the whole, more ceramic forms typical of the Iron Age IIA (e.g., Arie's Types CP1, CP4, and BoR1) than those characterizing the Iron Age IIB (e.g., Arie's Types CP5),[37] was uncovered in Stratum IVA.

Table 6: The stratigraphy of Tel Dan

Period	Stratum	Area A	Area T
Iron Age IIB	II	Gate compound; unnamed structure in Hussot; destruction	Small-scale modifications in the architecture of Stratum III; destruction
	III	Gate compound; Structure A in Hussot	
		Gate compound; Structure B in Hussot	Bamah B (+ Bamah A as an underground element); large altar; casemate enclosure; yellow floor
Iron Age IIA	IVA	Gate compound; Structure C in Hussot	Domestic remains; olive oil installation; a small altar
	Occupational gap throughout most of the Iron Age IIA		
Iron Age I	IVB	-	Fragmentary construction
	V	Pit 5009	New construction
	VI	-	Pits and reused architecture

3.2.3 Tel Tannim

Tel Tannim (Tell el-Wawiyat) is located *ca.* 1.5 km to the east of Kiryat Shmona.[38] During salvage excavations at the site during the 1980s and 1990s, two Iron Age I strata were exposed, both destroyed by fire (Strata X and IX).[39] According to D. Ilan, these layers are contemporary to Strata V and IVB at Tel Dan.[40] An exciting find from this site was a subterranean bell-shaped silo sub-divided by a stone slab at the bottom of the narrow shaft; this slab created the illusion of a smaller silo which Ilan proposed should be interpreted as an attempt to hide large quantities of grain.[41]

---

[36] *Pace* Greer 2017, n. 20; Ilan/Greer 2021, n. 8; Thareani 2019b.
[37] For instance, no torpedo jars have been published thus far from Stratum IVA contexts.
[38] Ilan 1999, 162–171; Ben-Ami 2003, 232–236; IAS 7, no. 75.
[39] Onn 1988; Onn *et al.* 1995; Avshalom-Gorni/Getzov 2001; idem 2003.
[40] Ilan 1999, 160–161.
[41] Ilan 1999, 161. For a section drawing, see Onn *et al.* 1995, fig. 10.

3.2.4 Kiryat Shmona South

A salvage excavation at Kiryat Shmona South, located in the southern sector of the modern city, revealed an Iron Age I settlement above a Middle Bronze Age fortress.[42] Several domestic structures, silos, and a tomb with four individuals were exposed during the excavation (Stratum IV), but only a small ceramic assemblage from mixed and unclear contexts was associated with the settlement.[43] Nevertheless, a complete Phoenician Bichrome jug found in the tomb seems to date the settlement to the late Iron Age I.[44] Noteworthy among the finds from this settlement is a bronze scepter (or mace-head), which was also discovered in the aforementioned tomb.[45] In contrast to other sites in the Hula Valley and nearby regions, the settlement of Kiryat Shmona South was not destroyed at the end of the Iron Age I.

3.2.5 Tel Anafa

Tel Anafa (Tell el-Akhdar) is a medium-size tell site located *ca.* 2.5 km to the northeast of Shamir.[46] Excavations at the site exposed finds mainly from the Hellenistic and Early Roman periods.[47] Earlier remains were also encountered here (e.g., wall fragments and sherds). Iron Age pottery from mixed loci includes Iron Age I and Iron Age IIA ceramic forms, mainly bowls and cooking pots.[48] A single Cypriot Black-on-Red fragment[49] and an Assyrian-style vessel were also found at the site.[50]

3.2.6 Tel Hazor

There is little doubt that Tel Hazor (Tell el-Qadeh) was one of the most important sites in the southern Levant, extending over *ca.* 80 hectares. It is located on the border between the Hula Valley and the Korazim Plateau and controls the main route leading from the Jezreel and Beth-Shean Valleys to the northern Levant (Figure 23; for a proposed stratigraphic correlation, see Table 7).

Aside from a short excavation at the beginning of the 20th century, the first systematic excavations of the site took place in the 1950s and 1960s by Y. Yadin on behalf of the Hebrew University of Jerusalem. In contrast to other large-scale projects carried out at that time, the data collected by the expedition were quickly published and became a reliable source for discussing the settlement history of the site.[51] While the excavations resumed during the 1990s added much to our knowledge regarding the archaeology and history of Tel Hazor,[52] over the years, the archaeological and historical interpretations

---

[42] For the final report on the Iron Age remains, see Covello-Paran 2012.
[43] Covello-Paran 2012, 103.
[44] Covello-Paran 2012, 114.
[45] See more in Section 11.2.2.
[46] Dayan 1962, 23; Ilan 1999, 161–171; Zuckerman 2003, 232–245; IAS 11, no. 17.
[47] Herbert 1992.
[48] Dever/Harrison 2017.
[49] Dever/Harrison 2017, 321–322.
[50] Dever/Harrison 2017, 321.
[51] Yadin *et al.* 1958; idem 1960; idem 1961; Yadin 1972.
[52] Ben-Tor/Ben-Ami/Sandhaus 2012; Ben-Tor *et al.* 2017. See summary in Ben-Tor 2016.

of the remains have also been challenged by many scholars.[53] Points of contention were, as always, chronological and historical matters, many of which are discussed below.

Figure 23: Aerial view of the western sector of Tel Hazor with the main areas excavated during the Hebrew University of Jerusalem projects (Ben-Tor 2020, 1: b)

a. Strata XIII–XII/XI

Most scholars agree that during the Late Bronze Age (Stratum XIII), Tel Hazor extended over the entire mound and the lower city. The city of this period includes monumental architecture, particularly the remains of a massive building understood by some as a ceremonial palace (i.e., the official residence of the city's ruler with some spaces dedicated to cult-related activity)[54] and by others as a temple (i.e., a structure fully devoted to cult-related activity).[55] In the lower city, the excavations revealed two temples, two gate complexes, and a few domestic buildings (Area 210). Despite the prosperity of the city, in fact, probably as a result of it,[56] Hazor was ultimately destroyed. Most scholars date the destruction of the Stratum XIII city to the 13th century BCE. A. Ben-Tor emphasized in his studies the exposure of a fragment of an Egyptian offering table with the name of a high-ranking officer of Ramesses II, which was dated to *ca.* 1240–1230 BCE, in the ruins.[57] Assuming that the destruction occurred a short while after the arrival of this artifact to Tel Hazor, he ascribed the violent event to the second half of the 13th

---

[53] Finkelstein 1999b; Herzog/Singer-Avitz 2006, 178–180; Sergi/Kleiman 2018, n. 9.
[54] Bonfil/Zarzecki-Peleg 2007; Ben-Tor 2016, 93–104; idem 2020.
[55] Zuckerman 2010.
[56] According to N. Na'aman (2011, 337), it is possible that the exceptional human and physical resources invested by the rulers of Hazor in cult-related activity, e.g., the construction of monumental temples, led to tension with marginal groups that abandoned their duty to the city in the time of crisis.
[57] Ben-Tor 2016, 116–117. S. Zuckerman (2003, 259–95) noted that the reading and date of the object are uncertain and argued for an earlier date, at the beginning of the 13th century BCE.

century BCE. P. Beck and M. Kochavi, in contrast, suggested an earlier date in that century, relying on the assumption that the ceramic assemblages originating from the destruction of Canaanite Hazor are earlier than those found in the destruction of Aphek in the Sharon. The latter event was dated to *ca.* 1230 BCE based on a letter sent from Ugarit found at the site.[58] Nevertheless, the main problem with both suggestions is that they assume that datable objects discovered in the destruction layers provide the latest possible date for the events, whereas they supply, in fact, only a terminus post quem. In other words, the destruction of Canaanite Hazor (and Tel Aphek) could have happened many years after the arrival of the mentioned objects, closer to the end of the 13th century or even the early days of the 12th century BCE.[59]

Following the destruction of the Late Bronze Age city, a relatively weak settlement prevailed at the site (Strata XII/XI). Evidence for the new settlement is limited to a few refuse pits and domestic architecture, which was established directly over the ruins of the previous city in several places.[60] A notable feature of these strata is an open-air cult place near the devastated Late Bronze Age temple (or ceremonial palace). S. Zuckerman suggested interpreting this evidence as a ruins' cult.[61] Despite the poor nature of the remains, the Iron Age I remains at Tel Hazor still attracted the attention of scholars who debated: 1) the number of phases between the destruction of the Late Bronze Age city (Stratum XIII) and the construction of the Iron Age IIA city (Stratum X), 2) the exact date of the remains within the greater Iron Age I sequence, and 3) the identity of the settlers. Y. Yadin, who established the site's stratigraphic sequence, divided the remains into two distinct strata based mainly on the finds from Area B. In his view, the rural settlement was constructed at the beginning of the 12th century BCE, immediately after the destruction of the Late Bronze Age city, and it existed for nearly two centuries. Eventually, this poor settlement developed into the fortified city of Stratum X.[62] In other

---

[58] Beck/Kochavi 1986; Zuckerman 2003, 259–295.

[59] Finkelstein 1995, n. 15. S. Bechar (2017, 242) showed that the ceramic assemblages from Stratum XIII should be equated with Strata VIIB and VIIA at Tel Megiddo. As the latter strata were recently radiocarbon-dated to between the late 13th and second half of the 12th centuries BCE (Finkelstein *et al.* 2017, 274–275), placing the destruction of Canaanite Hazor in the early 12th century BCE is quite probable. For various views on the destruction process of the city, see Ben-Tor/Rubiato 1999; Schäfer-Lichtenberger 2001; Finkelstein 2005; Ben-Tor/Zuckerman 2007; Zuckerman 2007; Ben-Tor 2016, 118–26; Benz 2019; Millek 2020, 157–159.

[60] Ben-Tor/Ben-Ami/Sandhaus 2012, 1–2; Ben-Tor 2016, 126–131. For limited evidence for activity in the lower settlement, see Yadin 1972, 200; Yadin *et al.* 1989, 297.

[61] Zuckerman 2011; Ben-Tor/Ben-Ami/Sandhaus 2012, 8–13; Ben-Ami 2013, 101–102; Na'aman 2016a. For the "cult room" discovered during the old excavation in Area B, see Yadin *et al.* 1989, 80–82. I. Finkelstein (2000a, 234–235) argued that the incense burners found in Building 3283 might have been used as part of a domestic cult (see also Zuckerman 2011, 390). While this interpretation may be correct, one should still note that at least one of these cultic vessels (Yadin *et al.* 1961, pl. CCIV) has an exact parallel in the ceramic assemblage of the "southern temple" of Stratum XV (Bechar 2017, fig. 7.6, 1). As no similar examples are known from later periods, it may be presumed that some looting of Middle Bronze Age remains took place during the lifetime of Stratum XII/XI. Indeed, S. Zuckerman (2011, 390) also suggested that many of the objects found in the foundation deposit of Building 3283 were scavenged from the Canaanite royal precinct.

[62] For the conventional reconstruction, see Yadin 1972, 135–146.

words, he presumed a settlement and social continuity between the end of the 13th century and the beginning of the 10th century BCE. However, in the last years, the division of the remains into two distinct strata has been contested by several scholars, including the current excavators of the site, who note the absence of two clear superimposed floors. Consequently, scholars, particularly A. Ben-Tor and D. Ben-Ami, suggest merging Strata XII and XI into a single-phase designated Stratum XII/XI.[63] Indeed, only a few architectural features are directly overlaid or replaced each other (e.g., Pit 8508 and Installation 8411), probably representing minor changes in the village.[64]

A more challenging task is the exact dating of the remains. Based on data from the old excavations and partial data from the new ones, I. Finkelstein argued that Stratum XII/XI should be dated earlier within the Iron Age I sequence – presumably to the late 12th century BCE.[65] In his view, Tel Hazor remained abandoned during the late Iron Age I, dated by him to the late 11th century and 10th century BCE. A. Ben-Tor, D. Ben-Ami, and D. Sandhaus contested Finkelstein's higher dating and maintained its 11th century BCE date.[66] Past attempts to date Stratum XII/XI have not differentiated between material originating from the floors of this stratum or material found in the many pits that characterize the strata.[67] Dating this settlement based on items found in the pits is problematic, as ultimately, they were used to dispose of broken vessels[68] but not necessarily sealed at the end of their use; thus, these pits are likely to include sherds from earlier[69] or later periods.[70] Based on pottery originating from the floors of Stratum XII/XI, one can make the following observations: 1) the typological composition of secure contexts is indeed different from that of Stratum XIII, lacking several types typical of the Late Bronze Age IIB (e.g., carinated bowls, cooking pots with a carinated stance, decorated pottery, and imports),[71] 2) the composition of the assemblage is also far from that of the Iron Age IIA, as evident in the absence of red-slipped and hand-burnished vessels from secure loci,[72] and 3) the ceramic assemblage of Stratum XII/XI also lacks many of the characteristic types of the late Iron Age I ceramic horizon (e.g., biconical cooking jugs, storage jars with an elongated body and carinated shoulder, "jar-jugs," and Phoenician Bichrome Ware). All of these types appear in late Iron Age I strata from sites nearby (e.g., Tel Dan), and thus their absence cannot be explained as a regional phenomenon.

---

[63] Finkelstein 2000a, 233–235; Ben-Tor/Ben-Ami/Sandhaus 2012, 1–2, 7.
[64] Finkelstein 2000a, 234; Ben-Tor/Ben-Ami/Sandhaus 2012, 7.
[65] Finkelstein 2000a, 235–236.
[66] Ben-Ami 2013; Ben-Tor/Ben-Ami/Sandhaus 2012; Ben-Tor 2016.
[67] E.g., Finkelstein 1988, 98–101; idem 2000a; Ben-Tor/Ben-Ami/Sandhaus 2012, 21–26.
[68] Ben-Ami 2001, 166; idem 2003, 31–33.
[69] E.g., Ben-Tor/Ben-Ami/Sandhaus 2012, fig. 1.6, 12.
[70] E.g., Yadin et al. 1961, pl. CLXIV, 8; Ben-Tor/Ben-Ami/Sandhaus 2012, fig. 1.10, 1–3.
[71] For similar observations, see, e.g., Yadin 1972, 129–130; Finkelstein 2000a, 236; Ben-Ami 2001, 165. Note that the presence of shallow bowls in the floor assemblages of Stratum XII/XI (e.g., Ben-Tor/Ben-Ami/Sandhaus 2012, fig. 1.1, 3; 6) may suggest their continuous production and mark some continuity between the ceramic traditions of Strata XIII and XII/XI.
[72] All red-slipped and hand-burnished vessels found in Stratum XII/XI originated from problematic loci, i.e., pits and fills (e.g., Ben-Tor/Ben-Ami/Sandhaus 2012, figs. 1.4, 2, 1.10, 1–4).

An additional comment should be made about the absence of the Philistine Bichrome Ware at Tel Hazor. Such sherds were found at Tel Dan, Tel Kinrot, and recently also at Tel Abel Beth-Maacah.[73] In her book on the material culture of the Philistines, T. Dothan mentions that Philistine sherds were unearthed both during an unpublished salvage excavation and the old excavations in Area A at Tel Hazor.[74] However, none of these sherds were ever published. Equally important is the fact that more than twenty years of intensive excavations at the site have not revealed a single Philistine vessel. Given the appearance of this ware in nearby sites, cultural segregation of some sort cannot explain the absence of this ware at Tel Hazor, and this phenomenon should be understood as a chronological indicator, suggesting an earlier date for Stratum XII/XI. One cannot ignore, of course, the absence of Late Bronze Age style cooking pots among the published pottery of Stratum XII/XI,[75] as well as the paucity of painted material; this might push the date of this stratum forward into the Iron Age I.

In short, the small village of Stratum XII/XI existed only for a brief time and was already abandoned at the beginning of the Iron Age I. Dating it to somewhere around the Late Bronze Age III-Iron Age I transition is a possibility, which constrains the gap between the destruction of the city and its reoccupation.[76]

b. Strata X–IX

After the abandonment of Stratum XII/XI, Tel Hazor remained abandoned for nearly 100–150 years.[77] The settlement of the Iron Age IIA did not resemble the previous one at all. Not only did the architecture of Stratum X include major construction projects with monumental and residential features, but the material culture comprised many new ceramic forms with little connection to those of Stratum XII/XI.[78] The most prominent change of this period was the construction of a casemate wall around the western sector of the upper mound, which was accompanied by the building of a monumental and ashlar-made six-chambered gate, similar to those discovered at Tel Megiddo (Gate 2156) and Tel Gezer (the so-called Solomonic gate). Both the old and renewed excavations exposed residential/industrial quarters near the gate area, including continually renovated structures,[79] in what seems to be an organic development. Having said that, restorable vessels found on the floors of Stratum X may suggest a confined traumatic event within the town[80] a few decades before the one associated with the end of Stratum IX.[81]

---

[73] Ilan 1999, 93–95; pls. 7, 3; 48, 3; 59, 1; 7–8; Panitz-Cohen/Mullins 2016, 159; Tynjä 2017, 153–154, 184, 232–233, 263. See also Section 9.3.2.

[74] Dothan 1982, 90.

[75] E.g., Bechar 2017, Type CP3.

[76] Both Y. Yadin (1972, 131–132) and S. Geva (1984, 160) dated Stratum XII to the 12th century BCE and presumed a shorter gap, of only several decades, between the destruction of Stratum XIII and the Iron Age I village.

[77] Finkelstein 2000a, 237–239.

[78] Ben-Tor/Ben-Ami/Sandhaus 2012, 2, 108.

[79] Yadin 1972, 135.

[80] Ben-Tor/Ben-Ami/Sandhaus 2012, photos 2.3–2.5, 2.15, 2.25–2.26.

[81] Yadin 1972, 143.

Conventionally, the construction of the city of Strata X–IX was dated to the early 10th century BCE and was regarded as one of the finest examples of the monumental building projects of the United Monarchy.[82] Following the Low Chronology, I. Finkelstein proposed down-dating the construction of this settlement by nearly 100 years to the days of the Omrides.[83] In reaction, A. Ben-Tor and D. Ben-Ami[84] argued the following: 1) the ceramic assemblages found associated with the casemate wall and the gate demonstrate that the original absolute dates of these features should be maintained, and 2) that squeezing Strata X–IX and their sub-phases (Strata XB, XA, IXB, and IXA) into the first half of the 9th century BCE cannot be justified. Finkelstein responded to both arguments.[85] First, he argued that attributing the pottery found in association with the gate to the "10th century BCE" was based on its association with the "10th century BCE gate." Second, he dismissed the "dense stratigraphy" argument, claiming that the high chronology basically did the same thing in squeezing the same strata within the 10th century BCE. Lastly, he suggested that the history of border sites may be more complicated than that of inland sites, such as Tel Megiddo.[86] Z. Herzog and L. Singer-Avitz[87] supported his scenario, associating Strata X and IX with their Jezreel Compound Phase.[88] However, unlike the Jezreel enclosure, the well-defined layers of both Strata X and IX at Tel Hazor date both to the late Iron Age IIA, and a similar stratigraphic sequence characterizes other sites in the Northern Kingdom, such as Tel Rehov (Strata V–IV) and Tel Megiddo (Levels Q-5 and Q-4).[89] At these sites, the earlier layer seems to represent a pre-Omride stage, which parallels Stratum VIIb at Tell el-Far'ah North (the capital of the Northern Kingdom before Samaria).[90] This means that from an archaeological perspective, the construction of Strata X–IX could be dated to the late 10th/early 9th century BCE, similar to Stratum V at Tel Rehov or Level Q-5 at Tel Megiddo.[91]

c. Strata VIII–V

It is generally agreed that Stratum VIII represents a turning point in the history of Iron Age Hazor.[92] During this time period, a series of public structures were built across the site: 1) in the western margin of the site (Area B), Citadel 3090 was constructed, with several administrative buildings around it (for an illustration of the building, see Figure 24), 2) in the southwestern sector (Area L), the excavators revealed an elaborate water system,[93] 3) around the site, a new inset-offset city-wall replaced the casemate fortification wall of Strata X–IX, 4) many new domestic and administrative structures (e.g.,

---

[82] Yadin 1970; Ben-Tor/Ben-Ami/Sandhaus 2012, 3; Ben-Tor 2016, 132–146.
[83] Finkelstein 1996, with updates in idem 2010.
[84] Ben-Tor/Ben-Ami 1998.
[85] Finkelstein 1999b.
[86] For additional arguments, see Finkelstein 2011c, 235–237; idem 2013, 96.
[87] Herzog/Singer-Avitz 2006, 178–180; idem 183.
[88] For this term, see Section 1.4.2.
[89] Finkelstein/Kleiman 2019, 290.
[90] Kleiman 2018; Montero Fenollós/Caramelo 2021.
[91] Mazar *et al.* 2005; Mazar 2016 (Tel Rehov); Boaretto 2022 (Tel Megiddo).
[92] Ben-Tor/Ben-Ami/Sandhaus 2012, 154; Shochat/Gilboa 2019; Kleiman 2021.
[93] For the excavations of Area L, see Garfinkel 1997.

tripartite pillared buildings) were built, and the size of the settlement doubled, now also covering the eastern half of the upper mound, and 5) since the six-chambered gate of Strata X–IX became an internal gate within the new city, it is likely to assume that a new gate complex was built at the site, but its location remains unknown.

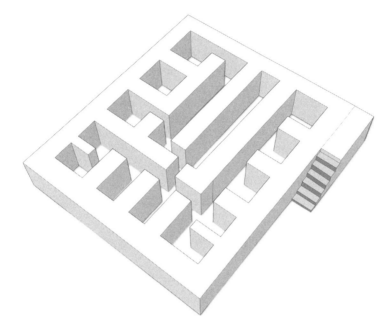

Figure 24: Reconstruction of the foundations of Citadel 3090, the largest Iron Age structure revealed at Tel Hazor (drawn with Trimble Sketchup Pro 2021 and based on Yadin et al. 1961, pl. xxxii, 1)

While from an architectural perspective, the basic town plan of Stratum VIII remained mostly unchanged until Stratum V, defining the chronological affinities of its ceramic assemblages is somewhat more difficult. During the early excavations, Y. Aharoni and R. Amiran[94] argued that the ceramic horizons at Iron Age II Hazor could be divided into two main sequences: Strata X–VIII and Strata VIII–IV. In absolute chronology terms, they assumed that the turning point was at the end of Stratum VIII, *ca.* 850 BCE. A review of the ceramic assemblage of Stratum VIII shows that this stratum still included many typical ceramic forms of the Iron Age IIA (e.g., cooking pots with vertical or inverted pinched rims) and only a few typical types of the Iron Age IIB (e.g., black juglets with a handle attached directly to the rim).[95] Accordingly, the best chronological

---

[94] Aharoni/Amiran 1958.
[95] For a review of the date of Stratum VIII, see Kleiman 2019a, 295–297; Shochat/Gilboa 2019.

slot for this stratum, in my view, is the final phase of the Iron Age IIA[96] rather than the Iron Age IIB.[97] In absolute chronological terms, this means the late 9th century BCE.[98]

The layout of Tel Hazor, as determined by the construction of Stratum VIII, changed minimally in Strata VII–V when floors were raised, and new buildings gradually replaced old ones. Unsurprisingly, the different excavation areas do not always present the same stratigraphic development. For instance, in Area A, it is possible to discern a substantial change between Strata VIII and VII, when the six-chambered gate and the casemate wall were decommissioned, and between Strata VII to VI, when the pillared building was built over. In contrast, in Area B, the stratigraphic sequence of Strata VIII–V reflects remarkable architectural continuity. The only significant change here was the removal of two volute capitals from the entrance to the citadel and their integration into a small poorly-built structure in the nearby courtyard (Building 3264).[99] Nevertheless, the city continued to flourish until its massive destruction at the end of the Stratum V, commonly assigned to the campaigns of Tiglath-Pileser III in 732 BCE (for a proposed stratigraphic correlation, see Table 8).

Table 7: The stratigraphy of Tel Hazor

Period	Stratum	Comments
Iron Age IIB	V	Citadel 3090 (reuse); insets and offsets wall (reuse); domestic remains in Areas A, A5, and G
	VI	
	VII	
Iron Age IIA	VIII	Citadel 3090 (construction); insets and offsets wall (construction); expansion of settlement to the east; domestic remains in Areas A, A5, and G
	IX	Six-chambered gate (construction); casemate wall (construction); domestic remains in Areas A and B
	X	
	Occupational gap in the early Iron Age IIA	
Iron Age I	Occupational gap in the late Iron Age I	
	XII/XI	Domestic remains; pits

3.2.7 Tel Ya'af

Tel Ya'af (Tell el-Kusab) is a medium tell site (*ca.* 2–3 hectares) on a basalt hill, *ca.* 1.5 km to the east of Rosh Pinna.[100] Around the hill, especially in the northwest, the remains of a fortification wall that was preserved to a height of four courses were observed. Additional (presumably ancient) architecture is visible at the top of the site. Iron Age pottery constituted *ca.* 87% of all the sherds found at the site during the survey carried out at Tel Ya'af. Y. Stepansky suggested that this site should be listed among the

---

[96] For a somewhat similar relative dating and detailed discussion, see Shochat/Gilboa 2019.
[97] E.g., Herzog/Singer-Avitz 2006, 179–180; Arie 2008, 36; Singer-Avitz 2018, n. 5.
[98] Finkelstein 1999b; Arie 2008; Sergi/Kleiman 2018; Shochat/Gilboa 2019.
[99] See also Section 10.2.2 and more details in Kleiman 2021.
[100] Dayan 1962, 26; Stepansky 1999, 32–33; IAS 18, no. 189.

possible candidates for the identification of Adama mentioned in the Hebrew Bible (Jos 19:36), together with Tel Nes and Tel Ya'af South (see below).[101]

3.2.8 Tel Ya'af South

Near Tel Ya'af, the remains of another small settlement on a low basalt hill were discerned.[102] A survey at the site revealed significant quantities of Iron Age sherds (about 77% of all the documented ceramics). Salvage excavations at the site were carried out in 2006 and 2013 and revealed architectural remains, most likely from the Iron Age IIB.[103] It is another candidate for the identification of biblical Adama.[104]

3.2.9 Rosh Pinna

Rosh Pinna (Ja'una) is located on a spur in the western sector of the modern settlement. Over the years, the site was the subject of several different salvage excavations.[105] During the fieldwork, two Iron Age strata were unearthed. The walls of the earlier stratum, which was dated to the timeframe of the Iron Age I–IIA, were established on bedrock.[106] Noteworthy finds from this occupational layer are fragments of painted red-painted plaster, which suggest the presence of a nearby lavish building. Burnt debris and restorable vessels from the Iron Age IIA signify the end of the settlement,[107] probably as part of the military campaigns of Aram-Damascus against the Northern Kingdom.[108] Above the destruction, the remains of a few wall fragments dated to the Iron Age IIB were found.[109]

3.2.10 Tel Nes

Tel Nes (Tell es-Sanjaq) is a small settlement on a basalt hill, *ca.* 2 km to the southeast of Rosh Pinna.[110] Around the site are the remains of a fortification wall. Iron Age pottery constituted *ca.* 20% of all sherds found during the survey of the settlement. Salvage excavations carried out at the site in 2002 and 2003 found fragments of cooking pots with an inverted stance and grooved rim, typical to the Iron Age IIB (but possibly beginning at the end of the Iron Age IIA).[111] Depression in this wall at the northwest may

---

[101] Stepansky 1999, 32–33; idem 2014, 105–106.
[102] Stepansky 1999, 34; IAS 18, no. 218.
[103] Hartal 2013; Berger 2013.
[104] Stepansky 1999, 34; idem 2014, 105–106.
[105] Stepansky 2008a; Hartal 2009a; Alexandre 2019. Most recently, a very detailed report on the archaeological research of Rosh Pinna was published (Stepansky 2019).
[106] Stepansky 2019, 7–11, 17. Despite the comprehensive report published by Y. Stepansky, this remarkable continuity seems to me a bit exceptional. It has no real convincing parallel anywhere in the region, and the excavations at Rosh Pinna were indeed limited in scope. A radiocarbon date from charcoal collected from the destruction provided a date in the late 10th and 9th centuries BCE (Stepansky 2008a; idem 2019, 34).
[107] Stepansky 2019, 17–33, fig. 16.
[108] Stepansky 2019, 34.
[109] Stepansky 2019, 18–19.
[110] Stepansky 1999, 36–37; IAS 18.
[111] Stepansky 2008b, n. 5.

signify the location of the entrance to the settlement. It is yet another possible candidate for the identification of biblical Adama.[112] Recent excavations at the site are focused on remains from the Chalcolithic Period found at the foot of the mound.[113]

3.3 Regional Synthesis

During the Late Bronze Age, the settlements in the Hula Valley were divided between two main clusters: one to the north of the lake (near Tel Abel Beth-Maacah and Tel Dan) and one to its south (in the vicinity of Tel Hazor). From a quantitative perspective, however, the number of sites in this period was relatively low, specifically around Canaanite Hazor (Figure 25).[114] Y. Stepansky assumed that this trend must be associated with the immense size of the Late Bronze Age city-state, which at that time, was home to nearly 20,000 people.[115] Further evidence for his conclusion may be gleaned from the fact that following the destruction of the city, the number of settlements in the Hula Valley, as well as in other nearby regions (e.g., the Golan Heights), more than doubled (Figure 26).[116] It is only reasonable to assume that the origin of the majority of new settlers is from the valley itself.[117] Archaeological data, especially from the stratigraphic sequences revealed in Tel Abel Beth-Maacah (Strata A6–A2) and Tel Dan (Strata VIIB–IVB), suggest that in the northern margins of the Hula Valley, the transition from the Late Bronze Age to the Iron Age I was gradual and included higher-degree of cultural and perhaps also political continuity (notwithstanding the destruction of Canaanite Hazor). While it is logical to assume that the large settlement revealed at Tel Abel Beth-Maacah became the regional center in the northern sector of the Hula Valley, the situation in the south, around the ruins of Canaanite Hazor, remains unclear. It could be dominated by Tel Abel Beth-Maacah as well, but Tel Kinrot, located *ca.* 15 km to the southwest, is also a possible candidate. In any event, a series of traumatic events towards the end of the Iron Age I suggests that the recovery of the local settlement system did not last long. Possible clues for the growing unrest in this region are the intensive hoarding of agricultural products in pits and silos – which may hint at political or social instability and a weak central authority[118] – and especially the destruction layers identified at Tel Abel Beth-Maacah, Tel Dan, Tel Tannim, and Rosh Pinna.

From the perspective of the excavated sites, it is possible to observe that following the destruction of the Iron Age I settlements, most of the mounds were abandoned, as not even a single stratum in this region can be assigned to the early Iron Age IIA with assurance. This means that the first sign of recovery in the Hula Valley is the construction of Stratum X at Tel Hazor in the early days of the Iron Age IIA (*ca.* 900 BCE). At

---

[112] Stepansky 1999, 32–33; idem 2014, 105–106.
[113] Rowan/Kersel/Hill 2018.
[114] For the general problem of human resources in the Late Bronze Age, see Bunimovitz 1994.
[115] Stepansky 1999, 94–95; idem 2014, 104–105.
[116] Stepansky 1999, 95–96; idem 2014, 105.
[117] See also Section 13.2.1.
[118] Following Ilan 1999, 120; idem 2008.

that time, it was the only urban center (or rather fortified stronghold) in this region. A few decades later, towards the end of the Iron Age IIA, the settlement system of the Hula Valley recovered dramatically (Figure 27), with the repopulation of many urban centers (e.g., Tel Dan and Tel Nes), a trend that continued in the Iron Age IIB (for a comparative stratigraphy of the excavated sites in the Hula Valley, see Table 8).[119]

Table 8: Comparative stratigraphy of excavated sites in the Hula Valley

Site	Late Bronze Age	Iron Age I	Iron Age II		
T. Abel Beth-Maacah	F-3?	A-6?, A-5–A-2	A-1		
T. Dan	VIIB	VIIA, VI–IVB	-	IVA	III–II
T. Tannim	Sherds	X–IX?	Sherds		
T. Hazor	XIV–XIII	XII/XI	- X–IX	VIII	VII–V
Rosh Pinna	-	Lower Phase	Upper Phase		

---

[119] Conventionally, scholars assume that Tiglath-Pileser III's campaigns in 732 BCE led to the abandonment of most of the settlements in the Hula Valley. This observation is almost certainly based on the absence of Iron Age IIC pottery in surveys. In this case, it should be reminded that the ceramic traditions of the Iron Age IIB did not disappear following the events and were maintained at least until the first decades of the 7th century BCE (see, e.g., Finkelstein 2012, 204). Since urban activity in this area was maintained by the Assyrians (e.g., Stratum I at Tel Dan), I see no reason why the countryside should have been abandoned in such a dramatic manner (see more in Section 13.4.5).

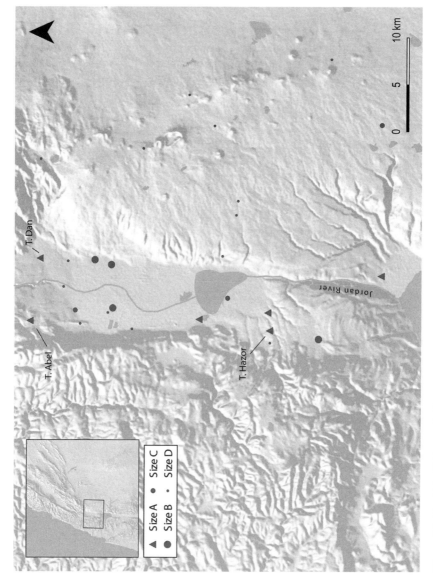

Figure 25: *The Hula Valley in the Late Bronze Age (created with QGIS 3.16 and World Shaded Relief of Esri 2014)*

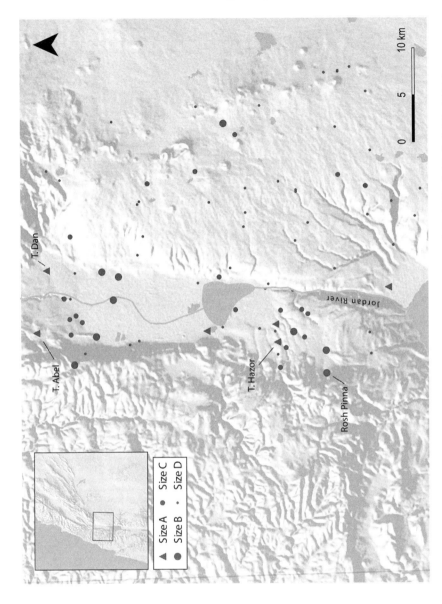

Figure 26: The Hula Valley in the Iron Age I (created with QGIS 3.16 and World Shaded Relief of Esri 2014)

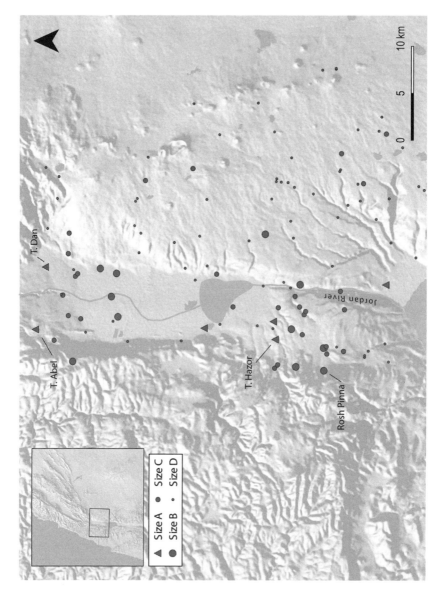

Figure 27: The Hula Valley in the Iron Age II (created with QGIS 3.16 and World Shaded Relief of Esri 2014)

4. The Sea of Galilee

4.1 Introduction

The Sea of Galilee is situated at a major crossroads in the southern Levant and has been an attractive territory for human activity throughout history.[1] During the Early Bronze Age, one of the first and largest urban centers in the southern Levant, Tel Beth Yerah, emerged on the lake's southwestern shore;[2] and several centuries later, an Egyptian pharaoh erected his royal stele at the fortified settlement of Tel Kinrot. Additionally, scholars identify some of the Iron Age II settlements that flourished around the lake with the Kingdom of Geshur, known to us from the Hebrew Bible (e.g., 2 Sam 3:3; 13:37–38; 14:32; 15:8).[3] Notwithstanding these periods of prosperity, the research of this region, especially excavations, reveals that it also suffered long periods of low settlement activity. This may have stemmed from the limited area suitable for agriculture around the lake which forced the locals to rely heavily on connections with nearby regions.

Figure 28: The southern shores of the Sea of Galilee merging into the Jordan Valley with the Golan Heights in the background (photographed by Z. Evenor / CC BY 2.0)

From a geological perspective, the Sea of Galilee and its shores are integrated into the Jordan Valley (Figure 28). Most of the territories around the lake enjoy *ca.* 400–500 mm

---

[1] For a *longue durée* overview of the history of the Sea of Galilee, see Zwickel 2017.
[2] For the excavations carried out at Tel Beth Yerah, see Greenberg *et al.* 2012.
[3] E.g., Na'aman 2012; Arav 2013; Sugimoto 2015b; Maeir 2017; Sergi/Kleiman 2018.

annual rainfall, with the exception of the southern shore, which receives only 300–400 mm, similar to the situation in the Beth-Shean Valley. While the total size of this region is *ca.* 230 sq km, the lake covers *ca.* 80% of this area (i.e., 190 sq km), which leaves a relatively small area of only 40 sq km for human habitation and agriculture. Nevertheless, the lake has its own advantages for the local economy (e.g., fishing), and it also served as a route for transporting commodities between the Golan Heights and the Galilee. All in all, only three areas around the lake have extended territories: 1) Tabgha Valley/'Ein Sheva) in the northwest, 2) Bethsaida/Betikha Valley in the northeast, and 3) the southern shores of the Sea of Galilee, which merge with the Jordan Valley. It is probably not coincidental that the three largest mounds of the region (Tel Kinrot, et-Tell/Bethsaida, and Tel Beth-Yerah) emerged in these areas.

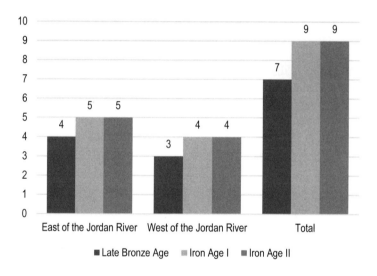

Figure 29: Settlement oscillations around the Sea of Galilee

4.2 Key Sites

The shores around the Sea of Galilee have not been completely surveyed. Some information, nonetheless, is included in IAS maps Nos. 36/1, 39, and 40.[4] To date, only 15 Iron Age sites are known from this region (Figure 29). In addition, over the years, several long-term archaeological projects have been carried out at the large tell sites located near the shores of the lake. Among them are the Land of Geshur Regional Project (focused on Tel Hadar and Tel 'Ein Gev), the Kinneret Regional Project (focused on Tel

---

[4] Unpublished data from the survey of IAS 36 were kindly provided to me by Y. Stepansky.

Kinrot), and the long-term excavation of et-Tell/Bethsaida.[5] However, none of these projects was fully published, and even preliminary data are limited or non-existent.

4.2.1 et-Tell/Bethsaida

The mound of et-Tell is one of the most prominent settlements in the central Levant, *ca.* 6–8 hectares in size.[6] In the historical literature, the site is mentioned as one of the possible candidates for the identification of Bethsaida Julias, a fishermen's village mentioned in the New Testament.[7] The ancient name of the site remains unknown, but several suggestions were put forward (e.g., Tzer or Geshur).[8] Victor Guérin was one of the first scholars to visit the site at the end of the 19th century and found it deserted.[9] He reported that the locals said that this had been the capital of the district (Butayha).

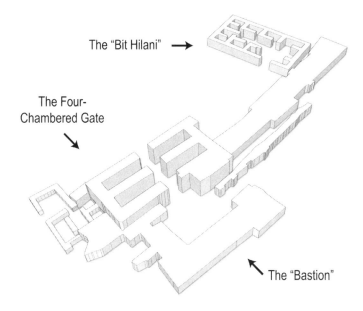

Figure 30: Reconstruction of the monumental remains associated with Stratum V at et-Tell/Bethsaida (drawn with Trimble Sketchup Pro 2021 and based on Arav 2013, fig. 3)

Excavations at the site commenced in 1987 by R. Arav. So far, the dig has exposed two main Iron Age strata: Stratum VI (attributed by the excavator to the Iron Age IIA) and Stratum V (attributed by the excavator to the Iron Age IIB; for a proposed stratigraphic correlation, see Table 9). The early preliminary reports associated the following features with Stratum VI: 1) a solid fortification wall with towers, which continued to be in use

---

[5] For a detailed analysis and discussion of the excavations of Tel Hadar, see Kleiman 2019a.
[6] Epstein/Gutman 1972, 276–277.
[7] E.g., Albright 1925, 10.
[8] Arav 2015 (Tzer); Na'aman 2012; idem 2014 (Geshur).
[9] Guérin 1987 [1880], 221–222.

during the subsequent occupational phase, 2) parts of the outer gate ("the bastion"), and 3) a structure found to the south of the gate complex of Stratum V ("the granary"). The association of some of these elements to Stratum VI, especially the solid fortification wall, has been questioned.[10] At any rate, this city was destroyed in a major conflagration, which resulted in more than a meter of burnt debris.[11] Hitherto, no ceramic assemblage from the floors has been presented, but radiocarbon dates for samples that supposedly originated from the floors of this stratum provided results around the mid-10th century BCE,[12] leaving little doubt regarding the affiliation of this stratum with the Iron Age I.

Figure 31: A view of the gate complex at et-Tell/Bethsaida (photographed by the author)

After the destruction, the site experienced an occupational gap of at least a century,[13] after which the settlement was constructed *de novo* (Stratum V, Figure 30). The new settlement included a solid fortification wall with towers, a monumental four-chambered gate, and a palace. In front of the gate, a moon/storm-god stele was erected (Figure 31).[14] The violent destruction of Stratum V has been attributed by the excavator to the

---

[10] For instance, the attribution of the fortification wall and parts of the outer gate to Stratum VI and its continued use during Stratum V depended on one of the walls of the granary, among the features that were associated with Stratum VI, which allegedly adjoined the fortifications (Arav 2004a, 19). However, the connection to the wall was never found and is absent in the most updated plans of this stratum (Arav 2013, fig. 2; idem 2018, fig. 4). See more in Sergi/Kleiman 2018, 5–7.

[11] Arav 2018, 85; idem 2020, 99.

[12] Sharon *et al.* 2007, Tables 7–8; Arav 2018, 85. According to R. Arav's (2020, 97) most recent report, the city of Stratum VI was built in the late 11th century and was destroyed in 920 BCE. It means that the city existed in parallel to Stratum IV at Tel Hadar, which undoubtedly belongs to the ceramic horizon of the late Iron Age I (Sergi/Kleiman 2018, 5–7; Kleiman 2019a, *passim*).

[13] Arav 2018, 85; idem 2020, 97.

[14] For other moon/storm-god steles found in the central Levant, see Section 10.4.

campaigns of Tiglath-Pileser III.[15] A complete cooking jug found in Stratum V may indicate that the event happened earlier than previously presumed, at the very end of the Iron Age IIA or in the early days of the Iron Age IIB.[16]

Table 9: The stratigraphy of et-Tell/Bethsaida

Period	Area A	Area B
Iron Age II	Stratum V (inset-offset wall and gate compound)	Stratum V (inset-offset wall and palace)
	Occupational gap throughout most of the Iron Age IIA	
Iron Age I	Stratum VI (domestic remains)?	Unexcavated/insufficient data

Note: The Iron Age IIA occupation possibility continued into the early days of the Iron Age IIB.

4.2.2 Tel Kinrot

Tell el-ʿOreimeh is situated on the northwestern shore of the Sea of Galilee (Figure 32). It is identified as the location of ancient Chinnereth (e.g., Jos 19:35). In the mid-19th century, Victor Guérin visited the site, noticing its prominent location and the remains of an ancient fortification wall.[17] Aside from some small-scale projects,[18] the first intensive excavation of the site commenced during the early 1980s, directed by V. Fritz (Seasons 1982–1985 and 1994–2001). In 2003–2008, the excavations resumed as the Kinneret Regional Project, a consortium of several academic institutes.[19]

A stratigraphic sequence of several strata dated to the Late Bronze and Iron Ages was revealed at the site (for a proposed stratigraphic correlation, see Table 10). The earliest layer relevant to our topic is Stratum VII, which was reached in a deep probe in Area H in the lower settlement.[20] In this probe, the remains of a small structure were revealed. A mixed assemblage of sherds from the Middle Bronze Age III and Late Bronze Age I was unearthed here. As the excavations progressed, it became clear that the early settlement was protected by a fortification line supported by a glacis, which was exposed mainly in Area G. In addition, there are two textual sources related to Chinnereth: 1) it is mentioned in Papyrus Hermitage 1116A, most likely as one of the city-states of northern Canaan,[21] and 2) at the site itself, at the beginning of the 20th century a fragment of an Egyptian royal stele dated from the 18th Dynasty was found on the surface, affiliated with the reign of Amenhotep II or Thutmose III.[22] Of note is that in contrast to other sites located in its vicinity (e.g., Tel Hazor and perhaps also Anaharath, maybe Tel

---

[15] Arav 2009a; idem 2009b; idem 2013, 14–15; idem 2018, 85.
[16] Arav 2009a, fig. 190, c. A review of the distribution of cooking jugs in stratified Iron Age sequences suggests that their production concluded a few decades before the destruction of Stratum V at Tel Hazor (Kleiman 2019a, 105–106). For a similar view, see also Ilan 2019b, 127–129.
[17] Guérin 1987 [1880], 143.
[18] E.g., Winn/Yakar 1984.
[19] For the old excavations, see Fritz 1990; for the new project, see Fritz 1999; Münger/Zangenberg/Pakkala 2011; Münger 2013; idem 2017.
[20] Fritz 1999, 95–98.
[21] Münger 2017, 117–118.
[22] Albright/Rowe 1928, and see also Section 12.3.1.

Rekhesh), the city is not mentioned at all in the Amarna Correspondence, which correlates well with the lack of Late Bronze Age II remains from the site.

The settlement reached its peak during the Iron Age I. During the excavations, two main construction episodes of a fortified town with minor differences between them were identified (Strata VI–V).[23] The settlement included a planned quarter which was exposed mainly in the lower city. In general, the material culture of these two strata was influenced by various traditions, including traditions originating in Syria and Transjordan.[24] Similar to other Iron Age I settlements nearby, Tel Kinrot was fiercely destroyed towards the end of the period.[25] Only limited remains were built directly over the ruins of the Iron Age I city, and these were interpreted as squatters' activity, which took place immediately after the destruction, still within the Iron Age I ("Stratum IV").[26]

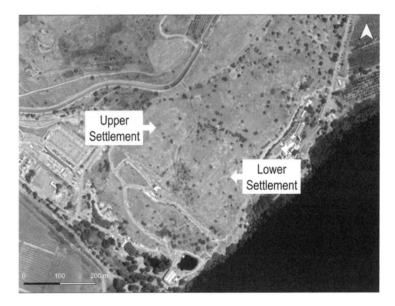

Figure 32: Satellite view of Tel Kinrot with the main sectors excavated by the various expeditions that worked at the site (created with QGIS 3.16 and Google Satellite)

The recent publication of the ceramic material from the new excavations of Tel Kinrot allows for some reassessment regarding the foundation of the Iron Age I settlement. According to the data presented by T. Tynjä,[27] Phoenician Bichrome vessels[28] and

---

[23] Fritz 1999, 98–103; Münger/Zangenberg/Pakkala 2011; Münger 2013; idem 2017.
[24] Münger 2013, 150.
[25] A single radiocarbon date from Stratum VI suggests a date for the foundation of the city in the late 11th century BCE (Fritz 1999, 112–114; but note this date is uncalibrated). Unpublished, short-lived samples from Stratum V point in this direction as well (S. Münger, personal communication).
[26] Münger/Zangenberg/Pakkala 2011, 87.
[27] Tynjä 2017.
[28] Tynjä 2017, 236–238, part of Type JG04, e.g., object no. 7250/3.

storage jars with elongated bodies and carinated shoulders[29] appear as early as Stratum VI. Based on ceramic data from stratified sequences at Tel Megiddo, E. Arie[30] argued that these are among the most indicative vessel types of the late Iron Age I in the northern valleys. It can therefore be suggested that Tel Kinrot was founded in the second half of the 11th century BCE and destroyed somewhere towards the mid-10th century BCE.[31]

After the destruction of the Iron Age I settlement and the subsequent squatters' phase, the site was abandoned for nearly 200 years. Iron Age II activity was observed only on the upper mound, where three distinct phases dated to this period were revealed. Stratum IV, the earliest of the three, included only meager remains. It was followed by the construction of a sizeable rectangular fortress (reconstructed by V. Fritz as 15 × 20 m) on the northeastern edge of the mound. Only a limited number of vessels were published from this stratum,[32] which represents a mix of Iron Age I and Iron Age II ceramic forms. It may be contemporary with Stratum III at Tel Hadar. Above these remains, a larger fortified compound (ca. 140 × 60 m) was constructed (Stratum II, Areas A–D). Excavations in Area D, located at the southern end of the upper mound, revealed a gate and a pillared building. In other sectors of the upper mound, different segments of a fortification wall were exposed, as well as two residential buildings. A rich ceramic assemblage of restorable vessels originating from the floors of the compound suggests an Iron Age IIB date.[33] A correlation between the destruction of this settlement and the campaigns of Tiglath-Pileser III in the second half of the 8th century BCE is reasonable.[34]

Table 10: The stratigraphic of Tel Kinrot

Period	Upper Settlement	Lower Settlement
Iron Age II	II (fortified compound)	Unstratified material
	III (large structure)	
	IV (old excavations)	
	Occupational gap throughout most of the Iron Age IIA	
Iron Age I	IV (new excavations)	IV (squatters' phase)
	V	V
		VI

4.2.3 Tel Hadar

Tel Hadar is a small 2.5 hectare tell-site on the eastern coast of the Sea of Galilee (Figure 33). It is located at the entrance to Wadi Samakh, halfway between Tel 'Ein Gev and et-Tell/Bethsaida. No well-founded identification has been suggested for Tel Hadar, although its location has led some to identify it with the unnamed hill next to where Jesus

---

[29] Tynjä 2017, 219–221, Type SJ02A.

[30] Arie 2006, 222, 227; idem 2013b, 519–520, 539.

[31] E. Arie's (2006, 230) attribution of Stratum VI to the early Iron Age I was primarily based on an earlier observation of the excavators (see, e.g., Fritz/Münger 2002, 12).

[32] Fritz 1990, pl. 60.

[33] Singer-Avitz 2014, 135–136, Table 2.

[34] Fritz 1990, 181. The Iron Age IIC remains include a Neo-Assyrian compound and are beyond the chronological framework of this study (Fritz 1990; Singer-Avitz 2014, 135–136).

is said to have fed the multitudes (Matthew 15:32–39; Mark 8:1–9).[35] As was the case of other nearby settlements, the first scholar to document the site was Victor Guérin, who visited the site on July 8, 1875. He described several huts, the fortification wall that surrounded the ancient town, and many graves, probably from the Ottoman period.[36] Nearly 80 years after Guérin's visit, the site was documented again during the Emergency Survey.[37] In the late 1980s and 1990s, Tel Hadar was excavated by M. Kochavi and P. Beck (1987–1998) as part of the Land of Geshur Regional Project. The objective of this project was to illuminate the history and material culture of the Golan Heights in the Bronze and Iron Ages (for a proposed stratigraphic correlation, see Table 11).[38]

Figure 33: Aerial view of Tel Hadar at the beginning of Moshe Kochavi and Pirhiya Beck's excavations (courtesy of the Institute of Archaeology of Tel Aviv University)

Following excavations at the site, it became clear that Tel Hadar was settled for the first time in the Late Bronze Age I or slightly earlier (Stratum VI). At this time, a massive fortification wall surrounded the settlement, and at the top of the mound, a rounded structure was built. This settlement was destroyed shortly after its foundation, as evidenced by destruction debris, including restorable vessels that covered the floors of the rounded structure. Afterward, the site was abandoned for several centuries.

---

[35] R. Bauckham (2015) suggested associating the site with Gargishta, which later became Gergesa, mentioned in the New Testament, instead of the conventional identification as Kursi (Guérin 1987 [1880], 216–218). This identification must be dismissed, as practically no sherds or any evidence for settlement activity dated to the late Hellenistic or Roman periods have been found at the site.

[36] Guérin 1987 [1880], 220.

[37] Epstein/Gutman 1972, 282–283, no. 146.

[38] Kochavi 1989; idem 1996; idem 1998; Yadin/Kochavi 2008. The Iron Age remains from the Tel Hadar excavations were studied by the author (Kleiman 2019a, 50–164).

Figure 34: Complete vessels on floors in Complex 296 ("the pillared building) at Tel Hadar, looking south (courtesy of the Institute of Archaeology of Tel Aviv University)

In the Iron Age I, as part of the resettlement of many sites around the Sea of Galilee (e.g., Stratum VI at Tel Kinrot),[39] Tel Hadar was also rebuilt (Stratum V). After a short time, the old fortifications were renovated, and in the southern sector of the site, a public quarter was constructed (Stratum IV). During this phase, a massive structure, including a granary with a large amount of wheat (Figure 77).[40] Based on more than 100 locally produced and imported vessels found in the quarter, the excavators presumed that the site functioned as a commercial center that controlled trade routes leading from the Mediterranean to the Golan Heights.[41] Of importance is a unique vessel originating from Euboea, one of the earliest Greek imports to the Levant in the Early Iron Age.[42] Stratum IV was destroyed in a conflagration, radiocarbon dated to the mid-10th century BCE (Figure 34).[43] There were very few signs of post-destruction activity,[44] and the settlement was abandoned for over a century until the late 9th century BCE (Stratum III).

The town plan completely changed in the Iron Age IIA, as new neighborhoods were built above the Iron Age I public quarter. For the first time, this occupational phase also saw the expansion of the settlement beyond the second millennium BCE fortification line (Figure 79), and a new solid fortification wall was built around this settlement. A typological study of the ceramic assemblages suggested that it was rebuilt at the end of the Iron Age IIA (parallel to Stratum IVA at Tel Dan and Stratum VIII at Tel Hazor)

---

[39] Sergi/Kleiman 2018; Kleiman 2019b.
[40] Kochavi 1998; Kislev 2015.
[41] Kochavi 1998; Yadin/Kochavi 2008.
[42] Kopcke 2002; Coldstream 2003. See also Section 9.3.4.
[43] Finkelstein/Piasetzky 2005; Scott *et al.* 2007, Table 5; Sharon *et al.* 2007, Tables 7–8.
[44] Kleiman 2019a, 60.

and was quickly abandoned only a few decades after its construction.[45] Following the abandonment, a residential quarter with a new architectural plan was built (Stratum II/I). However, it probably did not last long, and the settlement at Tel Hadar ultimately came to an end at the very end of the Iron Age IIA or in the early Iron Age IIB.

Table 11: The stratigraphy of Tel Hadar

Period	Stratum	Area AS	Area AN	Area B
Iron Age II	II/I	AS-2a	AN-2	B-2a
	III	AS-2b	AN-3	B-2b
				B-3
	Occupational gap throughout most of the Iron Age IIA			
Iron Age I	IV	AS-3	AN-4	B-4
	V	Unexcavated	AN-5	-
	-		-	

Note: The Iron Age IIA occupation possibility continued into the early days of the Iron Age IIB.

Figure 35: Aerial photo of Tel Soreg in Nahal 'Ein Gev (courtesy of the Institute of Archaeology of Tel Aviv University)

4.2.4 Tel Soreg

Tel Soreg (also known as Tel Afiq) is a small mound (less than one hectare in size) within Nahal 'Ein Gev (Figure 35), about half a kilometer to the west of Kibbutz Afiq. In the past, it was identified as the Aphek mentioned in 2 Kgs 13:17.[46] Excavations conducted from 1987 to 1989 revealed remains of several periods. Relevant to our subject is a few silos dated to the Iron Age I and the remains of a fortress, private houses, and agricultural installations dated to the Iron Age II. A burial cave that was used during

---

[45] Kleiman 2019a, 89–150.
[46] D. Ben-Ami cited in Kochavi 1993, 1410.

the Bronze and Iron Ages was also found here.[47] No pottery from the excavations has been published, but according to M. Kochavi, the Iron Age I ceramic assemblages include collared-rim pithoi similar to those found at Tel Hadar and the Irbid Plateau.

Figure 36: A view of Tel Dover at the entrance to the Yarmouk River (photographed by the author)

4.2.5   Tel Dover

Tel Dover (Tell Duweir) is located southeast of the Sea of Galilee, at the entrance to the Yarmouk Valley (Figure 36). It is a small settlement (*ca.* 2.5 hectares). Occasionally it is identified with Lo-Debar/Lidbir (Jos 13:26; 2 Sam 9:4–5; Amos 6:13).[48] The site is divided into an acropolis and a lower settlement.

In the late 1990s, salvage excavations were carried out in lower settlement and exposed remains from the Late Bronze and Iron Ages (for a proposed stratigraphic correlation, see Table 12).[49] According to A. Golani and S.R. Wolff's recent report on these investigations, the Late Bronze Age phase includes a large building that may have had a cultic or administrative function (Strata VIIIa–c).[50] Based on the presence of Chocolate-on-White and Cypriot White Slip vessels, this layer was dated to Late Bronze Age IB. No Late Bronze Age II remains were found at the site, and activity resumed only during the Iron Age I (Strata VIIa–d). A single burial, as well as a number of silos and domestic structures, were attributed to this period. These remains were divided into five phases, during which the lower city was used alternately for burial or habitation. At the

---

[47] Kochavi 1993.
[48] E.g., Younger 2016, n. 295. For a different view, see Finkelstein/Koch/Lipschits 2013, 143–145 with discussion and earlier bibliography.
[49] Rapuano 2001; Golani/Wolff 2018.
[50] Golani/Wolff 2018, 513.

end of the period, the lower settlement was abandoned. Later activity is evidenced by additional graves dated to the Iron Age IIA or slightly later (Stratum VIIf).[51]

Table 12: The stratigraphy of Tel Dover

Period	Upper Settlement	Lower Settlement
Iron Age II	Unexcavated	VIIf (burials)
		Occupational gap throughout most of the Iron Age IIA?
Iron Age I		VIIe (burials)
		VIId–b (residential quarter)
		VIIa (burials)

4.2.6 Tel 'Ein Gev

Tel 'Ein Gev (Khirbet el-'Asheq) is located in the northern sector of the modern kibbutz of the same name (Figure 37). In the winter of 1961, a ten-day excavation was carried out at the site on behalf of the Hebrew University.[52] Excavations resumed at the end of the 1980s as part of the "Land of Geshur Regional Project" and a consortium of several academic institutions (1990–2004).[53] Later excavations were conducted between the years 2009 and 2011 on behalf of Keio University in Japan, directed by D.T. Sugimoto (for a proposed stratigraphic correlation, see Table 13).

a. The Early Excavations

Three main areas were excavated by Hebrew University Expedition: Area A in the south and Areas B and C in the northwest. A detailed stratigraphic sequence was revealed only in Area A, although the limited excavated area made the interpretation of the results somewhat difficult. According to A. Mazar and his colleagues,[54] the occupation at the site commenced in the Iron Age IIA. During this period, the site was protected by a thick solid wall (Wall 21, which was associated with Stratum V). Later, in the Iron Age IIA, a casemate wall (Walls 15 and 19) was constructed above the fortification system of the previous stratum, but no floors were found (Stratum IV). Very few sherds, presumably from the Iron Age IIA, were published from these two occupational phases.[55]

More substantial remains were associated with Stratum III. During the lifetime of this stratum, the casemate wall of the previous stratum was transformed into an inset/offset wall and reinforced by a glacis. A small structure was built to the north of this fortification line. In the excavators' view, one of the rooms of this structure may have been used for cultic activities.[56] Restorable vessels found in the room suggest that the end of

---

[51] Golani/Wolff 2018, figs. 3, 13.
[52] Mazar et al. 1964.
[53] For the preliminary results on the excavations of Tel 'Ein Gev, see Kochavi 1989; Sugimoto 1999; idem 2015a; Miyazaki/Paz 2005; Hasegawa/Paz 2009; Hasegawa 2019.
[54] Mazar et al. 1964, 7.
[55] Mazar et al. 1964, fig. 4.
[56] Mazar et al. 1964, 12; see also Ahlström 1985.

this settlement was not peaceful. After this event, the settlement was rebuilt (Stratum II). No restorable vessels were associated with this phase, indicating that the settlement was abandoned rather than destroyed. Finally, the remains of Stratum I showed much architectural change; they were comprised of a single large building, the date of which is unclear, as it was found just below modern topsoil. Based on the absence of sherds from the Persian and Hellenistic periods, the excavators suggested dating the building to the late Iron Age. The excavations in Areas B and C were initiated in order to explore the nature of the acropolis of Tel 'Ein Gev.[57] Soundings carried out in these areas primarily revealed the remains of a citadel with *ca.* 1.35 m wide walls, which were preserved to a height of *ca.* 4 m. Four strata were identified here. The earliest one includes ovens and burnt debris (Stratum IV*). Above the debris, the walls of the citadel and a thick *ca.* 10 cm floor were revealed (Stratum III*). Two poorly-preserved strata were exposed above the citadel (Strata II* and I*).[58]

Figure 37: Satellite view of Tel 'Ein Gev with the main areas excavated by the various expeditions that worked at the site (created with QGIS 3.16 and Google Satellite)

b. *The Recent Excavations*

Excavations conducted at the site in the 1990s and 2000s extended the settlement history of the site and clarified some of the ambiguities surrounding the old excavations.[59] The renewed excavations focused mainly on two areas: Area F in the northeast and Area H in the northwest (near Area C of the 1961 excavations).

---

[57] Mazar *et al.* 1964, 14–18.
[58] The phasing of Areas B and C at Tel 'Ein Gev were marked with asterisks.
[59] Hasegawa/Paz 2009; Sugimoto 2015a.

Excavations in Area F focused on a horizontal exposure of the remains of two superimposed pillared buildings abutting a casemate wall and a tower (Strata JV and JIV). A sounding below the lower pillared buildings ("Locus 510") unearthed remains dating to the Iron Age I.[60] In Area H, three Iron Age strata were revealed. The earliest layer included a thick accumulation of destruction debris and some architectural remains dating to the Iron Age I (Stratum KIV). Equating this Iron Age I phase with the Hebrew University's Stratum IV* is possible.[61] Only a small ceramic assemblage has been published from the destruction of the Iron Age I settlement,[62] but it exhibits apparent similarities to the ceramic assemblages from the destruction of Stratum IV at Tel Hadar. A short-lived radiocarbon sample obtained from one of the floors of this stratum dates the destruction to the mid-10th century BCE and supports the ceramic observations.[63] Above the destruction debris, the excavators revealed the remains of a large building with a thick plaster floor. Due to later intrusions, no ceramic assemblages could be associated securely with the large building; its date is therefore based on its stratigraphic location between the destruction of Stratum KIV and a plaster floor that was built above the building, dated by the excavators to the Iron Age IIB (Stratum KII).

Table 13: The stratigraphy of Tel 'Ein Gev

Period	Area A	Area B and C	Area H	Area F
Iron Age II	MII (casemate wall and pillared building)	MII*	KII	JIV (casemate wall and later pillared buildings)
	MIII (casemate wall and "cult room")	MIII*	KIII	JV (casemate wall and earlier pillared buildings)
	MV–IV			
	Occupational gap throughout most of the Iron Age IIA			
Iron Age I	MV (solid wall)	MIV* (domestic remains and burnt material)	KIV (domestic remains and destruction debris)	Locus 510

Note: The Iron Age IIA occupation possibility continued into the early days of the Iron Age IIB.

A point of interest is the relative and absolute date of the Iron Age IIA settlement. In recent literature, this town is dated to either the entire span of the Iron Age IIA[64] or only to the late Iron Age IIA.[65] The only stratified ceramic assemblage associated with the Iron Age IIA settlement was found in Stratum III in Area A.[66] Only a few vessels included in this assemblage are indicative of high-resolution dating within the Iron Age

---

[60] Sugimoto 2015a, Table 2.
[61] Sugimoto 2015a, 206.
[62] Sugimoto 2015a, fig. 5.
[63] Sugimoto 2015a, 198; n. 2.
[64] E.g., Sugimoto 2015a.
[65] E.g., Finkelstein 2011c.
[66] Mazar et al. 1964, figs. 5–8.

IIA: 1) two holemouth jars,[67] a ceramic form that does not appear in early Iron Age IIA contexts,[68] 2) a single squat amphora with a ring base and thickened rim,[69] which has parallels in final Iron Age IIA or Iron Age IIB strata (e.g., Stratum IVA at Tel Dan or Stratum V at Tel Hazor),[70] and 3) two unpublished cooking pots with an inverted stance and shallow grooved rim.[71] According to the registration information found on these vessels, both should be attributed to Stratum III.[72] In this light, the construction of Stratum III of B. Mazar's excavations, and therefore the fortified settlement at Tel 'Ein Gev, should be dated to the end of the Iron Age IIA.

All told, the various excavations carried out at Tel 'Ein Gev exposed the same picture: an Iron Age I fortified settlement that ended in a large-scale traumatic event; a palatial Iron Age IIA city (with a citadel, pillared buildings, and a casemate wall) that terminated in a small-scale destruction event; and finally, a renovation of the previous settlement and subsequent abandonment during the early years of the Iron Age IIB.

4.3 Regional Synthesis

Only nine settlements from the Late Bronze and Iron Ages have been discovered around the Sea of Galilee. Most of them were located at a distance of 7–10 km away from each other. Moreover, it is possible that the mounds on the eastern shores of the lake (e.g., Tel Hadar and Tel 'Ein Gev) formed a cluster with sites situated in the southern sector of the Golan Heights (e.g., Tell Shuqayyif and Tell el-Hashash). While this study does not include settlements located in the Lower Galilee, it is likely that mounds located on the western shores of the lake formed a cluster with settlements in that region (e.g., Tel Rekhesh). These patterns reveal the high connectivity of the settlements which emerged around the lake, a trend that is also reflected in the material culture (see, e.g., the petrographic studies of the ceramic assemblages of Tel Hadar and Tel Kinrot).[73]

In the Late Bronze Age, seven mounds were settled around the Sea of Galilee (Figure 38). Some of these archaeological sites were new (e.g., Tel Hadar), while others existed since the Early Bronze Age (e.g., Tel Kinrot). The largest settlement was undoubtedly Tel Kinrot which covered an area of *ca.* 8 hectares. Nearly all the Late Bronze sites were also settled in the Iron Age I (Figure 39), and only two new settlements were founded in this period (Tel 'Ein Gev and Horvat Menorim). A somewhat similar settlement system also characterized the Iron Age II (Figure 40). In this period, only two sites were abandoned (Karei Deshe and Tell 'Ubeidiyah).[74] Another change that occurred in this period is the shift in the location of the regional center: from Tel Kinrot in the northwest

---

[67] Mazar *et al.* 1964, fig. 8, 7–8.
[68] Herzog/Singer-Avitz 2006, 168; Arie 2013a, 715.
[69] Mazar *et al.* 1964, fig. 7, 8.
[70] E.g., Arie 2008, Type AM1.
[71] These items were identified in my review of the pottery from B. Mazar's excavation in the IAA storage facility at Beit Shemesh (see a photo of these cooking pots in Kleiman 2019a, fig. 136).
[72] For the dating of these cooking pots, see Kleiman 2015, 190.
[73] Shoval *et al.* 2006; Erazo 2017. See also Section 13.5.2.
[74] Note the limited archaeological information concerning Tell 'Ubeidiyah.

to et-Tell/Bethsaida in the southeast; this transformation explains the concentration of many settlements around the Bethsaida/Betikha Valley.[75]

An interesting phenomenon related to the Sea of Galilee concerns the relationship between Tel Kinrot and et-Tell/Bethsaida. During the Bronze Age, Tel Kinrot was the most prominent site around the Sea of Galilee. A possible reflection of this status can be seen, for instance, by the erection of an Egyptian royal stele at the site.[76] A comparable pattern could be suggested for the Iron Age I, when the settlement at Tel Kinrot reached its zenith and expanded to the lower settlement. During this period, et-Tell/Bethsaida probably had a similar function to that of other secondary settlements in the area, such as Tel Hadar and Tel 'Ein Gev. However, in the Iron Age IIA, something changed, and et-Tell/Bethsaida became the largest site around the lake; the new function of et-Tell/Bethsaida did not last long, and only a few decades after its foundation, the city was destroyed in a fierce conflagration. In the Iron Age IIB, Tel Kinrot regained its prime position when a (north-Israelite?) fortress was built at the site (for a comparative stratigraphy of the excavated sites around the Sea of Galilee, see Table 15).[77]

Table 14: Comparative stratigraphy of excavated sites around the Sea of Galilee

Site	Late Bronze Age		Iron Age I				Iron Age II	
T. Kinrot	VII	Gap	VI	V	IV	Gap	III?	II
et-Tell/Bethsaida	VII?		VI				Early V	Late V
T. Hadar	VI		V		IV		III	II/I
T. 'Ein Gev	Unknown		MV/KIV/L. 510				MIII/KIII/JV	MII/KII/JIV
T. Dover	VIII		VIIa–VIIe				[gap?]	VIIf

---

[75] From a methodological perspective, the data from the Sea of Galilee provide a prime example of differences between excavation and survey results. According to the field surveys carried out around the lake, the location and number of settlements were more or less the same during the Late Bronze and Iron Ages. Henceforth, one could argue for continuity throughout these periods. However, the excavation results, especially those at Tel Kinrot and Tel Hadar, tell a different story. Both sites were occupied at the beginning of the Late Bronze Age and were then destroyed and abandoned for several centuries until the Iron Age I. After severe destruction episodes (Stratum V at Tel Kinrot and Stratum IV at Tel Hadar), these sites were abandoned again, but this time for only *ca.* 100–150 years. A similar settlement cycle is suggested for other sites in the region, such as et-Tell/Bethsaida.

[76] Albright/Rowe 1928, and see also Section 12.3.1.

[77] For similar shifts in political power in the Judean Shephelah, see Uziel/Shai/Cassuto 2014.

4.3 Regional Synthesis

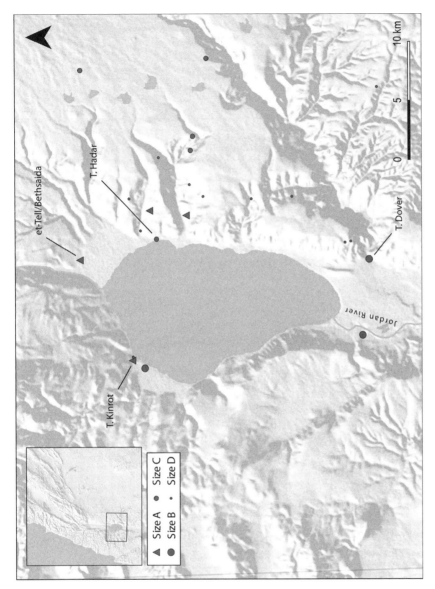

Figure 38: The Sea of Galilee in the Late Bronze Age (created with QGIS 3.16 and World Shaded Relief of Esri 2014)

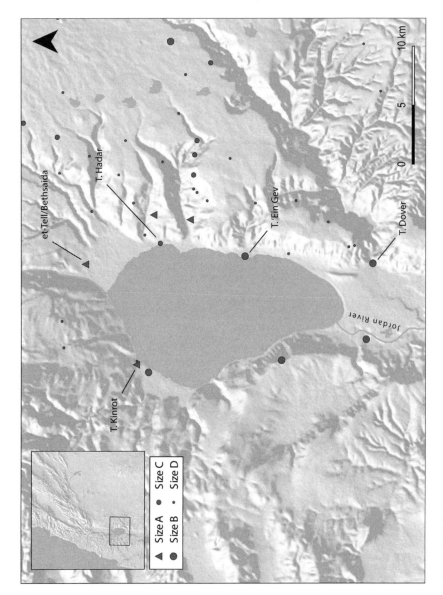

Figure 39: The Sea of Galilee in the Iron Age I (created with QGIS 3.16 and World Shaded Relief of Esri 2014)

4.3 Regional Synthesis

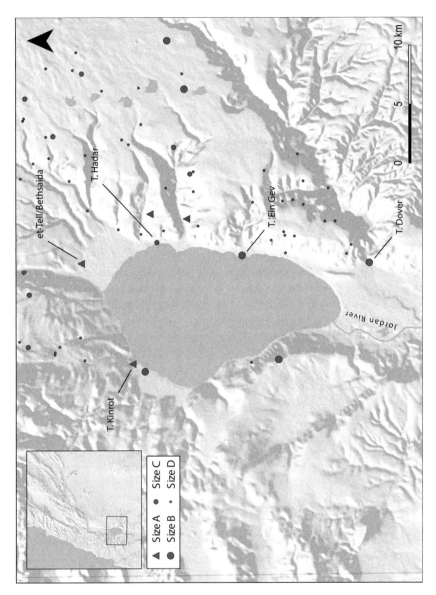

Figure 40: The Sea of Galilee in the Iron Age II (created with QGIS 3.16 and World Shaded Relief of Esri 2014)

5. The Golan Heights

5.1 Introduction

Historically, we know very little about the Golan Heights (el-Jawlan) during the Late Bronze and Iron Ages. Attempts to identify toponyms appearing in the Amarna Archive in this region, specifically the cities of the Land of Garu (Udumu, Aduru, Araru, Mishta, Magdalu, 'Eni-'Anabi, and Zarqu), are mostly to be dismissed based on both linguistic and archaeological grounds,[1] and later sources seem to refer to the Golan Heights only in general references to the Biblical Bashan (e.g., Amos 4:1). Nevertheless, the available textual data suggest that during the Late Bronze Age, the Golan Heights constitute a borderland between Hazor and 'Ashtaroth.[2] It is likely that this political division also characterized the region during the following centuries. Until not long ago, archaeological information on the settlement history of the Golan Heights was quite limited and derived mainly from Gottlieb Schumacher's work in the region at the end of the 19th century, and the Emergency Survey carried out in the late 1960s (by S. Gutman and C. Epstein).[3] The situation has certainly changed with the conclusion and publication of all the IAA field surveys in the Golan Heights.[4] However, and as evidenced below, a major problem with the archaeology of this region remains both the lack of excavations in general and the lack of stratified Iron Age sequences published in particular (especially in the large mounds located in the southern sector of the Golan Heights).

From a geographical perspective, the Golan Heights is a basalt plateau with clear boundaries (Figure 41). To the west, the edge of the plateau is demarcated by slopes in the direction of the Sea of Galilee. Its northern boundary is set at the southern slopes of Mount Hermon (Jabal esh-Sheikh) and Nahal Sa'ar (Wadi Hashba). The eastern and southern boundaries of the Golan Heights are the deep valleys of the Ruqqad and Yarmouk Rivers. In general, the Golan Heights are a fertile region, which enjoys an average annual rainfall of 400–950, but which varies significantly between its northern (1300–1000 mm), central (700–900 mm), and southern (400–600 mm) sectors. Water sources, including perennial streams and springs, are abundant throughout the region.

---

[1] For the problematic location of these settlements in the Golan Heights, see Excursus A.
[2] This situation is indicated by EA 364, which describes the complaint of Ayyab, the king of 'Ashtaroth, to the Egyptian Pharaoh. In the letter, Ayyab argues that the ruler of Tel Hazor has taken three of his towns. In N. Na'aman's view (1988, 181–182; Goren/Finkelstein/Na'aman 2004, 218), this shows that the two kingdoms bordered each other (see also Pakkala 2010, 163).
[3] Schumacher 1888; Epstein/Gutman 1972.
[4] Hartal 1989; idem 2014.

5.1 Introduction

Figure 41: A view of the Sea of Galilee from Tell Shuqayyif with the mountains of the Lower Galilee in the background (photographed by the author)

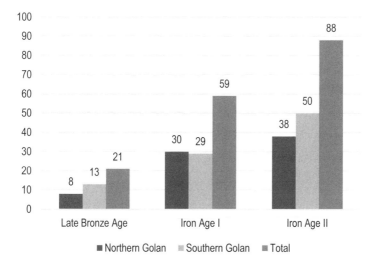

Figure 42: Settlement oscillations in the Golan Heights

5.2 Key Sites

Besides the Emergency Survey, the most relevant field surveys in the Golan Heights are those conducted by the IAA (especially by M. Hartal). Over the years, more than 100 Iron Age sites have been documented in the region (Figure 42). Some of these were also occupied during the Late Bronze Age. Most of the Iron Age sites (*ca.* 82%) are smaller than one hectare, which suggests that the region functioned as the rural hinterland of one of the nearby urban centers during this period. Most of the large settlements built on the plateau are located in the southwest, east of the Sea of Galilee (e.g., Tell Shuqayyif and Tell el-Hashash).[5] Only a limited number of excavations in the Golan Heights have yielded Iron Age remains. Most importantly, the largest sites in the region (e.g., Tell Shuqayyif, Tell el-Hashash, and Tell Abu Mudawwar) have not been excavated.

5.2.1 Horvat Sa'ar

Horvat Sa'ar is the northernmost Iron Age site recognized in the Golan Heights and may have been settled during the Middle and Late Bronze Ages.[6] It is situated on a hill near the western bank of Nahal Sa'ar, *ca.* 2 km to the northeast of the modern settlement Mas'ada. Iron Age I sherds were about 6.7% of all the sherds found at the site.[7] Of special note are several metal items which were found during a survey and dated to the Iron Age (e.g., a bronze dagger, a small bronze ingot, a horseshoe, an iron arrowhead, and other iron fragments).[8]

5.2.2 Mitzpe Golani

Mitzpe Golani is only a few kilometers from Horvat Sa'ar, and *ca.* 5 km to the east of Tel Dan. It is located on a basalt hill with steep slopes.[9] In 2005, a limited salvage excavation was carried out at the site and revealed the remains of an Iron Age II domestic structure with many indicative sherds.[10]

5.2.3 Bab el-Hawa

Bab el-Hawa (Tell el-Gharam) is among the largest settlements in the northern Golan (*ca.* 8 hectares) and is located less than 1 km north of Mount Bental (Figure 43).[11] For many years this site was known mostly for the late antiquity remains, which covered most of its surface. However, salvage excavations conducted between the years 1988 and 1990 and in 2009 by M. Hartal revealed the remains of superimposed structures

---

[5] Hartal 2014, 82.
[6] Epstein/Gutman 1972, 258; Hartal 1989, 19–20; IAS 8/3, no. 20.
[7] Hartal 1989, 19–20.
[8] Dar 1998, 245–246.
[9] Hartal 1989, 79; IAS 8, no. 79.
[10] Zingboym 2008, fig. 3.
[11] Epstein/Gutman 1972, 261; Hartal/Segal forthcoming; IAS 11/1, no. 53. I wish to thank M. Hartal for sharing with the unpublished report on the excavations of Bab el-Hawa.

dated to the Iron Age II, possibly representing parts of a fortress (Strata 3–2).[12] The earlier phase was destroyed by fire, but no restorable assemblages were uncovered. Below these strata, deposits with sherds from Bronze Age were exposed (Stratum 1). According to M. Hartal and O. Segal,[13] the pottery of Strata 3 and 2 is comparable to the ceramic assemblages from Stratum VIII at Tel Hazor. Of note is the presence of cooking pots and other ceramic forms with possible parallels in Syria (e.g., Tell Afis).

Figure 43: The view from Bab el-Hawa to Mount Bental (photographed by the author)

5.2.4 Metzad Yonathan

Metzad Yonathan (Qasr Tannuriya) is a small square-shaped fortress (*ca.* 26 × 26 m) near Nahal Tannuriya in the eastern Golan.[14] Soundings at the site by C. Epstein revealed a tomb that was dated to the Roman period.[15] Additional research of Metzad Yonathan in 1984 exposed the remains of a 1.75 m wide gate near the eastern sector of the fortress. Due to the exposure of Iron Age I sherds *ca.* 2 m below the modern surface, it has been suggested that the fortress dates to this period and that it was reused during the Roman period. However, the context of the sherds and their exact date is not entirely clear, and the evidence is insufficient for dating the whole structure.

5.2.5 Rujm el-Hiri

The megalithic site of Rujm el-Hiri is located about 5 km to the north of Tel Nov.[16] Recent excavations at the site, and detailed analysis of the settlement patterns around the site, suggest that construction of the monument occurred during the Chalcolithic

---

[12] Hartal 2009b.
[13] Hartal/Segal forthcoming.
[14] Epstein/Gutman 1972, 273; IAS 18/2, no. 62.
[15] Epstein 1976; idem 1984.
[16] Epstein/Gutman 1972, 277–278; Mizrachi *et al.* 1996; IAS 36/2, no. 56.

period.[17] Excavations also revealed evidence of later activity in the complex, specifically from the Late Bronze Age.[18] However, it cannot be excluded that some of the published sherds are actually from the Iron Age.[19] One way or another, the well-preserved monument probably continued to play a certain role in the life of the local communities also during the Late Bronze and Iron Ages.

Figure 44: Fortification remains at Tell Abu ez-Zeitun (photographed by the author)

5.2.6 Tell Shuqayyif

Tell Shuqayyif (el-Muskkerfawe) is situated at a strategic point on the path leading from the Sea of Galilee towards the Nuqra Plain.[20] It has a commanding view over its surroundings, especially on the Sea of Galilee and Nahal Kanaf (Figure 41). It is one of the largest mounds in the Golan Heights (*ca.* 7 hectares), comparable to the size of et-Tell/Bethsaida, located *ca.* 7.5 kilometers to the northwest. Except for a few villages in its immediate vicinity (e.g., Kfar ʿAkabya), the Iron Age settlement nearest to Tell Shuqayyif is Tel Hadar. An Ottoman village built on the southern sector of the site damaged the ancient remains, mainly due to the reuse of old construction materials. Currently, a fortification wall of unknown date is visible on the western sector of the settlement. Sherds from the Early Bronze Age, Middle Bronze Age, Iron Age I, and Iron Age

---

[17] Freikman 2012; Freikman/Porat 2017.
[18] Mizrachi *et al.* 1996, fig. 4.
[19] Mizrachi *et al.* 1996, fig. 4, 2, 6–7.
[20] Epstein/Gutman 1972, 281–282; Zingboym 2010; IAS 36/1, no. 84.

II suggest significant settlement activity at the site,[21] leading some scholars to consider it a candidate for the identification of the Aphek mentioned in 2 Kgs 13:17.[22]

5.2.7 Tell Abu ez-Zeitun

Tell Abu ez-Zeitun is a small oval fortress near Nahal Nov, *ca.* 1.5 km east of Tel Nov (Figure 44).[23] Y. Meitlis, who carried out a limited investigation here, noted that it was built of unworked basalt stones above an earlier site.[24]

Figure 45: The view from the shallow hill of Tel Nov to the southwest (photographed by the author)

5.2.8 Tel Nov

Tel Nov (Nab) is a low hill located south of the modern settlement bearing the same name (Figure 45).[25] The location of the site at the margin of Wadi Samekh may link it to the Sea of Galilee sites (e.g., et-Tell/Bethsaida and Tel Hadar) or, as an alternative, to the Nuqra Plain (e.g., Tell el-Ash'ari and Sheikh Sa'ad). Some scholars identified the

---

[21] A well-known find from Tell Shuqayyif is a lion statue found during the Emergency Survey (Epstein/Gutman 1972, 281–282). Shortly after the discovery, the statue was presented as the southernmost evidence of Neo-Hittite Iron Age monumental artwork (Epstein 1970). Unexpectedly, an additional survey in the early 1980s revealed the body of the very same sculpture in the village of Lawiyye, 1 km away from the lion head's original find-spot. Considering the new evidence and its possible comparison to a statue from the 'Ein Nashhut Synagogue (see, e.g., Hachlili 2013, 443–447, fig. IX-12, b), C. Epstein withdrew her former proposal (for her updated view, see idem 1982).

[22] Dothan 1975, 65.
[23] Epstein/Gutman 1972, 285; Meitlis 1999, 31; IAS 40/1, no. 24.
[24] Meitlis 1999, 31.
[25] Epstein/Gutman 1972, 285; Weksler-Bdolah 2000; IAS 40/1, no. 23.

site as 'Eni-'Anabi, mentioned in EA 256 as one of the cities of the Land of Garu,[26] but no Late Bronze Age remains have been found at the site.

The ruins of a pre-modern village and military construction are visible today on the surface of the site. In 1993, Tel Nov was excavated by S. Weksler-Bdolah.[27] During the excavation, two phases dated to the Iron Age II (Strata IVb and IVa) were exposed in a limited area (two squares). An installation and basalt-paved rooms were found, along with Iron Age II sherds. According to the excavator, a burnt surface at the bottom of the excavated area is to be associated with the earlier phase. A small ceramic assemblage was published from the excavation, including an undecorated grooved rounded bowl, a hemispherical red-slipped bowl, a krater with an out-folded rim, a cooking pot with pinched rim, a ridged jug, a ridged-neck jar, and a small decanter.[28] It probably dates to the late 9th/early 8th centuries BCE.[29]

Figure 46: Satellite view of Khirbet 'Ain et-Taruq (created with QGIS 3.16 and Google Satellite)

5.2.9 Khirbet 'Ain et-Taruq

Khirbet 'Ain et-Taruq is located *ca.* 2 km to the south of Tel Nov and remains unexcavated (Figure 46).[30] It is among the few sites with evidence of Late Bronze Age activity

---

[26] Ma'oz 1986, 148; Epstein 1993; Zwickel 2019, 270.
[27] Weksler-Bdolah 2000.
[28] Weksler-Bdolah 2000, fig. 5, 5–10.
[29] For recent excavations carried out to the west of Haspin, see Tzin/Bron/Kleiman forthcoming.
[30] Epstein/Gutman 1972, 286; Meitlis 1999, 31; IAS 40/1, no. 32.

in the southern Golan.[31] Due to its proximity to Tel Nov, where no Late Bronze Age sherds were found, N. Na'aman proposed that this might be the location of 'Eni-'Anabi, mentioned in EA 256 as one of the cities of the Land of Garu.[32]

5.3 Regional Synthesis

One of the obstacles standing in the way of reconstructing more accurately the settlement history of the Golan Heights during the Late Bronze and Iron Ages is the lack of detailed stratigraphic sequences from key sites (e.g., Tell Shuqayyif), as well from the smaller settlements (e.g., Tel Nov). However, more than 120 settlements from the Late Bronze and Iron Ages have been discovered thus far in the Golan Heights, and this provides substantial data for understanding the settlement history of this region. A review of the data from the surveys makes it clear that during the Late Bronze Age, the Golan Heights suffered a major decline in settlement activity (Figure 47). It makes sense to assume, nonetheless, that the region was not entirely devoid of human activity and was probably home to many archaeologically invisible semi-nomadic groups which interacted with the large urban centers of the Hula Valley (e.g., Tel Hazor) and the Nuqra Plain (e.g., Tell 'Ashtara). Settlement clusters existed only in the southwest, specifically in the vicinity of Tell Shuqayyif. Other settlements were dispersed in the landscape without a clear pattern (e.g., Khirbet 'Ain et-Taruq).

During the Iron Age I, the situation in the Golan Heights changed dramatically as the number of settlements in this region tripled itself (Figure 48). Most of the new settlements were small, usually measuring less than one hectare. In the southwest, near the Sea of Galilee, the settlement system strengthened.[33] Noteworthy are 12 new settlements that appeared in the southern part of the Golan Heights along an east-to-west axis (e.g., Metzad Yonathan), probably reflecting the existence of a route between the Sea of Galilee and the Nuqra Plain. The dramatic growth in the Late Bronze-Iron Age transition should probably be explained as a combination of transformation in subsistence strategies of the local semi-nomadic populations and the destruction of Canaanite Hazor towards the end of the Late Bronze Age IIB.

More changes occurred in the Iron Age II (Figure 49). In the northern Golan, the number of settlements nearly tripled itself, and in the south, the settlement system near Tell Shuqayyif and Tell el-Hashash grew stronger and expanded, mainly to the south, probably reflecting the decline of Tel Hadar as a commercial center vis-à-vis the development of the settlement at Tel 'Ein Gev. Lastly, some attention should also be drawn to the remains revealed during the limited excavations carried out at Bab el-Hawa and Tel Nov. Both sites seem to be dated to the Iron Age IIA/B transition and were destroyed not too long after their foundation. This is similar to the situation observed in the

---

[31] Late Bronze Age remains were observed near Tell edh-Dhahab, a large mound in the southern Golan, *ca.* 4 km to the northeast of Khirbet 'Ain et-Taruq (R. Beeri, personal communication).
[32] Na'aman 1977, 170.
[33] See also Hartal 2014, 82.

settlements that emerged around the Sea of Galilee (for a comparative stratigraphy of the excavated sites in the Golan Heights, see Table 15).

Table 15: Comparative stratigraphy of excavated sites in the Golan Heights

Site	Late Bronze Age	Iron Age I	Iron Age II
Mitzpe Golani	-	Sherds	Single structure
Bab el-Hawa	Sherds	-	2, 3
T. Abu ez-Zeitun	-	Fortress?	Sherds
Metzad Yonathan	-	Fortress?	-
T. Nov	-	-	IVb, IVa

5.3 Regional Synthesis

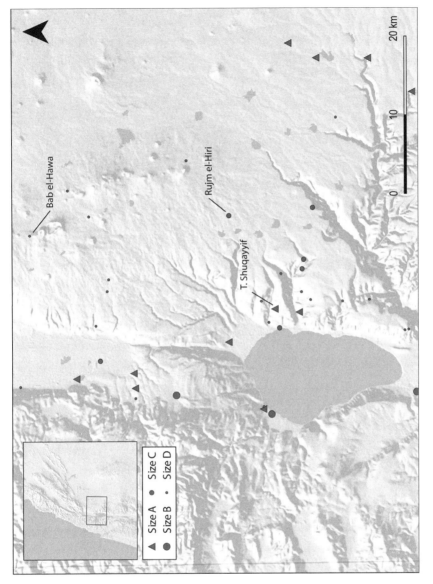

Figure 47: The Golan Heights in the Late Bronze Age (created with QGIS 3.16 and World Shaded Relief of Esri 2014)

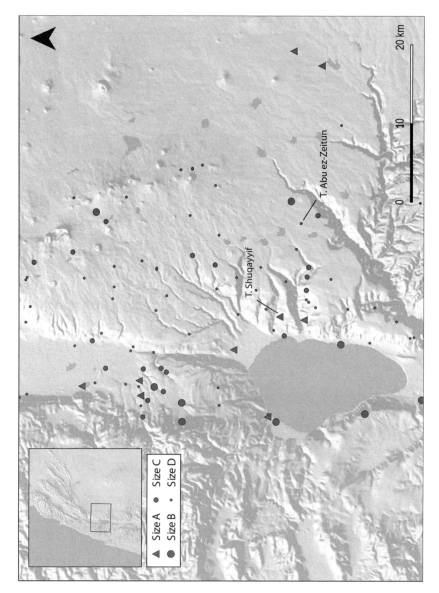

Figure 48: The Golan Heights in the Iron Age I (created with QGIS 3.16 and World Shaded Relief of Esri 2014)

5.3 Regional Synthesis

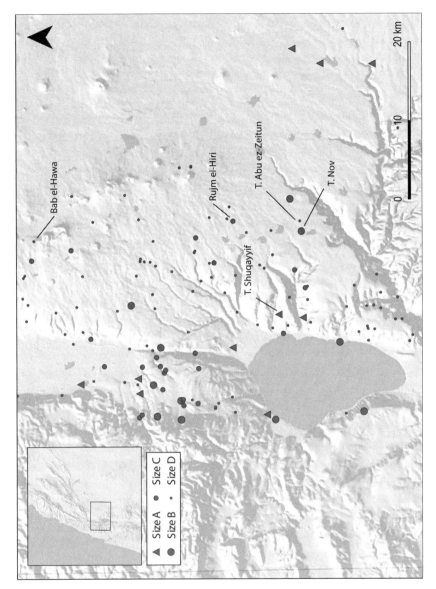

Figure 49: The Golan Heights in the Iron Age II (created with QGIS 3.16 and World Shaded Relief of Esri 2014)

Excursus A: The Cities of the Land of Garu and the Golan Heights

EA 256 mentions a revolt of the cities of the Land of Garu against 'Ashtaroth.[1] In the early 1960s, B. Mazar[2] proposed interpreting "Ga-ru" as a scribal error for "Ga-[šu]-ru." Following this suggestion, scholars have attempted to identify nearly all the cities mentioned in the letter within the area of the Golan Heights.[3] The linguistic issues derived from Mazar's suggestion, as well as from the following identifications, have been discussed at length and will not be repeated here.[4] However, there are two additional archaeological facts that should exclude most of the proposed identifications.

Table 16: Proposed identifications of toponyms mentioned in EA 256

Site Name	Proposed Identifications	Size (hectares)	Late Bronze Age Activity
T. Seluqie	Musunu	>1	No
T. 'Ain el-Hariri	Araru	>1	No
Bjuriyye	Magdalu	>1	No
T. Shuqayyif	Meshqu	5–7	Yes
el-Fakhuri	Magdalu	1–2	No
T. Nov	'Eni-'Anabi	3–4	No
T. Abu Mudawwar	Aduru	1–2	Yes
Kh. 'Ain et-Taruq	Zarqu; 'Eni-'Anabi	1–2	Yes
'Ain Umm el-Adam	Udumu	>1	No
Kh. 'Ayyun	Hayanu	>1	No

A review of the survey data from the Golan Heights shows that most of the sites correlated by scholars with the cities of the Land of Garu are usually smaller than 1–2 hectares (sometimes even less than one hectare) and thus can hardly be considered as the location of major settlements that could revolt so fiercely against 'Ashtaroth.[5] In addition, no Late Bronze Age sherds were found at many of the identified sites (Tell Seluqie, Tell 'Ain el-Hariri, Bjuriyye, el-Fakhuri, Tel Nov, 'Ein Umm el-Adam, and Khirbet 'Ayyun; see a summary of the archaeological data in Table 16). In this light, the cities of the Land of Garu should probably be sought somewhere to the south of 'Ashtaroth, especially in light of the convincing identification of Zarqu, one of the cities mentioned in EA 256, with Tell el-Fukhar and its substantial Late Bronze Age remains.[6] N. Na'aman's proposal to identify 'Eni-'Anabi with Khirbet 'Ain et-Taruq is possible from a linguistic perspective, as the site is not too far from Nab and as Late Bronze Age sherds were

---

[1] Rainey 2015, 1037–1039, 1571–1572.
[2] Mazar 1961, 20.
[3] E.g., Ma'oz 1986; idem 1992; Epstein 1993; Arav 2004a, 3–5; Zwickel 2019, 268–271.
[4] Pakkala 2010, 159–167; Na'aman 2012, 91–92.
[5] Note that the fact that 'Ashtaroth and Pihlu, two of the most important city-states to the east of the Jordan River, had to cooperate with each other, hints at a significant revolt (Na'aman 2011, 338)
[6] Kamlah 1993; Pakkala 2010, 160–161.

found there.[7] In my view, this location is a bit out of context, considering that it is located west of the Ruqqad River, which constitutes a natural border between the Golan Heights and the Nuqra Plain; the latter region seems to be the scene of events.

---

[7] Na'aman 1977, 170. As mentioned before, recently, Late Bronze Age remains were also observed in Tell edh-Dahab, a sizeable mound located *ca.* 4 km to the east of Tel Nov.

6. The Nuqra Plain

6.1 Introduction

Of all the regions discussed in this study, the Nuqra Plain is probably among the more challenging ones (Figure 50). Only a few details are known about its settlement history during the Late Bronze and Iron Ages.[1] In essence, the nature of the archaeological research of this region is somewhat similar to that of the Golan Heights, with extensive studies focused on the classical era but with very little data on earlier periods. Nonetheless, biblical and extra-biblical sources inform us that several important urban centers existed in the region, some of which can even be identified thanks to the preservation of the ancient names in modern toponyms (e.g., 'Ashtaroth or Busruna). In the Hebrew Bible, the Nuqra Plain constitutes part of biblical Bashan (e.g., Num 21:33; Deut 3:1; Jos 13:11–12; Amos 4:1; see also Ezek 47:17–18), together with the Argob (Deut 3:4; 1 Kgs 4:14), a toponym that seems to refer to the volcanic desert of the Laja.[2]

Figure 50: A view towards the western sector of the Nuqra Plain from Mount Bental, with Tell el-Hara in the background (photographed by A. Teicher / CC BY 2.5)

---

[1] For the archaeology of the Damascus Oasis, see Excursus B.
[2] Slayton 1992; Thompson 1992. For a different view, see Zwickel 2019, 274.

Like the Golan Heights, the Nuqra Plain is a volcanic plateau, *ca.* 300,000 hectares in size. It is bounded on the west by the Ruqqad River and a series of volcanic mounds (e.g., Tel Saki, Mount Peres, and Mount Varda), which separate it from the Golan Heights, and to the north by the Laja. Its eastern boundary is delineated by the western slopes of Jabal ed-Druz, an elevated volcanic field, and its southern boundary by the Yarmouk River. The region receives *ca.* 250 mm annual rainfall, making it one of the only regions in the central Levant vulnerable to short-term climate changes.[3]

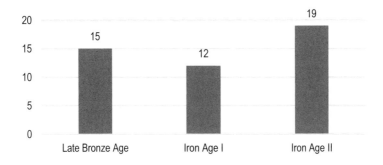

Figure 51: Settlement oscillations in the Nuqra Plain

6.2 Key Sites

In contrast to the situation west of the Ruqqad River, only a few sectors of the Nuqra Plain have been surveyed systematically,[4] and information on the Iron Age is particularly limited (Figure 51). Currently, most of the sites dating to this period are the large mounds of Tell ed-Dunayba, Sheikh Sa'ad, Tell 'Ashtara, Tell el-Ash'ari, Tell esh-Shihab, Dar'a, and Busra. Nearly all of these sites were visited by W.F. Albright at the beginning of the 20th century, who collected pottery from their surface and made general observations regarding their settlement history.[5] Needless to say, his chronological remarks, especially regarding the sub-phases of the Iron Age, should be treated with caution. Small-scale surveys carried out in the western sector of the Nuqra Plain, directly to the east of the Ruqqad River, revealed no signs of Iron Age activity.[6] This is a bit surprising considering the intense settlement activity in the Golan Heights at that time. Apparently, most of the Iron Age communities were located further to the east, specifically near the gorge of the Yarmouk River (e.g., Tell 'Ashtara and Tell el-Ash'ari) as well as along the northern part of the plain, just to the south of the Laja (e.g., Tell ed-Dunayba, Qarrasa, and Tell ed-Dabba).[7] Recently, a comprehensive reassessment of the

---

[3] Langgut/Finkelstein/Litt 2013, 164.
[4] Rohmer 2020, pl. II.
[5] Albright 1925.
[6] Barkay *et al.* 1974, 184.
[7] Braemer 1984; idem 1993.

settlement history of this region was published by J. Rohmer.[8] His work sheds new light on the history of southern Syria in the first millennium BCE and includes a detailed treatment of old data in addition to some previously unpublished information.

6.2.1   Tell ed-Dunayba

Tell ed-Dunayba is a large and imposing fortified tell site, located *ca.* 28 km to the northeast of Darʿa and *ca.* 18 km to the east of Sheikh Saʿad.[9] Apart from a few Iron Age sherds collected from the surface,[10] almost nothing is known about the Iron Age settlement. Due to its name, however, Tell ed-Dunayba is commonly regarded as the main candidate for the identification of Danabu, one of the cities of Aram-Damascus in the 9th century BCE.[11]

6.2.2   Qarrasa South

Qarrasa is located at the southern edge of the Laja. It is a relatively large mound, measuring *ca.* 6 hectares, and yielded remains from the Bronze and Iron Ages.[12] Soundings in the middle of the mound ("*Sondage* S9") and in its eastern sector ("*Sondage* S8") revealed Iron Age II sherds. In the former, the remains of a destroyed Iron Age structure with many complete vessels were exposed. In a preliminary report, the excavators of the site proposed a 7th century BCE date for the building.[13] However, more recently, J. Rohmer reexamined the pottery from the destruction layer and suggested an earlier date for the event, in the Iron Age IIB,[14] strengthening the identification of the site with Kurussa mentioned in the annals of Tiglath-Pileser III.[15]

6.2.3   Sheikh Saʿad

The ancient site at Sheikh Saʿad is located on a 12 m high hill in the midst of the modern village (Figure 52). It is one of the most important archaeological sites in southern Syria and is unanimously identified as biblical Qarnayim (Amos 6:13).[16] During the 7th century BCE, the site functioned as the capital of the Neo-Assyrian province Qarnini.[17]

In 1925, W.F. Albright visited the site and collected sherds from the Early and Middle Bronze Ages, as well from the Early Iron Age. Most of his observations were confirmed

---

[8] Rohmer 2020.
[9] Lehmann 2002, 177–178; Rohmer 2020, 114–118.
[10] Rohmer 2020, 114.
[11] Hasegawa 2012, 56; Younger 2016, 559–560; Lemaire 2019, 255; Rohmer 2020, 118.
[12] Braemer/Ibáñez/Shaarani 2011; Rohmer 2020, 190–213.
[13] Braemer/Ibáñez/Shaarani 2011, 37–38.
[14] Rohmer 2020, 202–209, 211, Table 2.3.
[15] Tadmor/Yamada 2011, 59; Rohmer 2020, 211–213, 437. For other options for locating ancient Kurussa, see the discussion in Lipiński 2000, 364; Younger 2016, 562.
[16] Braemer 1984; Hafthorsson 2006, 199–200; Rohmer 2020, 389–390.
[17] Younger 2016, 562–563. Another indication of its historical importance comes from the fact that in the late Ottoman period, Sheikh Saʿad replaced Busra as the seat of the local governor of the Hauran (Schumacher 1888, 10; idem 1889, 2, 22, 187–198).

in a later survey carried out at Sheikh Saʻad.[18] Despite the limited information on the site, two interesting finds indicating its importance in antiquity emerged already at the end of the 19th century. The first object is a stele of Ramesses II which was found by Gottlieb Schumacher in secondary use in the village mosque (the "Job Stone," according to the local folklore).[19] The second object is an orthostat depicting a striding lion, commonly considered the southernmost expression of Neo-Hittite monumental art. It was found on the mound but in secondary use.[20] Following the publication of the orthostat, excavations at the site began under the direction of Bedřich Hrozný in 1924. During these investigations, he identified three pre-Hellenistic layers, including what he understood to be a monumental building (although a later reevaluation of the excavation data suggested that this monumental building was, in fact, a Roman temple).[21] Unfortunately, much of the data collected during these excavations were not preserved, although an ongoing project is attempting to assemble and publish the surviving documentation.[22]

Figure 52: The village of Sheikh Saʻad at the end of the 19th century (Schumacher 1889, fig. 95)

---

[18] Albright 1925; Braemer 1984, 224.

[19] Giveon 1965, 197–200; Weinstein 1981, 21; Wimmer 2002. For a detailed textual discussion of the inscription engraved on the stele, see Younger 2020a. According to M. Dijkstra (2018, 71), in 2006, the monument was recovered from the collapsed mosque and brought to the Darʻa Museum.

[20] Contenau 1924, 207–210; Sader 1987, 270; Hafthorsson 2006, 199–200. For a different view on the date of the lion orthostat, see Aro 2016; Rohmer 2020, 391.

[21] Charvát 2015, 152; Rohmer 2020, 391–392.

[22] Bouzek 2019, 32–37. For a few pre-Hellenistic artifacts from the excavations, see Charvát 2015; Meynersen 2015. S. Velharticka kindly informed me that a large portion of the archival materials, which were stored in Castle Benesov (today in the Czech Republic), was destroyed in a fire in 1969.

6.2.4 Tell ed-Dabba

Tell ed-Dabba (or Dibbet Brekeh) is located in the northeastern sector of the Nuqra Plain, about 1 km to the south of the Laja (Figure 53). It is a large and fortified tell site (*ca.* 6 hectares).[23] Its identification is uncertain. E. Abou Assaf proposed identifying it with Tubu mentioned in EA 205.[24] However, this toponym is usually associated with Tayyiba, the assumed location of biblical Tob (Judg 11:3; 2 Sam 10:6, 8).[25] J. Rohmer cautiously proposed identifying Tell ed-Dabba as a viable option for Damascene Danabu along with Tell ed-Dunayba mentioned above.[26] Excavations conducted at Tell ed-Dabba focused on several architectural compounds across the site, but at present, the dating of the remains is not entirely clear as much of the material remains unpublished. Apart from a few sherds, there are no signs of Late Bronze Age activity; this may argue against identifying the site as the location of a major city-state. Published Iron Age remains are scarce, but clear evidence for activity in this period was found in the center of the mound and its eastern sector, where the excavations reached an Iron Age IIB phase, including domestic remains and Cypro-Phoenician pottery.[27] In addition, a large structure with thick walls was found together with many yet-unpublished pithoi and carved ivories, allegedly with parallels to those found in Samaria and Arslan Tash.[28]

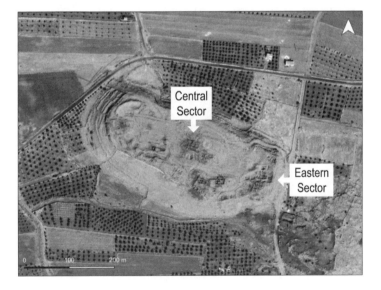

Figure 53: Satellite view of Tell Dabba with the location of excavated sectors that yielded Iron Age finds (created with QGIS 3.16 and Google Satellite)

---

[23] Braemer 1984, 242; Abou Assaf 2005; Rohmer 2020, 222–235.
[24] Abou Assaf 1974; Braemer 1984, n. 7.
[25] For problems with this identification, see Rohmer 2020, 233–235.
[26] Rohmer 2020, 235.
[27] Rohmer 2020, 224, 229–230, 232–233.
[28] The finds may suggest the existence of an Iron Age II palace (thus Rohmer 2020, 232).

6.2.5 Tell 'Ashtara

Located near one of the tributaries of the Yarmouk River, Tell 'Ashtara (biblical 'Ashtaroth) is among the largest and most important tell sites in the central Levant (Figure 54).[29] It measures *ca.* 8.5 hectares, surrounds by a moat and perhaps also a rampart, and rises to an impressive height of 18 m above the surrounding area. 'Ashtaroth is possibly mentioned in the Execration Texts and Thutmose III's list of conquered cities in Canaan.[30] EA 337 and 364[31] probably come from the site, and it was most likely the home of Biridashwa, mentioned in EA 197, and Ayyab, mentioned in EA 256.[32] During the Iron Age, the city's name was found on a relief exposed in Kalhu, which depicts its destruction by the Assyrians.[33] In the Hebrew Bible, 'Ashtaroth is said to be the capital of Og, the king of the Bashan (e.g., Deut 1:4; Jos 9:10, 12:4, 13:12). In other places, the city is nicknamed "Ashteroth-Karnaim" (Gen 14:5) or "Be'eshtera" (Jos 21:27).

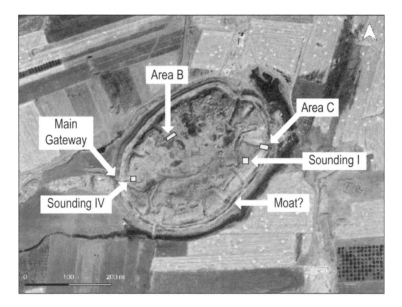

Figure 54: Satellite view of Tell 'Ashtara with the main areas excavated during E. Abou Assaf's project (created with QGIS 3.16 and Google Satellite)

---

[29] Albright 1925, 15; Abou Assaf 1968, 103–105; Lehmann 1996, 119; idem 2002, 52–53. For a high-quality plan of the site, see Rohmer 2020, fig. 4.20.
[30] Day 1992; Rohmer 2020, 394–395.
[31] Goren/Finkelstein/Na'aman 2004, 218–219, 221–223.
[32] For the correlations between these individuals and 'Ashtaroth, see Na'aman 1988. For provenancing EA 197 as Damascus, see Goren/Finkelstein/Na'aman 2004, 171.
[33] Tadmor/Yamada 2011, 144–145; Younger 2016, 650.

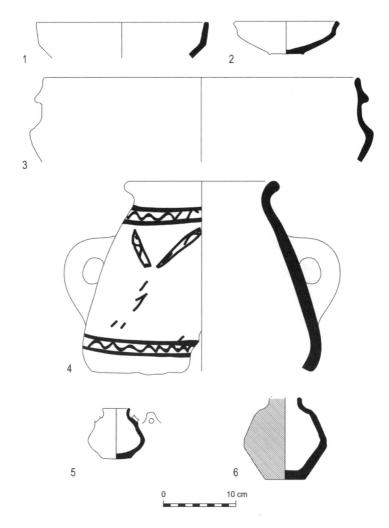

Figure 55: Selected Late Bronze and Iron Age vessels from Tell 'Ashtara (redrawn by the author based on Abou Assaf 1968, pls. I, 2; IV, 5; VI, 16; VII, 8 idem 1969, pl. III, 6, 8)

In 1966 and 1967, two short excavation seasons were carried out at Tell 'Ashtara by A. Abou Assaf (for a proposed stratigraphic correlation, see Table 17).[34] The main objective of the dig was to expose a gate compound allegedly identified on the western side of the mound and to examine the settlement history of the site.[35] Five soundings (I–V) and three larger areas (A–C) were excavated. Except for Sounding V and Area A, the latest layers in all the excavated areas were dated to the Iron Age II (most likely Iron

---

[34] For the preliminary reports, see Abou Assaf 1968; idem 1969.
[35] Abou Assaf 1968, 103–104.

Age IIB).³⁶ Below I describe only the areas that yielded Late Bronze and Iron Age finds (for selected pottery from the excavations, see Figure 55).³⁷

a. Sounding I

This area is located in the northeastern sector of the site.³⁸ Four layers were encountered here. In the uppermost layer, a series of walls built of worked and unworked stones was revealed (Layer I), constituting a few construction phases of a domestic structure, probably a part of a residential quarter. This layer appears to have been destroyed, as evident by a "smashed pithos" found *in situ*.³⁹ The pottery uncovered here includes rounded bowls with everted rims and carinated bowls with simple rims. Some of the bowls were red-slipped and burnished.⁴⁰ According to the published pottery, this layer must be dated to the Iron Age II. It is most likely the settlement that was destroyed by the Assyrians.

In Layer II, additional domestic remains were found, including evidence of heavy destruction by fire, with restorable vessels on the floors.⁴¹ The pottery uncovered here was significantly different from that of Layer I and included painted wares, Mycenean and Cypriot imports, as well as Philistine sherds.⁴² In E. Abou Assaf's view, this layer should be dated between 1200–1000 BCE.⁴³ In relative chronological terms, this means the Iron Age I (some of the reported imports must be understood, then, as residuals from an earlier phase). Below this phase, the remains of Layers III and IV were exposed. They included domestic structures and a workshop.⁴⁴ The separation of these layers was difficult. The description of the workshop (e.g., a furnace with bronze waste) suggests its use for metalworking.⁴⁵ The pottery of Layers III and IV included painted wares, and Mycenean and Cypriot imports, probably from the Late Bronze Age II.⁴⁶

b. Sounding IV

As mentioned above, the investigation of the southwestern sector of the mound was one of the main objectives of the excavations. In this area, the remains of a wide wall, next to an apparent natural entry into the settlement, were identified.⁴⁷ Sounding IV (ca. 13 × 11 m) was located to the north of the above-mentioned wall.

---

[36] Abou Assaf 1968, 121; idem 1969, 101.
[37] For a brief summary of the finds, see Lehmann 1996, 110.
[38] Abou Assaf 1968, 105–115.
[39] Abou Assaf 1968, plan II.
[40] Abou Assaf 1968, 106–107, pl. I.
[41] Abou Assaf 1968, 107–110, plan III.
[42] Abou Assaf 1968, 109–110, pl. II.
[43] Abou Assaf 1968, 110.
[44] Abou Assaf 1968, 110–112, plan IV.
[45] Abou Assaf 1968, 110–111; Akkermans/Schwartz 2003, 351; Younger 2016, 554.
[46] Abou Assaf 1968, 111–114, pls. III. Among the finds from the excavations of Tell ʿAshtara, the exposure of a domesticated camel was mentioned (Abou Assaf 1968, 114–115, fig. 29). Besides the fact that the appearance of domestic camels is now dated around the 10th century BCE (Sapir-Hen/Ben-Yosef 2013), the mandible found during the excavation belongs to a different species, cattle or caprine. I would like to thank A. Spiciarich for commenting on this photo.
[47] Abou Assaf 1968, 115–118.

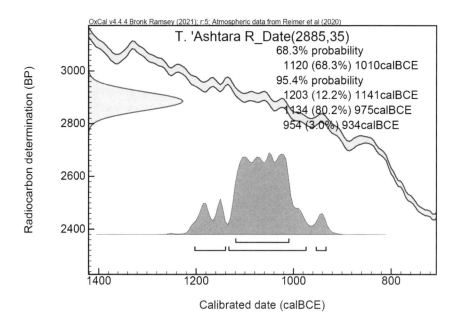

Figure 56: Radiocarbon result from Sounding IV at Tell 'Ashtara

The uppermost finds in this area were two parallel walls, which seem to constitute the remains of domestic structures (Layer 1).[48] The removal of some of these features revealed the remnants of installations of unknown function.[49] Additional features exposed in Sounding IV included a large oven and pithos full of burnt grape seeds (Layer 2). Radiocarbon dating of the seeds provided a date that ranges from the late 12th and 11th centuries BCE (Figure 56).[50] The pottery from the earliest phase encountered here included painted ware and Cypriot White Slip imports.[51] Another clue regarding the stratigraphic sequence comes from a bronze figurine from the Late Bronze Age, which was found in Layer 3.[52] It means that this layer should be dated to the Late Bronze Age. In the preliminary reports, E. Abou Assaf argued that the remains found in Sounding IV could be interpreted as an inner gate compound.[53] He was unsure of its stratigraphic affiliation but suggested that it may have functioned in the Late Bronze Age and was

---

[48] Abou Assaf 1968, 115–116, plan 5.

[49] Abou Assaf 1968, 116.

[50] The uncalibrated date is 2885±35 (Vogel/Waterbolk 1972, 53). In the original publication, the calibrated date is presented as *ca.* 935±100, but today the result is 1120–1010 BCE in 1 σ or 1203–934 BCE in 2 σ. It means the destruction occurred nearly a century before the events concluding settlement activity around the Sea of Galilee (e.g., et-Tell/Bethsaida VI, Tel Hadar IV, and Tel 'Ein Gev KIV).

[51] Abou Assaf 1968, 117–118, pls. 6–7.

[52] Abou Assaf 1968, 119, fig. 32.

[53] Abou Assaf 1968, 121. See also Schumacher 1914, 127, pl. XXXVI, b.

c. Area B

In Area B, located in the western sector of the settlement, three 6 × 8 m test trenches were excavated.[54] Apart from a few layers of superimposed and well-preserved walls, the main finds in this area were three shaft tombs covered by slabs. In one of the tombs, the remains of a small child were found above other human remains (Burial 2), and in another grave, the skeleton of a male was unearthed (Burial 3).[55] The pottery found in Area B suggests that most of the activity observed here should be dated to the Iron Age II.[56] Based on the necklace found on the skeleton in Burial 2, the excavator conjectured that it was earlier than the other graves. He proposed dating it to the late second millennium BCE, but no other evidence for this dating was provided.[57]

d. Area C

Additional test trenches were excavated in Area C, in the northeastern sector of the site near Sounding I. Three large walls and red-slipped pottery were found in one of the squares (Layer 1).[58] Two layers characterized by several deep silos were encountered below these remains (Layers 2A and 2B). The pottery associated with these layers included typical Iron Age I ceramic forms and decoration techniques,[59] as well as finds that are more characteristic of the Late Bronze Age.[60] We may assume that the upper silos (Nos. 1–4) date to the Iron Age I, while the lower silos (Nos. 5–6) date to the Late Bronze Age, but this dating is far from certain and should be regarded as tentative.

Table 17: The stratigraphy of Tell ʿAshtara

Period	Sounding I	Sounding IV	Area B	Area C
Iron Age II	I-1	IV-1	B-1 (mainly Burials 1–3)	C-1
Iron Age I	I-2	IV-2		C-2A (Silos 1–4)
Late Bronze Age	I-3	IV-3	B-2 (sherds)	C-2B (Silos 5–6)
	I-4			

---

[54] Abou Assaf 1969, 102–105, plan 2.

[55] Abou Assaf 1969, 103.

[56] Abou Assaf 1969, pl. 1, 8–9 (carinated bowls), 1, 5 (cooking pots with an inverted stance and a groove), 3 (strainer jug), and 6 (pyxis). It is also possible to mention the exposure of red-slipped items and a Black-on-Red bowl (idem 1969, 104–105, fig. 13). See also Rohmer 2020, 401–402.

[57] Abou Assaf 1969, 105. In addition, J. Rohmer (2020, 401) noted that parallels to the item in question could also be found in Iron Age contexts.

[58] Abou Assaf 1969, 105–108.

[59] Abou Assaf 1969, pl. II, 12, 20 (cooking pots with a pinched rim), 14 (strainer jug), 13, 16, and 17 (painted wares). These forms are typical of the ceramic horizon of the Iron Age I.

[60] Abou Assaf 1969, pl. II, 23 (carinated bowl), 19, and 25 (Cypriot White Slip ware).

6.2.6 Tell el-Ash'ari

Tell el-Ash'ari is a prominent mound situated south of one of the tributaries of the Yarmouk River, southwest of the modern village bearing the same name (Figure 57). Despite its impressive size (*ca.* 7.5 hectares) and location, the site is not sufficiently regarded in contemporary research and, in fact, largely ignored.[61]

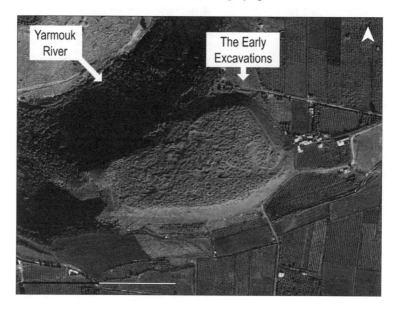

Figure 57: Satellite view of Tell el-Ash'ari near the Yarmouk River with the location of the early excavations carried out at the site by H. Seyrig (created with QGIS 3.16 and Google Satellite)

In 1925, W.F. Albright visited Tell el-Ash'ari and noted that the size of the mound was comparable to that of the nearby settlement at Tell 'Ashtarah, although situated in an even better ecological niche. He collected several sherds, dated them to the Late Bronze Age, and stressed the absence of sherds dated from the Early Iron Age.[62] The site was also active in earlier periods as a number of scholars describe a massive fortification wall built of large and roughly-hewn blocks as well as a gate complex. Both features are assumed to date to the Middle Bronze Age.[63] Evidence for Late Bronze Age II settlement came from a group of Mycenean vessels originating from an exposed tomb.[64] Excavations at the site in the first half of the 20th century also revealed a few remains from the

---

[61] Gottlieb Schumacher, for instance, visited the site in the late 19th century and concluded that Tell el-Ash'ari must be "the site of what was an impressive city in ancient days" (1889, 205–209).

[62] Note that W.F. Albright (1925, 15–16) reflected on whether his collection was indeed representative of the earlier periods due to the predominance of material from the Hellenistic period.

[63] Akkermans/Schwartz 2003, 320; Kropp/Mohammad 2006, 130–131; Rohmer 2020, 387–388. For the preliminary results of the 2010 excavations and general summary, see al-Mohammad 2015.

[64] Stubbings 1951, 83.

first millennium BCE, including a basalt moon/storm-god stele in secondary use within a Roman tomb, scarabs from the Egyptian 26th Dynasty, and Neo-Babylonian seals.[65]

While reconstructing the settlement history of Tell el-Ash'ari is difficult, the available evidence suggests that throughout the Bronze and Iron Ages, it was the location of a significant settlement. However, no identification of the site (e.g., Raphon) has gained consensus.[66] Considering its size, location, and remains (e.g., fortifications or imports), it is perhaps not too far-fetched to identify it as 'Eni-'Anabi, which appears in EA 256, Papyrus Anastasi I, and a topographical list from the days of Seti I.[67] Usually, this city is mentioned in conjunction with 'Ashtaroth (*ca.* 7 km to the north of Tell el-Ash'ari), Yeno'am (Tell esh-Shihab, *ca.* 7 to the southwest of Tell el-Ash'ari), and Zarqu (most likely Tell el-Fukhar; *ca.* 18 km to the southwest of Tell el-Ash'ari).

6.2.7 Sahem el-Jawlan

Sahem el-Jawlan is located about 8 km west of Tell 'Ashtara. It has been proposed as the location of biblical Golan, the northernmost city of refuge in the Hebrew Bible.[68] Nevertheless, the "Jawlan" component in the name of this site is most likely not genuine and originated from the need to differentiate the village from another settlement with a similar name. A salvage excavation carried out in 1992 in the modern village exposed a rock-cut tomb with more than 200 complete vessels and other small finds. According to P.M. Fischer, who analyzed the materials, burial activity here commenced at the beginning of the Late Bronze Age and continued until the beginning of the Iron Age.[69]

6.2.8 Tell esh-Shihab

Despite the apparent importance of Tell esh-Shihab, not much can be said about the site. It is located on the northern bank of Wadi el-Meddan (Figure 58). W.F. Albright visited the site in the early 20th century and noted its prominent location and impressive size; he also identified sherds from all the sub-phases of the Bronze Age but was uncertain regarding the existence of an Iron Age phase.[70] The most important find from the site is a fragment of a stele of Seti I, found in secondary use at the end of the 19th century (and considered lost already by Albright's visit to the region).[71] It hints at the importance of Tell esh-Shihab in the Late Bronze Age. The ancient name of the site is unknown. Y. Aharoni suggested identifying it with 'Eni-'Anabi,[72] while N. Na'aman proposed identifying it with the town of Yeno'am mentioned, for instance, in the Merneptah Stele.[73]

---

[65] Abd el-Kader 1931; Seyrig 1931, 589–591; idem 1959, 45–46; Rohmer 2020, 385–386.
[66] E.g., Albright 1925, 15–16. Recently, J. Rohmer (2020, 363–365) suggested identifying Raphon in Tell Hamed. For the identification of the Hellenistic settlement at Tell el-Ash'ari with Dion of the Decapolis, see Kropp/Mohammad 2006, 132.
[67] Aharoni 1979, 178–179; Na'aman 1977, 170.
[68] E.g., Arav 1992.
[69] Fischer 1997; idem 1998. See also Fischer/Keel 1995.
[70] Albright 1925, 16–17. See also Braemer 1984, 224.
[71] Weinstein 1981, 20–21.
[72] Aharoni 1957, 127–128.
[73] Na'aman 1975, 54–57; idem 1977.

Figure 58: Satellite view of Tell esh-Shihab (created with QGIS 3.16 and Google Satellite)

6.2.9 Dar'a

Dar'a is located *ca.* 10 km to the northwest of Ramtha, near the modern border between Jordan and Syria. It is identified with Edrei mentioned in Late Bronze Age texts (maybe also in EA 197)[74] and in the Hebrew Bible (e.g., Deut 3:1).[75] Past investigations at this settlement reported sherds from the Middle Bronze, Late Bronze, and Iron Ages.[76]

6.2.10 Tayyiba

Tayyiba is a large tell site, *ca.* 17 km southeast of Dar'a. Not much is known about this site, but it was probably settled during the Middle Bronze and Iron Ages.[77] No evidence of Late Bronze Age activity was found at Tayyiba, and that may cast some doubts on its common identification, as Tubu mentioned, for instance, in EA 205 (but the site is, of course, insufficiently explored).[78] Having said that, it is still regarded in research as the most convincing identification of biblical Tob (e.g., Judg 11:3; 2 Sam 10:6, 8).

---

[74] Goren/Finkelstein/Na'aman 2004, 224.
[75] Lipiński 2000, 366; Rohmer 2020, 413–414.
[76] Albright 1925, 16; Braemer 1984, 224; Rohmer 2020, 413–414.
[77] Abou Assaf 1974; Braemer 1984, 224.
[78] Goren/Finkelstein/Na'aman 2004, 215, 217–218; Finkelstein 2017, 184–185.

6.2.11 Busra esh-Sham

Busra esh-Sham is located *ca.* 37 km to the southeast of Darʻa. It is identified with Busruna mentioned in EA 197.[79] While the classical settlement is well-investigated, less is known about the earlier history of the site.[80] During the Middle Bronze Age, Busra was one of the largest sites in the southern Levant and may have reached an enormous size of *ca.* 21 hectares (but this does not mean, of course, that all of this area was settled). In later periods, the settlement must have shrunk, as excavations in the northwestern sector of the site did not reveal evidence of remains from the Late Bronze and Iron Ages.[81] Sherds from these periods were identified only during the survey of the site and in excavations in its southwestern sector.[82]

6.3 Regional Synthesis

As stated at the beginning of this chapter, the research of the Nuqra Plain in the Late Bronze and Iron Ages is under-developed. While J. Rohmer's recent study contributes significantly to the understanding of the local settlements and their material culture, the extent of information from this district cannot be compared easily to that of other nearby regions. Still, the review of the available archaeological and historical data demonstrates the existence of substantial mounds dated to the Late Bronze Age, which were the locations of important urban centers (e.g., ʻAshtaroth and Busruna). Most of them were situated on the margins of the plain (Figure 61). The evidence for settlement activity at many of the large mounds of this region correlates well with the historical sources, first and foremost the Amarna Letters, which indeed mention several local city-states. Some were identified with a high degree of certainty (Tell ʻAshtara and Busra), while the location of others has not been verified (e.g., Siribashani).[83] The existence of so many cities in the Nuqra Plain stands in contrast to the evidence from the Golan Heights, which apart from a few sites in the southwest, was the home of rural communities.

During the Iron Age I, the settlement pattern in the Nuqra Plain changed (Figure 62). The most drastic transformation occurred in the eastern and southern sectors of the region, where at least three large-scale sites were abandoned (e.g., Busra es-Sham, and Tayyiba). Some settlements were also deserted in the west (e.g., Tell esh-Shihab and Tell el-Ashʻari). The abandonment wave was accompanied by continued activity at two large-scale sites (Sheikh Saʻad and Tell ʻAshtara) and by the establishment of new sites (e.g., Dayr el-Asmar West). It is tempting to correlate the abandonment of sites in the east against the background of the "dry event" at the end of the Late Bronze Age, which

---

[79] Busra was the capital of the Roman province of Arabia and was also the seat of the governor of the Hauran in the Ottoman period before it was moved to Sheikh Saʻad (Schumacher 1888, 22).
[80] Dentzer *et al.* 2010, 139.
[81] Seeden 1986; idem 1988; H. Seeden cited in Sader 1987, 269.
[82] Braemer 1984, 224; idem 2002, 72; Dentzer *et al.* 2010, 142, n. 13; Rohmer 2020, 403.
[83] For possible identification of Siribashani in Izraa, see, e.g., Goren/Finkelstein/Na'aman 2004, 215. Note the absence of Late Bronze Age sherds in this location (Rohmer 2020, 118–119).

was assumed to have a more substantial impact on frontier regions, but the limited nature of the evidence must also be taken into account.[84]

Further development of the region occurred during the Iron Age II (Figure 63), when more than ten settlements were established (e.g., Tell el-Ash'ari, Qarrasa South, and es-Suwayda). All Iron Age I sites were resettled now, and renewed activity was initiated in a few large sites (e.g., Tell ed-Dabba). Also, in this case, some prominent sites are known only from texts, for instance, Helam is mentioned in 2 Sam 10:17 (for a comparative stratigraphy of the excavated sites in the Nuqra Plain, see Table 18).[85]

Table 18: Comparative stratigraphy of excavated sites in the Nuqra Plain

Site	Late Bronze Age	Iron Age I	Iron Age II
Qarrasa	-	-	Architecture
Sheikh Sa'ad	Sherds	Sherds?	Orthostat?
T. ed-Dabba	Architecture + sherds	Sherds?	Architecture
T. 'Ashtara	I-IV/III	I-II	I-I
	II-IV/III	II-II	II-I
	Sherds	Silos	C-I
T. el-Ash'ari	Burial	Sherds?	Stele
Busra	Sherds	-	Sherds

---

[84] Kaniewski *et al.* 2010; Langgut/Finkelstein/Litt 2013.

[85] It is commonly identified with modern Elmah, *ca.* 18 km to the northeast of Dar'a (e.g., Na'aman 2017b, 313). Currently, however, no Iron Age remains are known from the site.

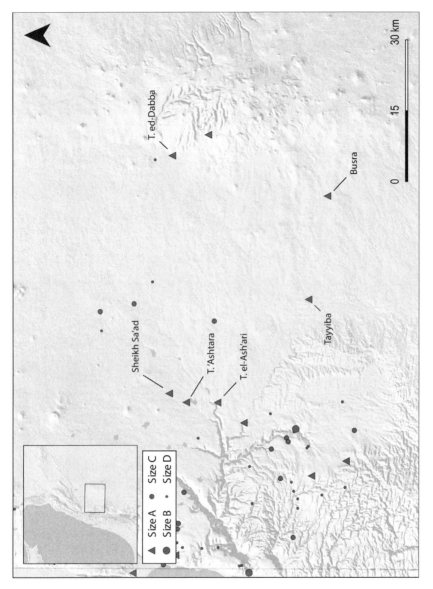

Figure 59: *The Nuqra Plain in the Late Bronze Age (created with QGIS 3.16 and World Shaded Relief of Esri 2014)*

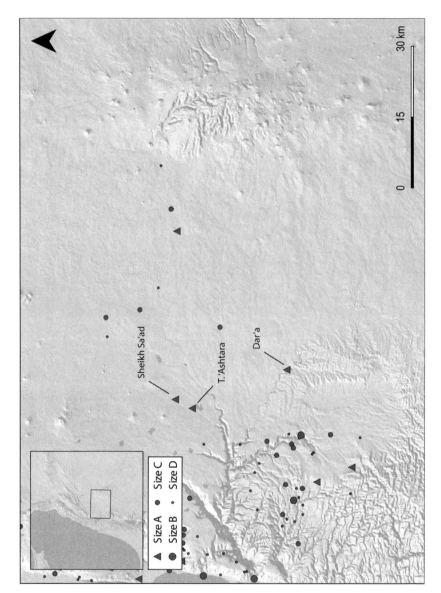

Figure 60: The Nuqra Plain in the Iron Age I (created with QGIS 3.16 and World Shaded Relief of Esri 2014)

6.3 Regional Synthesis

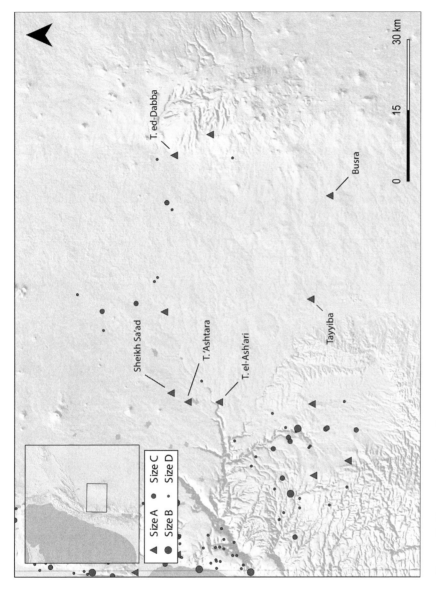

Figure 61: The Nuqra Plain in the Iron Age II (created with QGIS 3.16 and World Shaded Relief of Esri 2014)

Excursus B: In Search of the Archaeology of the Damascus Oasis

Very little is known about the archaeology of the Damascus Oasis (Figure 62).[1] In fact, even the exact location of the ancient city, the capital of Aram-Damascus, is not entirely clear. It is agreed that several hills in the midst of the old city may delineate the boundaries of the Iron Age settlement. According to R. Burns,[2] for instance, Tell el-Qantir, situated to the north of the so-called Straight Street (Midhat Pasha Suq/Suq et-Tawil) and northwest of the Umayyad Mosque, is the most favorable location for the Damascene palace of the Iron Age; this area, together with the Umayyad Mosque, measures *ca.* 6–8 hectares, a reasonable size for a prominent city like Damascus.[3] At present, the only pre-Hellenistic item revealed in the old city is a winged sphinx orthostat which was reused in the northeastern sector of the mosque.[4] It is assumed that this structure was built directly above a temple dedicated to Hadad-Ramman.[5]

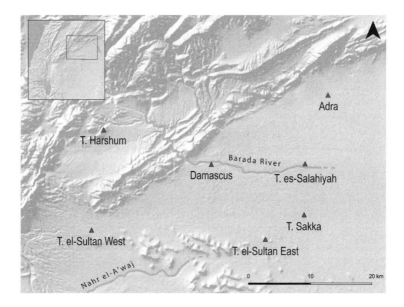

Figure 62: Iron Age settlements in the Damascus Oasis (created with QGIS 3.16 and World Shaded Relief of Esri 2014)

In the vicinity of Damascus, two main mounds have been investigated: Tell Sakka to the southeast of the old city[6] and Tell es-Salahiyah to its east (for a list of the Iron Age

---

[1] For discussions on the pre-Hellenistic city, see Pitard 1987, 1–5; Younger 2016, 553–554.
[2] Burns 2019, 27–28.
[3] Compare this with the size of Samaria in the Iron Age (*ca.* 8 hectares, see Finkelstein 2011b).
[4] See Section 10.3.1.
[5] Greenfield 1976, 197; Pitard 1987, 2–4; Younger 2016, 553–554.
[6] Taraqji 1999; idem 2015; idem 2016.

sites known from the Damascus Oasis, see Table 19).[7] The first site was mostly active in the Middle Bronze Age, but the excavations there revealed some evidence of Late Bronze Age activity as well (Stratum III). More tangible clues for Iron Age remains were exposed at Tell es-Salahiyah (also known as Tell Ferzad), which is mainly known in research as the find-spot of a figurative orthostat.[8] It is an impressive, possibly fortified, mound *ca.* 6 hectares in size. Iron Age finds were exposed during the excavations (e.g., Figure 63),[9] but its limited scope makes interpretation of the results difficult.[10]

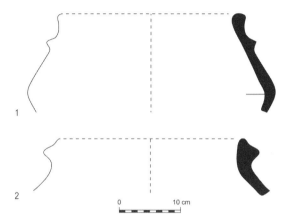

Figure 63: Selected Iron Age cooking pots from Tell es-Salahiyah (redrawn by the author based on van der Osten 1956, pl. 38, 5, 8, 16, 18)

Table 19: Iron Age settlements in the Damascus Oasis

Name	Size	Location	References
Damascus	A?	33°30'42.38"N, 36°18'24.30"E	Lehmann 2002, 138–162; Younger 2016, 553–557
T. es-Salahiyah	A	33°30'31.04"N, 36°28'11.66"E	van der Osten 1956; Lehmann 2002, 503
T. Sakka	A	33°26'25.12"N, 36°28'6.74"E	Taraqji 1999; idem 2015; idem 2016; Lehmann 2002, 503.
Adra	D	33°36'34.47"N, 36°30'34.51"E	Lehmann 2002, 9
T. el-Sultan (east)	D	33°24'17.86"N, 36°24'3.16"E	Zwickel 1990a, 352
T. el-Sultan (west)	D	33°25'6.25"N, 36°5'47.02"E	Zwickel 1990a, 353
T. Harshum	D	33°33'36.84"N, 36°7'12.50"E	Zwickel 1990a, 354

---

[7] van der Osten 1956.
[8] See Section 10.3.1.
[9] E.g., van der Osten 1956, pls. 38, 15–18, 21.
[10] E.g., Zwickel 2019, 301–302.

7. The Irbid Plateau

7.1 Introduction

During the early first millennium BCE, the area between Wadi Yarmouk and the 'Ajlun Highlands became one of the main locations for the territorial conflicts between Israel and Aram-Damascus (Figure 64). This region is one of the most fertile territories east of the Jordan Valley, and during the period, it was one of the main routes for the transportation of copper to Syria along the King's Highway. According to the Hebrew Bible, this territory was part of the Gilead,[1] as evidenced by toponyms such as Ramoth-Gilead (e.g., 1 Kgs 4:13). Archaeological data from this broader region are sparse, but most of the Irbid Plateau has been surveyed intensively.[2] Two key sites have been excavated and published (Tell el-Fukhar and Tell er-Rumeith), but information on other excavations in prominent settlements is currently limited (e.g., Tell Irbid and Tell el-Husn).[3]

Figure 64: A view over wide plain of the Irbid Plateau from Tell er-Rumeith (courtesy of I. Finkelstein)

---

[1] Finkelstein/Koch/Lipschits 2013 with earlier literature.
[2] See reviews of the data in Sauer 1986; Herr/Najjar 2001; idem 2008; Hindawi 2006, 16–69.
[3] For the results of surveys carried out in the vicinity of the plateau, see Hanbury-Tenison *et al.* 1984; Braemer 1993; Vieweger/Häser 2017, 24–54, 59–149; Rohmer 2020.

7.2 Key Sites

Several surveys have been carried out in the Irbid Plateau.[4] The most comprehensive project was conducted by S. Mittmann, who identified many archaeological sites dating to the Late Bronze and Iron Ages (Figure 65). Other survey projects focused on smaller areas and devoted significantly more time to each of the sites.[5] Until recently, none of the excavated stratified sites in the Irbid Plateau were sufficiently published, but this situation has changed now. Among the new studies, special mention should be given to the final publications of excavations conducted at Tell er-Rumeith and Tell el-Fukhar.[6] The latter provides us with a much better understanding of the Iron Age I, while the former clarifies issues related to the Iron Age II. Nevertheless, the lack of high-resolution data on the settlement history of Tell Irbid and Tell el-Husn, which are the largest mounds in the region, leaves a crucial gap in our knowledge of the cultural and settlement processes of the Irbid Plateau throughout the Late Bronze and Iron Ages.[7]

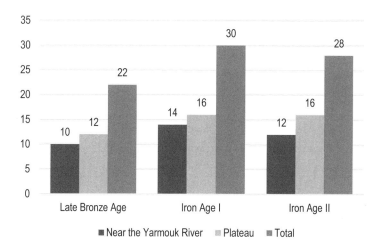

Figure 65: Settlement oscillations in the Irbid Plateau

---

[4] Glueck 1951; Mittmann 1970.

[5] E.g., Leonard 1987; Kamlah 2000; Lamprichs 2002; idem 2007.

[6] Barako/Lapp 2015 (Tell er-Rumeith); Strange 2015 (Tell el-Fukhar).

[7] One important excavated site, which is located beyond the geographical boundaries of this study but still should be mentioned, is Tell Zira'a. Long-term excavations at this site revealed impressive stratigraphic sequences dated from the Bronze and Iron Ages (Häser/Soennecken/Vieweger 2016; Vieweger/Häser 2017). Especially significant are the substantial remains from the Late Bronze Age, including a casemate wall (Stratum 14), which suggest that Tell Zira'a was perhaps the location of a small city-state. Activity in this settlement was maintained in the Iron Age I until the fierce destruction of Stratum 13 (most likely in the late phase of the period). In the view of the excavators, the site was rebuilt already in the Iron Age IIA (Häser/Soennecken/Vieweger 2016, 131).

7.2.1 Qwayliba

Surveys and excavations carried out in Qwayliba, identified with Abila of the Decapolis, exposed sherds from the Late Bronze and Iron Ages,[8] but the nature of the findings remains unclear. Some scholars suggest identifying this site with Yobilu, mentioned in EA 256 as one of the cities of the Land of Garu.[9]

7.2.2 et-Turra

One of the most enigmatic sites discovered during the field surveys carried out in the Irbid Plateau is et-Turra. It is located *ca.* 10 km to the north of Tell Irbid and *ca.* 6 km to the southeast of Tell esh-Shihab. No excavations have been carried out at the site, but it was surveyed by S. Mittmann, who documented sherds from the Iron Age II. Two notable items were found at et-Turra: an Egyptian stele of Ramesses II[10] and a moon/storm-god stele, probably from the Iron Age II.[11] Interestingly, the discovery of the Egyptian stele contradicts the result of the survey, which did not identify any sherds from the Late Bronze Age. This is, of course, possible, but one solution for this problem comes from S. Wimmer's suggestion that the stele may have actually originated from the nearby Tell esh-Shihab, where a stele of Seti I was found in the early 20th century.[12]

7.2.3 Tell el-Fukhar

Tell el-Fukhar is located *ca.* 11 km northeast of Irbid (Figure 66), only 800 m southeast of Tell es-Subba.[13] It is a relatively small mound but is located at a prominent position within Wadi esh-Shellaleh, one of the routes leading to southern Syria. Due to the proximity of Tell el-Fukhar to Khirbet ez-Zeraqon, where no Late Bronze Age remains were found, J. Kamlah proposed identifying it with Zarqu, mentioned in EA 256, as one of the cities of the Land of Garu.[14]

Excavations carried out at Tell el-Fukhar showed that the site was occupied during the Late Bronze Age II, Iron Age I, and Iron Age IIC.[15] No sherds dated to the Iron Age IIA or Iron Age IIB were found.[16] Iron Age I remains were limited to the area of the acropolis and were poorly preserved (Stratum VIB). However, according to the excavators, the possibility that the locals renovated the Late Bronze Age IIB fortification of

---

[8] Glueck 1951, 125–126; Zwickel 1990a, 331; Mare 1993, 2; Hafthorsson 2006, 204–205.

[9] E.g., Galil 1998, 375. Based on the proximity of the site to a settlement named ed-Dunaybah, E. Lipiński (2000, 352–353) reflected on whether the city of Danabu, mentioned in the royal annals of Shalmaneser III, should be located at the site, but ultimately rejected the identification.

[10] Wimmer 2002.

[11] Wimmer/Janaydeh 2011.

[12] Smith 1901; Wimmer 2002.

[13] Zwickel 1990a, 324; Kamlah 2000, 16–19.

[14] Kamlah 1993; Pakkala 2012, 160–161. In W. Zwickel's view (2019, 270), this identification is not convincing, partly because Tell el-Fukhar is located too far south (see also Strange 2015, 12, 420). In my view, the *ca.* 25 km separating Tell 'Ashtara and Tell el-Fukhar are not an obstacle.

[15] Strange 2015, 11–12, Table 13.

[16] Ottosson 2015, 26; Strange 2015, 44, 47, 71.

the acropolis cannot be excluded.[17] Evaluating the exact date of the Iron Age I occupation at Tell el-Fukhar is difficult, as most, if not all, of the published Iron Age pottery seems to originate from mixed loci.[18] Still, one should note that the indicative types of the late phase of the Iron Age I are absent at the site (e.g., storage jars with elongated bodies and carinated shoulders or Phoenician Bichrome Ware). A special find is a fragment of a Philistine bell-shaped krater, probably signifying the easternmost distribution of this ceramic tradition.[19] The excavations of Tell el-Fukhar also provide an important lesson in reconstructing the settlement history of the Irbid Plateau. S. Mittman's survey at the site revealed sherds from the Iron Age I and II,[20] which would suggest settlement continuity between these periods. However, the excavations demonstrate that the Iron Age II sherds date, in fact, to the Iron Age IIC and thus indicate an extended occupational gap of 300–400 years at Tell el-Fukhar after the Iron Age I.

Figure 66: Satellite view of Tell el-Fukhar (created with QGIS 3.16 and Google Satellite)

7.2.4 Tell Irbid

Tell Irbid is one of the largest sites in Transjordan. It is located in the center of the modern city and covers *ca.* 10 hectares (Figure 67). The site is commonly identified with biblical Beth-Arbel (Hos 10:14), but other identifications, such as Gintot[21] or Suhra

---

[17] Ottosson 2015, 15–16; for photos and a plan, see Strange 2015, pls. 3–5; 66.
[18] McGovern/Strange 2015.
[19] Strange 2015, pl. 154, 8.
[20] Mittmann 1970, 13.
[21] Lenzen/Knauf 1987.

(e.g., EA 334),[22] have also been suggested. W.F. Albright visited Tell Irbid at the beginning of the 20th century and collected sherds dated from all phases of the Bronze and Iron Ages.[23] Excavations of the site focused on its northern and eastern sectors, where several burial caves were unearthed.[24] While many of these tombs were dated to the Late Bronze Age (but some Middle Bronze Age III activity cannot be excluded), the use of some of them should be dated to the early phase of the Iron Age (Figure 68).[25] The latest ceramic forms in the assemblages from the Iron Age tombs include a black juglet,[26] which to the best of my knowledge does not appear in secure Iron Age I contexts,[27] and a Cypriot Black-on-Red juglet[28] which does not appear in the Levant before the late Iron Age IIA.[29] In addition, one can note the striking similarities between the pottery from these tombs and the pottery from the destruction of Stratum IV at Tel Hadar (especially the kraters with horizontal grooves on the neck).[30] Another important find from the tombs is a drummer figurine, which is typical of many Iron Age IIA contexts.[31]

Figure 67: Aerial view of Tell Irbid in the center of the modern city (Sauer 1986, fig. 7)

Excavations during the 1980s in the northern sectors of the mound revealed parts of the Bronze Age fortifications of the site (observed already by W.F. Albright) and a large

---

[22] Finkelstein 2014a, 149–150. For the provenance of EA 334, see Goren/Finkelstein/Na'aman 2004, 219–220 (but there with a preference towards Tell el-Husn).
[23] Albright 1929, 10.
[24] Dajani 1966; Lenzen 1986; Lenzen/Gordon/McQuitty 1985; Kafafi 2014; Fischer/Bürge/al-Shalabi 2015. For a summary of the history of research of the site, see Kafafi/Abu Dalu 2009.
[25] Tombs A–C in Dajani 1966.
[26] Dajani 1966, pl. XXXIII, 9.
[27] Cohen-Weinberger/Panitz-Cohen 2014, 409–410, *pace* Singer-Avitz 2016, 235.
[28] Dajani 1966, pl. XXXIV, 24.
[29] Gilboa/Sharon 2003; Georgiadou 2014, 383–384; more recently Kleiman *et al.* 2019.
[30] Kleiman 2019a, 103.
[31] Paz 2007, 102.

compound sealed by thick destruction debris.[32] One of the excavated rooms was interpreted as a Late Bronze Age temple, although it was probably a cult corner within a building with a different function (e.g., Complex 296 at Tel Hadar).

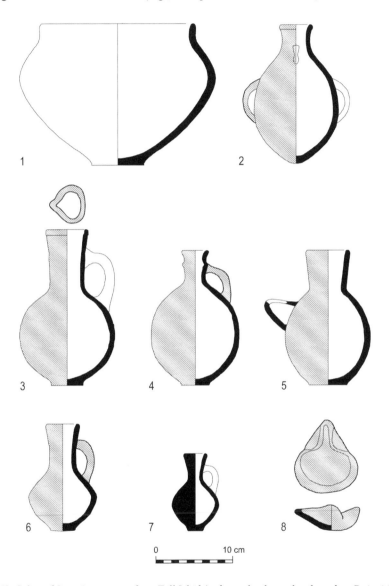

Figure 68: Selected Iron Age pottery from Tell Irbid (redrawn by the author based on Dajani 1966, pl. 32; red slip was added to the drawings based on the textual descriptions)

---

[32] Lenzen 1986.

Only a photo of the vessels found in the structure was published (Figure 69).[33] It shows seven vessels, including a rounded bowl with a simple rim, a cyma-shaped bowl, two goblets with globular bodies, a cup-and-saucer, a lamp, and a decorated stand. All of these vessels can be dated generally between the Late Bronze Age IIB and Iron Age I (although they perfectly fit within the Iron Age I, especially the goblet). Better clues for the destruction of the compound come from radiocarbon dating of carbonized grain from the destruction. It provides a date that ranges between the early 14th and mid-13th century BCE (cal. 1385–1230 BCE in 1 sigma; uncal. 3040±40).[34] The period that followed this event is even less clear. In C.J. Lenzen's view, the city existed until the late 9th century BCE, but virtually no information was published; to date, the survival of the settlement at Tell Irbid into the Iron Age IIA is supported only by the tombs dug by R.W. Dajani.[35]

Figure 69: Selected vessels from the cult room at Tell Irbid (Lenzen 1986, fig. 27)

7.2.5 Tell er-Rumeith

Tell er-Rumeith is located on a hill with a commanding view over its surroundings, *ca.* 15 km west of Irbid (Figure 70). It is a key site for studying the Irbid Plateau in the Iron Age II. The identification of the site is still unclear. Initially, N. Glueck proposed identifying it with biblical Ramoth-gilead,[36] a suggestion that was generally accepted in

---

[33] Lenzen 1986, fig. 27.
[34] Ambers/Matthews/Bowman 1989, 14.
[35] See also Section 11.2.8.
[36] Glueck 1943; idem 1951, 97.

research. E.A. Knauf suggested nearby Ramtha as a more reasonable identification as Ramoth-gilead, based on the problematic philological connection between the names Rumeith and Ramoth (and the small size of Tell er-Rumeith).[37]

Excavations at Tell er-Rumeith were focused on the eastern half of the hill and revealed a 50 × 50 m fortress.[38] Based on the preliminary reports, which described four Iron Age strata and four destructions (Strata VIII–V), as well as following a visit to the site, I. Finkelstein, O. Lipschits, and O. Sergi reevaluated the results of the old dig and correlated them with the historical developments in the Gilead during the 9th–8th centuries BCE.[39] According to their study, the recurring construction and destruction episodes of this fortress should be explained against the background of the rivalry between Israel and Aram-Damascus (for a proposed stratigraphic correlation, see Table 20).[40]

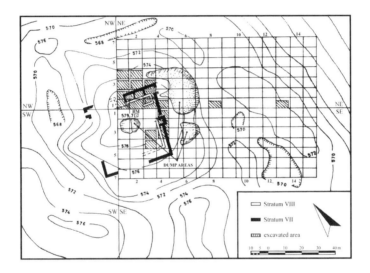

Figure 70: Plan of the fortresses of Strata VIII and VII at Tell er-Rumeith (Barako 2015b, 4.1)

More recently, the final report on the excavations was published by T.J. Barako and N.L. Lapp, who redefined the stratigraphic sequence of the site.[41] According to their new analysis, Stratum VIII marks the first substantial activity on the hill.[42] During the lifetime of this stratum, which was only partially exposed, a fortified compound was constructed directly on bedrock. Based on the ceramic evidence, Barako dates the

---

[37] Knauf 2001 followed by Finkelstein/Lipschits/Sergi 2013, 22–23; Barako 2015a, 6–8.

[38] See summaries of the excavations in N.L. Lapp 1992; Finkelstein/Lipschits/Sergi 2013, 9–11. For the preliminary reports, see P. Lapp 1963; idem 1968; idem 1975.

[39] Finkelstein/Lipschits/Sergi 2013.

[40] I. Finkelstein *et al.* also noted the existence of a moat and an outer rampart, an observation that was supported later in the final publication of the dig (Barako 2015b, 191).

[41] Barako/Lapp 2015.

[42] Note that some Late Bronze sherds were also found during the excavations and may suggest some small-scale activity on the prominent hill before the construction of Stratum VIII.

construction of Stratum VIII to the late 10th century BCE and attributes it to Solomon, or alternatively, to one of the early north-Israelite kings. In his view, this fortress was destroyed by the Aramaeans in the early 9th century BCE. After the destruction, new activity at the site commenced, indicated by the construction of Stratum VII. It included a casemate wall and a two-chambered gate. No apparent signs of destruction were identified at the end of this stratum (although a few complete vessels were associated with it and may allude to a small-scale disruption episode).[43] During the lifetime of Stratum VIIB, which followed Stratum VII, the settlement expanded beyond the fortification walls; this expansion was correlated with the construction of the moat and the rampart observed by I. Finkelstein and his colleagues.[44] This settlement was destroyed in a major conflagration which was dated to *ca.* 840–830 BCE and associated with either the battle of Ramoth-Gilead in 842/841 BCE or with the military campaigns of Aram-Damascus against the Northern Kingdom. After this event, the settlement was rebuilt again (Stratum VI). In several places, new floors were built, which were assigned to Stratum VIB. As with the earlier strata, ultimately, this phase was destroyed in fierce destruction, attributed to Tiglath-Pileser III's campaigns in the late 8th century BCE.

Table 20: Possible interpretations of the settlement history of Tell er-Rumeith

Reference	Stratum	Pottery	Built/Maintained	Destroyed
Scenario A	VIB	Iron Age IIB	Israel (Jeroboam II)	Aram-Damascus (Rezin)
	VI		Aram-Damascus (Hazael)	Israel (Jeroboam II)
	VIIB	Iron Age IIA	Israel (Omrides)	Aram-Damascus (Hazael)
	VII			
	VIII		Aram-Damascus (unknown)	Israel (Omrides)
Scenario B	VIB	Iron Age IIB	Aram-Damascus (Rezin)	Assyria (Tiglath-Pileser III)
	VI		Israel (Jeroboam II)	Aram-Damascus (Rezin)
	VIIB	Iron Age IIA	Aram-Damascus (Hazael)	Israel (Jeroboam II)
	VII			
	VIII		Israel (Omrides)	Aram-Damascus (Hazael)

Note: These scenarios are based on Finkelstein/Lipschits/Sergi 2013, Table 1, with changes according to the new data published by Barako/Lapp 2015.

Most of the dates proposed by T.J. Barako to the Iron Age strata at Tell er-Rumeith are reasonable.[45] Both Strata VIII and VII include ceramic forms typical of the late Iron Age IIA (e.g., holemouth jars and a single Cypriot Black-on-Red sherd found in Stratum VIII),[46] and therefore the construction of the earliest fortress is likely to be dated to the late 10th century or the beginning of the 9th century BCE, in parallel to Stratum X at Tel

---

[43] E.g., Barako 2015c, fig. 3.18, 1–2.
[44] Finkelstein/Lipschits/Sergi 2013, 13.
[45] Radiocarbon samples from the excavations (Crane/Griffin 1972, 218–219; Weinstein 1984, 351–352) were charcoal rather than short-lived samples, and thus the dating of the site depends solely on the pottery and historical considerations.
[46] Barako 2015c, fig. 3.42, 1.

Hazor, Stratum V at Tel Rehov, or Level Q-5 at Tel Megiddo. While Barako proposed that these strata were constructed by the Kingdom of Israel, the possibility that Aram-Damascus constructed the compound should not be discounted, especially given that Aram-Damascus seems to dominate the northern Gilead in the mid-9th century BCE (and certainly after the Battle of Ramoth-Gilead).[47] Iron Age IIB ceramic forms began to appear in Stratum VIIB,[48] hinting at its relatively late date within the Iron Age IIA sequence. In absolute chronology terms, the destruction of this settlement should probably be dated to the end of the 9th century or the beginning of the 8th century BCE (i.e., later than the mid-9th century BCE date advocated by Barako). The attribution of Strata VI and VIB to the Iron Age IIB and the attribution of the final destruction of the settlement to the Assyrian campaigns of the late 8th century BCE makes sense.[49]

Figure 71: Satellite view of Tell el-Husn (created with QGIS 3.16 and Google Satellite)

7.2.6 Tell Johfiyeh

Tell Johfiyeh is located *ca.* 7.5 southwest of Irbid. It is a small site and most likely constitutes part of the rural hinterland of the nearby Tell el-Husn. N. Glueck's survey of the site revealed sherds from the Iron Age.[50] Excavations at Tell Johfiyeh exposed finds from the Late Bronze and Iron Ages. Remains from the later period were discovered mainly on the top of the mound, where the remains of a modest Iron Age II farmstead

---

[47] Sergi 2016 with discussion and earlier bibliography.
[48] E.g., Barako 2015c, figs. 3.7, 1, 4 (wheel-burnished bowls); 3.10, 1 (a flat bowl).
[49] Finkelstein/Lipschits/Sergi 2013, 18; Barako 2015b, 194.
[50] Glueck 1951, 113.

were found below a structure from late antiquity.[51] According to R. Lamprichs, the builders of this farmstead reused massive walls from an earlier occupational phase. Ceramic assemblages from the excavations date to the Late Bronze Age, Iron Age I, and Iron Age II.[52] The lack of red-slipped and hand-burnished pottery, as well as the presence of many cooking pots with an inverted stance and grooved rim is notable[53] and may suggest an Iron Age IIB date for the renewal of settlement activity at this site.

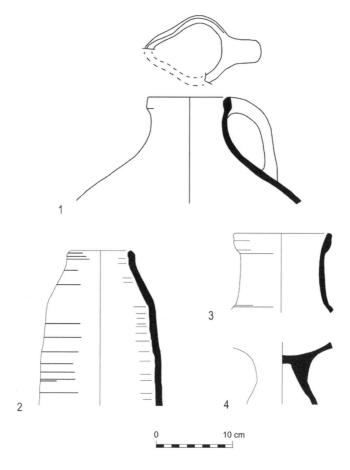

Figure 72: Selected Iron Age vessels from Tell el-Husn (redrawn by the author based on Leonard 1987, figs. 16, o, n; 18, a, c)

---

[51] Lamprichs 2002; idem 2007.
[52] Bastert/Hockmann 2008.
[53] E.g., Bastert/Hockmann 2008, fig. 13, 2–3.

7.2.7 Tell el-Husn

Tell el-Husn is located on the southern edge of the plateau, northeast of the 'Ajlun Highlands (Figure 71). Its size, estimated at *ca.* 5 hectares, and its imposing position relative to its surroundings, allude to its importance in antiquity. According to I. Finkelstein, I. Koch, and O. Lipschits,[54] this large tell-site may be identified with biblical Lidebir (e.g., Jos 13:26; 2 Sam 9:4–5; 17:27; Amos 6:13). Others, like A. Lemaire, considered it a possible candidate for the location of Ramoth-Gilead,[55] or Suhra mentioned in EA 334.[56] Only limited archaeological research on the Late Bronze and Iron Ages at the site has been carried out, but sherds dated from these periods were documented in surveys.[57] A salvage excavation on the margins of Tell el-Husn revealed some Late Bronze and Iron Age finds (Figure 72).[58] Distinctive among the finds are the remains of a casemate wall, the plan and date of which remain unclear.

7.3 Regional Synthesis

During the Late Bronze Age, there were more than 20 settlements on the Irbid Plateau (Figure 73), including two large mounds (Tell Irbid and Tell el-Husn) and one medium-size settlement (Tell el-Fukhar).[59] In this period, most of the settlements were dispersed across the landscape, with some small clusters in Wadi esh-Shellaleh (e.g., et-Turra, Tell el-Mughayir, and Tell es-Subba) and to the northwest of Tell Irbid (Tell ez-Za'faran, Khirbet Dabulya, and Jijjin). In contrast, the area around Tell el-Husn (on the plateau) was nearly void of settlements, with the exceptions of Tell Johfiyeh and Khirbet Umm el-Abar East. Although its ancient name remains uncertain, Tell Irbid, the largest settlement in the Irbid Plateau (and maybe even in the Transjordan), was almost certainly the regional center. Several small city-states seem to have existed to its north, near the Yarmouk River (e.g., Tell el-Fukhar). From time to time, these cities attracted the attention of the Egyptian Empire (see, e.g., Ramesses II stele from et-Turra). Following other scholars, I believe that many of the cities of the Land of Garu should be located in this area (e.g., Zarqu) rather than in the Golan Heights.[60] Our knowledge regarding the southern part of the Irbid Plateau in the Late Bronze Age is limited. Tell el-Husn could, in theory, constitute another city-state. Since virtually no settlements were identified in its surrounding, it may have served as the gateway to the plateau of the many settlements erected in the 'Ajlun Highlands during the Late Bronze and Iron

---

[54] Finkelstein/Koch/Lipschits 2012, 144–145.
[55] Glueck 1943; idem 1951, 164–165; Lemaire 2019, 253.
[56] Goren/Finkelstein/Na'aman 2004, 224.
[57] Glueck 1951, 161–165.
[58] Leonard 1987. For earlier remains, see, e.g., al-Bashaireh/al-Muheisen/ 2011.
[59] Recent investigations in Tell Ushayer, *ca.* 3 km to the west of Irbid, revealed substantial remains from the Late Bronze Age (Bonatz 2020). Although the site is quite prominent in the landscape, it is not mentioned by previous investigators of this region.
[60] Kamlah 1993; Pakkala 2010, 160–161.

Ages.⁶¹ If the settlement histories of Tell Irbid and Tell el-Fukhar reliably represent the cultural and historical processes that occurred in the plain at the end of the second millennium BCE, then sometime in the Late Bronze Age IIB, the local cities suffered severe destruction episodes, probably reflecting a regional crisis.⁶²

In the Iron Age I, the local communities recovered (Figure 74). While four settlements were abandoned, more than ten sites were founded. Most of the new settlements were established in either Wadi esh-Shellaleh (e.g., Khirbet ʿAin Ghazal, Isʿara, and Khirbet el-Mughayir East) or to the northwest of Tell Irbid, where a group of nine settlements was established around Tuqbul.⁶³ At both Tell el-Fukhar and Tell Irbid, new settlements were built above the ruins of the previous cities. In the former, the recovered town was short-lived. In the latter, in contrast, activity lasted for at least another century until it was abandoned sometime in the Iron Age IIA.⁶⁴

The settlement distribution of the Iron Age II is very similar to that of the previous period, with several new settled sites and a few abandoned ones (Figure 75). As was the case in the previous periods, the large mounds of the region were Tell Irbid and Tell el-Husn. Ramtha was probably another large settlement, but not much, in fact, nothing, is known about its ancient history. Our understanding of the regional processes in this period mostly depends on the interpretation of the excavations at Tell er-Rumeith.⁶⁵ Despite its small size, the dense stratigraphic sequence revealed at the site can be used to pinpoint cultural and historical transformations occurring regionally during the period. As mentioned above, the dates proposed for the different layers at the site can be generally accepted. However, the historical interpretation of a north-Israelite establishment of the early fortresses of Strata VIII and VII should be reevaluated, considering the probable control of Aram-Damascus over the Gilead in the mid-9th century BCE (2 Kgs 22). Its domination over the region in the 8th century BCE seems to be reinforced by the Assyrian sources (for a comparative stratigraphy of the excavated sites, see Table 21).

Table 21: Comparative stratigraphy of excavated sites in the Irbid Plateau

Site	Late Bronze Age I/II	Iron Age I	Iron Age IIA/B
T. el-Fukhar	City-state?	Fortified settlement?	Village?
T. Irbid	Cult Room + Tombs	Tombs	Tombs
T. er-Rumeith	Sherds	-	Strata VIII–VIB
T. Johfiyeh	Sherds	Sherds	Village

---

⁶¹ E.g., Der Burak, Khirbet Fara, or Sahra (Mittmann 1970, 60–61, 75–76).

⁶² Whether these events should be understood as the historical background for the erection of the royal stele of Ramesses II at et-Turra is uncertain.

⁶³ Note that the site is relatively small and has no apparent importance (Kamlah 2000, 13–16).

⁶⁴ If Tell Irbid is indeed identified with Beth-Arbel (Hos 10:14), then the abandonment of the site can be correlated with Shalmaneser III's campaigns in the region in the mid-9th century BCE.

⁶⁵ Lapp 1992; Finkelstein/Lipschits/Sergi 2013; Barako 2015c.

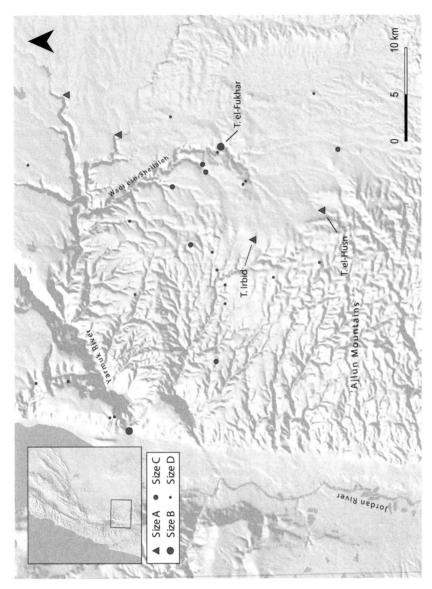

Figure 73: The Irbid Plateau in the Late Bronze Age (created with QGIS 3.16 and World Shaded Relief of Esri 2014)

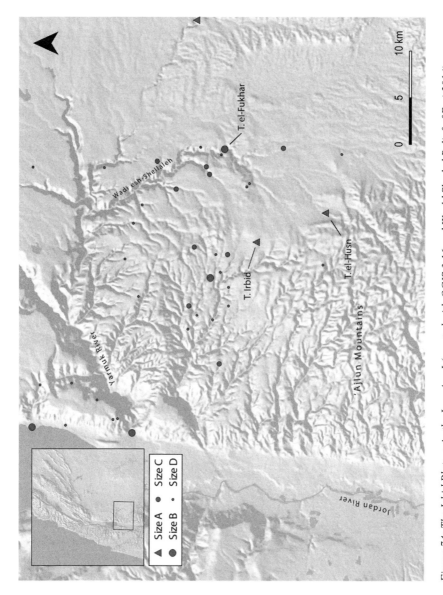

Figure 74: The Irbid Plateau in the Iron Age I (created with QGIS 3.16 and World Shaded Relief of Esri 2014)

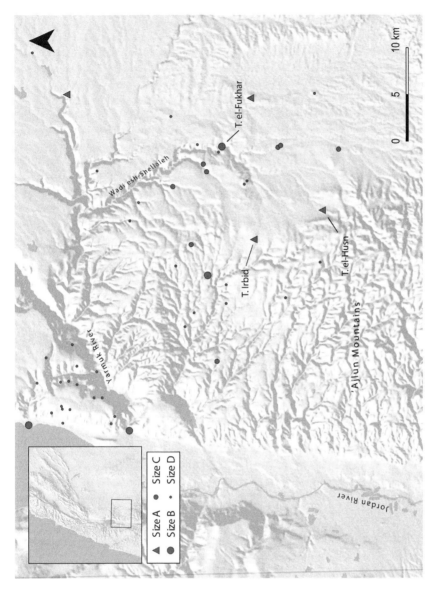

Figure 75: The Irbid Plateau in the Iron Age II (created with QGIS 3.16 and World Shaded Relief of Esri 2014)

Part II. The Material Culture

8. Architectural Styles

8.1 Introduction

Following the examination of the settlement history in the central Levant, we can now deal with the general characteristics of the local material culture: from architecture to inscribed objects. In this chapter, I discuss monumental structures (e.g., Citadel 3090 at Tel Hazor), distinct building types (e.g., pillared buildings and four-room houses), and residential quarters that were excavated in the central Levant. A review of the architectural evidence can help us to identify the intrusion of foreign traditions, political transformations, and even advanced urban and economic planning.

8.2 Monumental Structures

It is generally agreed that the construction or transformation of monumental structures can indicate substantial changes in social complexity (Table 22; Figure 76). Such buildings were a statement of political supremacy, sometimes functioning as the official seat of a local ruler and the center of power, and communicated messages of an ideological and symbolic nature.[1] Nevertheless, the identification of the exact function of these monumental buildings, administrative or religious, is not always straightforward. Perhaps the best example is Building 7050 at Canaanite Hazor. Even though this structure was well-preserved and completely exposed, there is still no agreement, even between the excavators themselves, on its purpose: a palace, a temple, or a ceremonial palace.[2]

Table 22: Public buildings in the central Levant

Designation	Description	References
Bamah B	T. Dan, Area T, Str. III–II. Ashlar-built structure at the top of the site (*ca.* 18 × 18 m)	Biran 1996, fig. 1.34
Building 8158	Hazor, Area A, Str. X. Stone-built structure in a neighborhood near the city-gate (*ca.* 16 × 15 m)	Ben-Tor/Ben-Ami/Sandhaus 2012, plan 2.3
Citadel 3090	Hazor, Area B, Str. VIII–V). Ashlar-built structure at the top of the site (*ca.* 21.5 × 25.5 m)	Yadin *et al.* 1989, plan XX
The Bit Hilani	et-Tell/Bethsaida, Area B, Str. V. Basalt-built structure near the city gate (*ca.* 15 × 28.25 m)	Arav/Bernett 2000, fig. 2

---

[1] E.g., Routledge 1997, 139–140; Faust 2012, 191–192; Sergi/Gadot 2017, 104–105.
[2] Bonfil/Zarzecki-Peleg 2007; Ben-Tor 2016, 93–104; idem 2020.

8. *Architectural Styles*

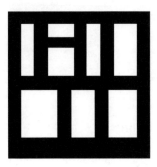
Bamah B at Tel Dan (Str. III–II)

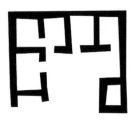
Building 8158 (Str. X)

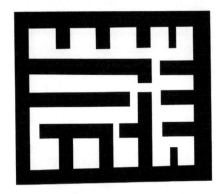
Citadel 3090 at Hazor (Str. VIII–V)

The Bit-Hilani at et-Tell (Str. V)

Figure 76: Sketches of Iron Age II public structures (adapted from Biran 1996, fig. 1.34; Yadin et al. 1961, Plan XX; Arav/Bernett 2000, fig. 2)

8.2.1 Bamah B at Tel Dan

During the excavation of Tel Dan, two superimposed monumental structures were discovered in Area T: Bamah A and Bamah B.[3] The full extent of Bamah A is unknown as Bamah B was built above it, and the later structure was not entirely removed during the excavation. Bamah A was built of ashlar blocks which were preserved to a height of two courses.[4] Even though many publications define Bamah A as a distinct feature,[5] it was probably no more than a support system for Bamah B.[6] Both structures were built together only after the domestic remains associated with Stratum IVA were taken out of use and sealed beneath the "yellow floor" of Stratum III. According to A. Biran, the entire structure continued to function also in Stratum II until the destruction of the site.

Perhaps the most intriguing question is the function of Bamah B. The excavator saw this structure as a renovation of the open-air sanctuary of Bamah A.[7] In contrast, I. Sharon and A. Zarzecki-Peleg drew attention to the administrative aspects of the compound (e.g., the casemate enclosure) and grouped Bamah B with other local monumental buildings (e.g., Palace 1723 at Tel Megiddo), which they termed "Lateral Access Podium Structures" (abbreviated as LAP).[8] Indeed, all the other parallels for Bamah B are usually interpreted by archaeologists as palaces and not as sanctuaries (e.g., Citadel 3090 at Tel Hazor or Building 338 at Tel Megiddo).[9] Considering the location of Bamah B at the top of the mound, the assumed function of similar buildings, its association with a cult place (e.g., the large altar), and evidence for connections with the Samaria Highlands (e.g., the stamp impression found in the compound), identifying it as the city palace during the Iron Age II is more than reasonable.

8.2.2 Building 8158 at Tel Hazor

Building 8158 is a large structure near the city gate of Tel Hazor. It is similar in plan to the so-called Bit-Hilani at et-Tell/Bethsaida (see below).[10] According to the excavators, this was the most prominent feature exposed in Stratum Xb, and it might have served an administrative function.[11] Building 8158's location in the midst of a densely-built neighborhood, however, suggests that its residents belonged to the upper echelon of the local

---

[3] Biran 1982; idem 1994, 159–214.

[4] Apart from Tel Hazor, Tel Dan is the only other site in the central Levant where ashlar masonry was observed during the period (the monumental building at et-Tell/Bethsaida was built of basalt).

[5] E.g., Biran 1994, 168; Sharon/Zarzecki-Peleg 2006, 154.

[6] For a similar proposal, see Davis 2013, n. 3.

[7] Biran 1982, 41; idem 1994, 189.

[8] Sharon/Zarzecki-Peleg 2006, 153–154. For an alternative, see Lehmann/Killebrew 2010.

[9] D. Ussishkin (1989) argued that Building 338 was a sanctuary and dated it to Stratum VA-IVB. Excavations carried out in the area of the building in 2014 reaffirmed its traditional association with Stratum IVA, as initially argued by the excavators of the Oriental Institute (Kleiman/Kaplan/Finkelstein 2016; Kleiman/Finkelstein 2018; for Ussishkin's responses, see idem 2017; idem 2018). It is still possible that Room 340 (the main excavated architectural unit) was used for a cultic activity, as argued by Gottlieb Schumacher, C.S. Fisher, and D. Ussishkin (see also Kleiman et al. 2017, 44).

[10] Considering that the structure had a large entrance hall in the east, its association with the four-room house (Ben-Tor/Ben-Ami/Sandhaus 2012, 53) is less likely in my view.

[11] Ben-Tor/Ben-Ami/Sandhaus 2012, 53.

population but were nevertheless not part of the ruling class. Additional data concerning the function of the building came from studies that revealed signs of iron production in its courtyard and bronze production in its western rooms.[12]

8.2.3 Citadel 3090 at Tel Hazor

Due to its impressive size, prominent location within the settlement, and relation to other structures, Citadel 3090 is undoubtedly the most lavish structure discovered in the central Levant. It was unearthed on the western edge of the upper mound (Area B). According to the excavators of the site, the construction of the structure should be attributed to Stratum VIII.[13] It is also among the best examples of the changes the city underwent following the partial destruction of Stratum IX. With slight modifications, activity in this structure continued until the destruction of the city (Stratum V).

The plan of Citadel 3090 consists of a rectangular building (*ca.* 25 × 21.5 m), which was situated on an elevated platform. Ashlar stones in the corners of the building included door jambs. Inner walls divided the building into 14 rooms. The entrance to the structure was either from the northwestern sector, where a series of stairs was discovered, or from the southeast, where a small tower-like structure and a ramp were found.[14] Support for the former may be gleaned from a long corridor that led to the stairs. It has been assumed that the volute capitals found in secondary use in Stratum VII originated from this corridor. Several well-built structures were constructed on either side of Citadel 3090. Some of them had the same architectural plan (e.g., Buildings 3100c and 3235). No structure was uncovered in front of the building, and the floor remnants found here should probably be reconstructed as a large courtyard. Another feature of the structure is a plaster layer that covers its walls from the inside and the outside; this phenomenon is comparable to the palace at et-Tell/Bethsaida (see below).[15]

Y. Yadin[16] interpreted the plan of the structure as a four-room house. Other scholars understood this building type as Assyrian-style,[17] Bit-Hilani,[18] or as part of the distinct LAP group.[19] In my view, I. Sharon and A. Zarzecki-Peleg's definition is the most convincing, as it takes into consideration details related to the construction techniques of these structures, as well as the marked differences between the LAPs and the palatial compounds uncovered in the northern Levant.

8.2.4 The Bit-Hilani at et-Tell/Bethsaida

The Bit-Hilani structure found during the excavations of et-Tell/Bethsaida was located in the center of the mound, to the east of the inset-offset fortification wall of Stratum

---

[12] Yahalom-Mack *et al.* 2014, 34.
[13] E.g., Yadin 1972, 169–179.
[14] Sharon/Zarzecki-Peleg 2006, 152–153.
[15] Arav 2013, 13, 19, 24.
[16] Yadin 1972, 170, followed by Shiloh 1973; Faust/Bunimovitz 2003 and others.
[17] Milson 1991, 47.
[18] Finkelstein 1999b, 61.
[19] Sharon/Zarzecki-Peleg 2006, 152–153.

V.[20] It is rectangular in shape (15 × 28.25 m) and was built of large basalt boulders directly on the bedrock. The entrance was from the southeastern sector of the building, and its internal design included 11 rooms, which were arranged around a central courtyard. Complete vessels were found on the floors of some of the rooms (especially in Room 7).[21] Despite its classification as Bit-Hilani, the structure appears to represent a variation of I. Sharon and A. Zarzecki-Peleg's LAP structures.[22] The best parallel for the structure is Building 101 at Tel 'Eitun, dated from more or less the same period.[23]

8.3 Other Building Types

Most structures excavated in the central Levant do not belong to a distinct building type that can be attributed to a specific type. Nevertheless, pillared buildings are found in four different sites in the central Levant (Tel Hazor, Tel Kinrot, Tel Hadar, and Tel 'Ein Gev) and seem to constitute an important architectural feature of this region. It is also interesting that clear examples of four-room houses, so popular in the heartland of the Kingdom of Israel (e.g., Tell el-Far'ah North), were found mostly at Tel Hazor. Other sites do not feature this type of building at all, not even in largely-exposed residential quarters (e.g., Tel Hadar). Moreover, apart from two structures found in Strata IX and VIII, both fragmentary, all four-room houses at Tel Hazor belong to Strata VIII–V.

8.3.1 Pillared Buildings

The exposure of Iron Age tripartite pillared buildings, i.e., long structures divided into three equal spaces by two lines of pillars in various regions in the Levant, has stimulated decades of intense discussion regarding their function.[24] Most scholars have interpreted these structures as storehouses, but military barracks, marketplaces, stables, and granaries have also been proposed. In an article published two decades ago, M. Kochavi[25] emphasized the location of many of the pillared buildings, especially Complex 296 at Tel Hadar (Figure 76),[26] in the vicinity of major highways; he consequently argued that

---

[20] Arav/Bernett 2000.

[21] It was argued that the Bit Hilani structure was used until the Hellenistic period (Arav/Bernett 2000, 52), but the exposure of complete vessels does not align with this conclusion.

[22] G. Lehmann and A.E. Killebrew (2010, 28) argued that the structure should not be associated with this group (nor with their "central hall tetra-partite" group) and that it was not monumental.

[23] Faust et al. 2017. In my view, the Tel 'Eitun structure should not be classified as a four-room house (Faust et al. 2017, 138–140; Faust/Sapir 2018, 4), merely because it had many more than four well-defined activity spaces (eight in its initial stage). One main difference between the Bit-Hilani at et-Tell/Bethsaida and Building 101 at Tel 'Eitun is the location of the entrance.

[24] E.g., Kochavi 1998; Cantrell/Finkelstein 2006, 643; Faust 2012, 101–102.

[25] Kochavi 1998, 471–477.

[26] Complex 296 is composed of two functionally distinct but architecturally inseparable units: a pillared building and a granary (Kleiman 2019a, 71–74). According to M. Kochavi (1996, 190), the walls found in this complex were almost entirely preserved, with some surviving to a height of ca. 2 m. All floors found within this complex were covered with thick burnt debris, clear evidence of its violent destruction. A pile of stones, which was preserved to a height of ca. 45 cm, blocked the entrance

these structures functioned as trading centers (*entrepôts*). In retrospect, the hope of finding a simple interpretation for these relatively generic structures (a hall with two rows of pillars) is problematic. In the central Levant, pillared buildings were found in several very different contexts (Table 23). Some are integrated into domestic contexts (e.g., the pillared buildings at Tel Hazor) while others into administrative ones (e.g., the pillared building at Tel 'Ein Gev). In addition, their construction techniques also vary. In some buildings, drafted stone monoliths were used as pillars (e.g., Tel Hazor), while in others, drum-built pillars were preferred (e.g., Tel Hadar). At Tel 'Ein Gev, buildings with monoliths and buildings with drum-pillars are attested in different parts of the city.

Figure 77: Complex 296 (the pillared building) at Tel Hadar, looking south (courtesy of the Institute of Archaeology of Tel Aviv University)

In brief, throughout the Iron Age, the architectural concept of a pillared building became popular among administrators and residents of many communities in the southern and central sectors of the Levant (it is less common in the northern Levant and Phoenicia) and was adopted by them for their specific needs: as a storeroom (as was the case of the buildings exposed at Tel Hazor, Tel Kinrot, Tel Hadar, and Tel 'Ein Gev), stable (as was the case of Tel Megiddo), or other unknown functions.

---

to the building. The main space of the building was divided into three long halls, which were separated by low wall segments. In between these partitions, drum-made pillars, which were placed on stone pillars, were inserted.

Table 23: Pillared buildings in the central Levant

Designation	Description	Ceramic Phase	Reference
B. 1873	Hazor, Area A, Str. VIII–VII	Final Iron Age IIA–Iron Age IIB	Ben-Tor/Ben-Ami/Sandhaus 2012, plans 3.9, 3.32, 4.2
B. 3699	Hazor, Area A, Str. VIII–V	Final Iron Age IIA–Iron Age IIB	Ben-Tor/Ben-Ami/Sandhaus 2012, plan 3.2
B. 71a	Hazor, Str. VIII–VII	Final Iron Age IIA–Iron Age IIB	Yadin *et al.* 1960, pls. CC–CCI
B. 683	T. Kinrot, Str. II, Area D	Iron Age IIB	Fritz 1990, fig. 23
B. 296	T. Hadar, Area AN, Str. IV	Iron Age I	Kleiman 2019a, plans 6–9
B. 395	T. Hadar, Area AN, Str. IV	Iron Age I	Kleiman 2019a, plans 6–7
W. 18	T. 'Ein Gev, Area A, Str. III (partial preservation)	Final Iron Age IIA	Mazar *et al.* 1964, fig. 2
LPB North	T. 'Ein Gev, Area F, Str. F-5	Final Iron Age IIA	Hasegawa/Paz 2009, fig. 1
LPB Center	T. 'Ein Gev, Area F, Str. F-5	Final Iron Age IIA	Hasegawa/Paz 2009, fig. 1
LPB South	T. 'Ein Gev, Area F, Str. F-5	Final Iron Age IIA	Hasegawa/Paz 2009, fig. 1
W. 5	T. 'Ein Gev, Area A, Str. II (partial preservation)	Iron Age IIB	Mazar *et al.* 1964, fig. 2
UPB North	T. 'Ein Gev, Area F, Str. F-4	Iron Age IIB	Sugimoto 2015a, fig. 16
UPB South	T. 'Ein Gev, Area F, Str. F-4	Iron Age IIB	Sugimoto 2015a, fig. 16

Note: B-building; LPB-lower pillared building; UPB-upper pillared building.

8.3.2 Four-Room Houses

The four-room house and its relationship to Israelite identity have been thoroughly discussed and debated. Nowadays, it is usually accepted that these structures, which include three long rooms and a broad backroom,[27] appeared in the southern Levant as early as the Iron Age I,[28] but became more popular in the Iron Age II.[29] Scholars even suggested that the unique plan of the building, which allowed equal access to all rooms through a central courtyard, indicates the egalitarian ideals of its dwellers.[30]

---

[27] Scholars have argued that the central space was an open-air courtyard intended to bring air and light into the structure (e.g., Shiloh 1973, 278). Others, in contrast, assumed that it was roofed, especially if the building had a second floor (Stager 1985, 15–16; Faust 2012, 215).

[28] See especially Mazar 2009b, 324.

[29] Shiloh 1973; Ji 1997; Faust 2012, 215.

[30] Faust/Bunimovitz 2003; Faust 2012, 213–229, but see Kletter 2016, 162, 164–165, 169.

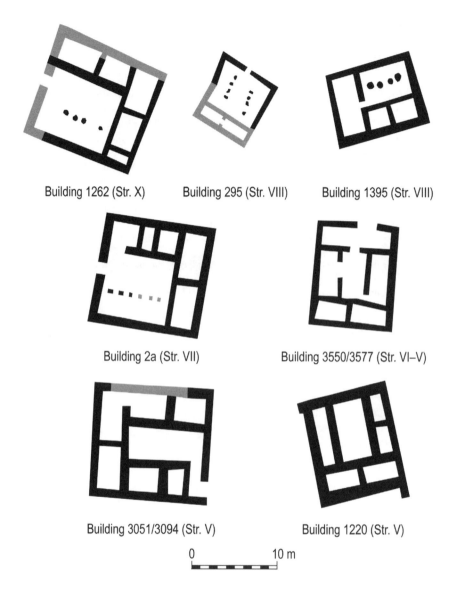

Figure 78: Schematic plans of four-room houses at Tel Hazor (adapted from Ben-Tor/Ben-Ami/Sandhaus 2012, plans 2.18, 3.7–3.8, 3.29–3.30, 4.5, 4.20–4.22, 4.24)

In any event, such houses became popular in the Samaria Highlands as early as the 10th century BCE (e.g., Strata VIIa and VIIb at Tell el-Farʿah North),[31] but the reasons that led to their popularity are still unclear. In the central Levant, four-room houses were

---

[31] For the residential quarters at Tell el-Farʿah North, see Chambon 1984, 19–52.

revealed mostly at Tel Hazor (Table 24; Figure 78).[32] The most obvious examples of these structures at this site were built near Citadel 3090 and near the old city gate. One structure was also exposed also in Area G, in the eastern part of the mound. The attribution of other structures excavated at the site to the four-room house type, especially those associated with Strata IX and VIII, is less clear.[33]

Table 24: Four-room houses in the central Levant

Building	Description	Date	Reference
B. 8382	Hazor, Area A, Str. X (*ca.* 13 × 13.5 m)	Late Iron Age IIA	Ben-Tor/Ben-Ami/Sandhaus 2012, plan 2.6
B. 1262	Hazor, Area A, Str. IX (*ca.* 13 × 12 m)	Late Iron Age IIA	Ben-Tor/Ben-Ami/Sandhaus 2012, plan 2.18; see Figure 78
B. 295	Hazor, Area A, Str. VIII (partial preservation)	Final Iron Age IIA	Ben-Tor/Ben-Ami/Sandhaus 2012, plan 3.7; see Figure 78
B. 1395	Hazor, Area A, Str. VIII (*ca.* 10 × 8 m)	Iron Age IIB	Ben-Tor/Ben-Ami/Sandhaus 2012, plan 3.8; see Figure 78
B. 2a	Hazor, Area A, Str. VII (*ca.* 13 × 12.5 m)	Iron Age IIB	Ben-Tor/Ben-Ami/Sandhaus 2012, plans 3.29–3.30; see Figure 78
B. 10054	Hazor, Area G, Str. VII–V (partial perseveration)	Iron Age IIB	Yadin *et al.* 1989, plan XXXI–XXXIII
B. 3550/3577	Hazor, Area A, Str. VI–V (*ca.* 12 × 9.5 m)	Iron Age IIB	Ben-Tor/Ben-Ami/Sandhaus 2012, plans 4.5 and 4.22; see Figure 78
B. 3051/3094	Hazor, Area A, Str. V (*ca.* 14 × 13.25 m)	Iron Age IIB	Ben-Tor/Ben-Ami/Sandhaus 2012, plans 4.20–4.21; see Figure 78
B. 1220	Hazor, Area A, Str. V (*ca.* 12 × 10 m)	Iron Age IIB	Ben-Tor/Ben-Ami/Sandhaus 2012, plan 4.24; see Figure 78
B. 3169a	Hazor, Area B, Str. V (*ca.* 12 × 9 m)	Iron Age IIB	Yadin *et al.* 1989, plan XXIV
B. 3148a	Hazor, Area B, Str. V (*ca.* 10 × 8.5 m)	Iron Age IIB	Yadin *et al.* 1989, plan XXIV
B. 452	T. Kinrot, Area C, Str. II (*ca.* 9 × 8 m)	Iron Age IIB	Fritz 1990, Abb. 23

---

[32] As mentioned in Section 6.2.5, J. Rohmer (2020, 396) suggested that one of the houses excavated at Tell 'Ashtara can be reconstructed as a four-room house, but this is only a possibility. Another possible example was reported from a 13th/12th century BCE context at Tell el-Fukhar (Ottosson 1993, 214, fig. 1; Ji 1997, 399), but the plan of the building is too fragmentary to be associated with a specific type. It could constitute an ordinary structure that employed stone-made pillars in its plan or even a tripartite pillared building similar to those revealed in Tel Hadar and Tel 'Ein Gev.

[33] E.g., Building 8158 in Area A (Ben-Tor/Ben-Ami/Sandhaus 2012, 53) and Citadel 3090 in Area B (Shiloh 1973, 277; for another view, see Finkelstein 1999b, 61). Building 8382 was located above the eastern part of the ruins of the Late Bronze Age Building 7050 and even integrated one of the pillar bases of the older structure into the floor of the new building. In the final report, the excavators defined this structure as a four-room house and suggested that it might have had an administrative function (Ben-Tor/Ben-Ami/Sandhaus 2012, 109). If this is indeed the case, then this building signifies the earliest example of this type exposed at Tel Hazor thus far.

Overall, the general impression from looking at the chronological and geographical distribution of the four-room houses is that this style was not adopted by the local societies of the central Levant (in contrast, e.g., to the pillared buildings which were observed in several settlements, see above). No evidence for this type was found in any Iron Age I context, and the sole example from the Iron Age IIA (i.e., Building 1262/8382 at Tel Hazor) is fragmentary, and other reconstructions can be suggested. The appearance of many four-room houses at Tel Hazor in the Iron Age IIB does not seem to be the product of natural development but may reflect an intrusive construction activity, maybe even state-supported. In my view, the best indication of this is the somewhat provocative construction of two four-room houses (Buildings 3148a and 3169a) in the front courtyard of Citadel 3090 at Tel Hazor.

8.4 Residential Quarters

Notwithstanding the importance of monumental structures and other individual buildings, looking at the design and development of residential quarters can also contribute to our understanding of social processes in the central Levant (Table 25). As will be shown below, in many cases, neighborhoods developed organically, with new units added according to the needs of the locals over time; this is evidenced by disorganized plans and the constitution of empty areas between structures. In other instances, it was clear that residential quarters were carefully designed from the outset. Indications for initial design can be found in the existence of clear complexes and streets.

8.4.1 Tell Kamid el-Loz

Fragmentary remains of two residential quarters dated from the Iron Age I were exposed at Tell Kamid el-Loz: one in the northern sector of the site[34] and another one on its eastern slope.[35] In both cases, medium residential structures (*ca.* 30–50 sq m) were built next to one another without evident pre-design. The houses revealed on the eastern slope were constructed of unworked stones of various sizes, and their floors were made of beaten earth.[36] No specific house plan can be identified at the site.

Table 25: Residential quarters in the central Levant

Site	Description	References
T. Kamid el-Loz	Two Iron Age I neighborhoods	Echt 1984, pl. 13; Heinz *et al.* 2010, pl. 4
T. Dan	One Iron Age I neighborhood	Ilan 2011, fig. 3, 7; idem 2019: plans 2–4
T. Dan	Two Iron Age II neighborhoods	Arie 2008, figs 1, 4–7

---

[34] Echt 1984, pl. 13.
[35] Heinz *et al.* 2010, pl. 4.
[36] Heinz *et al.* 2010, 120–121.

T. Hazor	Two Iron Age I neighborhoods	Yadin *et al.* 1989, plan XVIII; Ben-Tor/Ben-Ami/Sandhaus 2012, plans 1.1–1.7
T. Hazor	Two Iron Age II neighborhoods	Ben-Tor/Ben-Ami/Sandhaus 2012, plans 2.1, 2.8, 2.13, 2.21, 3.1, 3.13, 3.22, 3.36, 4.1, 4.15
T. Kinrot	One Iron Age I neighborhood	Münger 2017, figs. 3–5
T. Hadar	Two Iron Age II neighborhoods	Kleiman 2019a, plans 3, 10–17

8.4.2 Tel Dan

Domestic remains at the Iron Age I city of Tel Dan were primarily found in Area B, to the north of the gate complex, and were densely built, with very little evidence of initial design.[37] Residential quarters in the Iron Age II city are represented by the structures built to the east of the gate complex and to some extent also by the Stratum IVA remains in Area T.[38] In the first location, a series of four construction phases was exposed.[39] The houses that have been excavated here were well built and quite spacious. Most of them were nicely paved. Several prestige items were found in this quarter, hinting at the wealth of its residents.[40] In the second location, some industrial (e.g., the olive-oil installation) and cult-related (e.g., the "small altar") activities were conducted; this quarter was constructed at the end of the Iron Age IIA and was evacuated no more than a few decades after its establishment, probably due to the construction of the public compound of Strata III–II. Its plan is fragmentary, but the neighborhood appears to include at least one alley (e.g., Squares D/11–13), if not two (e.g., Square G/20). Note that no four-room houses were discovered at Tel Dan, although it was extensively excavated.

8.4.3 Tel Hazor

The excavations at Tel Hazor provide more examples of domestic architecture than any other site in the central Levant. Evidence from the Iron Age I (Stratum XII/XI) is relatively easy to interpret, as all the remains dated from this period were undoubtedly domestic, consisting of small units, tabuns, silos,[41] and even some cult corners.[42] Understanding the layout of the Iron Age II city (Strata X–V) is more difficult, as in many cases, administrative structures (e.g., the pillared buildings in Area A) were built next to small buildings. Moreover, recent studies suggest that bronze and iron production was carried out within residential quarters from the earliest Iron Age IIA phase at the site to the beginning of the Iron Age IIB.[43]

During the earlier stages of the Iron Age IIA (Strata X–IX), two new residential quarters were built at the site: one in Area B and another one south of the gate complex and

---

[37] Ilan 1999, 29–57; idem 2011, figs. 3, 7.
[38] Biran 1994, fig. 143; idem 2002.
[39] Biran 1999a; idem 1999b; idem 2002; Arie 2008, 12–14.
[40] E.g., Biran 1999a, figs. 7–8, for the bronze plaque, see Biran 1999b; Ornan 2006.
[41] E.g., Yadin *et al.* 1989, pl. XVIII; Ben-Tor/Ben-Ami/Sandhaus 2012, plan 1.1.
[42] E.g., Ben-Tor/Ben-Ami/Sandhaus 2012, 8–13.
[43] Yahalom-Mack *et al.* 2014. For evidence from other sites, see Ilan 1999, 47–50, 54–55.

west of the casemate wall (Area A5).[44] Two buildings in Area A seem to be more elaborate than the others (Buildings 9151 and 8382).[45] Building 9151 is relatively small (*ca.* 13 × 11 m) but seems to be a focal point for cult-related activity,[46] as evidenced by a unique four-horned terracotta altar, a stone basin, and fallen pieces of red-decorated wall plaster. Signs of bronze production were identified in nearly all the rooms of this building.[47] In contrast to other structures in this quarter, activity in this structure did not continue during Stratum IX although it was not abandoned.

As mentioned before, the construction of Stratum VIII led to significant alterations in the town plan of Tel Hazor. In Area B, Citadel 3090 and the surrounding structures were constructed above the domestic buildings of Stratum X–IX, which was evacuated, and the neighborhood of Area A was utterly transformed and built over by a large pillared building and other structures. Several new houses, which may have been used for domestic purposes, were built around the "mound of ruins" (the remains of Building 7050 of the Late Bronze Age). Production of iron and bronze continued during this period as well, albeit in different locations. With some modifications, the layout of the Stratum VIII neighborhood did not change drastically until the violent destruction at the end of Stratum V. A new feature of the settlement of Stratum VIII, however, was the expansion of the city to the east, especially evidenced by the fortification wall exposed in Areas G and M.[48] The expansion of settlement resulted in the construction of new residential quarters to the east of the casemate wall of Strata X–IX.[49] Most of the remains found here were attributed to Strata VI and V and seemed to reflect organic processes of construction, renovation, and destruction.

8.4.4   Tel Kinrot

One of the highlights of the excavations at Tel Kinrot was the extensive exposure on the eastern slope of the mound of a residential quarter dating to the Iron Age I.[50] Many residential units, sometimes separated by streets, were found here. In contrast to other Iron Age I residential quarters exposed in the central Levant (e.g., Tell Kamid el-Loz and Tel Dan), this neighborhood was most likely designed in advance; it shows, therefore, that the builders of the settlement must either have come from an urban center or at least had a clear, cognitive vision or concept of a city. Like all of Tel Kinrot, at the end of the Iron Age I, this quarter was violently destroyed and abandoned.

8.4.5   Tel Hadar

Two Iron Age IIA neighborhoods were found at Tel Hadar: one between the outer and inner fortification wall and another in the inner sector of the settlement (for a plan of the

---

[44] Yadin *et al.* 1989, plan XIX; Ben-Tor/Ben-Ami/Sandhaus 2012, plan 2.1.
[45] Ben-Tor/Ben-Ami/Sandhaus 2012, plans 2.3, 2.5 and 2.6.
[46] Ben-Tor/Ben-Ami/Sandhaus 2012, 65.
[47] Yahalom-Mack *et al.* 2014, 34.
[48] Yadin *et al.* 1989, 172–195; Ben-Tor 2016, 146–147.
[49] Ben-Tor/Ben-Ami/Sandhaus 2012, plan 4.15; Yadin *et al.* 1989, plans XIII–XI.
[50] Münger/Zangenberg/Pakkala 2011; Münger 2013; idem 2017.

latter, see Figure 79).[51] Residential units in these two neighborhoods were different from each other. The buildings found in the inner settlement were pillared and, in general, more spacious than those in the outer settlement. However, the functional distribution of the ceramic evidence does not suggest striking differences between the two neighborhoods (Table 26). Well-defined streets were detected in both locations, which shows that the architects of Stratum III at Tel Hadar set to work with a clear picture of an urban center (as was the case of Tel Kinrot in the Iron Age I). The construction of Stratum II/I, in contrast, witnessed a transformation in the plan of the town when flimsy domestic units replaced the organized and careful town planning of the previous stratum.[52]

Figure 79: Plan of the inner settlement at Tel Hadar (adapted from Kleiman 2019a, plan 10)

---

[51] Kleiman 2019a, 61–66, 77–81, plans 3, 10–13.
[52] Kleiman 2019a, 82–83, plan 14–17.

Table 26: Distribution of ceramic finds in Stratum III at Tel Hadar (Kleiman 2019a, Table 119)

Function	Outer Settlement				Inner Settlement					
	B. 114		B. 153		B. 451		B. 521		B. 545	
	N=	%=	N=	%=	N=	%=	N=	%=	N=	%=
Serving Vessels	9	33.3	4	30.7	14	17.9	11	44	7	22.5
Cooking Vessels	13	48.1	6	46.1	48	61.5	13	52	16	51.6
Storage Vessels	3	11.2	3	23.2	11	14.2	1	4	5	16.1
Cult Vessels	1	3.7	-	-	4	5.2	-	-	1	3.4
Varia	1	3.7	-	-	1	1.2	-	-	2	6.4
Total	27	100	13	100	78	100	25	100	31	100

8.5 Summary

A review of the architecture exposed in Iron Age strata across the central Levant illuminates various socio-cultural and political aspects of the local societies, particularly the following: 1) the date and nature of the local monumental structures, 2) the selective adoption of architectural styles, and 3) the organic development of some residential quarters as well as the pre-planned nature of others.

Hitherto, no monumental structure is known from the Iron Age I, but considering that massive fortifications did exist in this period (e.g., Tel Kinrot and Tel Hadar), it is reasonable to believe that such buildings were built in this period as well but have not yet been found (particularly at Tel Kinrot). Similarly, it may be assumed that a central monumental structure existed in Tel Hazor of the Iron Age IIA (especially in light of the exposure of elaborate buildings in residential quarters, e.g., Building 8158), but its exact location is unknown. It may have been removed during the construction of Citadel 3090, but excavations carried out in this area only identified poor domestic remains in Strata X–IX.[53] Interestingly, the three monumental structures that are known to us were erected at about the same time, around the late 9th/early 8th centuries BCE; the construction of two of these monumental structures, Citadel 3090 at Tel Hazor and the Bit-Hilani at et-Tell/Bethsaida, may have been stimulated by the Damascene authorities who ruled over the region in the late 9th century BCE. This does not mean that they originated from Aram-Damascus; their different construction style, as well as lifecycle, suggest that their residents were local rulers who probably remained in power also in the early 8th century BCE.[54] Additional indications for the selective adoption of cultural traits from nearby regions (e.g., the Jezreel Valley and the Samaria Highlands) come from the examination of the distribution of pillared buildings and four-room houses. While the former

---

[53] E.g., Building 3220 (Yadin 1989, plan XIX).

[54] J. Rohmer (2020, 71) drew attention to the unique pre-Hellenistic elements in the citadel area of es-Suwayda. He did not exclude the possibility that parts of the citadel, including its unique casemate features, date to the Iron Age II. Note that the reuse of Iron Age palatial compounds in the Hellenistic period have parallels at Tel Dan (Biran 1994) and at et-Tell/Bethsaida (Arav/Bernett 2000).

8.5 Summary

appeared in different sites throughout the Iron Age, the latter appeared mainly at Tel Hazor and probably not before the Iron Age IIB. It does not seem to be an integral feature of the local building style, and its appearance may even allude to either the presence of foreign social groups or to the limited adoption of external customs by the locals.

In addition, some residential quarters in the central Levant reflect clear and thoughtful design as evidenced by their careful construction (e.g., Tel Kinrot of the Iron Age I), while other quarters suggest an organic and unplanned development (e.g., Tell Kamid el-Loz of the Iron Age I). Also, at some sites, it was possible to observe an interesting shift in the function of specific areas (e.g., Tel Dan and Tel Hadar of the Iron Age II). At Tel Hadar, for instance, many domestic structures were built in the Iron Age IIA above the ruined administrative complex of the Iron Age I. An opposite shift was identified at Tel Hazor and Tel Dan. At both sites, palatial compounds were built above older residential neighborhoods.[55]

---

[55] This occurrence recalls the situation in the southern sector of Tel Megiddo, where the Palace 1723 enclosure was built above the remains of domestic structures that were evacuated (forcibly?) from it (Arie 2013a, 739–741; Finkelstein/Kleiman 2019, 285).

9. Ceramic Traditions

9.1 Introduction

Beyond relative chronology, an exploration of the processes of adoption or rejection of certain ceramic traditions can indicate the willingness of local societies to assimilate external cultural influences. Until recently, very few ceramic assemblages were available from Iron Age settlements located in the central Levant. Nonetheless, several new publications of old and new projects enrich our knowledge of pottery traditions in this region. Among the most essential assemblages that should be mentioned here are Tell el-Ghassil, Tel Dan, Tel Hazor, Tel Kinrot, Tel Hadar, and Tell er-Rumeith. Additional ceramic assemblages, more limited in size, are known from Tell Hizzin, Tell Kamid el-Loz, et-Tell/Bethsaida, Tel 'Ein Gev, Tell 'Ashtara, Sahem el-Jawlan, Qarrasa, Tell Irbid, and Tell Johfiyeh (Table 27). Admittedly, not all of the ceramic assemblages listed here originate from well-stratified sequences, and the lack of quantitative ceramic data from secure contexts constitutes a general problem.

And still, the available information allows us to characterize the ceramic profile of the central Levant in the Iron Age in a sufficient manner. In what follows, I review the main typological affinities and decoration techniques of local and imported wares found in Iron Age contexts in the central Levant, mainly based on the rich and stratified ceramic assemblages exposed during the excavations of Tel Hadar. Parallels for the discussed types were drawn mainly from the detailed sequences of Tel Dan and Tel Hazor.

Table 27: Published ceramic assemblages in the central Levant

Site	Region	References
T. Hizzin	Lebanese Beqaa	Genz/Sader 2008
T. el-Ghassil	Lebanese Beqaa	Joukowsky 1972
T. Kamid el-Loz	Lebanese Beqaa	Marfoe 1995; Heinz *et al.* 2004; idem 2010
T. Dan	Hula Valley	Ilan 1999; idem 2019a; Arie 2008
T. Hazor	Hula Valley	Yadin *et al.* 1961; Ben-Tor/Ben-Ami/Sandhaus 2012
Rosh Pinna	Hula Valley	Stepansky 2019
T. Kinrot	Sea of Galilee	Fritz 1990; Münger 2013; Tynjä 2017
et-Tell/Bethsaida	Sea of Galilee	Arav 2009a
T. Hadar	Sea of Galilee	Kleiman 2019a
T. 'Ein Gev	Sea of Galilee	Mazar *et al.* 1964; Sugimoto 2015a
Sahem el-Jawlan	Nuqra Plain	Fischer 1997
T. 'Ashtara	Nuqra Plain	Abou Assaf 1968; idem 1969
Qarrasa	Nuqra Plain	Rohmer 2020
T. Irbid	Irbid Plateau	Dajani 1966; Kafafi 2014

| T. er-Rumeith | Irbid Plateau | Barako 2015c |
| T. Johfiyeh | Irbid Plateau | Lamprichs 2007; Bastert/Hockmann 2008 |

9.2 Local Wares

9.2.1 Serving Vessels[1]

In general, the three main bowl types that characterize the Iron Age settlements of the central Levant are rounded bowls, sometimes with a small carination in the upper wall (Type BL1), carinated ones with various rim designs (Type BL2), and shallow bowls, also known as "dishes" (Type BL3; see examples in Figure 80).

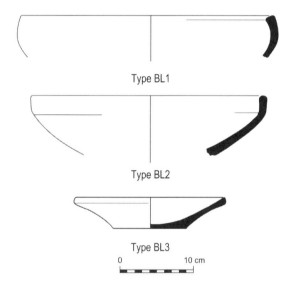

Figure 80: Bowl types (adapted from Kleiman 2019a, pls. 34, 1; 71, 1; Ben-Tor/Ben-Ami/Sandhaus 2012, fig. 6.4, 3)

Due to the numerous shapes in which both types appeared during the Iron Age, it is difficult to define clear chronological trends based exclusively on morphology. Nonetheless, detailed typological studies of large ceramic assemblages suggest that in the Iron Age IIA/B transition, the popularity of rounded bowls diminished.[2] This may be the result of increased production of the shallow bowls that appeared towards the end of the Iron Age IIA (e.g., Stratum IVA at Tel Dan or Strata VIII–VII at Tel Hazor) and were maintained in use in the Iron Age IIB.[3] Regarding the surface treatment of bowls, the impression is that red-slipped vessels were more popular in the Jezreel and Beth-

---

[1] For selected parallels of serving vessels in the central Levant, see Table 28.
[2] Zarzecki-Peleg/Cohen-Anidjar/Ben-Tor 2005, 239; Mazar 2006a, 327; Kleiman 2022a.
[3] Note that the lṭb[ḥ]y' bowl from Tel Dan (Avigad 1966) belongs to this type.

Shean Valleys than in the central Levant, although they appear in the Hula Valley and Irbid Plateau (more below).[4]

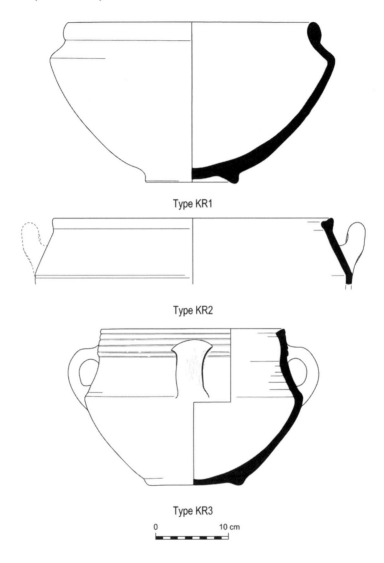

Type KR1

Type KR2

Type KR3

Figure 81: Krater types (adapted from Kleiman 2019a, pls. 15, 2; 27, 3; 62, 3)

Three main types of kraters were particularly common in the central Levant and are especially characterized by their rims and necks: folded-rim kraters (Type KR1), guttered rim kraters (Type KR2), and grooved neck kraters (Type KR3; see examples in Figure 81). The first type appeared in the Late Bronze Age IIB and was found in high

---

[4] Ben-Tor/Ben-Ami/Sandhaus 2012, fig. 5.1, 10, 15, 17; Barako 2015c, fig. 3.1, 1–2.

quantities in the Jezreel Valley in Iron Age I and IIA.[5] In the latter period, it is usually red-slipped and hand-burnished.[6] Not many examples of this type were found in Iron Age IIB contexts.[7] The other two types are more typical to Iron Age IIA–B contexts in the central Levant. At Tel Hazor, for instance, kraters with guttered rims appear in Strata X–IX but became dominant only towards the end of the period, during the lifetime of Stratum VIII.[8] Kraters with grooved necks were found at several sites in the central Levant, mainly east of the Jordan River (e.g., Tel Hadar and Tell Irbid). At least some of them were produced from clay sources that can be found in the central Jordan Valley.[9]

Table 28: Selected parallels to serving vessels

Type	Iron Age I	Iron Age IIA/B
BL1	T. Dan VI–IVB (Ilan 1999, Types Bh1–3); T. Hazor XII/XI (Ben-Tor/Ben-Ami/Sandhaus 2012, 21, figs. 1.2, 2; 1.4, 1); T. Kinrot VI–IV (Tynjä 2017, 143–146, BL02A); T. Hadar V–IV (Kleiman 2019a, 95–96, Types BL1–2)	T. Hazor X–V (Ben-Tor/Ben-Ami/Sandhaus 2012, 411, 414, 436, 438 Types BL Ia and Ic); T. Kinrot IV*–II (Fritz 1990, pl. 61, 3; 95, 6; 96, 1–2); T. Hadar III–II/I (Kleiman 2019a, 95–96, Types BL1–2)
BL2	Numerous examples, e.g., T. Hadar V–IV (Kleiman 2019a, 97–98, Types BL4a–c)	Numerous examples, e.g., T. Hadar III–II/I (Kleiman 2019a, 97–98, Types BL4a–c)
BL3	None	T. Dan IVA–II (Arie 2008, 17–18, Type BL3); T. Hazor VIII–V (Ben-Tor/Ben-Ami/Sandhaus 2012, 442, Type Bowl III); et-Tell/Bethsaida V (Arav 2009a, 73–75, figs. 1.75)
KR1	Numerous examples, e.g., T. Hadar IV (Kleiman 2019a, 101, Type KR1)	Numerous examples, e.g., T. Hadar III–II/I (Kleiman 2019a, 101, Type KR1)
KR2	None	T. Dan II (Arie 2008, Type KR3); T. Hazor X–VI (Ben-Tor/Ben-Ami/Sandhaus 2012, 419, 448–449, Type Krater III); et-Tell/Bethsaida V (Arav 2009a, 81–83, fig. 1.90, b); T. Hadar II/I (Kleiman 2019a, 104, Type KR4)
KR3	T. Hadar IV (Kleiman 2019a, 103, Type KR3c)	T. Hazor V (Yadin *et al.* 1958, pl. LVI, 25); T. Hadar III–II/I (Kleiman 2019a, 103, Type KR3c)

---

[5] Martin 2013, 368–369; Arie 2013b, 490–491.
[6] Arie 2013a, 686–687; Kleiman 2022a.
[7] Zarzecki-Peleg/Cohen-Anidjar/Ben-Tor 2005, 264; Mazar 2006a, 336.
[8] Ben-Tor/Ben-Ami/Sandhaus 2012, 419, 448–449). Note the presence of a similar vessel with an associated lid in Stratum V at et-Tell/Bethsaida (Arav 2009a, fig. 1.90, a–b), as well as the exposure of similar kraters in the Amuq Plain (e.g., Osborne 2011, pls. 4, 8–9; 20, 7).
[9] For the petrography of a grooved-neck krater from Tel Hadar, see Shoval/Beck/Yadin 2006.

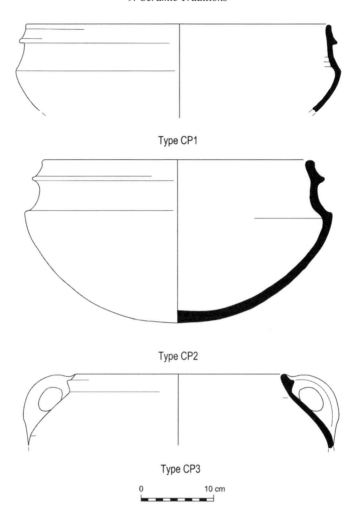

Figure 82: Cooking vessel types (adapted from Kleiman 2019a, pls. 6, 4; 36, 1; 78, 2)

9.2.2 Cooking Vessels[10]

During the Iron Age, three main vessels were used for cooking-related activities: pots, jugs, and baking trays.[11] Similar to other regions in the central and southern Levant (but

---

[10] For selected examples and parallels of cooking vessels, see Table 29.

[11] A distinct type of cooking pot was found in Stratum X at Tel Hazor (Ben-Tor/Cohen-Weinberger/Weeden 2017; Ben-Tor/Ben-Ami/Sandhaus 2012, fig. 2.11). It was made of reddish material, and its morphology differs from the local repertoire (but a petrographic examination of the item did not reveal its exact origin). The vessel is assumed to be imported from the northern Levant, but also there no sufficient parallels were found; this is unsurprising considering that most of the cooking wares of Syria in the Iron Age II were holemouth cooking pots (see, e.g., Lehmann 1996, pl. 83, Types 438a–b). At any rate, the most distinctive feature of the cooking pot is two stamp impressions with Luwian

in contrast to the situation in the northern Levant), open cooking pots certainly dominated the local ceramic assemblages. In the Iron Age I, the most popular types had either a triangular rim (Type CP1) or an inverted pinched rim (Type CP2). While the latter is usually associated with Iron Age IIA contexts, it already appeared in the Iron Age I (but probably in the later part of this period).[12] At the end of the Iron Age IIA, a new type of cooking pot with an inverted stance and grooved rim joined the repertoire (Type CP3), and in the following period, it became prevalent while the older types gradually disappeared, usually appearing only in sherd material (see examples in Figure 82).[13]

Less common were cooking jugs, which appeared in two primary forms: with an everted neck and thickened rim (Type CJ1) or with a straight neck and simple rim (Type CJ2; see examples in Figure 83). The first type is typical of the Iron Age I, while the second one is more common in the Iron Age IIA.[14] In the Iron Age IIB, the production of both types decreased dramatically or even ceased (most likely in the early days of the Iron Age IIB, as it does not appear in Strata VI and V at Tel Hazor).[15]

Baking trays appeared in earlier Late Bronze Age contexts and were also produced in the Iron Age (e.g., Figure 83).[16] An interesting local phenomenon is the marked differences between the baking trays of the Late Bronze Age IIB and those of the Iron Age, which suggest a certain change in the foodways of the locals with the transition to the Iron Age I.[17] A complete example found in Stratum V at Tel Hazor suggests that in the central Levant, baking trays were also produced in the Iron Age IIB.[18]

Table 29: Selected parallels to cooking vessels

Type	Iron Age I	Iron Age IIA/B
CP1	T. Dan VI–IVB (Ilan 1999, Type CP2–3); T. Hazor XII/XI (Ben-Tor/Ben-Ami/Sandhaus	T. Hazor X–IX (Ben-Tor/Ben-Ami/Sandhaus 2012, 423, Types CP IIa

signs on both of its handles, a rare appearance in the region to the south of the Homs Plain (for the Luwian inscriptions in the Kingdom of Hamath, see Hawkins 2016). According to M. Weeden (in Ben-Tor/Cohen-Weinberger/Weeden 2017), the signs on the vessel are unusual and unclear. Nonetheless, they seem to date from the late second millennium BCE and convey "king" and "to the woman Ha...." Based on the incomplete information, the authors cautiously suggested that the item may have been a gift from a king to a woman of high status. While a complete discussion of the life history of this particular item is beyond the scope of the current discussion, two comments are in place: 1) the careless production of the item, as seen especially in the attachment of the handles to the vessel's body (see, e.g., Ben-Tor/Cohen-Weinberger/Weeden 2017, fig. 1), as well as in the sloppy stamping, suggest that the cooking pot was a reject or the work of an apprentice; and 2) a radiocarbon date from the locus in which the vessel was found provide a date within the late 9th century BCE (Locus 8579, see discussion of the stratigraphic affiliation of the samples in Kleiman 2019a, 356–358; Shochat/Gilboa 2019, 378–379). I would like to thank D. Sandhaus for showing me the item.

[12] Arie 2006, 200; idem 2013a, 691–693; idem 2013b, 496.
[13] Finkelstein/Zimhoni/Kafri 2000, 310; Mazar 2006a, 344; Arie 2013a, 739; Kleiman 2022a.
[14] Arie 2013a, 695–697.
[15] Zarzecki-Peleg/Cohen-Anidjar/Ben-Tor 2005, 281; Mazar 2006a, Table 12.10; Ben-Tor/Ben-Ami/Sandhaus 2012, 456; Kleiman 2022a.
[16] E.g., Ben-Tor/Ben-Ami/Sandhaus 2012, fig. 4.12, 2.
[17] Compare Bechar 2017, Types BT1–BT2 and Ben-Tor/Ben-Ami/Sandhaus 2012, Type VI.
[18] Ben-Tor/Ben-Ami/Sandhaus 2012, fig. 4.12, 2.a

	2012, 22, fig. 1.1, 14, 1.2, 7–8); T. Kinrot VI–IV (Tynjä 2017, 194–196, Type CP02A); T. Hadar V–IV (Kleiman 2019a, 107–108, Types CP2a–b); T. 'Ein Gev KIV (Sugimoto 2015a, fig. 5, 3–4)	and IIc); T. Kinrot IV*–II (Fritz 1990, pls. 60, 6–7, 10; 85, 2, 4–6, 8; 87, 7–9, 11; 95, 11; 96, 4) T. Hadar III–II/I (Kleiman 2019a, 107–108, Types CP2a–b)
CP2	T. Dan VI–IVB (Ilan 1999, Type CP2–3); T. Hazor XII/XI (Ben-Tor/Ben-Ami/Sandhaus 2012, 22, figs. 1.4, 14; 1.7, 9); T. Kinrot VI–IV (Tynjä 2017, 192–194, Type CP02B); T. Hadar V–IV (Kleiman 2019a, 106–107, Types CP1a–b); T. 'Ein Gev KIV (Sugimoto 2015a, fig. 5, 5–7)	T. Dan IVA (Arie 2008, Type CP1); T. Hazor X–IX (Ben-Tor/Ben-Ami/Sandhaus 2012, 423, Type CP Ia and Ic); T. Kinrot IV*–II (Fritz 1990, pl. 62, 6; 85, 3, 7; 96, 5–6); T. Hadar III–II/I (Kleiman 2019a, 106–107, Types CP1a–b)
CP3	None	T. Dan IVA–II (Arie 2008, Type CP5); T. Hazor VIII–V (Ben-Tor/Ben-Ami/Sandhaus 2012, 453–456, Types Cooking Pot III–IV); T. Kinrot IV*–II (Fritz 1990, pl. 62, 2–4; 85, 11); T. Hadar III–II/I (Kleiman 2019a, 110, Type CP6)
CJ1	T. Dan VI–V (Ilan 1999, Types CJ1 and CJ2); T. Kinrot V–IV (Tynjä 2017, 197–198, Type CP04); T. Hadar V–IV (Kleiman 2019a, 110–111, Type CJ1)	None
CJ2	T. Hadar V–IV (Kleiman 2019a, 111, Type CJ2a)	T. Hazor X–IX (Ben-Tor/Ben-Ami/Sandhaus 2012, 424, Type CP6); T. Hadar III–II/I (Kleiman 2019a, 111, Type CJ2a)
BT	T. Dan VI–IVB (Ilan 1999, Types BTa–e); T. Hazor XII–V (Ben-Tor/Ben-Ami/Sandhaus 2012, figs. 1.1, 7); T. Kinrot V (Tynjä 2017, 197–198, Type BT02); T. Hadar IV (Kleiman 2019a, 112, Type BT1)	T. Hazor X–V (Ben-Tor/Ben-Ami/Sandhaus 2012, 457, Type Cooking Pot VI); T. Hadar III–II/I (Kleiman 2019a, 112, Type BT1)

9.2.3   Small Containers[19]

Generic jugs with a simple or trefoil rim characterized all phases of the Iron Age (Type JG1). The only noticeable change in their production over the Iron Age I/II transition is their decoration with red slip and occasionally also dense burnishing;[20] the production and decoration of some of these jugs in this region seem to be influenced by coastal traditions.[21] Another jug type popular in the central Levant included a distinctive strainer (Type JG2). Such jugs appeared at the beginning of the Late Bronze Age[22] and were produced until the end of the Iron Age IIA (see examples in Figure 84).[23]

---

[19] For selected examples and parallels of small containers, see Table 30.

[20] Yadin *et al.* 1958, pl. XLVI, 3; idem 1960, pls. LI, 16; LII, 18; idem 1961, pl. CLXXII, 4; CLXXVI, 5; CLXXVII, 15–16; CCVII, 19; CCVIII, 43; Ben-Tor/Ben-Ami/Sandhaus 2012, figs. 2.5, 21; 2.6, 30; 2.19, 6; 2.21, 8.

[21] Ben-Tor/Ben-Ami/Sandhaus 2012, 430, fig. 5.9, 5–7.

[22] Martin 2013, 389.

[23] For a single example for strainer jug in an Iron Age IIB context, see Fischer 2013, fig. 168, 2.

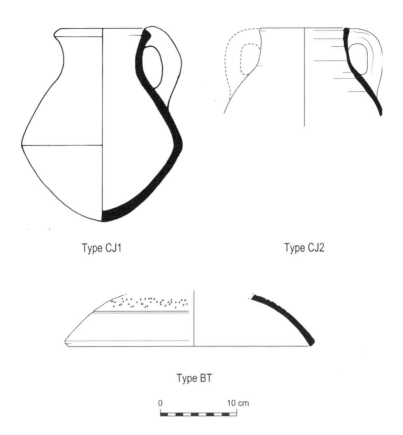

Figure 83: Cooking vessel types (cont.) (adapted from Kleiman 2019a, pls. 16, 7; 30, 3; 50, 8)

Dipper juglets were popular throughout the Iron Age (Type JT1). Again, the only noticeable change in their production occurred at the beginning of the Iron Age IIA, when some were red-slipped and hand-burnished.[24] Such vessels are rare in Strata X–IX at Tel Hazor, but the reason for this phenomenon is unclear.[25] Black juglets (Type JT2) appeared at the beginning of the Iron Age IIA and remained in use also in the Iron Age IIB. It is usually accepted that in the transition between the two periods, some typological modifications occurred in the production of black juglets. In earlier examples, the handle was attached directly to the neck of the juglet, while in later examples, it was attached directly to the rim.[26] Recently, E. Arie discussed the decoration of these juglets.[27] Based on the distinct dark gray fabric of the black juglets, he suggests that their dark color was the result of reduction firing rather than a dark slip. It is clear that black

---

[24] Arie 2013a, 704–705.
[25] Ben-Tor/Ben-Ami/Sandhaus 2012, 430; fig. 5.8, 15 (rare example).
[26] Amiran 1969, 256; Mazar 2006a, 369.
[27] Arie 2013a, 705–706.

juglets are an uncommon type in the central Levant, and only a few vessels were found in Strata X–IX at Tel Hazor (see examples in Figure 84).[28]

Table 30: Selected parallels to small containers

Type	Iron Age I	Iron Age IIA/B
JG1	T. Dan VI–IVB (Ilan 1999, Type JG1); T. Hazor XII/XI (Ben-Tor/Ben-Ami/Sandhaus 2012, 23, figs. 1.1, 23; 1.6, 6; 1.7, 11; 1.9, 14); T. Kinrot VI–IV (Tynjä 2017, 234–236, part of Types JG03A and JG03B, e.g., Objects Nos. 7454/2 and 7792/1); T. Hadar V–IV (Kleiman 2019a, 114, Type JG2)	T. Dan IVA–II (Arie 2008, Type J2); T. Hazor X–V (Ben-Tor/Ben-Ami/Sandhaus 2012, 429, 467, part of Type Jug I); T. Hadar III–II/I (Kleiman 2019a, 114, Type JG2)
JG2	T. Dan VI–IVB (Ilan 1999, Type J5); T. Hazor XII/XI (Ben-Tor/Ben-Ami/Sandhaus 2012, 23, fig. 1.6, 10); T. Kinrot V–IV (Tynjä 2017, 232–233, Type JG02C); T. Hadar V–IV (Kleiman 2019a, 114–115, Type JG3)	T. Hadar III (Kleiman 2019a, 114–115, Type JG3)
JT1	T. Dan VI–IVB (Ilan 1999, Type JT); T. Hazor XII/XI (Ben-Tor/Ben-Ami/Sandhaus 2012, fig. 1.9, 13); T. Kinrot VI–IV (Tynjä 2017, 244–247, Types JL02A and JL02B); T. Hadar V–IV (Kleiman 2019a, 116, Type JT1)	T. Dan II (Arie 2008, Type JT1); T. Hazor X–V (Ben-Tor/Ben-Ami/Sandhaus 2012, 430, 470–472, Type Juglet I*); T. Kinrot IV*–II (Fritz 1990, pl. 60, 11; 66, 11; 93, 10–14); T. Hadar III–II/I (Kleiman 2019a, 116, Type JT1)
JT2	None	T. Hazor VIII–V (Ben-Tor/Ben-Ami/Sandhaus 2012, 430, 472, Type Juglet II*); T. Kinrot II (Fritz 1990, pl. 88, 9; 93, 10–14; Tynjä 2017, 248–249, Type JL03); T. Hadar III (Kleiman 2019a, 116–117, Type JT2)

9.2.4 Storage Vessels[29]

Amphorae are quite rare in the ceramic repertoire of the southern Levant, although some examples of them can be found.[30] In the Iron Age I, a biconical amphora with a molded rim was the most common type (Type AM1).

---

[28] Ben-Tor/Ben-Ami/Sandhaus 2012, 430, 470; fig. 2.8, 27. An example found in a pit at Tel Hazor was attributed to Stratum XII/XI (Yadin *et al.* 1961, pl. CLXIV, 8–10). L. Singer-Avitz (2016, 235) argued that this item is among the earliest examples of black juglets. However, the Iron Age I village at Tel Hazor dates to the early phase of the period (Finkelstein 2000a). It was abandoned about a century before the earliest evidence for these juglets. It is likely that the example in question originated from Strata X or IX since the area is sealed by a Stratum VIII building (Yadin *et al.* 1989, plan XI). Note also a black juglet in a burial at Tell Irbid (Dajani 1966, pl. XXXIII, 9).

[29] For selected parallels of storage vessels, see Table 31.

[30] E.g., Levy/Edelstein 1972, fig. 11, 1–4, 6; Mazar *et al.* 2005, figs. 13.23, 11; 13.24, 11–12; 13.26, 1–2; Finkelstein/Zimhoni/Kafri 2000, fig. 11.28, 2; 11.33, 13–14; 11.35, 2; 11.41, 3–4, 6.

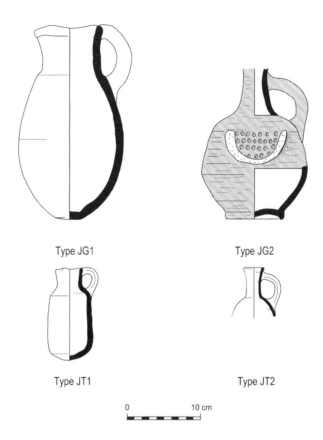

Figure 84: Small container types (adapted from Kleiman 2019a, pls. 3, 6; 17, 4; 56, 7; 73, 7)

It is present in many different sites in the central Levant, specifically those located along the Great Rift Valley (e.g., Tell el-Ghassil, Tel Dan, and Tel Hadar). While locally produced,[31] the manufacturers of this amphora type were most likely influenced by Syrian traditions.[32] At the end of the Iron Age IIA, a new amphora type appeared (Type AM2). Only a few examples, which were decorated in various ways, belong to this type and its distribution seems to be limited to the central Levant (see examples in Figure 85).[33]

---

[31] For a petrographic analysis of amphorae from Tel Hadar, see Shoval/Beck/Yadin 2006.
[32] For a comprehensive discussion, see Münger 2013. See also Kleiman 2019a, 118–119.
[33] For Syrian examples, see Pucci 2019, pl. 169, g; Riis/Buhl 1990, figs. 63, 426; 64, 427–428.

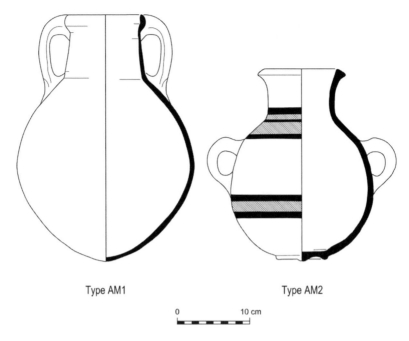

Figure 85: Small amphora types (adapted from Kleiman 2019a, pl. 40, 4; 59, 8)

Storage jars with an ovoid body and various kinds of molded rims were more abundant and found in large quantities in all sites in the central Levant (Type SJ1). A distinct type that should be mentioned here, in particular, has carinated shoulders and an elongated body (Type SJ2). It appeared in the late phase of the Iron Age I, but its production continued into the Iron Age IIA with slight typological variations.[34]

Perhaps the most interesting jar type appearing in the central Levant was the hippo storage jar (Type SJ3). It was defined for the first time by Y. Alexandre in the mid-1990s and has since attracted much attention.[35] It probably represents an Israelite administrative system that operated throughout the Iron Age II.[36] Genuine hippo jars, i.e., vessels that were produced from Lower Cretaceous, appear mainly at Tel Hazor (see examples in Figure 86), while the ridged jars from other sites, including those from et-Tell/Bethsaida and Tel Hadar, seem to be local imitations.[37]

---

[34] Arie 2006, 213–215; idem 2013a, 712; idem 2013b, 519–520. S. Shoval *et al.*'s (2006) petrographic examination of the single complete storage jar found in Stratum IV suggests that it was produced from clay sources that can be found in the western Galilee or Lebanon.

[35] Alexandre 1995; Gal/Alexandre 2000, 47; Arie 2013a, 715; Harush 2014.

[36] Kleiman 2017 with discussion and references.

[37] Ben-Tor/Ben-Ami/Sandhaus 2012, 427–428. For the petrographic results of the hippo jars exposed at et-Tell/Bethsaida, see Shuster 2009. A physical examination of two ridged storage jars found at Tel Dan (Arie 2008, fig. 11, 9–10) indicated that they are not made of the typical fabric used in the production of the hippo storage jars observed in Jezreel and Beth-Shean Valley. I would like to thank Y. Thareani for allowing me to investigate the vessels at the Hebrew Union College. A similar local

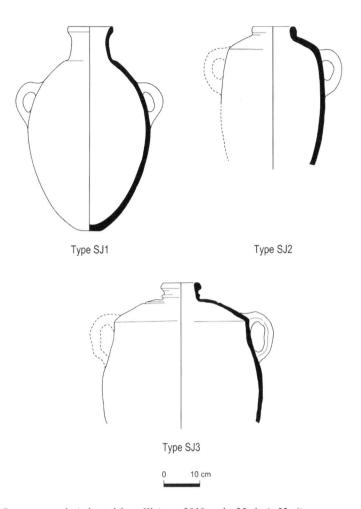

Figure 86: Storage vessels (adapted from Kleiman 2019a, pls. 25, 1, 4; 52, 4)

Noteworthy is that in the past, the appearance of collared-rim pithoi (Type CRP) in Iron Age I contexts in the central Levant has been interpreted as evidence for the presence of Israelite populations in the far north.[38] Today, however, it is agreed by most scholars that these vessels were already produced in the Late Bronze Age IIB and that they reflect the development of the local ceramic industries (see an example in Figure 87).[39]

---

provenance is suggested for the jars discovered in Tel Hadar. Note that the šd'l inscription from this site was probably executed on such a jar (Kleiman 2019a, 161–163, pl. 100).

[38] E.g., Biran 1994, 132–134.

[39] For studies that deal with the morphological and chronological aspects of the collared-rim pithoi, see Finkelstein 1988, 275–285; Killebrew 2001; Arie 2006, 215–216; Ilan 2019a, 108–110.

Figure 87: Collared-rim pithos from Stratum IV at Tel Hadar (photographed by the author)

Table 31: Selected parallels to storage vessels

Type	Iron Age I	Iron Age IIA/B
AM1	T. Dan VI–IVB (~Ilan 1999, pls. 3, 6; 5, 6; 53, 5); T. Kinrot VI–V (Tynjä 2017, 222–223, Type SJ03); T. Hadar IV (Kleiman 2019a, 118–119, Type AM1); T. 'Ein Gev KIV (Sugimoto 2015a, fig. 5, 10)	T. Hadar III–II/I (Kleiman 2019a, 118–119, Type AM1) (rare)
AM2	None	T. Dan IVA (Arie 2008, 26, Type AM1); T. Hazor V (Ben-Tor/Ben-Ami/Sandhaus 2012, fig. 4.17, 11); T. Hadar II/I (Kleiman 2019a, 119–120, Type AM2); T. 'Ein Gev MIII (Mazar *et al.* 1964, fig. 6, 8); T. Soreg (unpublished)
SJ1	Numerous examples, e.g., T. Hadar V–IV (Kleiman 2019a, 120–122, Types SJ1a–d)	Numerous examples, e.g., T. Hadar III–II/I (Kleiman 2019a, 120–122, Types SJ1a–d)
SJ2	T. Kinrot VI–IV (Tynjä 2017, 219–221, Type SJ02A); T. Hadar IV (Kleiman 2019a, 123, Type SJ3)	None
SJ3	None	T. Dan IVA–II (Arie 2008, Type SJ4); T. Hazor X (Ben-Tor/Ben-Ami/Sandhaus 2012, 426–428, Type Storage Jar V); T. Kinrot IV*–II (Fritz 1990, pl. 66, 9–10; 87, 19); T. Hadar III–II/I (Kleiman 2019a, 124–125, Type SJ5)
CRP	T. Dan VI–IVB (Ilan 1999, Type PCR); T. Hazor XII/XI (Ben-Tor/Ben-Ami/Sandhaus 2012, 23, figs. 1.1, 18–19; 1.9, 1–3); T. Kinrot VI–IV (Tynjä 2017, 206–207, Type PT01A); T. Hadar V–IV (Kleiman 2019a, 126, Type PT1)	None

9.2.5 Cult-Related Vessels[40]

An interesting feature of central Levantine ceramic traditions was the use of many different cult-related vessels. From the end of the Bronze Age to the Iron Age IIA, the most common vessel used for public and domestic rituals was a chalice with a flaring rim (Type CH1),[41] sometimes with drooping petals or pointed knobs.[42]

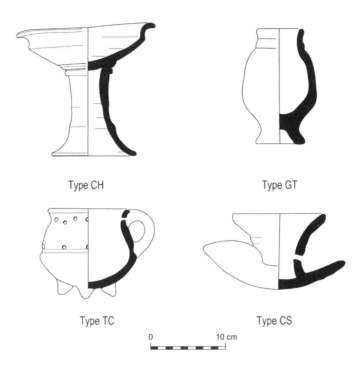

Figure 88: Cult-related vessel types (adapted from Kleiman 2019a, pls. 21, 6; 32, 5; 38, 5; 51, 10)

---

[40] For selected examples and parallels of cult-related vessels, see Table 32.
[41] Arie 2013a, 689–690; idem 2013b, 493.
[42] Faßbeck 2008; see also Kleiman *et al.* 2017, 29.

Figure 89: Shrine model from Stratum IV at Tel Hadar (photographed by the author)

In the Iron Age IIB, the production of these vessels probably ceased, or at the very least, diminished significantly (all the examples documented in Strata VII–V at Tel Hazor, for instance, are sherds and may have originated from one of the earlier strata).[43] Goblets, in contrast, are found in limited numbers in the region and only in Iron Age I contexts.[44] A unique type of perforated goblet, which looks like an attempt to combine the features of chalices/goblets and tripods cups into one vessel, was observed in Stratum IVB at Tel Dan and in Stratum IV at Tel Hadar.[45] D. Ilan raised the possibility that they may have been used as a strainer.[46] Additional parallels for these unique vessels were found in the Amuq Plain[47] and the highlands.[48] Also, cup-and-saucers were very rare in the region.[49] Apart from two examples found in Stratum X at Tel Hazor, this type seems to vanish

---

[43] Zarzecki-Peleg/Cohen-Anidjar/Ben-Tor 2005, 260; Mazar 2006a, 334; Ben-Ami/Sandhaus/Ben-Tor 2012, 445; Ben-Tor/Zarzecki-Peleg 2015, 139; Kleiman 2022a.

[44] E.g., Kleiman 2019a, pls. 32, 5; 33, 1–3. In other regions, goblets can also be found in Iron Age IIA contexts (see, e.g., Singer-Avitz 1989, fig. 7.5, 15–17; Kleiman 2015, fig. 34, 11). One of the examples found at Tel Hadar was sampled for petrography (Shoval/Beck/Yadin 2006). It was produced from clay sources that can be found between Wadi Samekh and the Yarmouk.

[45] Ilan 2019a, fig. 3.69, 7; 3.73, 3; Kleiman 2019a, pl. 33, 1–3.

[46] Ilan 2019a, 103.

[47] Osborne 2011, pl. 11, 4; Pucci 2019, fig. 87.

[48] Wampler 1947, pl. 79, 1814–1815.

[49] For discussion and parallels, see Uziel/Gadot 2010.

after *ca.* 900 BCE. In contrast, tripod cups used for burning incense[50] were common in the central Levant. They appeared as early as the Iron Age I but gained popularity in the Iron Age IIB in parallel to the disappearance of the chalices. In this period, their geographical distribution encompassed the entire Levant (see examples in Figure 88).[51]

It is also possible to mention here the shrine models ("snake houses") found in various Late Bronze and Iron Ages strata in the central Levant (e.g., Tell Kamid el-Loz, Tel Dan, Tel Kinrot, and Tel Hadar) and beyond (e.g., Tell Munbaqa, Ugarit, Tell Zira'a, Tel Deir Alla, Tel Rehov, Tel Megiddo, and Ashkelon; see, e.g., Figure 89).[52] None of the examples are identical to one another, meaning that these relatively rare items were produced by demand. Having said that, the models found at Tel Dan, Tel Hadar, and Tell Zira'a share some similarities, especially in the design of their upper parts.

Table 32: Selected parallels to cult-related vessels

Type	Iron Age I	Iron Age IIA/B
CH	T. Dan VI–IVB (Ilan 1999, Type CH1); T. Kinrot VI–V (Tynjä 2017, 167–169, Types CL02A and CL02B); T. Hadar IV (Kleiman 2019a, 127–128, Type CH1)	T. Hazor X–V (Ben-Tor/Ben-Ami/Sandhaus 2012, 445); T. Kinrot IV* (Fritz 1990, pl. 84, 8); T. Hadar III–II/I (Kleiman 2019a, 127–128, Type CH1)
GT	T. Dan IVB (Ilan 1999, pl. 17, 11); T. Kinrot VI–V (Tynjä 2017, 172, Type G01); T. Hadar IV (Kleiman 2019a, 128–129, Types GT1a–b)	None
TC	T. Dan V–IVB (Ilan 1999, pls. 14, 2; 28, 1); T. Hadar IV (Kleiman 2019a, 129–130, Type TC1)	T. Dan II (Arie 2008, Type TC1); T. Hazor X–V (Ben-Tor/Ben-Ami/Sandhaus 2012, 418, 442, Type BL VIb); T. Hadar III (Kleiman 2019a, 127–128, Type CH1)
CS	T. Dan IVB (Ilan 1999, pl. 18, 3); T. Hazor XII/XI (Ben-Tor/Ben-Ami/Sandhaus 2012, 24, fig. 1.9, 16); T. Hadar IV (Kleiman 2019a, 130, Type CS1)	T. Hazor X (Ben-Tor/Ben-Ami/Sandhaus 2012, fig. 2.5, 13, 23)

9.3 Imported Wares

9.3.1 Phoenician Wares

Phoenician Bichrome ware appeared in the central Levant towards the end of the Iron Age I (Table 33). Complete vessels are known from Stratum IVB at Tel Dan, Strata VI and V at Tel Kinrot, and Stratum IV at Tel Hadar. Additional examples, but from less secure contexts, can be found at Tell el-Ghassil, and Tell Kamid el-Loz. In the Iron

---

[50] For a discussion of the function of tripod cups, see Daviau 2001, 207; Mazar 2006a, 373; Arie 2013a, 719. It can be noted here that two examples with clear soot marks in their interior were found at Tel Hadar (Kleiman 2019a, pls. 44, 25; 51, 10).
[51] See references in Zwickel 1990b.
[52] See parallels and discussion in Nissinen/Münger 2009.

II, the only site with secure evidence of Phoenician Bichrome Ware is Tel Hazor. Only a few vessels were published from the Nuqra Plain and the Irbid Plateau.[53]

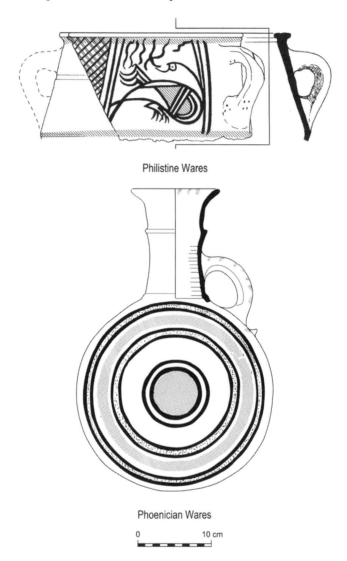

Philistine Wares

Phoenician Wares

0   10 cm

Figure 90: Imports (adapted from Ilan 2019a, pl. 3.120, 8; Kleiman 2019a, pls. 22, 1)

---

[53] E.g., Rohmer 2020, 208, fig. 2.131 (Qarrasa); Barako 2015c: fig. 3.38, 7 (Tell er-Rumeith).

9.3.2 Philistine Wares

Imports from Philistia, or local imitations of such wares,[54] are underrepresented in the pottery of the central Levant. Examples are known from a few sites in the Hula Valley, such as Tel Dan and Tel Kinrot (note their absence from Tel Hazor),[55] with a rare example from Tell el-Fukhar in the Irbid Plateau (Table 33).[56] A sherd with a spiral motif was found at Tell 'Ashtara, signifying a sole appearance of this ware in southern Syria.[57]

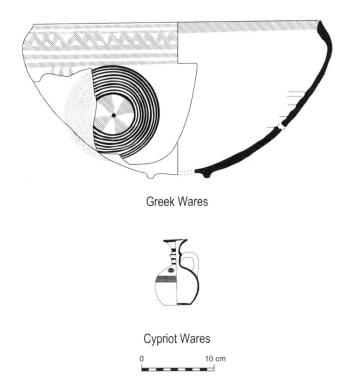

Figure 91: Imports (cont.) (adapted from Genz/Sader 2008, pl. 6, 3; Kleiman 2019a, pls. 22, 2)

9.3.3 Cypriot Wares

During the Iron Age I, Cypriot items are very rare in the central Levant (Table 33). This is not surprising since such imports are also rare in settlements located much closer to the coast, such as Tel Megiddo.[58] Most of the Cypriot or Cypriot-influenced examples in this region are wavy-band pithoi, which according to A. Gilboa, might even allude to

---

[54] Petrographic studies of Philistine sherds from Tel Kinrot and Tel Dan suggest a local production (Martin 2017, 211; Ben-Shlomo 2019; Zuckerman 2019).
[55] Ilan 2019a, 102, 122; Zukerman 2019; Tynjä 2017, 151–154, 184, 239.
[56] Strange 2015, pl. 154, 8.
[57] Abou Assaf 1968, 120, pl. 5
[58] Arie 2013b, 529.

the presence of Cypriot potters on the Phoenician coast.[59] Examples of these pithoi were found mainly in Tel Dan.[60] In the later phases of the Iron Age IIA, Cypriot imports reached the Lebanese Beqaa, the Hula Valley, and even the Irbid Plateau.[61] As in other regions, the most popular Cypriot import belongs to the Black-on-Red Ware.[62] Vessels of this ware were only found in large quantities at Tel Hazor.[63] Excavations of other sites in the central Levant unearthed only a few examples at each site (e.g., Tel Dan and Tel Abel Beth-Maacah).[64] This is unsurprising since the main distribution of the Black-on-Red Ware in the southern Levant was during the first half of the 9th century BCE,[65] and Tel Hazor is indeed one of the only sites that were certainly active at this time. Tell er-Rumeith, which was settled in this period, is located in the far east, away from the main harbors. Other Cypriot ceramic products (e.g., white-painted and bichrome wares) have been found only seldomly in the region (e.g., at Tel Hadar).[66]

9.3.4 Aegean Wares

Very few Aegean imports arrived at the central Levant during the Iron Age. The only published example is a restorable krater discovered in Stratum IV at Tel Hadar.[67] In J.N. Coldstream's view,[68] this vessel originated from Euboea and imitated a bronze bowl or cauldron. From a chronological perspective, he concluded that it represents a transitional type that should be assigned to the transition between the middle and late Protogeometric Period (*ca.* 950 BCE). G. Kopcke,[69] in contrast, attributed the item to the Attic Early Geometric Period or to the end of the late Protogeometric Period (*ca.* 900 BCE).[70]

Following the reassessment of the materials from the excavations of Tel Hadar,[71] several new observations constrain the date of the vessel: 1) the ceramic assemblage of Stratum IV represents an advanced stage of the late Iron Age I, but with very few signs of developed Iron Age IIA ceramic traditions (i.e., this stratum is earlier Stratum VB at Tel Megiddo or Stratum VI at Tel Rehov), 2) the radiocarbon dates from the destruction of Stratum IV (and from the destruction of other nearby sites, e.g., et-Tell/Bethsaida and Tel 'Ein Gev) concentrate around the mid-10th century BCE,[72] and 3) the lebes is earlier in date than the vessels exposed recently in Level Q-5 at Tel Megiddo, which is

---

[59] Gilboa 2001.
[60] Ilan 2019a, 113–114. See, though, Joukowsky 1972, pl. I, 16, 21–22; III, 8, 16; XIII, 1–4, 13.
[61] E.g., Genz/Sader 2008, pl. 6, 2–3; Baramki 1964, figs. 17, 1; 37, 1; Ben-Tor/Ben-Ami/Sandhaus 2012, fig. 5.10, 6–10; Barako 2015c, 89, figs. 3.37, 8; 3.42, 1.
[62] Schreiber 2003; Gilboa 2015, 487; Kleiman *et al.* 2019.
[63] Note our limited knowledge of the Iron Age IIA in the Lebanese Beqaa.
[64] Arie 2008, 27.
[65] Gilboa 2015, 488.
[66] Kleiman 2019a, pl. 80, 4–5.
[67] Recently, two sherds were also found at Tel Abel Beth-Maacah (Panitz-Cohen 2022, n. 5).
[68] Coldstream 1998, 357; idem 2003, 253.
[69] Kopcke 2002.
[70] For other views, see Fantalkin 2001; Lemos 2002, 25; Waldbaum 2015, 511.
[71] Kleiman 2019a, 50–164.
[72] Finkelstein/Piasetzky 2005; Scott *et al.* 2007, Table 5; Sharon *et al.* 2007, Tables 7–8.

radiocarbon-dated the late 10th/early 9th century BCE (it also features ceramic forms typical of the late Iron Age IIA).[73] Considering these points, Coldstream's dating of the vessel to the transition between the middle and late protogeometric Period (*ca.* 950 BCE, according to the low chronology of Greece) is probably the most accurate one.

Beyond the chronological issues, the exposure of a rare Aegean vessel in a small community such as Tel Hadar suggests that there was contact between coastal sites and the emerging Sea of Galilee settlements in the Iron Age I. It is also reasonable to assume that Tel Hadar was not the final destination of this prestigious item, and it probably made its way to some unknown location in the Golan Heights or in southern Syria.

Table 33: Long-distance imported wares in the central Levant

Type	References
Phoenician Bichrome Ware	T. Hizzin (Genz/Sader 2008, pl. 5–7, 9); T. el-Ghassil (Joukowsky 1972, pls. II, 35?; XI, 29); T. Kamid el-Loz (Heinz *et al.* 2010, fig. 8, b, d); T. Dan IVB (Ilan 2019a, figs. 3.64, 3; 3.66, 5; 3.68, 2); Kiryat Shmona South (Covello-Paran 2012, 114); T. Hazor X–V (Ben-Tor/Ben-Ami/Sandhaus 2012, figs. 5.9, 8–9, 11, 16–17; 5.10, 1–5); T. Hadar IV–II/I (Kleiman 2019a, pls. 4, 1; 22, 1; 28, 3; 34, 4; 39, 5; 44, 3–4; 49, 5; 62, 9)
Philistine Bichrome Ware	T. Dan VI (Zukerman 2019, figs. 4.15, 1–6; 4.16, 9–13); T. Kinrot (Tynjä 2017, 151–154, 184, 239); T. el-Fukhar (Strange 2015, pl. 154, 8)
Cypriot Bichrome/White-Painted Ware	T. Hizzin (Genz/Sader 2008, pl. 6, 4 [burial]); T. el-Ghassil (Joukowsky 1972, pls. I, 8?; IV, 4?; IX, 12; XI, 37?); T. Dan (Ilan 2019a, fig. 3.33, 4); T. Hadar (Kleiman 2019a, pl. 80, 4–5), T. er-Rumeith VIIB (Barako 2015c, 3.42, 3–4)
Cypriot Black-on-Red Ware	T. Hizzin (Genz/Sader 2008, pl. 6, 2–3 [burial]); T. Ghassil (Baramki 1964, figs. 17, 1; 37, 1; Joukowsky 1972, pls. I, 1–2; XI, 34; XXV, 25); T. Abel Beth-Maacah (Panitz-Cohen/Mullins/Bonfil 2015, 51 [without figure]); T. Dan IVA (Arie 2008, 27, fig. 11.6); T. Hazor X–V (numerous examples, e.g., Ben-Tor/Ben-Ami/Sandhaus 2012, fig. 5.10, 6–10); T. Anafa (Dever/Harrison 2017, 321–322, PH 190); T. Kinrot (Fritz 1990, 131, pl. 66, 16); et-Tell/Bethsaida V (Arav 2009a, figs. 1.105–1.106); T. Hadar (Kleiman 2019a, pl. 80, 6); T. 'Ein Gev (Mazar *et al.* 1964, 22; fig. 11, 1; pl. 8, b–c); Bab el-Hawa (Hartal/Segal forthcoming, fig. 12, 10); T. 'Ashtara (Abou Assaf 1969, fig. 13); T. er-Rumeith (Barako 2015c, 89, figs. 3.37, 8; 3.42, 1); T. Irbid (Dajani 1966, pl. XXXIV, 24 [burial])
Aegean/Euboean Ware	T. Hadar IV (Kleiman 2019a, pls. 22, 2; 92); T. Abel Beth-Maacah (unpublished, see Panitz-Cohen 2022, n. 5).

9.4 Decoration Techniques

Red slip is one of the hallmarks of the Levantine ceramic industries of the Iron Age II.[74] In some regions, however, this surface treatment already appeared in small quantities in

---

[73] Fantalkin *et al.* 2020; Fantalkin/Kleiman/Mommsen 2022.
[74] Arie 2006, 224–225; Zarzecki-Peleg/Cohen-Anidjar/Ben-Tor 2005, 254.

the Iron Age I.[75] While most of the red-slipped items found in Iron Age I contexts in the central Levant originate from dubious contexts,[76] several fragments were found in the secure context of Stratum IV at Tel Hadar, below thick destruction debris. These sherds may indicate an early appearance of this surface treatment in the central Levant or alternatively suggest a somewhat later date for the destruction of the site.[77] Generally speaking, the frequency of red-slipped vessels in the central Levant is unclear, as all detailed studies that consider the chronology and nature of this surface treatment were carried out at sites located in either the Jezreel or the Beth-Shean Valleys.[78] Moreover, published quantitative studies are scarce in this region. Consequently, in Table 34, I compare the published data on red-slipped bowls from Tel Megiddo, Tel Beth-Shean, Tel Hadar, and Tel Hazor. Data from the latter site was calculated from the published drawings and thus should be regarded as tentative. It is also possible to observe that in the Iron Age, the frequency of red-slipped bowls at sites in the Jezreel and Beth-Shean valleys was higher than at Tel Hazor and Tel Hadar. The low frequency of red-slipped vessels is, therefore, another feature of the ceramic workshops of the central Levant.[79]

Table 34: Frequency of red-slipped bowls

Site	Iron Age IIA (according to sub-phases)						Iron Age IIB		References
	N=	%=	N=	%=	N=	%=	N=	%=	
T. Hazor*	-	-	47	28.4	78	29.4	132	40.3	Ben-Tor/Ben-Ami/Sandhaus 2012
T. Hadar	-	-	-	-	12	20.6	1	9	Kleiman 2019a
T. Beth-shean	-	-	No count		-	-	1136	94.2	Mazar 2006a
T. Megiddo	220	59.7	145	-	-	-	193	82.1	Arie 2013a; Kleiman 2022a

Note: No quantitative data are available for the ceramic assemblages retrieved from the excavations at Tel Hazor. The numbers in this table are based on the published drawings and should be regarded as tentative. I omitted from this counting red painted rims that are abundant in Strata VIII–V.

Some decorative styles are distinct to the central Levant and were rarely observed in other nearby regions. For instance, horizontal grooves appeared on kraters from excavated sites on the eastern shore of the Sea of Galilee[80] and were also observed in several surveyed sites in the Golan Heights (e.g., Tell el-Khashash)[81] and the Irbid Plateau (e.g., Tell Irbid, Khirbet el-Mughayir East, and Tell es-Subba).[82] In Tel Hazor, it appeared

---

[75] Mazar 1998; idem 2015, 10 *contra* Holladay 1990.
[76] E.g., Ben-Tor/Ben-Ami/Sandhaus 2012, fig. 1.4, 2.
[77] Kleiman 2019a, 136–137, pl. 48, 1–2.
[78] Zarzecki-Peleg/Cohen-Anidjar/Ben-Tor 2005; Mazar 2006a; Arie 2013a.
[79] Despite the low number of published vessels from the Golan Heights, the distribution of red-slipped items in this region was relatively low, and so far, only a single red-slipped item was published from this region (Weksler-Bdolah 2000, fig. 5, 5). For a count of all the published Iron Age pottery from the Golan Heights, see Kleiman 2019a, 19–20.
[80] Sugimoto 2015b, fig. 5a; Kleiman 2019a, 138–139, Table 45.
[81] IAS 40, no. 15, fig. 7, 11; IAS 44, no. 52, fig. 14, 7.
[82] Dajani 1966, pl. XXXIV, 1; Kamlah 2000; Lamprichs 2007, pls. 27, 2; 64, 1–3; 87, 1–7.

only rarely.[83] Another decoration technique observed in this region is the use of reed impressions. It is found chiefly on multi-handled kraters, altars, and shrine models.[84]

9.5 Summary

While the current format does not allow a detailed typological study of the ceramic traditions of the central Levant, a review of the main vessel types observed in this region is quite instructive (for a representative assemblage, see Figure 92).

Figure 92: An Iron Age I ceramic assemblage from Tel Hadar (Kleiman 2019a, fig. 80)

As already noted by S. Münger,[85] in the Iron Age I, the vessels used by the local populations were similar to those found in the southern Levant (e.g., Stratum VI at Megiddo). Exceptions are selected Syrian-influenced vessels, such as the biconical amphorae observed, especially at Tel Kinrot and Tel Hadar. Long-distance imports from the coast (e.g., Phoenician Bichrome Ware or Philistine Pottery) are present in the ceramic assemblages of several sites (e.g., Tel Dan and Tel Kinrot) but in relatively small quantities. Of note here is the exposure of the Euboean krater at Tel Hadar. Despite the fact that we are dealing here with a single item, it has chronological and historical importance since only a few Aegean vessels have been found in the Levant from the 11th to 10th centuries BCE.[86] At the very least, this item suggests the existence of a commercial route between southern Syria and the coast. In the Iron Age II, the local ceramic traditions were very similar to those observed in the southern Levant (e.g., the Jezreel

---

[83] E.g., Yadin *et al.* 1958, pl. LVI, 25.
[84] Ben-Tor/Ben-Ami/Sandhaus 2012, photo 2.16; Kleiman 2019a, pls. 15, 4; 78, 5.
[85] Münger 2013.
[86] For other protogeometric items in the Levant, see Maeir/Fantalkin/Zukerman 2009 (Tell es-Safi); Mazar/Kourou 2019, fig. 4, 1 (Tel Rehov); Pucci 2019, pls. 122, b; 123, a (Chatal Hoyuk).

Valley). However, several important ceramic features of the period were only partially adopted in the central Levant. In particular, red slip and hand burnishing were not so common, as mainly observed at Tel Hazor and Tel Hadar (although quantitative data is available only from the latter site). Black juglets, a prominent feature of the ceramic industry of the southern Levant, are also rare in the regions under discussion. Finally, the presence of hippo storage jars in Stratum X at Tel Hazor, which were produced in eastern Samaria, should be highlighted; these vessels are the earliest tangible evidence of contact between the Hula Valley and the highlands in the early first millennium BCE.

10. Monumental Art

10.1 Introduction

Monumental art has an important place in the establishment of political power, group identity, and collective memory.[1] Nevertheless, its definition is invariably complex, considering that objective measures (e.g., energy expenditure) for the characterization of monuments are not always taken as primary criteria.[2] In the case of the objects discussed in this chapter, the energy invested in their creation and design, the careful selection of raw materials for production, the public context in which they were discovered, as well as depictions of similar objects in ancient Near Eastern art, justify their definition as monumental artworks.

10.2 Architectural Elements

10.2.1 Capitals

Volute capitals, also known as "proto-Aeolic capitals," are among the most prominent examples of southern Levantine monumental art, with examples found in nearly all the local kingdoms.[3] However, the dating of these monumental features is debated.

According to the traditional interpretation, volute capitals made their first appearance during the time of David and Solomon.[4] In line with the ongoing debate over the chronology of the Iron Age, scholars suggested lowering the date of the earliest examples to the first half of the 9th century BCE and understanding them as representative of the monumental art of the Omride Dynasty.[5] While this dating is possible, the only

---

[1] Sergi/Gadot 2017, 104–105; Hermann 2019, 399–405.

[2] Trigger 1990. For methodological issues in defining monuments, see Osborne 2014a; idem 2014b, 195–197; Hegeneuer/van der Heyden 2019.

[3] For reviews of the distribution, chronology, and meaning of the volute capitals in the southern Levant, see Shiloh 1979; Lipschits 2011; Franklin 2011.

[4] Shiloh 1979, 88–91.

[5] Finkelstein 2000b; Lipschits 2011. Dating the volute capitals found in northern Israel throughout the years according to their context is indeed a challenge (see, e.g., Kletter 2015). It must be remembered that the earliest examples were usually found in the vicinity of structures dating from the Iron Age IIA (e.g., Palace 1723 at Tel Megiddo or Citadel 3090 at Tel Hazor) and never in the vicinity of earlier buildings (Shiloh 1979, 21). This is especially true for the capitals found in Samaria and Tel Hazor, where no significant Iron Age I strata exist, and for Tel Megiddo and Tel Dan, where massive destruction layers mark a clear stratigraphic division between the remains of the two periods.

published items that can be assigned to a pre-8th century BCE date were unearthed at Tel Hazor (two examples) and maybe also at Tel Dan (one example, with two more items from the 8th century BCE). At Tel Hazor, the two capitals were reused in Stratum VII Building 3264 in Area B (Figure 93),[6] but it is generally accepted that they originated from the original construction phase of Citadel 3090, which dated to the end of the Iron Age IIA (Stratum VIII).[7] A similar date should also be proposed for the capitals found at Tel Dan. According to the preliminary reports, two of the capitals found at the site were uncovered in debris lying on the flagstone pavement to the east of the gate complex, and another one was in secondary use within the upper gate (Figure 21). The construction of the latter structure is assigned to Stratum II. This means that the capital found in secondary use within the gatehouse must be attributed to either Stratum IVA or Stratum III.[8] As the architectural differences between these strata are unclear in the gate area, attributing the capitals to the Stratum IVA, which represents the construction of the city in the late 9th century BCE,[9] is more likely.

While the manufacture of most of the volute capitals discovered in the southern Levant is similar,[10] their styles are not exactly the same. Relying on the examples known at the time, Y. Shiloh composed a typological system based on the depicted motifs and identified five types of volute capitals.[11] According to his classification, most of the objects found in northern Israel belonged to several closely-related types (designated Types A–C), while the two items unearthed at Tel Hazor belonged to a different type characterized by the distinct depiction of a "central triangle" behind the volute-shaped motifs and not in front of them ('Type D'). To date, the only other example belonging to this group is the one discovered in secondary use at Tel Dan. Due to the exposure of volute capitals at several major sites in northern Israel (Table 35), scholars have assumed that the objects found at Tel Hazor represent a north-Israelite monumental product.[12] Nevertheless, the possible affiliation of Stratum VIII with Aram-Damascus, coupled with the distinct style of the volute capitals found at the site and their unique depositional history, hint that these items may actually constitute a rare example of Damascene monumental art. Additional clues for this scenario come from the close parallel found at Tel Dan which was not settled during the Omride period.

The possible use of volute capitals in Aram-Damascus should not be so surprising considering their popularity in other territorial kingdoms in Israel, Judah, Ammon, and Moab. Moreover, the rare monumental items that are known from the heartland of the Aramaean kingdom suggest a variety of cultural influences, including from Phoenicia

---

[6] Yadin et al. 1961, pls. XLVIII 1–3; XLIX, 1–3; CCCLXII–CCCLXIII.

[7] Betancourt 1977, 29; Shiloh 1979, 1; Mazar 1990, 412; Lipschits 2011, 206; Ben-Tor 2016, 162. As no other monumental building was found in Area B, an earlier dating for the two examples in the first half of the 9th century BCE (e.g., Finkelstein 2000b, 118) is a bit forced. Furthermore, the exposure of a 2.45 long lintel about 5 m away from their findspot (Yadin 1972, 171; Yadin et al. 1989, 99) strengthens the idea that they were used at the entrance of the nearby citadel.

[8] Biran 1994, 241; Thareani 2016a, 179.

[9] Arie 2008. See also Section 8.4.2.

[10] Shiloh 1979, 14–17, 60; Shiloh/Horowitz 1975, 39.

[11] Shiloh 1979, 17–20.

[12] E.g., Mazar 1990, 412; Finkelstein 2000b, 118; Lipschits 2011, 222; Ben-Tor 2016, 162.

and the Syro-Anatolian kingdoms of the northern Levant.[13] Given our inability to pinpoint the absolute date of the earliest examples of volute capitals in northern Israel, the question of who influenced whom will probably remain open. Nevertheless, the pristine volute capitals found at Tel Hazor (as well as one found at Tel Dan), and the fact that they are the only examples that can with any certainty be ascribed to the pre-8th century BCE, suggests that it was Aram-Damascus that influenced the monumental architecture of Israel, and not *vice versa*.

Figure 93: Volute capitals in secondary use at Tel Hazor (Yadin 1975, 167)

Another important aspect of the capitals found at Hazor is their archaeological context. Shortly after the excavation of the capitals, Y. Yadin explained their unique findspots against the background of squatter activity in the area of the citadel.[14] His interpretation, however, cannot be accepted. First, the relocation of these 1.5–2-ton objects from the citadel to Building 3264, a distance of c. 7 m, must have consumed significant energy and human resources, unlikely to be invested in the construction of "wind blockers" for an oven. Second, and more importantly, the excavations carried out at Tel Hazor over the last three decades have convincingly demonstrated the high degree of cultural and architectural continuity in the city from its remodeling in Stratum VIII to its total destruction in Stratum V.[15] Apart from some small-scale architectural changes observed mainly in Area A, the basic features of the city (e.g., the citadel, the water system, and the fortification system) remained unchanged.

---

[13] Winter 1981, 102; Börker-Klähn 1982, 225; Schroer 2018, 440.
[14] Yadin 1959a, 79; idem 1959b, 11; idem 1972, 171, n. 6.
[15] Ben-Tor/Ben-Ami/Sandhaus 2012, 2–3; Ben-Tor 2016, 146; Shochat/Gilboa 2019.

In this light, Yadin's reconstruction of a squatter phase in the political hub of the city is highly unlikely. It is more likely that the removal of the volute capitals from Citadel 3090 and their integration into Building 3264 should be understood as part of an intentional attempt to alter the original message of the volute capitals; instead of communicating the political power of those who created and erected them, the capitals' new message may have been to signify a public commemoration of their defeat.[16] A similar explanation could be proposed for the volute capital integrated within the upper-gate complex at Tel Dan.

Table 35: Volute capitals in northern Israel

Type	Examples	Comments
A	M1, M2, M3/M8, M6, M7, M9, M13, S1, S2 and S3	Nearly all the examples of this type from Tel Megiddo were exposed in the area of Building 338 of Stratum IVA. Nos. S1–S3, like most of the other examples from Samaria, were found in the eastern sector of the acropolis. For the possibility that M3 and M8 are, in fact, the same object, see Ussishkin 1989, 160. Y. Shiloh (1979, Table 2) noted that the style of M3 is identical to that of M2.
B	M4 and M5	Both M4 and M5 were reused in Stratum III architecture (Shiloh 1979, 2, n. 14) dated to the Iron Age IIC. According to D. Ussishkin (1970), these items were installed in Palace 1723 of the late Iron Age IIA.
C	D2 and M10	Note that while the find-spot of M10 is uncertain (Shiloh 1979, 3, n. 18), its parallel from Tel Dan was found in the destruction layer of the Iron Age IIB city (Thareani 2016a, 179). For the association of D2 with Type C, see Lipschits 2011, 207.
D	D1, H1, and H2	The three items from Tel Hazor and Tel Dan were reused in Iron Age IIB structures. Notably, the capitals from Tel Hazor must be associated with Stratum VIII (at the end of the Iron Age IIA), and there is no late Iron Age IIA stratum at Tel Dan (Arie 2008).
Undefined	D3, M12, S4, S5, S6, S7, and possibly G1	For the volute capital from Tel Gezer, see Brandl 1984.

Note: D-Tel Dan; G-Gezer; H-Hazor; M-Megiddo; S-Samaria.

10.2.2 Pillars

During the Iron Age, three types of stone-made pillars were observed in the central Levant. The first type is a drum-made pillar, observed mainly on the eastern shore of the Sea of Galilee in both the Iron Age I and II.[17] The second type is a hewn monolith, which is featured in nearly all of the tripartite buildings. The earliest examples of this pillar type in the central Levant are found in Stratum VIII at Tel Hazor and Stratum F-5 at Tel

---

[16] For a detailed description, see Kleiman 2021.
[17] Mazar *et al.* 1964, pl. 3; Kleiman 2019a, fig. 39; see also Harrison 2009, fig. 3.

'Ein Gev,[18] but these are known at sites further south like Tel Megiddo already at the beginning of the late Iron Age IIA (Level Q-5).[19]

The third type is decorated pillars which have only been found at Tel Dan (Table 36). Two examples were exposed in mixed contexts in Area T[20] and another in Area A, below the destruction debris of the Iron Age IIB city. Similar to the pumpkin-shaped pillar bases described below, these objects are considered to represent a Syro-Anatolian or Mesopotamian influence on the material culture of the central Levant.[21]

10.2.3 Bases

Most of the pillar bases found in the central Levant were undecorated.[22] Elaborate examples are the three pumpkin-shaped bases, which adjoined the canopied structure, found next to the city-gate of Tel Dan in the western sector of Area A (Table 36; see location in Figure 21).[23] Similar items are known from Mesopotamia and Syria.[24]

Table 36: Decorated pillars and bases at Tel Dan

#	Description	References
1	Decorated pillar (*ca.* 140 × 40 cm), mixed context	Thareani 2016a, pl. 1, 1
2	Decorated pillar (*ca.* 42+ × 28 cm), mixed context	Thareani 2016a, pl. 1, 2
3	Decorated pillar (*ca.* 25+ × 28 cm), mixed context	Thareani 2016a, pl. 1, 3
4	Decorated base (*ca.* 53 cm), destruction layer, Str. II	Biran 1971, 8
5	Decorated base, destruction layer, Str. II	Not illustrated
6	Decorated base, destruction layer, Str. II	Not illustrated

10.3 Figurative Orthostats

Orthostats are known from the Early Bronze Age in the Ancient Near East, but they became a prominent feature of the monumental art of Syria, Anatolia, and Mesopotamia in the Iron Age.[25] In marked contrast to these cultural spheres, only a few orthostats were found in the central Levant (e.g., Sheikh Sa'ad) or in nearby regions (e.g., Tell es-Salahiyeh; Table 37). It is notable that no Iron Age figurative orthostat has been discovered in the well-investigated Hula Valley, or especially at Tel Dan (this is in marked contrast to the situation in Late Bronze Age, e.g., Stratum XIII–XIV at Tel Hazor).

---

[18] E.g., Yadin *et al.* 1960, 6–7, pls. I, IV–V; Sugimoto 2015a, fig. 16; Hasegawa 2019, 213–217. For the other pillared building, see Kochavi 1998; Cantrell/Finkelstein 2006.

[19] Lamon/Shipton 1939, figs. 8–9; Kleiman *et al.* 2017, pl. 4, a; Homsher/Kleiman 2022.

[20] Biran 1971, 8; Thareani 2016a, 177–179, 191; pl. 1, 4.

[21] According to Y. Thareani (2016a, 177), the items found at Tel Dan are comparable to objects discovered in Arslan Tash (Thureau-Dangin *et al.* 1931, pl. XLIV, nos. 92–93).

[22] E.g., Ben-Tor/Ben-Ami/Sandhaus 2012, plan 3.2; photos 3.1–3.2 (Building 3699).

[23] Biran 1971, 8.

[24] Thareani 2016a, 177; pl. 1, 1–3.

[25] See, e.g., Orthmann 1971; Gilibert 2011.

Table 37: Figurative orthostats in southern Syria

#	Site	Description	References
1	T. es-Salahiyeh	Ruler orthostat; almost complete example (114.3 × 76.2 × 17.78 cm); found out of context	Contenau 1924; Bossert 1951, no. 485; Börker-Klähn 1982, no. 249
2	Damascus	Winged sphinx orthostat; complete example (70 × 80 × 31–51 cm); found in secondary use in the Umayyad Mosque of Damascus	Abd el-Kader 1949; Winter 1981
3	Sheikh Sa'ad	Striding lion orthostat; complete example (130 × 250 × 100 cm); found in an unclear context	Contenau 1924; Aro 2016

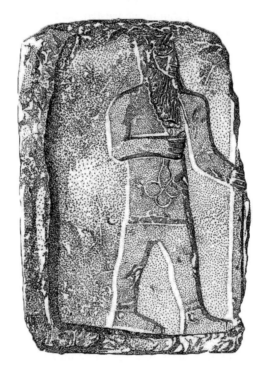

Figure 94: Ruler orthostat from Tell es-Salahiyeh (Börker-Klähn 1982, no. 249)

10.3.1 The Ruler Orthostat from Tell es-Salahiyeh

This orthostat was discovered in a village located on the western sector of the mound in the summer of 1852 by J.L. Porter (Figure 94).[26] The sculpture, which was unusually executed in yellow limestone, depicts an unknown authoritative figure dressed in a kilt and sandals. It is bearded and holds a clover-shaped item in its right hand (maybe an up-

---

[26] Porter 1885, 383–384.

turned lily?). In the left hand, the figure grips an elongated item, probably a staff. Several features in the stele allude to its production by an unskilled artisan. J. Börker-Klähn, for instance, drew attention to the fact that the top of the preserved section is at the same height as the forehead of the figure, which means that the artist did not correctly calculate the space needed for it.[27] The dating of the item is uncertain and depends on the interpretation of the motifs depicted in the relief: Aramaean/North Syrian[28] or Assyrian.[29] Its best parallel comes from Tell Ahmar in Syria.[30] This example was found in a context assigned to the reign of Ahuni (mid-9th century BCE).[31]

10.3.2   Winged-Sphinx Orthostat from Damascus

The only pre-Hellenistic item originating from the capital of Aram-Damascus is an orthostat of a winged sphinx found in secondary use during the renovation of the Umayyad Mosque in the old city.[32] I. Winter described the iconographic features of the orthostat as a walking female sphinx wearing the Egyptian double crown, which is in a Phoenician style.[33] It is usually dated to the timeframe of the 9th and 8th centuries BCE.[34]

10.3.3   Lion Orthostat from Sheikh Saʻad

A single striding lion orthostat is probably the most famous piece of monumental artwork found in the central Levant (Figure 95).[35] The item was discovered in an unclear context prior to B. Hrozný's excavation at Sheikh Saʻad. In contemporary research, this orthostat is considered the most southern expression of the Neo-Hittite/Luwian monumental artwork. The provincial features of the statue,[36] as well as the Assyrian influence on it,[37] were recognized long ago. S. Aro demonstrated its association with Assyrian provincial art, notwithstanding its evident unique style.[38] In her view, the orthostat

---

[27] Börker-Klähn 1982, 225.
[28] E.g., Galling 1953, 184–185.
[29] E.g., Contenau 1924, 210; Börker-Klähn 1982, 225.
[30] Orthmann 1971, 534–535; pl. 54, a; Börker-Klähn 1982, no. 252.
[31] Thureau-Dangin/Dunand 1936, pl. IX, 1. Due to its fragmentary state, the identity of the figure depicted in the example from Tell Ahmar is uncertain. D. Ussishkin (1967, 190) and W. Orthmann (1971, 535) suggest identifying it as a soldier/warrior.
[32] Abd el-Kader 1949.
[33] Winter 1981, 102.
[34] E.g., Abd el-Kader 1949, 193; Schroer 2018, 440 with a list of parallels made of ivory.
[35] A figurative stele (39 × 25 cm) associated with southern Syria was found in the early 20th century and is exhibited today in the Vorderasiatisches Museum in Berlin (Bossert 1951, 33, no. 484; Börker-Klähn 1982, 243–244, no. 294). Its exact provenance is unknown, but it is assumed to have been found in southern Syria. I. Winter (1981, 102) considered the depicted motifs, particularly the Egyptianized crown, to be associated with Phoenician art (compare with the figure depicted on a scarboid found near Tel Dan, Avigad/Sass 1997, 441, no. 1165). For the late date of the lion orthostat found in Tell Shuqayyif, see Section 5.2.6.
[36] Contenau 1924, 208–209.
[37] Isserlin 1961.
[38] Aro 2016.

should be dated to the 7th century BCE, when Sheikh Saʻad was transformed into the provincial capital of the region by the Assyrians.

Figure 95: Lion orthostat from Sheikh Saʻad (by High Contrast / CC BY 3.0 DE)

10.4 Moon/Storm-God Steles

Steles made of basalt depicting a warrior bull with crescent-shaped horns seem to represent genuine monumental artwork of Iron Age communities in the central Levant. So far, five steles of this group have been discovered (Table 38; see, e.g., Figure 96).[39] Their iconographic features were discussed at length by M. Bernett and O. Keel, who argued that the figure depicted in these steles represents the moon-god.[40] Nonetheless, T. Ornan contended that throughout the first millennium BCE, bull representations were

---

[39] Another moon/storm-god stele is said to have come from the area of Gaziantep in southern Turkey, nearly 450 km to the north of the other examples. Scholars were troubled by this exceptional occurrence. It has been suggested, then, that these monuments may have been Hazael's "border steles," which explain their presence at both edges of the Levant in the timeframe of the late 9th and early 8th centuries BCE (B. Brandl cited in Sass 2017, n. 18). Intriguing as it is, this proposal currently raises more questions than it would solve (e.g., why the steles are not identical, why only one stele was found in the northern Levant). In my view, it is easier to understand the northern piece as reflecting contacts between the two halves of the Levant, perhaps between different cult centers.

[40] Bernett/Keel 1998; see also Arav 2020.

used to depict both moon and storm gods, their interchange likely intentional.[41] Regarding spatial distribution, the steles were found between the Sea of Galilee and Jabal ed-Druz, on both sides of the Yarmouk River (et-Tell/Bethsaida, Tell el-Ash'ari, 'Awas, and ed-Turra).[42] Contextual information for most of the steles is lacking, but the two examples found at et-Tell/Bethsaida suggest that these steles were situated at the entrance to the city, but other locations within the settlement cannot be excluded.

Figure 96: Moon/storm-god stele from Stratum V at et-Tell/Bethsaida (photographed by the author)

In 2019, a new stele was found in a Stratum VI context at et-Tell/Bethsaida.[43] If the object was indeed found in situ, then we have good evidence for the continuation of artistic and religious traditions from the Iron Age I into the Iron Age IIA.

---

[41] See the detailed discussion in Ornan 2001.

[42] Recent excavations to the west of Haspin in the Golan Heights unearthed a large boulder with a distinct engraving of a moon/storm-god figure, similar to the one identified in various sites in the central Levant (for a preliminary report, see Tzin/Bron/Kleiman forthcoming). Near the stone, a small offering table, a drummer figurine, and a few other small items were found. The dating of the finds is still unclear and demands further research, but in its vicinity, sherds from the Middle Bronze Age II and Iron Age were found. I would like to thank B. Tzin and A. Bron for allowing me to mention these finds prior to the publication and especially for showing me the pottery from his dig. I added this site to Appendix A but did not change the maps and general statistics (e.g., Figure 42).

[43] Arav 2020, 98–100.

Table 38: Moon/storm god steles in the central Levant

#	Site	Region	Description	References
1	et-Tell/Bethsaida	Sea of Galilee	Complete example (115 × 59 × 31 cm), Stratum V	Bernett/Keel 1998, 1–7
2	et-Tell/Bethsaida	Sea of Galilee	Complete example (no measurements), Stratum VI	Arav 2020, 100
3	Haspin	Golan Heights	Schematic engraving on a rock (88 × 60 × 45 cm)	Tzin/Bron/Kleiman forthcoming
4	T. el-Ash'ari	Nuqra Plain	Complete example (88 × 35 × 30 cm), secondary use in a Roman period tomb	Bernett/Keel 1998, 8–9
5	'Awas	Jabal ed-Druz	Complete example (80 cm in height), secondary use in an Ottoman house	Bernett/Keel 1998, 9–10
6	et-Turra	Irbid Plateau	Almost complete example (58+ × 43 × 26 cm), out of context	Wimmer/Janaydeh 2011

10.5 Summary

The limited corpus of monuments in the central Levant vividly reflects the divergence of local culture from the prevailing art of Syro-Anatolian kingdoms of the northern Levant (e.g., the Kingdom of Unqi/Patin or even the Kingdom of Hamath).[44] Furthermore, the individual expressions of the local artwork support the limited familiarity of local artists with the production of monumental items (e.g., the Tell es-Salahiyeh orthostat) or reveal the impact of nearby cultures (e.g., the Damascus orthostat or the decorated pillars and bases found at Tel Dan). Apparently, the locals favored other types of monumental artworks, such as the moon/storm-god steles found in several different sites in northeastern Israel, southern Syria, and northern Jordan, and seem to reflect a genuine local tradition (as particularly evident by the new sketches documented near Haspin). Such items may have also been produced throughout the Iron Age, as the new stele found at et-Tell/Bethsaida appears to indicate.

Lastly, and most importantly, in some instances, apparent similarities can be observed between the local artworks of the central Levant and those found in urban centers in the Jezreel Valley and the Samaria Highlands (e.g., drafted pillars and volute capitals). This does not necessarily mean that the Northern Kingdom controlled the regions under discussion as often assumed in regard to the Hula Valley, but rather that the monumental art of Israel and Aram-Damascus belonged to the same cultural milieu.[45] The case of the two volute capitals found in secondary use at Stratum VIII at Tel Hazor shows, nonetheless, that a detailed examination of the lifecycle of individual objects can disclose, at times, their possible origin.

---

[44] See, e.g., Orthmann 1971; Gilibert 2011.
[45] See also Rohmer 2020, 542–543.

11. Mortuary Practices

11.1 Introduction

Mortuary practices are regarded in archaeological and anthropological literature as a primary tool to investigate socio-cultural aspects and, in particular, group identity.[1] Archaeological evidence for burial practices in the central Levant is sufficient and provides us with a unique snapshot of the approaches of the locals to the dead. Examples of burials were found in more than ten sites (Table 39). Of these sites, four locations seem to have been used exclusively for burial purposes (Tell es-Safa, Kir'ad el-Baqq'ara South, Jaz'ir, and Khirbet el-Lawziyeh). All of them are located in the Korazim Plateau, and they must have been used, at least partly, for the burial of the residents of Tel Hazor[2] or by populations that lived outside of the city. Additional evidence for burials was discovered within some settlements (e.g., Tel Kinrot) or on their margins (e.g., Kiryat Shmona South). It is also possible to mention that in many of the burial caves discovered in the central Levant, there was evidence of continuous activity between the Bronze and Iron Ages (e.g., Tel Soreg or Tell Irbid), and only a few burial caves were abandoned in the transition (e.g., HaGoshrim).[3]

Table 39: Burials in the central Levant

#	Site	Type(s)	Age/Sex	Offering	References
1	T. Hizzin	-	No data	Pottery	Genz/Sader 2008
2	Kiryat Shmona South	D	Adult (18–25) Adult (18–25) Adult (30–40) Adult (50–60)	Pottery; metal	Covello-Paran 2012
3	T. es-Safa	A, B, C	No data	Pottery	IAS 18, no. 28
4	T. Mashav Northwest	B	No data	Pottery; metal	IAS 18, no. 4
5	Kir'ad el-Baqq'ara South	B, C	No data	Pottery	IAS 18, no. 32
6	Jaz'ir	E	No data	Pottery	IAS 18, no. 20
7	Kh. el-Lawziyeh	B, C	No data	-	IAS 18, no. 138
8	T. Kinrot	A	Adult (20–30, female)	Pottery; varia (necklace)	Münger 2013

---

[1] Faust 2012, 32; Fantalkin 2008, 19–23; Lehmann/Varoner 2018, 257–263.
[2] Stepansky 2014, 103.
[3] For this site, see IAS 7, no. 66.

#	Site	Type	Individuals	Finds	Reference
			Child (4)		
9	T. Soreg	B	No data	-	Kochavi 1993
10	H. Menorim	A	No data	Pottery; metal; varia (bead)	Braun 2001
		A	No data	Pottery	
		A	No data	Pottery	
11	T. Dover	A	Adult (20–25, female)	Pottery; metal	Golani/Wolff 2018
		D	Adult (20–25, female)	-	
			Child (2–3)		
			Adult (40–60, male)		
			Adult (40–50, female)		
			Adult (18–25, female)		
			Adult (30–40, female)		
			Child (1–1.5)		
		A	Adult	Pottery; metal	
			Adult		
		A	Juvenile/infant	Pottery	
			Juvenile/infant		
			Juvenile/infant		
12	T. 'Ashtara	C	No data	-	Abou Assaf 1969
		C	Child	Varia (necklace)	
			No data		
		C	Mature (male)	Varia (turtle shell and antlers)	
			Child		
13	Sahem el-Jawlan	B	No data	Pottery; metal	Fischer 1997
14	T. Irbid	B	No data	Pottery; metal	Dajani 1966
		B	No data	Pottery; metal	
		B	No data	Pottery	
		B	Adult (30, female)	Pottery; metal; ivory items	Fischer/Bürge/al-Shalabi 2015

Note: A-cist burial; B-simple cave; C-shaft tomb; D-reused silo; E-cremation.

11.2 Intramural Burials

11.2.1 Tell Hizzin

M. Chehab's excavation at Tell Hizzin revealed at least three tombs. Unfortunately, the surviving documentation is insufficient to illustrate their location or layout.[4] According to the reanalysis of the dig materials by H. Genz and H. Sader, the inventory of one of them, Tomb 7B, included, *inter alia*, three Iron Age II Cypriot juglets (one White Painted Ware and two Black-on-Red Ware).[5] This tomb seems to correspond to G. Lehmann and O. Varoner's Group 2 (burials with meager finds but with special items such as Cypriot imports).[6] Based on the Cypro-Geometric III/IV imports found in it, the burial should be dated to either the Iron Age IIA or Iron Age IIB.

11.2.2 Kiryat Shmona South

A single chamber tomb with a *dromos* was found during the salvage excavations carried out at Kiryat Shmona South.[7] Initially, the chamber probably functioned as a silo. Similar burials were discovered at Tel Soreg and Tel Dover (see below). Four individuals were uncovered during the fieldwork: three in the chamber and another one in the *dromos*. Exceptional among the finds from this burial is a bronze scepter (or mace-head). A. Yasur-Landau,[8] who published the object, stressed the contradiction between the prestige item, which may have belonged to a ruling figure, and the otherwise poor finds from the settlement in general and the tomb in particular. He suggested that the intent behind the deposition of the object might have been to create an "invented biography" for the deceased. While this is possible, it is not entirely clear how the people who buried the individuals acquired the item and whether or not there was some violence against an actual ruling figure involved in the process (such a scenario would match well with the general insecurity issues observed in this region during the period). The pottery from the tomb and from the settlement shows that it was used in the late Iron Age I.

11.2.3 Tel Kinrot

Salvage excavations carried out at this site suggest that the necropolis of Tel Kinrot was probably located northeast of the city.[9] Two Iron Age I cist tombs, one of them with funerary jars and pots, were excavated in the southeastern sector of the lower settlement.[10] The most notable funerary-related find from Tel Kinrot is an intact burial of a young woman and a child below the floors of one of the Iron Age I houses excavated in the lower city.[11] Apart from a pierced shell pendant, no other offerings were found

---

[4] Genz/Sader 2008, 192.
[5] Genz/Sader 2008, pl. 6, 1–4.
[6] Lehmann/Varoner 2018, 259.
[7] Covello-Paran 2012.
[8] Yasur-Landau 2012a, 204.
[9] Münger 2013, 161.
[10] Winn/Yakar 1984.
[11] Münger 2013, 162–163, fig. 6.

together with the deceased.[12] This burial fits G. Lehmann and O. Varoner's Group 1.[13] It probably dates to the late Iron Age I with the rest of the city (Strata VI–IV).[14]

11.2.4 Horvat Menorim

Three simple cist burials were discovered during salvage excavation.[15] According to E. Braun, the excavator, the preservation of skeletons was poor, but complete vessels were found in all burials, in addition to two small items (e.g., a bead and a metal knife/sickle). G. Lehmann and O. Varoner included these burials in their Group 3.[16] These are the only graves that can be dated with assurance to the Iron Age IIA in the central Levant (excluding the problematic evidence from Tell Hizzin).[17]

11.2.5 Tel Soreg

A single burial cave with a *dromos* was discovered on the northern slope of Tel Soreg.[18] It was used from the Middle Bronze Age to the Iron Age II. It is the second burial with a *dromos* identified in the central Levant (for Kiryat Shmona South, see above). Most of the data concerning this cave have not been published.

11.2.6 Tel Dover

Iron Age burials were exposed during the salvage excavations carried out at Tel Dover.[19] The earliest burial was dated to the Iron Age I and assigned to Stratum VIIa. It included a shallow cist burial surrounded by boulders.[20] Within the tomb, the remains of a young woman were found together with a copper alloy bowl and two ceramic vessels. The excavators assumed that the burial belonged to a stage that preceded the construction of the residential quarter of Strata VIIb–VIId. Considering the evidence from Tel Kinrot (see above),[21] it is also possible that the woman was actually buried under the floor of one of the domestic buildings, but this interpretation cannot be confirmed.

Another concentration of burials was attributed to a later phase of the Iron Age I. According to A. Golani and S.R. Wolff,[22] some silos were reused for burials during this period. In one silo, seven individuals were found. Aside from the reused silos, there was also a built tomb that contained two mature individuals. Finally, a cist tomb containing three juveniles/infants was found at the site, dated to the Iron Age IIB. The copious evidence of burial practices at Tel Dover is surprising considering the small size of the settlement and the limited excavated area (with remains from the Late Bronze and Iron

---

[12] Münger 2013, 162.
[13] Lehmann/Varoner 2018, 258.
[14] For the dating of Strata VI–IV at Tel Kinrot, see Section 4.2.2.
[15] Braun 2001.
[16] Lehmann/Varoner 2018, 260.
[17] For the pottery, see Braun 2001, 177–178.
[18] Kochavi 1993, 31.
[19] Golani/Wolff 2018.
[20] Golani/Wolff 2018, 513.
[21] Münger 2013, 162–163, fig. 6.
[22] Golani/Wolff 2018, 514.

Ages). This site was located at the junction of major highways and probably was not used solely by the residents of Tel Dover but may also have served semi-nomad groups living in, or passing through, this region.

11.2.7 Tell 'Ashtara

During the second season of excavation at Tell 'Ashtara, three shaft tombs were found in the western sector of the settlement (see, e.g., Figure 97).[23] Each of the graves was covered by flat slabs. Only two tombs were investigated in detail. In Tomb no. 2, the remains of a child in full articulation were found. Below these remains, additional human bones were found. A somewhat different picture emerged from the excavation of Tomb no. 3, where a skeleton of a male in articulation was found next to a turtle shell. About 1.5 m below this skeleton, a deer antler was exposed together with a small human skeleton (unspecified gender). Aside from a necklace found in the child's tomb, no other apparent grave goods were exposed. The three tombs were dated to the Iron Age II (most likely before the destruction and abandonment of the city in the late 8th century BCE).

Figure 97: A skeleton in full articulation at Tell 'Ashtara (Abou Assaf 1969, fig. 8)

11.2.8 Tell Irbid

Three hewn burial caves with Iron Age vessels were found during excavations on the eastern slope of Tell Irbid, almost certainly the location of the necropolis of the city, in

---

[23] Abou Assaf 1969.

the 1960s (Tombs A–C, Figure 98).[24] In Tomb C, a 60 cm high bench was found with a human skeleton of unspecified sex lying on it. The pottery revealed in the tombs indicates that the caves were used during the late Iron Age I and Iron Age IIA.[25]

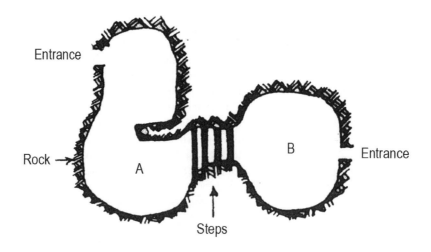

Figure 98: Burial caves at Tell Irbid (adapted from Dajani 1966, pl. XXXV)

11.3 Burials Sites

11.3.1 Tell es-Safa

More than 60 caves, spread across an area of nearly 15 hectares, were found at Tell es-Safa (Figure 99). A rescue excavation carried out at the site revealed a 3.5 × 5 m rock-cut cave at the bottom of which two pits were dug.[26] In one of the pits, a skeleton was found. The pottery from the cave was dated to several eras: Middle Bronze Age II, Iron Age I, and the Roman period. Note that one whole jug from the cave, which was presented as belonging to the Middle Bronze Age II, is also attested in secure Iron Age I contexts (e.g., Stratum IV at Tel Hadar).[27] It is unknown whether the evidence for Middle Bronze Age activity in this cave is based solely on this vessel.

---

[24] Dajani 1966. A fourth tomb, designated Tomb D, dates to the Late Bronze Age (Dajani 1964). More recently, another tomb was excavated near these caves (Fischer/Bürge/al-Shalabi 2015). See also the Middle Bronze Age III/Late Bronze Age I pottery from two burials dug in 1968 (Kafafi 2014).
[25] Dajani 1966, pls. XXXII–XXXIV. See also Figure 68.
[26] Edelstein 1975; IAS 18, no. 28.
[27] Compare IAS 18, fig. 4.28, 1 with Kleiman 2019a, pl. 17, 4 (see also Section 9.2.3).

11.3 Burials Sites

Figure 99: The burial site of Tell es-Safa (created with QGIS 3.16 and Google Satellite)

11.3.2 Jaz'ir

Soundings to the south of Tel Hazor revealed a few structures and 20 cremation burials from the end of the Iron Age IIA (or a bit later).[28] These remains are rare in the central Levant and may suggest that the deceased were not locals. The closest evidence of cremation at an inland site comes from Hama and Tell en-Nasriyeh in the Homs Plain (*ca.* 225 km to the north).[29] Either a north Levantine origin or, more likely, the Phoenician coast (*ca.* 40 km to the west) for the people buried in Jaz'ir are possibilities.[30]

11.3.3 Kir'ad el-Baqq'ara South

About 20 hewn caves were discovered at the site during a field survey.[31] Ovoid and rectangular-shaped shafts led into a few of these caves, which were ultimately used for domestic purposes. The pottery from the site dates to the Iron Age I and II.

11.3.4 Khirbet el-Lawziyeh

About ten hewn caves, spreading over an area of less than half a hectare, were documented at Khirbet el-Lawziyeh.[32] Presumably, these caves were initially used for burial but were later transformed into a storage space (as suggested for Kir'ad el-Baqq'ara

---

[28] Ben-Tor 1993; IAS 18, no. 20.
[29] For the cremation cemeteries excavated in central Syria, see Riis 1948; Tenu 2015.
[30] The results of these soundings are being prepared for final publication by A. Ben-Tor and D. Sandhaus. I would like to thank both for showing me the pottery from this excavation.
[31] IAS 18, no. 32.
[32] Stepansky 2014, 103; IAS 18, no. 138.

South, see above). The pottery collected at the site dates mainly to the Iron Age I–II, Persian and Hellenistic periods.

11.3.5 Sahem el-Jawlan

A hewn burial cave (*ca.* 7.5 × 7.5 m) was discovered near the modern village of Sahem el-Jawlan.[33] In the tomb, nearly 80 complete vessels were discovered, among other finds (e.g., jewelry, figurines, and metal objects). The pottery from the tomb dates to the end of the Late Bronze Age or the beginning of the Iron Age I.

11.4 Summary

Considering the limited data on the archaeology of the central Levant, the relatively abundant evidence for mortuary practices is quite surprising. In fact, it is comparable to the burial distribution in the Jezreel Valley, the Galilee, and other nearby regions.[34] Unusual phenomena relating to mortuary practices identified in this area are: 1) the reuse of silos for burial (e.g., Kiryat Shmona South and Tel Dover), a practice that was not identified elsewhere in the southern Levant, 2) the female burials with a child (e.g., Tel Kinrot) or without (e.g., Tell 'Ashtara), and 3) the appearance of cremation burials near Tel Hazor, probably at the end of the Iron Age IIA or the early days of the Iron Age IIB. One can also emphasize the documentation of several burial sites (e.g., Tell es-Safa) that may have been used by nearby urban centers (e.g., Tel Hazor) or even semi-nomads who lived in their vicinity (e.g., Tel Dover). In brief, the various burial practices (e.g., grave style and offerings) identified in Iron Age settlements in the central Levant probably hint at the social diversity of the local populations.

---

[33] Fischer 1997; idem 1998.
[34] Bloch-Smith 1992, fig. 15; Lehmann/Varoner 2018, figs. 13–14.

12. Writing and Literacy

12.1 Introduction

The exposure of inscriptions, or more commonly inscribed objects, in archaeological sites may allude to an advanced stage of literacy or the presence of literate individuals in settlements or ceramic workshops (e.g., royal administration), revealing connections between different cultural spheres (Aram, Israel, Phoenicia), and provide a rare snapshot into various aspects of a given society (e.g., personal names). Here, I focus on the archaeological aspects of inscribed objects (e.g., context, distribution, and quantity) found in the central Levant (Figure 100). Paleographic and linguistic aspects of these items, including differentiation between script types, have been extensively discussed in other places and are situated beyond the scope of the current study.[1]

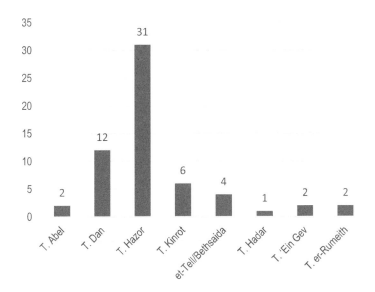

Figure 100: Inscriptions and other inscribed objects

---

[1] See, e.g., Delavault/Lemaire 1979; Dobbs-Allsopp *et al.* 2005; Renz/Röllig 1995; Sass 2005, 85–88; idem 2016; Rollston 2008; Finkelstein/Sass 2013; Sass/Finkelstein 2016. For the cultural background of the emergence of writing in the Iron Age Levant, see also Malena 2020.

12.2 Inscribed Objects

12.2.1 Distribution, Quantity, and Dating

Inscribed objects in the central Levant are plentiful compared to more investigated regions such as the Jezreel Valley (Table 40; Appendix B; see, e.g., Figure 102 and a distribution map in Figure 104).[2] Most of them are concentrated in the Hula Valley. No items are known from the Lebanese Beqaa,[3] Golan Heights, or the Nuqra Plain (and only two alphabetic signs are known from the Irbid Plateau), but this makes sense considering the limited research of these regions.[4] From a chronological perspective, not even a single inscription in the region was found in a secure context dated earlier than the end of the 9th century BCE, even in well-investigated sites such as Tel Hazor (Figure 101);[5] this situation stands in contrast to the evidence documented in the Beth-Shean Valley[6] but is similar to other regions controlled by the Northern Kingdom in the 10th–9th centuries BCE (e.g., Stratum V at Tel Megiddo,[7] or Stratum VIII/VII at Tel Gezer).[8]

The presence of stamped storage jars in the central Levant should also be noted (see, e.g., Figure 103). In recent years, the many stamped handles exposed in Iron Age Judah (i.e., the LMLK administrative system) have been discussed extensively.[9] In this light, it is surprising that the discovery of stamp impressions in pre-732 BCE contexts in the

---

[2] For catalogs of Iron Age inscriptions, see Delavault/Lemaire 1979; Renz/Röllig 1995; Avigad/Sass 1997; Dobbs-Allsopp et al. 2005; Finkelstein/Sass 2013. Several items were unearthed (or rediscovered) after the publication of these studies: one handle with an alphabetic sign from Tel Dan (Greer 2011, 69); two inscriptions from Tel Abel Beth-Maacah (Panitz-Cohen/Mullins/Bonfil 2015, 51; Yahalom-Mack/Panitz-Cohen/Mullins 2018, 152; Yahalom-Mack et al. 2021); three lost inscriptions from Yigael Yadin's excavations at Tel Hazor (Mendel 2011), one inscription from Tel Hadar (Kleiman 2019a, 161–163, pl. 100), an unpublished inscription from Tel 'Ein Gev (see details in idem, 397), and two alphabetic signs from Tell er-Rumeith (Lapp/Cooper 2015). I excluded from the database a yet-unpublished sherd with three ink marks found in et-Tell/Bethsaida (Arav 2004b).

[3] For possible alphabetic signs at Tell Kamid el-Loz, see Heinz et al. 2010, 21, fig. 10.

[4] Only two items are known from the Irbid Plateau (Lapp/Cooper 2015, figs. 11.4–11.5).

[5] Inscription no. 4440 at Tel Hazor was found in Locus 3273 (Yadin et al. 1961, pl. CCCLVII, 1). It represents an open space in Square E/9 that was attributed to Stratum IX. According to the loci list, Locus 3273 ranges between 234.35–234.15 m.a.s.l. (Yadin et al. 1989, 115), only a few centimeters above a floor that was assigned to the Late Bronze Age (Locus 3305) but more than a meter below the floor of Stratum VIII (no floor associated with Stratum X–IX was found in this area). This means that the sherd most likely originated from an undetected pit or other disturbance in Square E/9; this is not surprising considering the changes that occurred in the area of the citadel (e.g., Building 3148a). Regarding the stratigraphic affiliation of Inscription no. 2712/1, see Finkelstein/Sass 2013, n. 111.

[6] Ahituv/Mazar 2013; idem 2014.

[7] Sass/Finkelstein 2016. Due to my familiarity with the stratigraphic challenges of the southeastern sector of Megiddo (Area Q), I believe that the association of the Megiddo Jug inscription with Level Q-5, dated to ca. 900 BCE, is more likely (see also Vanderhooft 2017). Its association with a later phase, Level Q-4, as suggested by B. Sass and I. Finkelstein, is, of course, not out of the question.

[8] Note the late 10th/early 9th century BCE calendar found by R.A.S. Macalister at Tel Gezer. For other inscriptions found in the Judean Shephelah, see Rollston 2008; Maeir/Eshel 2014; Garfinkel et al. 2015; Sass/Finkelstein 2021; Eshel et al. in press. See also the inscriptions found in Horvat Rosh Zayit and Kefar Veradim (Gal/Alexandre 2000, 133–134; Alexandre 2002).

[9] E.g., Lipschits/Sergi/Koch 2010; Ussishkin 2011; Finkelstein 2012; Na'aman 2016c.

Kingdom of Israel has largely been ignored, especially since they seem to depict an immature form and could have inspired its development.[10] Nine impressions are known from the north: five examples from Tel Dan (zkryw, l'mdyw [three items], and ly[...]), one example from et-Tell/Bethsaida (zkryw), one example from Tel Dothan (lšmryw), and two examples from Samaria (lyd'yw and an undeciphered one).[11]

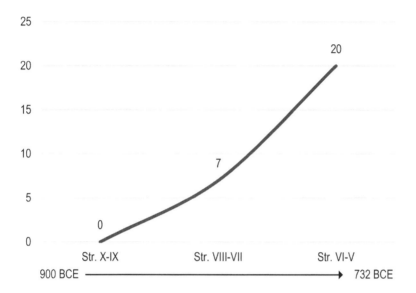

Figure 101: Number of inscribed objects in Hazor according to strata (three unprovenanced items and one surface find, all are probably from Strata VI–V, are excluded)

12.2.2 The Function of the Inscribed Objects

The possible function of inscribed items found in the central Levant, mostly storage jars and bowls, remains unanswered. However, any explanation of this phenomenon must first address where and when the vessel was inscribed. Inscriptions written in ink or incised after firing provide little information, as they could have been executed anywhere at any time. In contrast, pre-fired incised inscriptions indicate that literate individuals, or people who acted on their behalf, were present in some of the ceramic workshops that produced the jars. As it is highly unlikely that literacy was common among the potters themselves during the Iron Age,[12] we must, therefore, assume that the individual(s) in question originated from the literate sectors of society, namely the royal administration of Israel (or Aram-Damascus). It is possible, then, that the names inscribed on storage jars, especially those that appear to be produced in a central place

---

[10] See details and discussion in Kleiman 2017.
[11] The association of the undeciphered stamp impression with Samaria is uncertain.
[12] Note that the education of scribes, even those who practiced alphabetic writing, was a demanding process that deployed over a few years (Rollston 2006, 68).

(e.g., the hippo jars or the torpedo jars[13]), reflect the allocation of certain quantities of vessels to specific individuals, clans, or settlements.[14] Other inscribed items, such as bowls and jugs, may suggest dedication or ownership; they may indicate a different pervasiveness of literacy among the local societies of the central Levant.

Figure 102: Selected inscribed storage jars: 1) šd'l nz'' from Tel Hadar (Kleiman 2019a, pl. 100), 2) lmkbrm from Tel Hazor (Yadin et al. 1960, pl. CLXIX, 5), 3) lšky' from Tel 'Ein Gev (photographed by the author), and 4) ink inscription from Tel Hazor (Yadin et al. 1960, pl. CLXIX, 6)

---

[13] One of the two ink inscriptions found in the central Levant (Yadin *et al.* 1960, 73; pls. CLXIX, 6; CLXX, 6) was written on a torpedo jar, as is evident in the sharply carinated shoulder and the elongated body of the vessel; petrographic studies suggest that at least some of these jars were produced in Phoenicia (Ballard *et al.* 2002, 160). For other inscriptions that may have been executed on torpedo jars, see Yadin *et al.* 1961, pl. CCCLVII, 11; Mendel 2011, fig. 3 (and compare with Pritchard 1988, figs. 2, 12; 3, 17–18 in Sarepta, similarly executed on such containers).

[14] Only a few inscribed items have been sampled for petrographic research in the central Levant (Tel Hadar, Tel Dan, and et-Tell/Bethsaida), meaning that the exact origin of many of these vessels is currently unknown. In the case of the single examined inscription at Tel Hadar, the results suggest a local production (L. Bouzaglou, personal communication). Of importance is that the stamped handles found at Tel Dan and et-Tell/Bethsaida were shown to be produced in the Samaria Highlands (Y. Goren cited in Brandl 2009, 171).

12.2.3 The Content of the Inscriptions

Most of the inscriptions found in the central Levant are short. However, they often consist of personal names, which can illuminate the social background and beliefs of the local societies (Table 41).[15] Interestingly, the limited corpus from the Hula Valley and the Sea of Galilee consists of inscriptions written in Hebrew and Non-Hebrew scripts[16] and includes a few groups of theophoric names: names with the component yw (e.g., dlyw, zkryw, and 'mdyw), names with the component 'l (e.g., 'lplṭ, bn'l, and šd'l), names with the component b'l (e.g., b'lplṭ), and names with other components (e.g., mkrbm; see a summary of the theophoric suffixes in Table 42).[17] As the stamped zkryw and 'mdyw jars were most likely produced in the Samaria Highlands, the only local Yahwistic names are bnyw, dlyw, and […]yw (pending that they were produced in the central Levant and not elsewhere).

Figure 103: One of the 'mdyw stamp impressions found at Tel Dan (Biran 1988, 16)

---

[15] The Iron Age dating of the mky and 'kb' inscriptions, which were found during the excavations of et-Tell/Bethsaida, is uncertain (B. Sass, personal communication).
[16] Delavault/Lemaire 1979; Naveh 1989; Sass 2016.
[17] For the distribution of theophoric names in the southern Levant, see Golub 2014, 635.

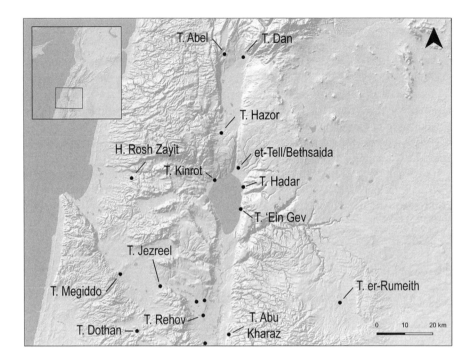

Figure 104: Settlements with inscriptions and inscribed objects from the 9th and 8th centuries BCE in the central Levant and nearby regions (created with QGIS 3.16 and World Shaded Relief of Esri 2014)

Table 40: Inscriptions and inscribed objects in the central Levant

Site	Royal Inscriptions	Inscribed Objects	Stamp Impressions	Seals	Total
T. Abel		2			2
T. Dan	1	5	5	1?	12
Hazor		31			31
T. Kinrot		6			6
et-Tell		3	1		4
T. Hadar		1			1
T. 'Ein Gev		2			2
T. er-Rumeith		2			2
Total	1	52	6	1	60

Table 41: Personal names in the central Levant

#	Name	Site(s)	Additional Features	References
1	bnyw בניו	T. Abel	Ownership/dedication prefix	Yahalom-Mack et al. 2021
2	'mṣ אמץ	T. Dan	Ownership/dedication prefix	Biran 1994, 255, fig. 215
3	b'lplṭ בעלפלט	T. Dan	Ownership/dedication prefix; similar personal name in T. Kinrot	Biran 1994, 262, fig. 218
4	zkryw זכריו	T. Dan, et-Tell	-	Biran 1994, 255, fig. 213
5	'z' עזא	T. Dan?	Ownership/dedication prefix	Avigad/Sass 1997, 411, no. 1165
6	'mdyw עמדיו	T. Dan	Ownership/dedication prefix	Biran 1994, 199–201, fig. 158; see also Figure 103
7	'lm[lk/tn] אלמןלך\תן	T. Hazor	Same inscription as yrb['l/m]; torpedo storage jar?	Yadin et al. 1960, 73, pls. CLXIX, 6, CLXX, 6 see also Figure 103, 4
8	bn'l בנאל	T. Hazor	Torpedo storage jar?	Mendel 2011, 330, fig. 3
9	Dlyw דליו	T. Hazor	Ownership/dedication prefix	Yadin et al. 1960, 74–75, pl. CLXXII
10	yrb['l/m] ירבןעל\ם	T. Hazor	Same inscription as 'lm[lk]; torpedo storage jar?	Yadin et al. 1960, 73, pls. CLXIX, 6, CLXX, 6; see also Figure 103, 4
11	mkbrm מכברם	T. Hazor	Ownership/dedication prefix; uncertain reading	Yadin et al. 1989, 72–73, pls. CLXIX, 5; see also Figure 103, 2
12	pd[y/h] פדן י\ה	T. Hazor	Ownership/dedication prefix	Naveh 1989, 347; Yadin et al. 1961, pl. CCCLVII
13	pqḥ פקח	T. Hazor	Ownership/dedication prefix; commodity (smdr)	Yadin et al. 1960, 73–74, pls. CLXXI–CLXXII
14	[...]yw יו[...]	T. Hazor	Fragmentary inscription (only the theophoric suffix was preserved)	Naveh 1989, 347; Yadin et al. 1961, pls. CCCLVII, 11, CCCLVIII, 11
15	'lplṭ אלפלט	T. Kinrot	Ownership/dedication prefix; same personal name in T. Dan	Fritz 1990, 116–117, pl. 100, 1
16	mky מכי	et-Tell	Exceptionally large letters	Arav 1999, 91, fig. 36
17	'qb' עקבא	et-Tell	-	Arav 1995, 17–18, fig. 11
18	šm שם	et-Tell	Ownership/dedication prefix	Savage 2009, figs. 3.1–3.2
19	šd'l שדאל	T. Hadar	With title (nz')	Kleiman 2019a, 161–163, pl. 100 see also Figure 103, 1

Table 42: Theophoric elements in the central Levant

#	Element	Site(s)	N=	%=
1	[...]'l אל[...]	T. Dan, T. Hazor, T. Kinrot, T. Hadar	4	28.5
2	[...]bʻl בעל[...]	T. Dan	1	7.2
3	[...]yw י[...]	T. Abel, T. Dan, T. Hazor, et-Tell	8	57.1
4	[...]rm רם[...]	T. Hazor?	1?	7.2
Total		T. Abel, T. Dan, T. Hazor, et-Tell	14	100

12.3 Royal Inscriptions

12.3.1 Egyptian Inscriptions

Four fragments of Egyptian royal inscriptions dated from the Late Bronze Age were discovered in the central Levant: Thutmosis III/Amenophis's Stele from Tel Kinrot, Ramesses II's Stele from Sheikh Saʻad (also known as "Job Stone"), Seti I's Stele from Tell esh-Shihab, and Ramesses II's Stele from et-Turra (Table 43). To this corpus, one can add two fragments found beyond the research area, in the vicinity of Damascus: one to the south of the city (the "el-Kiswa" stele of Ramesses II) and another one to its east (the "el-Meyda'a Stele" of a high-ranking officer in the army of Seti I).[18] No post-13th century BCE Egyptian steles have been found east of the Phoenician coast, and the list of Shoshenq I (biblical Shishak) list does not include toponyms to the north of the Jezreel Valley, where a fragment of his stele was found.[19]

Table 43: Egyptian monumental inscriptions in the central Levant

#	Site	Region	Ruler	Reference
1	T. Kinrot	Sea of Galilee	Thutmosis III/ Amenhotep II	Albright/Rowe 1928
2	Sheikh Saʻad	Nuqra Plain	Ramesses II	Schumacher 1891
3	T. esh-Shihab	Nuqra Plain	Seti I	Smith 1901
4	et-Turra	Irbid Plateau	Ramesses II	Wimmer 2002

---

[18] Also Merneptah, Ramesses II's successor, carried out a military campaign in the central Levant regardless of the exact identification of Yenoʻam, maybe Tell esh-Shihab. For the cultural contacts between Egypt and Canaan, see Schipper 2012, 31–35; Koch 2021, *passim*. For the distribution of Egyptian items in Canaan of the Late Bronze Age, see Levy 2017.

[19] The fragment was found in Gottlieb Schumacher's dump during the Oriental Institute excavations but is said to have come from the northeastern sector of the upper mound, i.e., the area of Palace 6000 and Stable Compounds 403 and 407 (Breasted 1929; Harrison 2004, 7–8). Note that the investigations of this area by Yigael Yadin (Zarzecki-Peleg 2016, 53–70) and by the new excavations (Kleiman/Dunseth 2022) did not reveal any clue for significant 10th century BCE activity here. The only possible exception to this rule is the poorly-preserved and difficult to interpret Building 6107 (Zarzecki-Peleg 2016, 10, 53–57, 61–62, 326; see also Wightman 1984; Kleiman *et al.* 2017, n. 145).

| 5 | el-Kiswa | Damascus Oasis | Ramesses II | Taraqji 1999 |
| 6 | el-Meyda'a | Damascus Oasis | Officer of Seti I | Lagarce 2010 |

12.3.2 The Tel Dan Inscription

To date, the only monumental Iron Age inscription discovered in the central Levant was found during the Hebrew Union College excavations at Tel Dan in 1993 (one fragment) and 1994 (two additional fragments of the same inscription).[20] Since its initial publication, the content of the inscription and its historical implications have been discussed intensively.[21] Nearly everyone classifies the stele as a summary inscription that details the victory of its anonymous author over the kings of Israel and Judah, as well as events that preceded his reign, a common practice in royal inscriptions.[22] Most scholars attribute the monument to Hazael of Damascus (although some assigned it to Hazael's son, Ben-Hadad).[23] From a broader perspective, the erection of the stele is contemporaneous with the emergence of monumental alphabetic inscriptions in other places in the Levant (e.g., the Mesha Stele).[24] Fascinatingly, and as already noted in the past,[25] the Tel Dan inscription also included several details that do not align with other biblical and extra-biblical sources. In particular, scholars stressed the reference to the author's father as a king, which seems to contradict the portrayal of Hazael in Assyrian sources as a "son of nobody"[26] and the execution of kings of Israel and Judah, who, according to the Book of Kings were killed by Jehu (2 Kgs 9). Attempts were made to resolve these issues in various ways. Regarding Hazael's genealogy, it has been suggested that Hazael's father was the ruler of Beth-Rehob, i.e., he originated from a prominent family.[27] Concerning the responsibility for the killing of the kings of Israel and Judah, it has been proposed that the author credited himself for the act of Jehu, who served as his messenger.[28]

In this study, which focuses on the archaeological remains, it is more productive to concentrate on the contextual aspects of the inscription while adopting the conventional reading of the stele.[29] According to A. Biran's last report of the archaeological evidence from the excavation in the city-gate area,[30] all three fragments of the stele were found to the east of the gate complex, integrated into the final construction phase in the Hussot.[31] It is quite likely that this phase should be equated with Stratum II, which ended

---

[20] For the inscriptions from Byblos, see Sass 2017 with earlier bibliography.
[21] For the *editio princeps*, see Biran/Naveh 1993; idem 1995, and for further discussions, see, e.g., Halpern 1994; Schniedewind 1996; Lemaire 1998; Na'aman 2000; Yamada 2000, 309–320; Galil 2001; Hafthorsson 2006, 49–65; Ghantous 2013; Blum 2016; Frevel 2018a, 136, 138, 248–250 with updated references therein.
[22] Na'aman 2000, 98–99.
[23] E.g., Galil 2001.
[24] Sass 2016, 222; idem 2017.
[25] E.g., Biran/Naveh 1995; Halpern 1994; Schniedewind 1996; Na'aman 2000.
[26] Yamada 2000, 188–190.
[27] Na'aman 1995a, 388–390.
[28] Halpern 1994, but see Na'aman 2000, 102.
[29] E.g., Na'aman 2000.
[30] Biran 2002.
[31] Biran 2002, 6, figs. 1.6–1.7.

with the destruction of the city by the Assyrians in the second half of the 8th century BCE. Since Stratum IVB is undoubtedly too early for the inscription, it can be dated to either Stratum IVA or Stratum III. The former phase is a more likely option, as the inscription was probably erected as part of the construction of the city.[32]

A fascinating issue is the lifecycle of the Tel Dan Stele. Since three related parts of the stele were found in roughly the same place, it is very likely that the stele was erected not too far from their find-spot, and the natural place for such a monumental inscription is, of course, the entrance to the city. More than 30 years ago, W. Zwickel[33] insightfully proposed that the canopied structure, which was revealed between the inner and the outer gates of the city (Figure 21), was not a cult place[34] but rather the location of a royal stele. Writing before the discovery of the Tel Dan inscription, he suggested that this was the place of a stele belonging to Jeroboam I. His proposal was based on an emphasized depression found in the platform, as well as on comparanda from the Ancient Near East. A similar conclusion was also reached by I. Finkelstein, who made a direct reference to the royal stele found during the excavations,[35] and, more recently, also by the D. Ilan and J.S. Greer.[36] It can be concluded, then, that with the occupation of the city by Israel in the early 8th century BCE (Stratum III), the stele must have been shattered (and thrown outside of the gate complex to the east). Parts of it were used later for the construction of new extramural buildings. A somewhat similar lifecycle probably is revealed in the secondary use of a volute capital in the upper gatehouse; both processes constitute archaeological evidence for political transformations in the city.[37]

12.4 Summary

The distribution of the epigraphic evidence in the central Levant shows that throughout most of the 10th–9th centuries BCE, literacy was limited to the core areas of the Kingdom of Israel (e.g., Beth-Shean Valley) and did not diffuse into remote strongholds such as Tel Hazor.[38] In this case, the absence of such items from Samaria – the capital – is odd but may derive from the nature of the excavations carried out at the site in the early 20th century. Evidence of literacy in the central Levant can be discerned only from the late 9th century BCE (e.g., Tel Dan, Tel Hazor, and Tel 'Ein Gev), a trend that may be

---

[32] Arie 2008, 35.
[33] Zwickel 1990b, 226.
[34] Biran 1993, 329; Blomquist 1999, 63; Thareani 2016a, 177.
[35] Finkelstein 2013, 128.
[36] Ilan/Greer 2021, 163.
[37] For the capital, see Section 10.2.1 and more details in Kleiman 2021, 12.
[38] It has been suggested that during the 10th–9th centuries BCE, the Beth-Shean Valley was an independent enclave (Finkelstein 2016b; for a more nuanced proposal, see Arie 2017). Other scholars (e.g., Mazar 2016; idem 2020b, 122–123; idem 2021, 263–264) argued against this scenario and interpreted the region as part of the north-Israelite kingdom since its constitution. In my view, there is no substantial evidence for disconnecting the Beth-Shean Valley from the Northern Kingdom nor historical logic. Moreover, the archaeological data (e.g., pottery and inscriptions), especially from Tel Rehov, suggest that this region was part of the heartland of this polity (more in Sergi 2019; Mazar 2020b).

correlated with the expansion of the political control of Aram-Damascus during the reign of Hazael of Damascus. He was also responsible for the erection of one of the few monumental inscriptions found in the southern Levant and may even have played a pivotal role in the spread of such monuments across the Levant at the end of the 9th century BCE.[39] Recently M. Amadasi Guzzo discussed the limited corpus of inscriptions that can be associated with Aram-Damascus and noted their shared attributes. She proposed interpreting this as evidence for a Damascene scribal school.[40] The data from the central Levantine settlements, especially from the Hula Valley, support her suggestion.

In contrast, the stamp impressions, originating from Iron Age IIB contexts, already reflect clear economic and political contacts with the Kingdom of Israel (and not with Aram-Damascus). This is suggested by the north-Israelite names that appeared on these impressions (e.g., zkryw) and by the petrographic results which located the production of the stamped jars in the Samaria Highlands. Such contacts were probably generated during the renewed territorial expansion of the Kingdom of Israel to the central Levant in the days of Jeroboam II. Related as well to this process is the Tel Dan Stele. As the royal inscription probably served as a symbol of the Damascene control over the Hula Valley, it is hardly surprising that in the early 8th century BCE, the stele was smashed and removed from its original location (the canopied structure in the gate complex?). Parts of it were disposed of downslope, where these pieces were integrated within the walls of new houses built in the Iron Age IIB.[41]

---

[39] Sass 2017, 115–116.
[40] Amadasi Guzzo 2019, 162–163.
[41] From a methodological point of view, this provides additional archaeological evidence for the identification of the military conflicts between Israel and Aram-Damascus (see more in Kleiman 2021).

Part III. Synthesis

13. Between Local and Foreign Rulers

13.1 Introduction

In this study, I discussed the contribution of the archaeological research for clarifying issues related to the settlement history and material culture of Iron Age communities in the central Levant. Detailed reassessment of the data from the field suggests that throughout the 12th–8th centuries BCE the local societies modified their lifestyle in accordance with the shifting historical circumstances but at the same time maintained their independent cultures and experienced distinct historical developments. Moreover, with the new dataset presented in this study, it is possible to provide a nuanced narrative for the local populations, to highlight the results of their encounters with the foreign rulers of the territorial kingdoms, and lastly, to examine several long-term trends in the central Levant (demography, economy, literacy, cult, and identity): from the dawn of the Iron Age to the collapse of Israel and Aram-Damascus in the 8th century BCE (Table 44).

Table 44: Comparative stratigraphy of selected excavated sites in the central Levant

Site	Iron Age I (ca. 1150–950 BCE)		Iron Age IIA (ca. 950–800 BCE)		Iron Age IIB (ca. 800–650 BCE)	
T. Hizzin	Sherds		←Tomb + Sherds→			
T. el-Ghassil	5–1		←Sherds→			
T. Kamid el-Loz	4–3		←Sherds→			
T. Abel	A5–A2		←A1→			
T. Dan	VI–V	IVB	Gap	IVA	III–II	I
T. Hazor	XII/XI	Gap	X–IX	VIII	VII–V	II
T. Kinrot	Gap	VI–IV	Gap	III	II	I
et-Tell	Gap	VI	Gap	V		
T. Hadar	Gap	V–IV	Gap	III	II/I?	
T. ʿEin Gev	Gap	KIV	Gap	KIII	KII?	
Mitzpe Golani	←Sherds→		←Structure→			
Bab el-Hawa		Gap		2	3?	
T. Nov		Gap		IVb	IVa?	
T. el-Ashʿari	←Uncertain→		←Moon/storm-god stele→			
T. ʿAshtara	←I-II/IV-II→		←I-I/IV-I/C-1→			
Sheikh Saʿad		←Uncertain→			Lion Orthostate	
T. Irbid		←Tombs→				
T. er-Rumeith		←Gap→	VIII/VII	VIIB	VI–VIB	

13.2 From Crisis to Collapse

13.2.1 The Crisis Days at the End of the Late Bronze Age

During the 13th century BCE, at least three major city-states were located in the central Levant: Kumidi in the Lebanese Beqaa, Hazor in the Hula Valley, and 'Ashtaroth in the Nuqra Plain. A fourth city-state was possibly centered at Tell Irbid, but our knowledge of the Late Bronze Age remains at this site is limited to incomplete data retrieved from the margins of the mound and from its necropolis.[1] All of these city-states were surrounded by semi-independent towns, including the cities of the Land of 'Amqi (e.g., Hasi) in the Lebanese Beqaa and the cities of the Land of Garu in the vicinity of the Yarmouk River (e.g., Zarqu). In addition, one must take into account invisible semi-nomad groups, which lived outside the cities and maintained economic and socio-political connections with the city-states,[2] and the Land of Upi, which at that time controlled large parts of southern Syria.[3]

One of the most discussed issues related to the end of the Bronze Age in the central Levant is the date of the destruction of Canaanite Hazor, probably the largest city that emerged in this region, and the historical background of this event. As described earlier, the dates suggested for the destruction range across the entire 13th century BCE. A bit later date, in the early 12th century BCE, cannot be excluded. More enigmatic is what led to the destruction of the city. Based on the biblical evidence (Jos 11:10–13), it has been argued that the Israelite tribes were responsible for the burning of Canaanite Hazor.[4] Other proposals suggested additional candidates, including the Egyptians, the Sea Peoples, rival city-states, or the local population itself. None of these suggestions have gained consensus to date. The only details agreed upon are that Canaanite Hazor was destroyed around the 13th century BCE by human agents and that there were no substantial attempts at rebuilding the metropolis after the event.

No less interesting, albeit less discussed, is the fate of 'Ashtaroth, the enemy of Hazor to the east. Based on EA 256, scholars concluded that the two cities competed for political control over the territories situated between them, including the lands around the Sea of Galilee, the Golan Heights, and probably even parts of the Yarmouk River. Indeed, the data presented in this study reinforces this picture while showing that no urban center, and very few rural settlements, existed in the area between the Hula Valley and the Nuqra Plain; it also means that the city-states of the Land of Garu should be sought elsewhere, most likely between the Yarmouk and the northern sector of the Irbid Plateau (e.g., Tell el-Fukhar).[5] To date, there are no sources that refer to Late Bronze Age 'Ashtaroth after the 14th century BCE. Still, we know that several Egyptian campaigns were directed at its periphery during the 13th century BCE:

---

[1] See Section 7.2.4.

[2] See, e.g., Rainey 2015, 18–32.

[3] Na'aman 1988, 184–185.

[4] Yadin 1972, 106–109. Beyond other issues relating to this suggestion (especially the date of the biblical accounts and the connection between material culture and ethnicity), it is possible to add that the data presented here suggest minimal contact with southern regions prior to the Iron Age IIA.

[5] For a possible exception, see Na'aman 1977, 170 (see more in Excursus A).

- At least one campaign during Seti I's reign (1300–1290 BCE), evidenced by the royal stele found at Tell esh-Shihab, located *ca.* 13.5 km to the southwest of Tell 'Ashtara and the leading candidate for the location of Yeno'am.
- One or more campaigns during Ramesses II's reign (1290–1224 BCE). Indication for these events are the royal stele found two decades ago at et-Turra, located *ca.* 18 km to the south of Tell 'Ashtara, and the Job Stone found by Gottlieb Schumacher at Sheikh Sa'ad, located *ca.* 4 km to the northeast of Tell 'Ashtara.
- At least one campaign during Merneptah's reign (1224–1214 BCE). It is evidenced by the Israel Stele and was partially directed against Yeno'am (see above).

Excavations at Tell 'Ashtara revealed some remains from the Late Bronze Age, but the limited scope of the investigation hinders any fundamental understanding of the nature of the site during the late 13th–12th centuries BCE.[6] The only clear destruction event exposed during the excavations occurred in the 11th century BCE, at least a century later.[7] In this light, it is possible that 'Ashtaroth survived the Egyptian campaigns into southern Syria.[8] The situation in the Lebanese Beqaa and Irbid Plateau is less clear. In the former, the palatial area at Tell Kamid el-Loz seems to have been abandoned, but tangible signs of a crisis do appear in some areas at the site.[9] In the latter, Tell Irbid seems to have been destroyed. Radiocarbon dates from a destruction layer exposed in its northern margin during excavations in the 1980s, as well as the ceramic assemblages found in the cult room, suggest that the event occurred around 1200 BCE, more or less in parallel to the destruction of Canaanite Hazor.

Looking at the central Levant from a long-term perspective, the Late Bronze Age events seem to mark the beginning of a decline of local political institutions. In contrast to the city-states in the Jezreel Valley (e.g., Stratum VIA at Tel Megiddo)[10] and in the Samaria Highlands (e.g., Stratum XI at Tell Balata), Tell Kamid el-Loz never regained its former status, and Tel Hazor only became a regional center again a few centuries after its destruction, and even then, on a much more limited scale.

13.2.2 New Canaan in the Central Levant?

Nearly 20 years ago, I. Finkelstein highlighted the continuous settlement activity and cultural continuity in the northern valleys following the destructions associated with the end of the Late Bronze Age and nicknamed it New Canaan (sometimes called Revived Canaan).[11] In the central Levant, a slightly different trajectory followed. However, this is not a surprise considering that Tel Hazor, one of the largest urban centers in the region, was severely destroyed and did not immediately recover. In the Iron Age I,

---

[6] See Section 6.2.5.

[7] Vogel/Waterbolk 1972, 53. For the radiocarbon results, see Appendix C.

[8] Additional disturbances in the Nuqra Plain may be hinted at by the abandonment of Busra after the Late Bronze Age. At present, no Iron Age I sherds and with only a few sherds from the Iron Age II, it is obvious that the city did not relive its heyday in the early first millennium BCE.

[9] See Section 2.2.9.

[10] Finkelstein 2003; Arie 2011, *passim*.

[11] Finkelstein 2003. For a different view, see Ben-Tor 2003.

continuous activity can be observed in all the excavated sites in the Lebanese Beqaa, especially at Tell Kamid el-Loz and Tell el-Ghassil. The only substantial change is the decline of Tell Kamid el-Loz as a regional center. Rebuilding episodes at Tell el-Ghassil, most likely one of the city-states of the Land of 'Amqi (Enishasi?), suggest, however, some continuity in the political structure in the center of the Lebanese Beqaa. Our knowledge of other nearby sites is limited, as no excavations have been conducted in the large mounds near Tell Kamid el-Loz (Tell Dalhamiya, Tell es-Sirhan, Tell Barr Elyas, or Tell Dayr Zanun). One of them likely functioned in this period as a new regional power. It is difficult to say, though, if new polities really appeared in this region or not.[12]

As for the south, it is clear that the destruction of Canaanite Hazor changed the political landscape of the Hula Valley. In contrast to the scanty remains characterizing this site in the Iron Age I, nearby settlements, such as Tel Abel Beth-Maacah and Tel Dan, exhibited strong activity during this period. This, in turn, suggests that a certain cultural continuity characterizes the region during the Late Bronze/Iron Ages transition. At this point, it is difficult to define the political organization of Tel Abel Beth-Maacah and Tel Dan in the Iron Age I, but the two sites could have constituted: 1) two neighboring city-states, 2) a single polity centered in Tel Abel Beth-Maacah (or less-likely at Tel Dan), or 3) the southern extent of a polity situated in the Lebanese Beqaa or in the northern Levant (i.e., Palastin/Walastin, probably also a less-likely scenario).[13]

The situation around the Sea of Galilee was different, as the region was only sparsely settled in the Late Bronze Age. Tel Kinrot, which was abandoned for nearly 300 years, was resettled during the Iron Age I and quickly developed into a major well-planned and fortified center with long-distance connections.[14] Excavations at all the other mounds in this region (e.g., Tel Hadar or Tel 'Ein Gev) revealed similar evidence of rapid urbanization. The formation of a dense network of sites around the Sea of Galilee during the 11th century BCE suggests that we are probably dealing with the emergence of a territorial polity that was restricted in geographical scope and time (dubbed the "Kinnereth Polity").[15] Setting its center at Tel Kinrot, the largest settlement in the region at that time, seems logical. While the recovery of the urban culture around the Sea of Galilee in the Iron Age I is generally linked to the fall of Canaanite Hazor,[16] the fact that roughly two centuries elapsed between the destruction of the latter and the rise of the Kinnereth Polity makes this direct connection unlikely. It then seems appropriate to ask, who controlled the area around the Sea of Galilee and the important highway that crossed it[17] after the 13th century BCE? Further, what stimulated the sudden rise of urban sites in this region 100–150 years later? One possible answer, admittedly not conclusive,

---

[12] For the history of the Aramaean kingdom of Beth-Rehob, see Younger 2016, 192–204.

[13] For a historical overview of the newly-reconstructed Kingdom of Palastin/Walastin, see Hawkins 2011; Weeden 2013; Galil 2014 (see also the comments in Sass 2010). As of today, the southernmost evidence for this kingdom was found in Meharde and Sheizar (Sinzar of EA 53), in the vicinity of Hama (Hawkins 2000, 415–419), *ca*. 230 km to the north of Tel Abel Beth-Maacah and Tel Dan.

[14] See Sections 4.4.2, 9.3.1, 9.3.2, and 9.3.4.

[15] Finkelstein 2013, 32; Sergi/Kleiman 2018; Kleiman 2019b.

[16] E.g., Fritz 1999, 94; Stepansky 1999, 95–96, Finkelstein 2000a; idem 2013, 32.

[17] Oded 1971; Aharoni 1979, 53; Kochavi 1998.

may be sought in the information provided in EA 256, which emphasized the rivalry between Hazor and 'Ashtaroth, as well as in the archaeological data that demonstrated the limited number of settlements between them in the Late Bronze Age as opposed to the appearance of many new settlements in the Iron Age I (especially in the Golan Heights). If 'Ashtaroth survived the events that led to the demise of Tel Hazor, one could speculate that the territorial control around the Sea of Galilee shifted at the beginning of the Iron Age I eastward. As previously mentioned, intense 13th century BCE settlement activity in the Nuqra Plain is hinted at by the recorded Egyptian campaigns to the region. In this regard, the rise of the Kinnereth Polity may reflect the fall of 'Ashtaroth.

13.2.3 The Collapse of the Urban Societies in Canaan

Despite the development of many Iron Age I settlements in the central Levant, their heyday was short, and activity at nearly all urban centers concluded with violent and total destruction (Table 45; Figure 105).[18] Multiple Iron Age I destructions identified only in Tell Kamid el-Loz, Tel Abel Beth-Maacah, and Tel Dan suggest that clashes in the Lebanese Beqaa and Hula Valley were more intense than in the southern parts of the country (e.g., the Jezreel Valley). Well-excavated urban centers in the Golan Heights, the Nuqra Plain, and the Irbid Plateau are scarce, and thus it is unsurprising that no Iron Age I destructions are known from these regions to date.

Despite the fact that Iron Age I destructions are known throughout Canaan, from the Lebanese Beqaa in the north to the Judean Shephelah in the south, very little has been written about the regional extent of the phenomenon.[19] Excavators of Iron Age I destructions usually considered them as reflecting one or more of the following scenarios: 1) David's wars against Israel's neighbors,[20] 2) Shoshenq I's campaigns,[21] 3) an earthquake,[22] or 4) the violent expansion of highlanders into the lowlands.[23]

Radiocarbon dates from various sites in the northern valleys (e.g., Tel Megiddo, Tell el-Hammeh, and Tel Hadar) show that the destruction of Iron Age I settlements extended over several decades,[24] a process that probably ended before *ca.* 950 BCE. Logically, then, single military campaigns or earthquakes should be dismissed. Perhaps the only common denominator for all Iron Age I destructions is that all of the urban centers of the period were replaced with the appearance of territorial kingdoms several decades later. Of course, some of the destructions could have been caused by conflicts between city-states, rebellion by oppressed populations, or even attacks of uprooted groups living outside of the cities. However, the systematic destruction of the urban landscape and the substantial changes introduced to the same regions in the following periods suggest that the attacks on the Iron Age I cities were not entirely arbitrary. In this light, the real

---

[18] For classification of destruction events, see Finkelstein 2009; Kreimerman 2017, 175–176.
[19] For some exceptions, see Finkelstein/Piasetzky 2007a; Yasur-Landau 2012b.
[20] Mazar 1985, 46–47; Harrison 2004, 108.
[21] Watzinger 1929; Finkelstein 2002, 120–122.
[22] Mazar 1985, 127; Thomsen/Zwickel 2011; Münger/Zangenberg/Pakkala 2011, 77.
[23] Finkelstein/Piasetzky 2007a, 256–258; Finkelstein 2013, 32–36.
[24] Finkelstein/Piasetzky 2007a, 249–256; Finkelstein/Piasetzky 2011.

question is not who destroyed the settlements but who benefited from the new situation, and in that case, the answer is clear: the elites that constituted the territorial kingdoms.

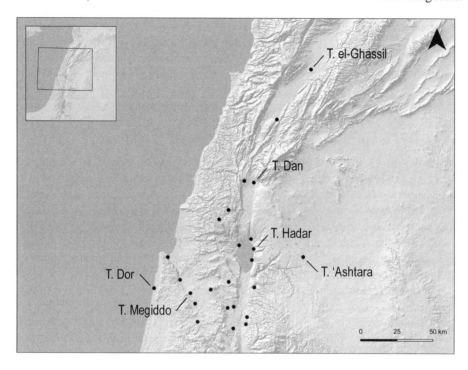

Figure 105: Iron Age I destruction layers in the central Levant and nearby regions (created with QGIS 3.16 and World Shaded Relief of Esri 2014)

Table 45: Late Iron Age I destructions in the central Levant and in nearby regions

Site/Stratum	Pottery	Radiocarbon Dates
T. el-Ghassil I/II-1	Joukowsky 1972	None
T. Kamid el-Loz 1	Marfoe 1995	None
T. Dan IVB	Ilan 2019a	Ilan 2019a
T. Abel Beth-Maacah A2	Unpublished	Unpublished
T. Kinrot V	Tynjä 2017	Fritz 1999
et-Tell/Bethsaida VI	Unpublished	Finkelstein/Piasetzky 2005; Scott *et al.* 2007; Sharon *et al.* 2007
T. Hadar IV	Kleiman 2019a	Finkelstein/Piasetzky 2005; Scott *et al.* 2007; Sharon *et al.* 2007
T. 'Ein Gev KIV	Sugimoto 2015a	Sugimoto 2015a
T. 'Ashtara	Abou Assaf 1968	Vogel/Waterbolk 1972, 53
T. Zira'a	Unpublished	Vieweger/Häser 2017
T. Abu-Kharaz	Fischer 2013	Wilde/Fischer 2013

T. Sasa	Stepansky/Segal/Carmi 1996	Stepansky/Segal/Carmi 1996
H. Avot	Braun 2015	None
T. Rekhesh	Paz et al. 2010	Unpublished
T. Yoqne'am	Zarzecki-Peleg 2005	Sharon et al. 2007
T. Megiddo VIA	Arie 2006; idem 2013b	Toffolo et al. 2014
T. Beth-Shean S-2	Panitz-Cohen 2009	None
T. el-Hammeh Lower	Cahill 2006	Sharon et al. 2007

13.3 Foreign Invasions and their Consequences

13.3.1 An Early Bird? Shoshenq I's Campaign(s) to Canaan

From the 10th century BCE on, the central Levant experienced a series of foreign invasions. In contrast to the Egyptian campaigns of the 13th century BCE, the presence of foreigners in the landscape was more visible and more permeant. Ironically, there is no evidence of Egyptian intervention in the central Levant at that time. In fact, the available data hint that the Egyptians refrain from entering this region.

Over the years, numerous scholars have dealt with Shoshenq I's list of his campaign (or campaigns) to Canaan in the second half of the 10th century BCE (mentioned in 1 Kgs 14:25).[25] Of importance for the current study is that the campaign(s) did not seem to reach beyond the Jezreel and Beth-Shean Valleys; this is evident from the absence of cities located in the central Levant on the list. Moreover, it is possible that the Shoshenq I stele at Megiddo,[26] the "capital" of the Jezreel Valley, was erected in order to commemorate the northernmost point seized by the Egyptians; this was a common practice in the Ancient Near East.[27] Egyptian inability to reach northeastern Israel and southern Syria suggests that these regions were controlled by a strong entity; a conflict with it might have put the immediate objectives of the Egyptian campaign(s) at risk (e.g., the copper trade network). This may indicate initial manifestations of statehood in southern Syria during the early first millennium BCE.[28]

13.3.2 Political Statements in the Landscape

The destruction of the late Iron Age I cities in the central Levant also led to the abandonment of nearly all the urban centers: from the Lebanese Beqaa to the Nuqra Plain. At the time of writing, the exact dating of the Iron Age II phases at Tel Abel Beth-

---

[25] See, e.g., Na'aman 1998; Finkelstein 2002; Ben-Dor Evian 2011; Schipper 2012, 35–36.

[26] D. Ussishkin (1990, 71–74) was among the first to stress the problem with the idea that Shoshenq I destroyed Stratum VIA at Tel Megiddo and then erected his stele over the ruins. He suggested, instead, that the stele was installed within a living city, that of the Iron Age IIA. His view is reinforced by a reevaluation of the finds from Ta'anach, suggesting that the site, which is mentioned in Shoshenq I's list, was not occupied during the Iron Age I (Arie 2011, 294).

[27] Na'aman 1992, n. 11; idem 1998, 265.

[28] Kleiman 2019b.

Maacah is still uncertain,[29] but the critical analysis of the Iron Age II strata at Tel Dan certainly left the site without an early Iron Age IIA phase.[30] A similar pattern characterizes the settlements around the Sea of Galilee, where no strata dated to the early Iron Age IIA were discovered.[31] The evidence from other regions (e.g., the Golan Heights, the Nuqra Plain, and the Irbid Plateau) is not sufficiently clear to determine the situation in the early Iron Age IIA.

The next phase in the history of the central Levant occurred around 900 BCE, with the construction of two fortified strongholds: one at Tel Hazor in the Hula Valley (Stratum X) and another at Tell er-Rumeith in the Irbid Plateau (Stratum VIII). It is probably not a coincidence that both Tel Hazor and Tell er-Rumeith exhibited very weak or no settlement activity during the Iron Age I, while other sites, which were prominent during this period, remained unsettled in the early and late phases of the Iron Age IIA (e.g., Tel Dan and Tel Kinrot). From a social perspective, the construction of Tel Hazor and Tell er-Rumeith, and their unique architectural reconfiguration (e.g., casemate walls and moats) are likely to represent the emergence of new elites, which were most likely supported by the monarchs of Israel and Aram-Damascus. The dominance of these new groups does not necessarily mean that the former elites, who lost their political status following the destruction of the Iron Age I settlements, disappeared from the landscape, but rather that during the late Iron Age IIA, they were no longer visible in the archaeological record. Possible evidence for their ongoing presence and for local political tension may be identified in the small-scale traumatic events observed in the stratigraphic sequences of Tel Hazor (Stratum X)[32] and Tell er-Rumeith (Stratum VIII).[33] With no well-published Iron Age II remains in the Lebanese Beqaa, the Golan Heights, or the Nuqra Plain, it is very difficult to reach any conclusions regarding the transformations carried out in these regions.

13.3.3 The Archaeology of the Days of Hazael

Hazael's reign (*ca.* 842–805 BCE) represents a turning point in the history of the Iron Age Levant. Biblical and extra-biblical sources suggest that Hazael ascended to the throne sometime before the Battle of Ramoth-gilead in *ca.* 842/841 BCE. He was most likely not the rightful heir to the throne of Damascus, although he may have belonged to a royal family.[34] Despite the rebellion, Hazael seems to have maintained the policies of his predecessor and resisted Assyrian attempts to impose their dominance over the local kingdoms in the Levant. He kept these policies even when most of Aram-Damascus's allies abandoned it and submitted to the empire. Ultimately, after the campaign(s) of 838/837 BCE, the Assyrians left southern Syria, and Aram-Damascus began exerting its political control in the Levant.

---

[29] See Section 3.2.1.
[30] See Section 3.2.2.
[31] See Section 4.2.1.
[32] See Section 3.2.6.
[33] See Section 7.2.5.
[34] Na'aman 1995a (but for a different view, see Younger 2016, 602, n. 193).

While the history of the kingdom during Hazael's reign has been discussed extensively,[35] research into the physical remains related to his rule is under-explored. The main factors leading to the exposure of his actions in the archaeological record were the down-dating of the Iron Age IIA destruction layers, which were associated previously with Shoshenq I's campaign(s), to the second half of the 9th century BCE, and especially their interpretation as the consequences of conflicts between Israel and Aram-Damascus (Table 46; Figure 106).[36] Additional support for the involvement of the Aramaeans in the southern Levant comes from the excavations at Tell es-Safi (Philistine Gath).[37] A massive destruction layer was exposed at the site, radiocarbon dated to the second half of the 9th century BCE.[38] The correlation of this destruction with Hazael's campaign to Gath (2 Kgs 12:18) is accepted by nearly all scholars.[39]

Destructions or rapid abandonments that may be associated[40] with Hazael's campaigns were found in several regions: the Hula Valley (e.g., Stratum IX at Tel Hazor and Rosh Pinna), the Lower Galilee (e.g., Stratum II/I at Horvat Rosh Zayit), the Beth-shean Valley (e.g., Stratum IV at Tel Rehov and Stratum S-1 at Tel Beth-Shean), the central Jordan Valley (e.g., Phase C at Pella), the Jezreel Valley (e.g., the Jezreel Compound, Stratum VA-IVB at Tel Megiddo, and Stratum XIV at Tel Yoqne'am), northwestern Samaria (e.g., Stratum IX at Tel Dothan), the Central Coastal Plain (e.g., Stratum A7 at Tel Aphek and Stratum XIV at Tel Michal), Philistia (e.g., Stratum A3 at Tell es-Safi and Stratum I at Tel Zayit), and maybe even in the Judean Shephelah (e.g., Stratum IV at Tel Lachish), the Beer-Sheba Valley (e.g., Tel Arad XI), and the southern coastal plain (e.g., Stratum VII at Tel Sera'). Needless to say, accepting the reconstruction of the territorial expansion of Aram-Damascus to the south does not mean that every Iron Age IIA destruction layer in the southern Levant must be attributed to Hazael's campaigns. For instance, discussing the destruction of Stratum VIIb at Tell el-Far'ah North (biblical Tirzah), I proposed that neither the dating of the event nor its abandonment mechanism really fits the pattern emerging from the analysis of other destruction

---

[35] For historical reevaluations of Hazael's reign, see Pitard 1987, 145–160; Lipiński 2000, 376–390; Kahn 2007, 70–72; Younger 2016, 591–632; idem 2020b; Frevel 2018b, 219–220; idem 2019a.

[36] Na'aman 1997, 126–127; Finkelstein 2009, 118, 121–122; Kleiman 2016.

[37] Maeir 2004; idem 2012, 26–49; idem 2020, 21–34 and earlier references therein.

[38] A deep trench found outside the settled area was interpreted as a moat dug by the Aramaeans (Maeir/Gur-Arieh 2011; Gur-Arieh/2020). For an alternative view, see Ussishkin 2007.

[39] Note that unlike Shoshenq I's campaign to Canaan, the territorial expansion of Aram-Damascus and its political supremacy in the 9th century BCE are reinforced by the inscribed items found in Eretria, Samos, and Arslan Tash (Röllig 1988; Bron/Lemaire 1989; Epha'l/Naveh 1989; Na'aman 1995a, 381–384; Hafthorsson 2006, 43–44; Hasegawa 2012, 58–62; Ghantous 2013, 65–73; Younger 2016, 627–630; Amadasi Guzzo 2019, 162–163, n. 35), the Tel Dan stele (Biran/Naveh 1993; idem 1995; Blum 2016), perhaps also by a stele fragment from Tell Afis (Amadasi Guzzo 2014), the royal annals of Shalmaneser III (Pitard 1987, 146–151; Yamada 2000) and by a few accounts in the Hebrew Bible (Hafthorsson 2006, 137–184; Hasegawa 2012; Ghantous 2013; for detailed discussion in Younger 2016, 591–632). These are several different types of sources that, more or less, corroborate each other.

[40] Note that this does not mean the Hazael's army necessarily destroyed these sites, but rather that their settlement activity was affected by the conflict (Kleiman 2016, 71), and see more below.

layers associated with Hazael's campaigns in the north.[41] Similarly, I. Finkelstein questioned whether the destruction of Stratum 4 at Kadesh Barnea (*ca.* 95 km to the southwest of Tell es-Safi), which dates to the late 9th century BCE, matches the scope of Hazael's activity in the Levant.[42]

Based on the ceramic evidence, especially the appearance of ceramic forms usually associated with Iron Age IIB contexts, the southern destructions (e.g., Stratum A7 at Tel Aphek or Stratum A3 at Tell es-Safi) seem to occur two or three decades after the northern ones (e.g., Stratum IX at Tel Hazor or Stratum VA-IVB). In my view, this occurrence points to the complex nature of Hazael's subjugation of the southern Levant, which had many different ideological and economic motives.[43] Moreover, the different destruction mechanisms of the Iron Age IIA settlements seem to reflect the diversity of the Damascene policy.[44] Most of the north-Israelite cities were partly destroyed (e.g., Stratum IX at Tel Hazor or Stratum VA-IVB at Tel Megiddo). The only northern settlements that suffered massive destruction was Tel Rehov and sites located in its surroundings (e.g., Tel Beth-Shean, Tel Amal, and Tell el-Hammeh).[45] Similar heavy destructions were identified in Tell es-Safi/Gath and its surroundings (e.g., Tel Zayit, Tel Goded, and possibly also Tel Burna). The Judahite towns and fortresses in the Judean

---

[41] Kleiman 2018. In contrast to the north-Israelite settlements located in the northern valleys (e.g., Tel Megiddo, Tel Rehov, and Tel Hazor), no destruction between Building Periods 1 and 2 was identified during the excavations at Samaria (see, e.g., Franklin 2004). In this light, a risky Damascene campaign into the Samaria Highlands – only to destroy Tirzah – is less probable. Instead, it is more reasonable to consider the destruction of the city within its regional context as the possible result of internal political conflicts between the highlanders themselves. Potential evidence for the tension between clans in the northern highlands and central authority is the rapid shifts in the locations of the capital after centuries of stability under Shechem (1 Kgs 15:21; 16:23–24), frequent political assassinations (e.g., 1 Kgs 15:27; 16:9) and even the Samaria Ostraca (Niemann 2008). For the renewed excavations at Tell el-Far'ah North, see Montero Fenollós/Caramelo 2021.

[42] Finkelstein 2010b, n. 4. For Hazael's activity in the south, see Maeir 2012, 26–49; Lehmann/Niemann 2014, 88–89; Lehmann 2019; Kleiman 2016, 64–65, 69; for a detailed reassessment of the Iron Age IIA settlements in the Negev, see Golding-Meir 2015. Regarding Judah, I already stressed in an earlier work that the Judahite settlements were not violently destroyed following Hazael's campaign, maybe indeed due to Jehoash's earlier surrender to the Aramaean king (2 Kgs 12:19). Instead, their rapid abandonment occurred shortly afterward, probably to be connected with the impact of the destruction of the Kingdom of Gath on the region (Kleiman 2016, 71).

[43] Possible support for this scenario could be found in the enigmatic addition to 2 Kgs 13:22 in the Lucianic recension of the Septuagint ("And Hazael took the foreigner from his hand from the sea of the evening to Aphek"). It provides possible additional evidence for the correlation of the destruction of Aphek in the Sharon with Hazael's campaigns against the Kingdom of Israel and, moreover, with Jehoahaz's reign (Lipiński 2000, 386; Kleiman 2015, 227–228; Frevel 2018a, 219). In the last years, however, the corrupted nature of the verse was discussed in detail by both M. Richelle (2010) and S. Hasegawa (2014), who subsequently questioned its conventional interpretation.

[44] Kleiman 2016, 65–69. See also Frevel 2018b; idem 2019a.

[45] Based on his excavations at Tel Rehov, A. Mazar (2016, 110) proposed that the violent destruction of Stratum IV was the result of the site being Jehu's hometown (or the territory of his family or clan). Apart from the exceptional prosperity of the city in the 10th and 9th centuries BCE, he noted the occurrence of the name Nimshi in several inscriptions discovered in the Beth-Shean Valley (two at Tel Rehov and another one at Tel Amal). In the Hebrew Bible, Nimshi is presented as the father of Jehu (1 Kgs 19:16; 2 Kgs 9:20; 2 Chr 22:7) and in other places as his grandfather (2 Kgs 9:2,14).

Shephelah (e.g., Tel Lachish) and the Negev (e.g., Tel Arad), in contrast, were abandoned rapidly at the end of the Iron Age IIA and not destroyed.

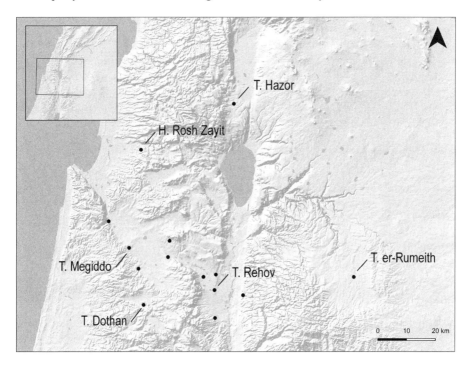

Figure 106: Iron Age IIA destructions/rapid abandonment events in the central Levant and nearby regions (created with QGIS 3.16 and World Shaded Relief of Esri 2014)

It would be a mistake, however, to limit Hazael's actions to violent events. In fact, the archaeological record from the central Levant shows that major developments occurred in this region during the last third of the 9th century BCE. Among these changes are the construction of at least two fortified royal cities in the Hula Valley (Stratum IVA at Tel Dan and Stratum VIII at Tel Hazor),[46] the establishment of a new polity around the Sea of Galilee, and even the spread of sophisticated monumental artwork and literacy.[47] In this respect, the regions discussed here present substantial differences from other territories in the Levant, which suffered an apparent decline during Hazael's reign.[48]

---

[46] See Sections 3.2.2 and 3.2.6.

[47] See Sections 12.2.1 and 12.3.2.

[48] Excavations carried out at Tel Megiddo suggest an occupational gap following the partial destruction of Stratum VA-IVB; Finkelstein/Zimhoni/Kafri 2000, 319; Kleiman 2022a, 940, 947–948. A single possible exception to this rule is Level K-2a in the southeastern sector of the site (Arie 2013a, 741–742). Other settlements that suffered a noticeable decline in this region are Tel Yoqneʻam (Stratum XIII), Tel Jezreel (post-Jezreel Compound phase), and Tel Taʻanach (Stratum III).

Table 46: Late Iron Age IIA destructions in the central Levant and nearby regions

Site/Stratum	Pottery	Radiocarbon
T. Hazor IX	Ben-Tor/Ben-Ami/Sandhaus 2012	Sharon *et al.* 2007
Rosh Pinna	Stepansky 2019	Stepansky 2019
T. er-Rumeith VIIB	Barako 2015b	Crane/Griffin 1972
H. Rosh Zayit I	Gal/Alexandre 2012	Sharon *et al.* 2007
T. Beth-Shean S-1	Mazar 2006a	None
T. Amal IV	Levy/Edelstein 1972	None
T. Rehov IV	Panitz-Cohen 2016	Mazar *et al.* 2005
Pella C	Edwards *et al.* 1990	Unpublished
T. el-Hammeh Upper	Cahill 2006	Sharon *et al.* 2007
T. Megiddo VA-IVB	Arie 2013a	Toffolo *et al.* 2014
T. Yoqne'am XIV	Zarzecki-Peleg/Cohen-Anidjar/Ben-Tor 2005	Sharon *et al.* 2007
T. Ta'anach IIA	Rast 1978	None
T. Dothan IX	Master *et al.* 2005	Master *et al.* 2005

13.4 Shifting Alliances

13.4.1 The Rise and Fall of the Kingdom of Geshur[49]

The Kingdom of Geshur is a remarkable example of a small polity that emerged and quickly disappeared in the central Levant. And yet, many details concerning this kingdom are debated.[50] In the Hebrew Bible, Geshur is mentioned in several texts (e.g., 2 Sam 3:3; 13:37–8; 14:32; 15:8), which situate the kingdom within the political and cultural sphere of Aram-Damascus (2 Sam 15:8).[51] Further evidence of the "Aramaean" classification of this kingdom comes from W.F. Albright's proposal to understand *gtr* mentioned in the Table of Nations (Gen 10:23) as an original Aramaic variant of the name of Geshur.[52] The name of this kingdom generally does not appear in extra-biblical texts[53] Conventionally, and despite the limited sources, scholars locate the territory of the Kingdom of Geshur around the Sea of Galilee and the Golan Heights.[54] Most agree that the monumental remains found at et-Tell/Bethsaida indicate that it functioned as

---

[49] Parts of the ideas expressed here were developed by the author together with O. Sergi.

[50] For previous discussions relating to the history of the Kingdom of Geshur, see Pakkala 2010; idem 2013; Na'aman 2012; Arav 2013; idem 2018; Sergi/Kleiman 2018; Frevel 2018a, 215–216.

[51] For the biblical narratives, see Sergi/Kleiman 2018, 10–13 with earlier references.

[52] Albright 1956, 12; Na'aman 2012, 89.

[53] For the problematic reconstruction of the name ga-[šu]-ru in EA 256, see Excursus A. Another attempt to identify the name Geshur was proposed based on an analysis of the inscriptions of Shalmaneser III's 838 BCE campaign against Aram-Damascus (Na'aman 2002b, 205–207).

[54] E.g., Kochavi 1989; Lipiński 2000, 335–336; Na'aman 2002b, 206–207; idem 2012; Arav 2013; idem 2018; Younger 2016, 204–213.

the capital of the kingdom from the early 10th century to the second half of the 9th century BCE, when it was annexed by Aram-Damascus.[55]

A few years ago, O. Sergi and I discussed the archaeology and history of the Sea of Galilee, challenged the conventional dates of key layers, and emphasized the occupational gap of all the settlements located around the Sea of Galilee during both the early and late phases of the Iron Age IIA, i.e., the ceramic horizons of Strata VB and VA-IVB at Tel Megiddo.[56] We suggested, then, an alternative scenario where the kingdom of Geshur emerged only following Hazael's occupation of the southern Levant in the late 9th century BCE. In our view, his political rule over this region was not direct but rather carried out in the form of patron-client relations. When the historical circumstances changed, the local leaders – the king of Geshur among them – shifted loyalties. Following the complete analysis of the ceramic data from Tel Hadar, some modifications in our historical reconstruction are needed.[57] During the work, I noticed that the ceramic assemblages originating from the (partial) destruction of Tel Hadar, as well as the assemblage from the more considerable destruction of et-Tell/Bethsaida, are not precisely parallel to those exposed within the destruction of Stratum V at Tel Hazor (e.g., they lack typical ceramic forms such as torpedo storage jars). Moreover, cooking jugs which do not usually appear in Iron Age IIB destruction layers in northern Israel, appear in the et-Tell/Bethsaida and Tel Hadar assemblages.[58] A similar conclusion was reached independently by D. Ilan.[59] In other words, sites located around the Sea of Galilee were partially destroyed at the very end of the Iron Age IIA or in the early days of the Iron Age IIB (*ca.* 800 BCE), hinting that the ruler of the Kingdom of Geshur did not acquiesce willingly during the renewed territorial expansion of the north-Israelite kings.

13.4.2 The Days of Joash and Jeroboam II

During the early 8th century BCE, the Northern Kingdom enjoyed a second period of prosperity and territorial expansion.[60] Royal endeavors to promote the kingdom's economy and control over a more extensive territory can be seen in the renovation of key cities, the establishment of the horse industry at Tel Megiddo,[61] the foundation of a fortified seaport at Tel Dor,[62] the construction of a royal trading outpost at Kuntillet ʿAjrud in Sinai,[63] and the development of olive oil industry in the Samaria Highlands.[64] The

---

[55] E.g., Na'aman 2012, 94–95; Arav 2013; idem 2018; Mazar 2014, 368; Sergi and Kleiman 2018, 5–7; Frevel 2018, 215. J. Pakkala (2010) contested the standard reconstruction and noted that the available sources do not allow us to locate this kingdom at all; he did agree, however, that such a kingdom had existed in the early first millennium BCE (see also idem 2013).
[56] Sergi/Kleiman 2018; Kleiman 2019b.
[57] See Section 4.2.3.
[58] See Section 9.2.2.
[59] Ilan 2019b, 127–129.
[60] For the paucity of historical data from the 8th century BCE, see Section 1.3.4.
[61] Cantrell/Finkelstein 2006.
[62] Gilboa/Sharon/Bloch-Smith 2015.
[63] For the excavations at Kuntillet ʿAjrud, see Meshel 2012.
[64] Eitam 1979; idem 1983; Finkelstein 2013, 132.

recovery of Israel at that time, at the expense of Aram-Damascus, is also mentioned in several biblical accounts (e.g., 2 Kgs 13:14–19, 25; 14:23–24; Amos 6:13).[65]

Despite the great advances of the north-Israelite kingdom at the time, the archaeological visibility of its renewed expansion into the central Levant is only rarely acknowledged.[66] While scholars emphasized the rhetorical character of some biblical narratives related to the campaigns against Aram-Damascus, as well as their confusing style and the late date of composition (e.g., 2 Kgs 13:14–19, 25),[67] it is still hardly possible that Joash and Jeroboam II achieved their unprecedented territorial expansion peacefully. Understanding the abandonment mechanism of archaeological layers dated to the late 9th/early 8th century BCE (e.g., Stratum IVA at Tel Dan, Stratum VIII at Tel Hazor, and Stratum III at Tel Hadar) is essential for this matter. Indeed, except for the destruction of Stratum V at et-Tell/Bethsaida, no wholesale destructions were observed at the end of the 9th/early 8th century BCE. However, this does not mean that the sites in question continued to prosper without disturbance until the Assyrian campaigns of the late 8th century BCE. At Tel Dan, for instance, the end of Stratum IVA is marked by a forced evacuation of a neighborhood in Area T (see, e.g., Isa 22:10), which resulted in the exposure of more than 40 complete vessels associated with signs of a conflagration below the "yellow floor" assigned to Stratum III.[68] A. Biran interpreted the evidence as indicating a traumatic event and attributed it to Ben-Hadad I's campaign. In view of E. Arie's re-dating of this stratum, it is more likely that Joash or Jeroboam II were responsible for the end of Stratum IVA at Tel Dan,[69] for the shattering of the royal stele stood at the entrance to the city,[70] and for the transformation of Area T into a royal enclosure.[71]

At the end of Stratum VIII at Tel Hazor, which coexisted with Stratum IVA at Tel Dan, a peaceful transition was observed.[72] During the new excavations, for instance, no clear sign of destruction was observed at the end of this stratum,[73] and complete or restorable vessels were infrequent, comprising only ca. 10% of all the published items. Only one substantial change occurred at the end of Stratum VIII: the volute capitals adorning the corridor leading to Citadel 3090 were removed from their original location and were integrated into a poorly-built structure assigned to Stratum VII.[74]

The situation around the Sea of Galilee was different. As mentioned above, the ceramic assemblages of several sites in this region (e.g., Stratum V at et-Tell/Bethsaida, Stratum III at Tel Hadar, and Stratum MIII at Tel 'Ein Gev) should be dated to the very end of the Iron Age IIA rather than to the Iron Age IIB. Put it differently, these strata are contemporaries of Stratum VIII at Tel Hazor and not Stratum V (conventionally

---

[65] Finkelstein 2013, 129–140; Younger 2016, 635–636.
[66] Finkelstein/Piasetzky 2007b, 272; Finkelstein/Lipschits/Sergi 2013, 19–20.
[67] Miller 1966; Richelle 2010; Hasegawa 2012, 80–82, 107–115; Younger 2016, 636.
[68] Biran 1994, 166–168, 181–183, figs. 129–131; Arie 2008, figs. 9–13.
[69] See Section 3.2.2.
[70] See Section 13.3.2.
[71] See Sections 8.2.1 and 12.3.2. This scenario corresponds to A. Berlejung's (2009) attribution of the construction of the shrine to Jeroboam II in the early 8th century BCE.
[72] Yadin 1972, 179.
[73] Ben-Tor/Ben-Ami/Sandhaus 2012, 154. See discussion in Section 3.2.5.
[74] See Section 10.2.1 and Kleiman 2021.

assigned to Tiglath-Pileser III's campaigns against Israel and Aram-Damascus in 732 BCE).[75] This means that in contrast to previous reconstructions,[76] the towns around the Sea of Galilee were destroyed (some of them only partially) in the late 9th/early 8th century BCE. The fortified settlement at et-Tell/Bethsaida, almost certainly the local capital, was demolished and abandoned,[77] while peripheral settlements and strongholds like Tel Hadar and Tel 'Ein Gev were rapidly abandoned (or partially destroyed). After the destruction, only sporadic and short-lived occupations were recorded in the destroyed towns (e.g., Stratum II/I at Tel Hadar and Stratum MII/KII at Tel 'Ein Gev).[78] Apparently, the renewed expansion of the Kingdom of Israel into the central Levant in the days of Joash and Jeroboam II was not a homogenous process. Settlements were thoroughly destroyed (e.g., Stratum V at et-Tell/Bethsaida), partially ruined (e.g., Stratum IVA at Tel Dan), and rapidly abandoned (e.g., Stratum III at Tel Hadar), or even remained unscathed (e.g., Stratum VIII at Tel Hazor). The multifaceted expression of the transition to the Iron Age IIB in the research area should be understood as a reflection of the diversity of the political institutions, which struggled between their loyalty to Aram-Damascus and the threat of the Northern Kingdom.[79]

In regard to other regions discussed in this study, it must be admitted that currently, we have very few clues for settlement activity in the Lebanese Beqaa in the Iron Age IIB (including whether or not Israel extended its political rule into this region as suggested, for instance, by 2 Kgs 14:25), but this is the result of the limited archaeological research in this region, specifically at the sites of Tell Qasr Labwa, Tell Dalhamiya, Tell es-Sirhan, Tell Barr Elyas, and Tell Dayr Zanun.[80] In the Irbid Plateau, the excavations of Tell er-Rumeith[81] demonstrated that the site was destroyed in the late 9th/early 8th century BCE. In theory, this could have happened during the north-Israelite occupation of the region, which would mean that the later reoccupation of the plateau by Aram-Damascus was not associated with destruction or that the last destruction of the site should be associated with a Damascene attack rather than the result of Tiglath-Pileser III's campaign against Aram-Damascus.

Following the death of Jeroboam II (*ca.* 747 BCE), the political supremacy of the Northern Kingdom began deteriorating.[82] In the Hebrew Bible, this period is vividly illustrated by a series of rebellions and, specifically, the inability of the new kings to establish stable dynasties (2 Kgs 15:10, 14, 16, 25, 30).[83] In such a chaotic reality, it is appropriate to ask whether the Kingdom of Israel was able to control efficiently all the territories conquered by Jeroboam II, encompassing the area between the Lebanese Beqaa in the north (e.g., Labwa) and the desert in the south (e.g., Kuntillet 'Ajrud or Etzion-

---

[75] E.g., Yadin 1972, 115, 198; Ben-Tor/Ben-Ami/Sandhaus 2012, 2–3.

[76] E.g., Arav 2009b; idem 2013, 26; Zwickel 2019, 298.

[77] See Section 4.2.1.

[78] See Sections 4.2.3 and 4.2.6.

[79] For a similar case in the Judean Shephelah, see Maeir/Shai 2016.

[80] See Sections 2.2.2, 2.2.7, and 2.2.8.

[81] See Section 7.2.5.

[82] For the last days of the Northern Kingdom, see Hasegawa/Levin/Radner 2019.

[83] Nevertheless, it is certainly possible that the biblical authors intensified the described events for ideological reasons (Frevel 2019b).

Geber).⁸⁴ This question is interesting in particular in the case of the central Levant, since 2 Kgs 15:29 is usually considered an authentic remark that reflects Tiglath-Pileser III's campaigns in 732 BCE against Israelite cities in the north (Ijon, Abel Beth-Maacah, Janoah, Kadesh, and Hazor).⁸⁵

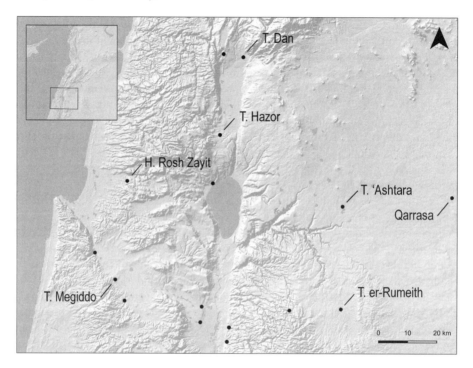

Figure 107: Iron Age IIB destructions in the central Levant and nearby regions (created with QGIS 3.16 and World Shaded Relief of Esri 2014)

Indeed, over the years, scholars have usually assumed that most of the territories conquered by Israel from Aram-Damascus in the early 8th century BCE, especially the Hula Valley and the Irbid Plateau, remained in north-Israelite hands until the fall of Samaria.⁸⁶ A different view on this matter was presented about 25 years ago by N. Na'aman, who discussed the implications of two summary inscriptions from the days of Tiglath-Pileser III.⁸⁷ In contrast to the past views, he proposed that Rezin of Damascus conquered the Gilead before the Assyrian campaigns of 732 BCE (Table 47; Figure 107) and postulated

---

⁸⁴ For the excavations at Kuntillet 'Ajrud, see Meshel 2012. Ezion-Geber is identified Tell el-Kheleifeh. For a reevaluation of the old excavations carried out at the site by N. Glueck, see Pratico 1985; more recently, Finkelstein 2014b.

⁸⁵ See exegetical comments in Frevel 2019b, 329–330, 333 (particularly on the inclusion of the Gilead in the list). For an alternative view regarding the north-Israelite control in the northern valleys in the late 8th century BCE, see, e.g., Irvine 1994.

⁸⁶ Ben-Tor 2016, 166; Thareani 2016b, 257–258; Yahalom-Mack/Panitz-Cohen/Mullins 2018.

⁸⁷ Na'aman 1995b. For the inscriptions, see Tadmor/Yamada 2011, 105–107.

that the decline of Israel already began towards the end of Jeroboam II's reign. In theory, a similar scenario can also be considered for the Marj 'Ayyun and the Hula Valley.[88]

Table 47: Iron Age IIB destructions in the central Levant and nearby regions

Site/Stratum	Pottery	Radiocarbon
T. Dan II	Thareani 2016b; idem 2018	A flat section in the calibration curve ("Hallstatt Plateau"). No accuracy can be reached between ca. 750–400 BCE.
T. Hazor V	Ben-Tor/Ben-Ami/Sandhaus 2012	
T. Kinrot II	Fritz 1990	
H. Rosh Zayit	Gal/Alexandre 2000	
T. 'Ashtara	Abou Assaf 1968; idem 1969	
Qarrasa	Rohmer 2020	
T. er-Rumeith VIB	Barako 2015b	
T. Johfiyeh Village	Lamprichs 2007	
Pella B	Edwards *et al.* 1990	
T. Abu Kharaz XIV	Fischer 2013	
T. Beth-Shean P-7	Mazar 2006a	
T. Rehov III	Mazar/Panitz-Cohen 2020	
T. Ta'anach V?	Rast 1978	
T. Megiddo IVA	Kleiman 2022a	
T. Yoqne'am XII	Zarzecki-Peleg/Cohen-Anidjar/Ben-Tor 2005	

13.4.3 What Happened after 732 BCE?

More than 300 Iron Age sites were documented in the regions discussed in this study, about half are small and rural settlements, while others are large mounds.

Currently, the common opinion is that the fall of Samaria and Damascus in the second half of the 8th century BCE was a watershed in the settlement history of the central Levant and that the rural hinterland in the central Levant was largely abandoned in this period.[89] This view is primarily based on the absence of Iron Age IIC pottery in many of the surveyed villages and on the assumption that the ceramic traditions of the Iron Age IIB in the north disappeared in 732 BCE (or slightly thereafter). Both assertions, however, need reexamination. First, it is clear that the distinction between Iron Age IIB and Iron Age IIC sherds can be deceiving as some ceramic forms were used in both periods (e.g., carinated bowls, torpedo storage jars, and decanters).[90] This is especially true when considering the small number of sherds discovered in many of the surveyed sites. Second, the idea that all the local workshops in the central Levant stopped producing certain ceramic forms following the destruction of some of the urban centers (e.g., Stratum V at Tel Hazor) is irrational. For instance, in the Judean Shephelah, the

---

[88] I am grateful to A. Fantalkin for drawing my attention to the ambiguity surrounding the days of Rezin. We intend to deal with this issue in detail elsewhere. Note that the Assyrian annals suggest that the Lower Galilee remained in north-Israelite hands (Tadmor/Yamada 2011, 61–63).

[89] Hartal 1989, 123; idem 2014, 83; Gal 2009; Faust 2015, 768–770, 776; idem 2021, *passim*.

[90] Singer-Avitz 2014, Table 1. In my view, also the distinction between the ceramic forms of the Iron Age IIA and Iron Age IIB is not always easy, specifically in small sherd collections.

ceramic industry maintained its activity through the violent events associated with the Late Bronze Age/Iron Age I transition.[91] Many scholars have also noted that the Iron Age IIB ceramic traditions did not necessarily disappear with the 701 BCE destruction of the administrative centers of the Kingdom of Judah (e.g., Stratum III at Tel Lachish), that the transition to the ceramic traditions of the Iron Age IIC was gradual, and that it occurred sometime in the early 7th century BCE.[92]

In principle, the rural settlements in the central Levant could have survived until some point in the 7th century BCE (if not until the Neo-Babylonian period). Further support for this scenario is the continuous activity in many of the large mounds of the region during the Assyrian period (Table 48).[93] Even in the Nuqra Plain, no large-scale changes occurred, as following the destruction of Tell 'Ashtara, the regional center moved to the nearby settlement of Sheikh Sa'ad.[94]

Table 48: Regional centers in the central Levant in the Iron Age

Region	Iron Age I	Iron Age IIA/B	Iron Age IIC
Hula Valley	T. Abel Beth-Maacah?	T. Hazor	Ayyelet haShahar (near T. Hazor)
Sea of Galilee	T. Kinrot	et-Tell/Bethsaida	T. Kinrot
Nuqra Plain	T. 'Ashtara?	T. 'Ashtara	Sheikh Sa'ad

Note: The situation in the Lebanese Beqaa and Irbid Plateau in the Iron Age II is unclear.

13.5 The Long-Term Perspective

13.5.1 Demographic Changes

Based on a calculation of the total built-up area in each period, as reflected in settlements sizes, it is possible to estimate roughly the demographic changes that occurred in the central Levant from the end of the Late Bronze Age to the Iron Age II, or in other words, before and after the emergence of the territorial kingdoms of Israel and Aram-Damascus (Table 49).[95] Based on the available data, we can conclude that most of the regions discussed in this study exhibited moderate demographic changes throughout the period.

---

[91] For a comprehensive discussion of the changes in the ceramic industries of the Judean Shephelah in the transition between the Late Bronze and Iron Ages, see S. Kleiman 2021.

[92] E.g., Finkelstein 2012.

[93] Thareani 2016b (Tel Dan); Fritz 1990 (Tel Kinrot); Kletter/Zwickel 2006 (Ayyelet haShahar).

[94] On the Assyrian policy in the Hula Valley, see Faust 2015, 768–769, 775–780; idem 2021; Thareani 2016b; idem 2018; idem 2019c. Nonetheless, and as mentioned above, the available archaeological evidence suggests less dramatic changes in the central Levant.

[95] See, e.g., Stager 1985; Broshi/Finkelstein 1992; Bunimovitz 1994. While the methodological challenges standing in the way of demographic reconstructions of past societies have been frequently highlighted over the years (e.g., Geva 2014, 131–134 with references to earlier studies), I have chosen to present the numbers as they are, without further manipulations. A single exception to this rule is the addition of the lower city of Tel Hazor, which was the home of *ca.* 15,000 people in the Middle and

Notable trends were observed in the settlement systems of the Lebanese Beqaa, which reached a zenith in the Iron Age I, and of the Golan Heights, which recovered impressively after a depression lasting most of the Late Bronze Age. In the Hula Valley, the settlement system declined in the Iron Age I, but this is almost certainly the result of the destruction of Canaanite Hazor and especially the abandonment of its lower city. Some of its former residents must have found refuge in nearby regions such as the Galilee Mountains, the Lebanese Beqaa, and the Golan Heights (and probably also in the newly-established urban centers of Tel Abel Beth-Maacah and Tel Kinrot).[96] All three regions indeed show a population increase in the Iron Age I.[97] In the following period, the Iron Age II, the settlement system in the Hula Valley recovered, and the overall population size in this period was very similar to the one observed during the Middle and Late Bronze Ages.[98] Another significant settlement drop occurred in the Nuqra Plain during the Iron Age I. Considering that this region is ecologically sensitive, specifically in the rate of annual rainfall (*ca.* 250 mm), environmental reasons for the observed decline are not out of the question, especially when bearing in mind that the "dry event" of the late second millennium BCE was indeed assumed to affect such zones.[99] However, in this case, too, the settlement system already recovered in the following period.[100] In contrast to the regions mentioned above, the Sea of Galilee and Irbid Plateau exhibited remarkable demographic stability throughout the Late Bronze and Iron Ages.

Table 49: Demographic changes in the Late Bronze and Iron Ages.

Region	Middle Bronze Age I/II		Late Bronze Age I/II		Iron Age I		Iron Age II	
	Built-up area	Settled population	Built-up area	Settled population	Built-up area	Settled population	Built-up area	Settled population
Lebanese Beqaa	150	37,500	120	30,000 20%↓	150	37,500 25%↑	115	28,750 25%↓
Hula Valley	70	30,000	50	27,500 8%↓	80	20,000 27.5%↓	100	25,000 25%↑
Sea of Galilee	10	2,500	25	6,250 150%↑	30	7,500 20%↑	30	7,500 no change

Late Bronze Ages, to the calculation. Needless to say, the numbers discussed above represent only a rough estimation of the demographic changes that occurred in the central Levant.

[96] Fritz 1999, 94. See also Stepansky 1999, 95–96; Gadot 2017, 108; Kleiman 2019b, 298–300.

[97] For the Galilee Mountains, which were not discussed here, see Frankel *et al.* 2001.

[98] Past studies (e.g., Broshi/Finkelstein 1992, 50, Table 1) state lower numbers for the population size of the Hula Valley in the Iron Age II (*ca.* 18,750 people). I believe that the reason for this discrepancy is the progress in the field research of the valley in the last three decades, which naturally resulted in the discovery of many more new settlements (e.g., Stepansky 1999; idem 2014).

[99] See, e.g., Langgut/Finkelstein/Litt 2013, 164.

[100] A word of caution is needed regarding the observed changes in the Nuqra Plain. Large territories in this region remained *terra incognita* from an archaeological perspective (see especially Rohmer 2020, 27–28, pl. II), and thus the information at hand may not be representative after all.

Golan Heights	50	12,500	25	6,250 50%↓	55	13,750 120%↑	70	17,500 30%↑
Nuqra Plain	70	17,500	70	17,500 no change	20	5,000 70%↓	65	16,250 225%↑
Irbid Plateau	25	6,250	35	8,750 40%↑	40	10,000 15%↑	40	10,000 no change

Note: All the numbers appearing in this table were rounded to avoid giving a false impression of accuracy. In the calculation process, I used the average size categories specified in Appendix A and a density coefficient of 250 people per hectare (following Broshi/Finkelstein 1992).

Needless to say, these data should not facilitate any argument regarding settlement continuity in the central Levant, as the excavation results (see, e.g., the transition between Strata IV and III at Tel Hadar)[101] shows that the opposite is true – many sites in the discussed regions suffered occupational gaps of 100–150 years, especially in the Iron Age IIA. Nevertheless, it is possible to cautiously suggest that the overall number of settled populations in the central Levant was more or less stable and that the region did not experience major positive or negative migration waves that could influence its social structures and cultural traditions drastically.

13.5.2 Economic Aspects

The collapse of many of the Bronze Age city-states in the central Levant towards the end of the 13th century BCE, especially Kumidi and Hazor,[102] naturally led to a fundamental change in the economic organization of the surviving settlements through time.[103] Particularly apparent is the gathering of agricultural commodities in subterranean installations such as silos (i.e., stone-lined pits) and simple pits in the Iron Age I.[104] Conventionally, scholars have interpreted these pits against the background of the subsistence economy of the local inhabitants.[105] D. Ilan, who examined this phenomenon in detail at Tel Dan and other sites in the Hula Valley (e.g., Tel Tannim and Tel Hazor),[106] suggested that the construction of pits and silos in this period may reflect regional insecurity and complicated relations with a central authority (see, e.g., 2 Sam 17:18–19; Jer

---

[101] See Section 4.2.3.

[102] See Section 13.2.1.

[103] Note that most of the data concerning economic aspects originate from the settlements of the Hula Valley and the Sea of Galilee and is more limited to other regions discussed in this study.

[104] Most of the Iron Age I silos were discovered in the Hula Valley, but this is probably the result of our insufficient information concerning the other regions discussed here. For several silos discovered in Tel Hadar, see Kleiman 2019a, 70, 85, Plans 4–5, 20.

[105] E.g., Finkelstein 1988, 264–269; Ilan 1999, 617–621. According to this view, stone-lined pits were used for bulk storage, while the simple ones, like those found at Hazor, were used for storage of goods in ceramic containers such as storage jars (Gadot 2009, 100). Note that the pits exposed in Stratum XII/XI have unique characteristics (see detailed description in Ben-Tor/Ben-Ami/Sandhaus 2012, 18–20; Ben-Ami 2013, 101) and may actually be understood as evidence of ancient looting of the remains of the Late Bronze Age settlement following the destruction (Kleiman 2022b, 32–34).

[106] See Sections 3.2.2, 3.2.3, and 3.2.6.

41:7–8).¹⁰⁷ The fact that Tel Dan and other nearby sites in the central Levant (e.g., Tell Kamid el-Loz, Tel Abel Beth-Maacah, and Tel Tannim) were destroyed at least twice in the Iron Age I may indeed support his suggestion.¹⁰⁸ In any case, in the later days of the Iron Age I, many of the local sites, particularly Tel Abel Beth-Maacah and Tel Kinrot,¹⁰⁹ recovered and, with them, the local economy and cross-regional trade (although some long-distance imports are known earlier in the period).¹¹⁰ Excavations at several settlements across the central Levant revealed evidence of trade relations with the west, mainly reflected in the importation of pottery that was produced on the Phoenician coast (e.g., wavy-band pithoi or Phoenician Bichrome Ware), as also confirmed by the petrographic research of rich ceramic assemblages unearthed at Tel Kinrot and Tel Hadar.¹¹¹ Noteworthy, of course, is the exposure of the rare protogeometric vessel at Tel Hadar, which was produced in Euboea in Greece and most likely made its way to the east, maybe to southern Syria.¹¹² The massive quantities of grains exposed at the site¹¹³ suggest that western products may have been exchanged for agricultural products, presumably grown in the Golan Heights. The reconstruction of a central east-to-west commercial route in the central Levant should not surprise us, as this was most likely the economic incentive from the very beginning for the settlement of populations in the limited available territories around the Sea of Galilee (Figure 108).¹¹⁴

In the Iron Age IIA, the economic organization of the local populations in the central Levant underwent another radical change, and again, this followed the destruction of prominent urban centers. Our information on this period, as already mentioned several times, derives mainly from two key settlements: Tel Hazor (Strata X–IX) and Tell er-Rumeith (Strata VIII–VII).¹¹⁵ Both seem to function as isolated, fortified strongholds built on the ruins or in the vicinity of prominent Bronze Age city-states and were not strictly urban centers (notwithstanding the residential quarters exposed at Tel Hazor).¹¹⁶ Only a few vessels were sampled for petrography from the rich ceramic assemblages exposed in Strata X and IX at Tel Hazor,¹¹⁷ but those that were examined indicate a clear connection to the highlands for the first time; this evidence reinforces what seems to be a scholarly consensus regarding the control of the Northern Kingdom over the Hula Valley at that time. Additionally, one can note exceptional quantities of imported wares at the site in this period, including Cypriot and Phoenician vessels,¹¹⁸ hinting at the renewal of the trade (and social) relations between the local settlements and one or more of the Phoenician city-states. Lastly, it is possible to note that the abandonment of most

---

¹⁰⁷ Ilan 2008; idem 2019a, 597–598. See also Kleiman forthcoming.
¹⁰⁸ See Sections 2.2.9, 3.2.2, and 3.2.3.
¹⁰⁹ See Sections 3.2.1 and 4.2.2.
¹¹⁰ See Section 9.3.3.
¹¹¹ See Sections 9.2.4 and 9.3.1.
¹¹² See Section 9.3.4.
¹¹³ See Section 4.2.3.
¹¹⁴ See also Section 13.2.2.
¹¹⁵ See Sections 3.2.6 and 7.2.5.
¹¹⁶ See Section 8.4.3.
¹¹⁷ Aznar 2005, 221, 273–274.
¹¹⁸ See Sections 9.3.1 and 9.3.3.

of the traditional settlements in the central Levant during most of the Iron Age IIA (e.g., Tell Kamid el-Loz, Tel Dan, and Tel Kinrot) probably reflects changes in the subsistence economy of many of the local populations, many of whom may have kept living in the vicinity of the abandoned mounds but remained archaeologically invisible. From the end of the period and until the collapse of Israel and Aram-Damascus in the late 8th century BCE, it is possible to observe the recovery of many of the local settlements, for instance, Tel Dan (Stratum IVA), Tel Hazor (Stratum VIII), and several sites around the Sea of Galilee (e.g., Stratum V at et-Tell/Bethsaida, Stratum III at Tel Hadar, and Stratum MIII at Tel 'Ein Gev). In contrast to the situation in the Iron Age I, this time, the economic engine of the Sea of Galilee was most likely situated at et-Tell/Bethsaida rather than in Tel Kinrot; this change was probably not incidental and may reflect the shifting orientation towards Aram-Damascus, as well as the existence of intensive settlement activity in the Hula Valley, especially at Tel Hazor.[119]

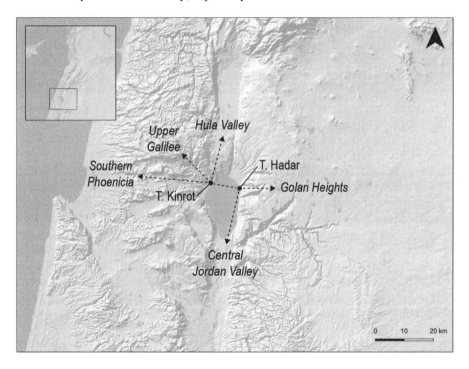

Figure 108: Cross-regional contacts in the Iron Age I in the central Levant according to the petrographic studies carried out at Tel Kinrot and Tel Hadar (created with QGIS 3.16 and World Shaded Relief of Esri 2014)

---

[119] See also Sergi/Kleiman 2018, 7–10. Note that following the destruction of Stratum V at et-Tell/Bethsaida, most likely the result of the north-Israelite re-occupation of the region (see Section 13.4.2), the regional center of the Sea of Galilee seemingly moved back to Tel Kinrot (Strata II–I).

13.5.3 Dissemination of Writing

The data presented in this study also shed light on the question of the local literacy rates and distribution of alphabetic writing. As is the case of many other regions across the Levant, the physical evidence for literacy among the central Levantine communities in the early first millennium BCE is not very impressive, notwithstanding their geographical proximity to Phoenicia (in the west) and the Beth-Shean Valley (in the south).[120] From a chronological perspective, the review of the data, particularly from Tel Hazor, has demonstrated a moderate increase in the number of epigraphic finds from the late 9th century to the second half of the 8th century BCE. Not even a single letter can be dated confidently to an earlier context.[121] In my view, this trend alludes to the contribution of Aram-Damascus in the spread of alphabetic writing in the central Levant (and thus to another positive outcome of Hazael's reign, see above). Apart from the royal inscription discovered at Tel Dan, most of the inscriptions found in the discussed regions are very brief and usually contain a personal name (e.g., zkryw), sometimes with a title (e.g., šd'l nz''), or in rare cases, the type of commodity sent to a specific individual (e.g., lpkḥ smdr).[122] There have been no ostraca found to date in the central Levant, but these are generally rare in the territories controlled by the Northern Kingdom and, naturally, also in Aram-Damascus.[123] The longest inscription in the region was found at Tel Hazor on a shoulder of a torpedo jar, which was presumably produced in Phoenicia; it may have been sent to a north-Israelite high official that resided in the city at that time.[124]

Past studies of the epigraphic evidence from the central Levant, especially from the Hula Valley and around the Sea of Galilee, have particularly emphasized the existence of Hebrew and non-Hebrew inscriptions in these regions.[125] This situation suggests that the local societies may have been multilingual, as should be expected for regions between a few influential cultural spheres.[126] That being said, one must also remember that

---

[120] See Sections 12.2 and 12.4. For the contacts with the Phoenician coast, see also Section 13.5.2.

[121] For the problematic interpretation of Sherd No. D2338, on which two Proto-Canaanite letters were ostensibly written, see Sass 2005, 55; Finkelstein/Sass 2013, n. 23. Note again that large sections of the city of Strata X–IX at Tel Hazor, generally agreed to represent the first half of the 9th century BCE (or slightly before), were exposed during the renewed excavations (see, e.g., Ben-Tor/Ben-Ami/Sandhaus 2012, plans 2.1, 2.8, 2.13, and 2.21). And still, no inscriptions were associated with either of these strata (and compare Strata V and IV at Tel Rehov, Aḥituv/Mazar 2013; idem 2014).

[122] See Sections 10.2.1 and 12.2.3.

[123] But for ostraca from Tel Beth-Shean, see Mazar 2006b. Note that such items are also unknown from the Gilead, a territory that was certainly controlled by Aram-Damascus in the 8th century BCE. To date, the only inscriptions believed to have originated from the Damascus Oasis are Hazael's Booty inscriptions (e.g., Amadasi Guzzo 2019), for which, see Section 1.3.3 with references.

[124] Yadin *et al.* 1960, pls. CLXIX, 6; CLXX, 6. See Section 12.2.2.

[125] E.g., Naveh 1989; Delavault/Lemaire 1979; Dobbs-Allsopp *et al.* 2005; Sass 2016.

[126] A. Berlejung (2019, 252–265, and especially 260–261) discussed in detail multilingualism in past societies and concluded that this phenomenon "…was not the exception, but the rule – especially in urban centers." The finds from the central Levant support her conclusion. Most importantly, she challenged the common perception which tends to correlate one language/script with one people (or political entity) as hinted, for instance, in the Aramaic (or more accurately, non-Hebrew) inscriptions found in Stratum VIII at Tel Hazor (Finkelstein 1999b, 61), the recently-exposed inscription from Tel

most of the inscriptions found in the central Levant were inscribed (or stamped) on storage jars as part of administrative activity.[127] This means that the inscriptions were written by literate elites or under their supervision, who sent products to other elites. In other words, the language used in regional or cross-regional communications should not necessarily reflect on the entire population, which must have been largely illiterate.

13.5.4 Cult-Related Activity

Evidence for official/public cult in the central Levant was relatively meager and, as always, difficult to interpret. In some cases, it was clear that the initial justification for the definition of specific central structures as temples, i.e., structures that are predominantly devoted to cult,[128] was weak from the very beginning (e.g., the so-called temple excavated at Tell el-Ghassil) or relied on earlier (biblical) preconceptions (e.g., Bamah B at Tel Dan).[129] Hitherto, the best evidence for public cult-related activity in the central Levant was identified at the city gate of et-Tell/Bethsaida, where a moon/storm god stele was found near a small platform, its original place of use.[130] Interestingly, this site also provided the most solid indication for the survival of a particular cult practice from the Iron Age I into the Iron Age IIA; this phenomenon becomes even more remarkable when considering the occupational gap that et-Tell/Bethsaida experienced in the second half of the 10th and first half of the 9th centuries BCE, indicating social continuity in this region through the Iron Age I/II transition.[131] Important as well is the fact that parallels for the figures depicted on the steles found at this site were discovered in several different regions in the central Levant: in the Golan Heights (the fortified complex near Haspin), the Nuqra Plain (Tell el-Ashʻari), Jabal el-Druz ('Awas), and the Irbid Plateau (et-Turra). These examples demonstrate that the worship of the represented deity was practiced across the central Levant rather than being limited to a single region.[132]

More common cult-related features in the central Levant were small rooms with cult paraphernalia, which were identified at Tel Dan, Tel Hazor, Tel ʻEin Gev, Tell Irbid, and maybe also Tel Hadar.[133] In most cases, these architectural units contained a modest assemblage of ceramic vessels that were seemingly used for rituals, such as chalices, goblets, tripod cups, stands, and shrine models (but the buildings in which these rooms were found could have had another function).[134] In addition, the finds from Tel Abel Beth-Maacah, Tel Dan, and Tel Hazor suggest that this cult-related activity was

---

Abel Beth-Maacah (Yahalom-Mack *et al.* 2021) and the Aramaic inscriptions discovered in several sites around the Sea of Galilee (Arav 2013, 3).

[127] Kleiman 2017, 364.

[128] As noted in Section 8.2, deciphering the function of central/monumental structures, even if highly preserved and well investigated, is not invariably easy. See also the discussions relating to the social context of cult in past societies in Koch 2020; Halbertsma/Routledge 2021 and bibliography therein.

[129] See Sections 2.2.6 and 8.2.1.

[130] Another public cult-related building was exposed near Haspin in the Golan Heights, but the analysis of the results of this excavation was not accomplished yet. See more in Section 5.2.8.

[131] See Section 4.2.1.

[132] See Section 10.4.

[133] See Sections 3.2.2, 3.2.6, 4.2.3, 4.2.3, 4.2.6, and 7.2.4.

[134] See Section 9.2.5.

frequently associated with metallurgy, a known phenomenon in the ancient Near East, with several recently-discovered examples from the Levant.[135] Other indications for the local cult practices can be deduced from the personal names documented in the central Levant, which include theophoric elements of several deities such as El or Baʻal and even a few Yahwistic names (e.g., bnyw, dlyw, and zkryw).[136] While it is indeed natural to see the latter group as indicating a connection to the Northern Kingdom, as particularly evident by the fact that some of the inscribed jars were produced in the Samaria Highlands and sent to selected settlements in the central Levant,[137] it must be remembered that a limited number of such names were also documented in central Syria (e.g., ʻAzaryau and possibly also Yau-biʼdi; see also 2 Sam 8:10).[138] Perhaps, this was the result of the north-Israelite reoccupation of the Hula Valley and the (temporary) territorial expansion into the Lebanese Beqaa in the days of Jeroboam II, which turned the Kingdom of Israel and Hamath into neighboring polities for the first time.[139]

Lastly, it can be mentioned that the burial practices identified in the central Levant – in the Hula Valley as well as in the Nuqra Plain – mostly correspond to the funerary customs observed in other regions in the southern Levant (e.g., the Jezreel Valley).[140] In this case, the absence of cremations from this region, apart from a few examples discovered near Tel Hazor (in Jazʼir), is noteworthy and clearly differentiates the funerary customs of the locals from those of Phoenicia and the northern Levant.[141]

13.5.5 A Central Levantine Cultural Sphere?

Conventional reconstructions of the archaeology and history of the Levant in the early first millennium BCE usually acknowledge the existence of three broad cultural spheres: 1) the south Levantine culture, predominantly represented by the kingdoms of Israel and Judah, and to a lesser extent also by the desert polities of Ammon, Moab, Edom,[142] 2)

---

[135] See, e.g., Yahalom-Mack/Panitz-Cohen/Mullins 2019 (Tel Abel Beth-Maacah); Ilan 2019a, 618–619, 631–632 (Tel Dan); Yahalom-Mack et al. 2014 (Tel Hazor). See also Yahalom-Mack et al. 2017 (Tel Megiddo); Workman et al. 2020 (Tell es-Safi/Gath).

[136] Note that the diverse theophoric names documented in the discussed regions should not necessarily be correlated with different social (or ethnic) groups. Perhaps the best evidence for this can be found in the admittedly much later archives of al-Yahudu (from the Persian period), which indicate the diversity of theophoric names even in the same families (Schipper 2018, 75; and see also the situation at Elephantine in idem, 82–85). We may assume, then, that the same phenomenon also occurred from time to time in the seemingly less socially-cohesive Iron Age communities of the central Levant.

[137] See Section 12.2.3.

[138] Dalley 1990; Zevit 1991, but for some reservations, see Niehr 2019, 383–385. From the biblical narrative of 2 Sam 8:3–11, we learn that Toʻiʼs son was named Joram (note that Toʻi is not necessarily a Luwian name as commonly thought, and see Lipinski 2000, 339; Naʼaman 2017b, 323–324). In contrast, the parallel account in 1 Chr 18:10, as well as the version in the Septuagint, read Hadoram (see also Ant. 7.107). While scholars usually preferred the latter versions (i.e., they tend to understand the reading of Hadoram as the genuine version), this might not be the case after all, as evidence for Yahwistic names in the Kingdom of Hamath does exist, even if limited in scope.

[139] See Section 13.4.2.

[140] See Sections 11.2 and 11.3.

[141] For burial practices in Phoenicia, see Sader 2019, 216–248; for inland Syria, see Tenu 2015.

[142] See, e.g., the geographical regions discussed in Gitin 2015.

the coastal culture of the Phoenician city-states, which stretched from the Carmel Coast in the south to ʿAmrit in the north,[143] and 3) the north Levantine culture of the Neo-Hittite and Aramaean kingdoms.[144] Against this background, it is unsurprising that the cultural affiliation of most of the central Levantine communities, and to some degree also of Aram-Damascus, was determined according to modern political divisions and outdated ethnic affiliations or remained undecided and thus largely untreated.[145]

In this study, I have demonstrated the unique settlement history and the material culture of the local Iron Age communities of the central Levant. On the one hand, it is clear that the local material culture (e.g., burial practices), as well as general developments (e.g., the destruction wave of the Iron Age I/II transition), were significantly different from those observed in the city-states of the north (e.g., the Hama Citadel, Tell Afis, and Tell Tayinat) or even the coast (e.g., Tyre and Sidon). On the other hand, it does not entirely resemble the cultural traits and settlement sequences observed in the well-excavated north-Israelite settlements of the south (e.g., Tel Megiddo, Tel Rehov, and Tel Dor), as especially evident in their very fragmented occupational histories.[146] Consequently, past and ongoing debates regarding the north-Israelite or Damascene (sometimes referred to as Aramaean) affiliation of the local material culture become superfluous.[147] In reality, the archaeological data show that the development of the material culture of the central Levant was affected by local as well as cross-regional processes (e.g., the destruction of Canaanite Hazor) and combined elements borrowed from other nearby regions with local ones.[148] This is not to say that the central Levantine societies were politically independent in the early first millennium BCE, as the opposite is clearly true here. Historical and biblical sources, as well as many clues in the material culture, indicate that along the 10th–8th centuries BCE, the historical trajectory of the central Levantine societies was primarily shaped by continuous but everchanging contacts between the local populations and foreign entities, such as Israel and Aram-Damascus, both ultimately also impacting its history of research.

---

[143] Sader 2019, 4–8. For southern Phoenicia, see Gilboa 2005; idem forthcoming.

[144] Gilibert 2011; Niehr 2014; Osborne 2014b; and especially idem 2021, *passim*.

[145] The best example of this approach is the continued insistence on the cultural (and political) association of the Hula Valley and nearby regions exclusively with the south Levantine polities, although the northern influences on this region were frequently noted in research for both the Late Bronze and Early Iron Ages (e.g., Bonfil/Zarzecki-Peleg 2007; Zuckerman 2010; Münger 2013). Regarding the problematic concept of ethnicity, see Berlejung 2019, 254–256; Maeir 2021, both with references.

[146] For similar conclusions, see recently Rohmer 2020.

[147] E.g., Finkelstein 1999b; Ben-Tor 2000; Thareani 2016a; Yahalom-Mack *et al.* 2021.

[148] As was nicely summarized by Y. Thareani (2019a, 197) in regard to the material culture of Tel Dan, perhaps one of the more debated sites in the central Levant: "…a complex picture in which diverse northern cultural influences coexisted alongside continuing local cultural traditions."

14. Conclusions

Despite the fact that many mounds have been excavated in the central Levant, and hundreds of sites have been documented in field surveys, the archaeology and history of the region throughout the Iron Age remained relatively obscure. In most cases, the development of the local societies was discussed as part of the political history of the elite groups thriving in the Samaria Highlands and the Damascus Oasis, and not in their own right. My main objective in this book was to demonstrate the distinct settlement and cultural processes the indigenous populations experienced and to argue that their history should be understood as a continuous discourse between the locals and the foreign powers that ruled over them. As in many other cases throughout history, these negotiations were successful at times and resulted in prosperity, while on other occasions, these encounters were devastating and led to the destruction of local institutions.

Based on the surviving remains, the events at the end of the Late Bronze Age, first and foremost the destruction of Egyptian-affiliated city-states such as Hazor and Kumidi, should be taken as a turning point in the history of the central Levant. These events had long-term effects on the development of the local societies in the following centuries. During the 12th–10th centuries BCE, the political power was apparently distributed among smaller territorial formations, for example, the putative Kinnereth Polity that flourished around the Sea of Galilee. While these polities enjoyed some economic prosperity and succeeded in developing long-distance contacts and trade with remote regions (e.g., the Phoenician coast), recurring traumatic events indicate that the region suffered from poor security conditions and feeble control of central authority over the countryside. Ultimately, and as part of a cross-regional process, which extended from the Lebanese Beqaa to the Judean Shephelah, the urban societies in Canaan collapsed. Evidence of the traumatic events in the central Levant can be found in the heavy destructions documented in nearly all the excavated urban settlements (e.g., Tell el-Ghassil, Tel Dan, Tel Kinrot, and Tel Hadar). Regardless of the particular reasons that led to the destruction of each site, these were the elite groups residing in the Samaria Highlands and the Damascus Oasis that harnessed the situation in their favor and changed the socio-political landscape in a significant way. The first signs of their active involvement in the central Levant are visible from *ca.* 900 BCE and can especially be seen in the establishment of fortified strongholds in key locations that were sparsely settled or abandoned during the Iron Age I, such as Tel Hazor (Strata X–IX) in the Hula Valley and Tell er-Rumeith (Strata VIII–VII) in the Irbid Plateau. Historical considerations suggest that the former stronghold was built under the auspices of the north-Israelites, while the construction of the latter was probably supported by Aram-Damascus (or controlled directly by it). Despite the resources invested in the construction and preservation of these control points, cultural traits from the heartland of the Kingdom of Israel, and maybe also from Aram-Damascus, were only partially adopted by the locals who operated in these sites (e.g., ashlar masonry, four-room houses, and wide use in red-slipped wares).

In the second half of the 9th century BCE, a new chapter in the history of the central Levant began with the territorial expansion of Aram-Damascus during Hazael's reign. Besides the destructions associated with the military conflicts between Israel and Aram-Damascus, the impact of the Damascene rule over the central Levant seems to be primarily positive. It includes, for instance, the renovation of old cities (e.g., Tel Hazor), the establishment of new polities (e.g., the Kingdom of Geshur), the introduction of novel artworks (e.g., the volute capitals in Tel Dan and Tel Hazor), and even the spread of literacy (e.g., the inscriptions found in Tel Dan, Tel Hadar, and Tel 'Ein Gev). However, this period of affluence did not last long. Already in the late days of the 9th century BCE (or a bit later), the shifting circumstances in the Ancient Near East, especially the resumption of the military campaigns of the Neo-Assyrian Empire to the west in the days of Adad-Nirari III, stimulated a new north-Israelite expansion to the central Levant, naturally, at the expanse of Aram-Damascus. The results of this process can be discerned in the archaeological record, *inter alia*, in the destructions of the settlements around the Sea of Galilee (especially the severe destruction of Stratum V at et-Tell/Bethsaida) but also in the removal of symbols of Damascene statehood like volute capitals from the citadel of Tel Hazor or the shattering of the royal stele erected at Tel Dan.

While Aram-Damascus regained its political power within several decades and reoccupied territories in the central Levant (e.g., the Irbid Plateau), the entire region faced the new policies of the Neo-Assyrian kings of the second half of the 8th century BCE, particularly the extreme measures taken toward rebellious kingdoms. Eventually, this process led to the destruction of many cities, including Hazor and 'Ashtaroth, which lost their prominent status forever. But this was not the end of the local political institutions, as the center of gravity moved now to other local settlements in the region, and life in the central Levant evidently continued, even after the fall of Samaria and Damascus.

Appendices

Appendix A: Iron Age Sites

In this appendix, I present a catalog of all the surveyed and excavated Iron Age sites discovered in the regions discussed throughout this study. A few general comments concerning the composition of the list are in place:

1. Information on most of the sites included in this catalog was gathered from several comprehensive works published throughout the years with some minor additions (e.g., the fortified complex discovered near Haspin in the Golan Heights).[1]
2. I divided the excavated sites into three categories: well-investigated sites (single asterisk), well-investigated sites but with an insufficient representation of Bronze and Iron Age remains (two asterisks), and partially-excavated sites (three asterisks).
3. Geographical references are given as decimal degrees, which can be easily copied to many online services (e.g., Google Maps), similar to the system employed by the *Wissenschaftliche Bibellexikon im Internet* (WiBiLex).
4. Estimations of maximal settlement size are given according to the following categories: A (*ca.* 5–7 hectares), B (*ca.* 3–4 hectares), C (*ca.* 1–2 hectares), and D (less than 1 hectare). In uncertain cases, or when an insignificant number of Iron Age sherds was found in a large settlement, the smallest category was used. Whenever it was possible, I remeasured the size of the settlement in QGIS using satellite imagery.
5. The differentiation between the Late Bronze Age III and Iron Age I ceramic forms is difficult in sherd collections.[2] Consequently, many sites that were dated to the latter period could belong to the former. In the central Levant, a similar problem exists regarding the differentiation between Iron Age IIA and Iron Age IIB types.[3] In order to overcome these issues, I divided the sites into broad timeframes: Middle Bronze Age I/II (#1), Late Bronze Age I/II (#2), Late Bronze Age III/Iron Age I (#3), and Iron Age IIA/B (#4). Uncertain cases in which the differentiation between the subphases of the Iron Age was not possible were included in a separate category (#5).

---

[1] Marfoe 1995 (for the Lebanese Beqaa); the website of the Israel Archaeological Survey (for the Hula Valley, Sea of Galilee, and the Golan Heights); Braemer 1993; Rohmer 2020 (for the Nuqra Plain); Mittmann 1970; Kamlah 2000 (for the Irbid Plateau). I was also assisted by the data provided in Zwickel 1990a and Lehmann 2002. References to other works (e.g., final reports) were provided in particular cases. Note that I preferred to exclude from the catalog sites with problematic dates, e.g., sites that were surveyed by Nelson Glueck (see details in Sauer 1986; Finkelstein 1988, 114–116).

[2] Arie 2011, 316. A. Mazar (2009a) includes all of this timeframe within his Iron Age I.

[3] This is also one of the reasons for the debate over the exact dating of Stratum IVA at Tel Dan (Arie 2008; Thareani 2016a), Stratum VIII at Tel Hazor (Finkelstein 1999; Ben-Tor 2000), as well as the settlements that emerged around the Sea of Galilee (Sergi/Kleiman 2018; Mazar 2020b).

6. Published pottery figures were available only for a fraction of the survey sites included in the catalog, and only a few of the surveyors described their dating criteria.[4] As a result, in nearly all cases, the dating of the surveyors had to be trusted blindly.

A.1. The Lebanese Beqaa

#	Name	Location	Size	1	2	3	4	5	References
1	Kh. Busaybis	34°24'32.09 N, 36°25'43.10 E	D	+	+	+	+		Marfoe 1995, 280, no. 374
2	el-Hirmil Old Town Center	34°23'48.61 N, 36°22'59.08 E	B	+	+	+	+		Marfoe 1995, 280, no. 375
3	el-Hirmil Wadi el-Jawz	34°23'18.92 N, 36°23'38.29 E	D	+				+	Marfoe 1995, 281, no. 376
4	Marah el-Wazza	34°16'50.99 N, 36°21'24.66 E	D	+	+	+			Marfoe 1995, 277, no. 362
5	Ras Baalbek	34°15'32.55 N, 36°25'6.60 E	D	+				+	Marfoe 1995, 278, no. 367
6	T. Haql el-Jami'	34°14'47.61 N, 36°20'53.77 E	D	+	+	+	+		Marfoe 1995, 273–274, no. 348
7	T. Sugha	34°13'31.19 N, 36°20'10.20 E	D	+	+	+			Marfoe 1995, 370–371, no. 343
8	Haql el-Bayda	34°12'49.44 N, 36°20'17.65 E	D	+	+	+	+		Marfoe 1995, 274, no. 349
9	Labwa North	34°11'59.65 N, 36°21'8.06 E	C		+			+?	Marfoe 1995, 272–273, no. 346
10	T. Qasr Labwa (Labwa)***	34°11'59.76 N, 36°20'37.70 E	A	+	+	+	+		Marfoe 1995, 271–272, no. 344
11	T. Labwa South	34°11'40.39 N, 36°20'58.55 E	A	+?	+?	+?	+		Marfoe 1995, 272, no. 345
12	T. el-'Ayyun	34° 9'38.53 N, 36°16'26.63 E	A	+	+	+	+		Marfoe 1995, 264–265, no. 322
13	T. el-Husn	34° 9'7.48 N, 36°15'58.26 E	C	+	+		+		Marfoe 1995, 266, no. 325
14	T. el-Mathani	34° 8'35.30 N, 36°16'16.92 E	B	+	+	+			Marfoe 1995, 265, no. 323
15	T. en-Naba'	34° 8'26.04 N, 36°16'22.15 E	C			+	+		Marfoe 1995, 265–266, no. 324
16	T. 'Ain Ahla	34° 8'19.87 N, 36°17'11.54 E	D	+	+	+	+		Marfoe 1995, 266–267, no. 326

---

[4] For exceptional cases, see Marfoe 1995, 21–24; Stepansky 1999; Kamlah 2000.

Appendix A: Iron Age Sites 237

#	Name	Location	Size	1	2	3	4	5	References
17	T. 'Ain Sha't	34° 8'2.69 N, 36°13'56.12 E	B	+	+	+	+		Marfoe 1995, 260–261, no. 309
18	Riha Station	34° 7'13.38 N, 36°12'3.21 E	D	+			+		Marfoe 1995, 262, no. 313
19	T. Maqna	34° 4'53.43 N, 36°12'43.96 E	D	+	+	+	+		Marfoe 1995, 257, no. 294
20	T. el-'Alaq	34° 1'40.11 N, 36° 6'17.56 E	C	+?		+	+		Marfoe 1995, 251, no. 270
21	T. Hawsh es-Safiya	34° 1'30.51 N, 36° 8'18.00 E	B	+		+			Marfoe 1995, 256, no. 292
22	T. Nab' Litani	34° 0'49.03 N, 36° 6'1.82 E	C		+?	+	+		Marfoe 1995, 250, no. 268
23	Baalbek**	34° 0'25.22 N, 36°12'15.89 E	A	+		+?	+?		Marfoe 1995, 255–256, no. 291
24	T. el-Hadat	33°59'58.00 N, 36° 4'4.96 E	B	+?		+	+		Marfoe 1995, 250, no. 269
25	T. 'Ain es-Sa'uda	33°59'50.73 N, 36° 5'58.76 E	C		+		+		Marfoe 1995, 243–244, no. 340
26	T. Majdalun	33°59'47.76 N, 36° 7'20.30 E	B	+?		+	+		Marfoe 1995, 242, no. 234
27	T. Duris	33°59'14.66 N, 36°10'47.72 E	C	+		+	+?		Marfoe 1995, 245, no. 249
28	T. Mas'ud	33°58'57.03 N, 36° 4'18.88 E	C	+		+	+		Marfoe 1995, 243, no. 237
29	T. Hizzin (Hasi)***	33°57'54.28 N, 36° 6'14.74 E	B	+	+	+	+		Marfoe 1995, 241, no. 232; Genz/Sader 2008
30	T. 'Ain el-Basha	33°57'52.78 N, 36° 4'51.97 E	C	+	+?			+	Marfoe 1995, 243, no. 239
31	T. Hashbe (Hashabu)	33°56'49.40 N, 36° 3'13.86 E	A	+	+	+	+		Marfoe 1995, 240–241, no. 231
32	T. el-Ghassil*	33°55'14.21 N, 36° 4'17.32 E	B		+	+	+		Marfoe 1995, 241–242, no. 333; Joukowsky 1972
33	T. 'Ain Sharif	33°53'29.51 N, 36° 1'35.08 E	A	+	+	+	+		Marfoe 1995, 235, no. 206
34	T. Rayyaq	33°51'15.31 N, 36° 1'13.01 E	B	+?		+			Marfoe 1995, 235–236, no. 207
35	T. Jita	33°49'14.91 N, 35°50'9.56 E	C	+?	+?			+?	Marfoe 1995, 287, no. 400
36	T. 'Ain Saufar	33°49'22.81 N, 35°54'20.10 E	D		+		+		Marfoe 1995, 231, no. 186

#	Name	Location	Size	1	2	3	4	5	References
37	T. Dalhamiya	33°49'6.12 N, 35°57'32.49 E	A	+	+	+	+		Marfoe 1995, 227–228, no. 177
38	T. Chtaura/Jedithe	33°48'50.28 N, 35°51'3.60 E	B	+	+	+	+		Marfoe 1995, 223, no. 160
39	T. T'albaya	33°48'39.34 N, 35°52'35.83 E	C		+	+	+?		Marfoe 1995, 227, no. 174
40	T. Karmita	33°48'25.21 N, 35°54'11.24 E	C			+			Marfoe 1995, 228, no. 179
41	T. 'Aqaibi	33°48'22.47 N, 35°55'31.47 E	D				+		Marfoe 1995, 228, no. 178
42	T. Ta'nayil	33°47'53.24 N, 35°52'3.10 E	D	+	+			+?	Marfoe 1995, 222–223, no. 158
43	T. el-Maj-dub/Ayyub	33°47'41.88 N, 35°53'38.56 E	C			+			Marfoe 1995, 229, no. 180
44	T. Qabb Elyas	33°47'37.18 N, 35°49'17.77 E	C	+	+?	+	+?		Marfoe 1995, 223, no. 159
45	T. es-Sirhan	33°47'21.95 N, 35°56'35.33 E	A	+	+	+	+		Marfoe 1995, 226, no. 173
46	T. Nab' el-Fa'ur	33°46'52.88 N, 35°58'8.19 E	B	+?		+			Marfoe 1995, 230, no. 183
47	T. el-Mahada	33°46'51.49 N, 35°57'51.37 E	C			+			Marfoe 1995, 229, no. 182
48	T. Barr Elyas	33°46'32.11 N, 35°54'12.88 E	A	+	+	+	+		Marfoe 1995, 227, no. 176
49	T. Dayr Zanun	33°45'9.40 N, 35°55'3.31 E	A	+	+	+	+		Marfoe 1995, 225–226, no. 170
50	T. 'Ain el-Khanzira	33°43'16.23 N, 35°54'45.82 E	C	+	+?	+			Marfoe 1995, 217–218, no. 140
51	T. Bir Dhakwa	33°42'10.18 N, 35°52'28.29 E	B	+	+	+	+		Marfoe 1995, 209, no. 105
52	T. ed-Dar	33°41'31.24 N, 35°47'41.12 E	A	+	+			+?	Marfoe 1995, 209–210, no. 106
53	T. er-Rahib	33°41'2.35 N, 35°53'42.08 E	C	+		+	+		Marfoe 1995, 218, no. 142
54	T. Satiya South	33°40'17.53 N, 35°52'58.40 E	B	+		+?			Marfoe 1995, 219, no. 143
55	T. Ghazza	33°40'4.09 N, 35°49'34.57 E	B	+?		+			Marfoe 1995, 210, no. 107
56	T. 'Ain el-Fawqa	33°38'54.80 N, 35°52'26.64 E	C	+		+			Marfoe 1995, 201, no. 66
57	T. el-Jisr	33°38'23.92 N, 35°46'42.91 E	B	+	+	+			Marfoe 1995, 197, no. 51

#	Name	Location	Size	1	2	3	4	5	References
58	T. Kamid el-Loz (Kumidi)*	33°37'25.71 N, 35°49'16.50 E	A	+	+	+	?		Marfoe 1995, 196–197, no. 50; Heinz 2016
59	Siret ed-Diyab	33°32'11.19 N, 35°35'6.89 E	D				+		Marfoe 1995, 188, no. 14
60	T. ez-Zeitun	33°28'12.64 N, 35°44'52.99 E	C	+	+	+	+		Marfoe 1995, 18, no. 12
61	T. Dibbin (Ijon)	33°20'40.07 N, 35°35'26.53 E	A	+?	+	+	+		Marfoe 1995, 185, no. 1

A.2. The Hula Valley

#	Name	Location	Size	1	2	3	4	5	References
62	Nahal Misgav	33°15'39.21 N, 35°33'55.19 E	D					+?	IAS 7, no. 5
63	T. Abel Beth-Maacah*	33°15'31.52 N, 35°34'51.03 E	A	+	+	+	+		IAS 7, no. 16; Yahalom-Mack/Panitz-Cohen/Mullins 2018
64	T. Dan*	33°14'54.76 N, 35°39'8.20 E	A	+	+	+	+		IAS 8, no. 46; Ilan 2019a
65	Giv'at haShoket	33°14'22.90 N, 35°34'6.46 E	C	+			+		IAS 7, no. 29
66	Kh. Mamzie	33°13'56.99 N, 35°37'15.61 E	D			+	+		IAS 7, no. 35
67	Kh. Sanbariyeh	33°13'51.26 N, 35°37'12.33 E	C			+	+		Dayan 1962, 25
68	T. Beit Ahu	33°13'31.93 N, 35°35'47.44 E	C			+	+		Dayan 1962, 21
69	T. Hasas	33°13'28.77 N, 35°37'11.61 E	A	+	+	+	+		IAS 7, no. 55
70	T. Barum	33°13'27.62 N, 35°34'43.31 E	C			+			IAS 7, no. 45
71	H. Mezudat Honin	33°13'16.06 N, 35°32'39.34 E	B			+	+		IAS 7, no. 59
72	T. Qata'an	33°13'12.14 N, 35°38'56.69 E	D		+	+	+		Dayan 1962, 25
73	'Ein Shkitan	33°13'9.52 N, 35°36'2.01 E	C			+			IAS 7, no. 64
74	Tahunat et-Tabgha***	33°13'5.75 N, 35°38'29.63 E	C	+			+		IAS 8, no. 89
75	T. Katlit	33°12'57.34 N, 35°38'39.83 E	C				+		IAS 8, no. 92
76	T. Tannim North	33°12'50.46 N, 35°35'31.42 E	D					+	IAS 7, no. 61

#	Name	Location	Size	1	2	3	4	5	References
77	T. Tannim***	33°12'46.89 N, 35°35'34.11 E	C	+	+	+	+		IAS 7, no. 75
78	'Ein 'Aked	33°12'37.53 N, 35°33'25.48 E	D	+		+			IAS 7, no. 72
79	Giv'at Shhomit	33°12'29.20 N, 35°34'38.81 E	D	+	+		+		IAS 7, no. 74
80	Kiryat Shmona South***	33°11'57.02 N, 35°34'34.43 E	B	+		+			Gadot/Yasur-Landau 2012
81	T. Qalil	33°11'35.63 N, 35°39'0.76 E	B		+	+	+		Dayan 1962, 26
82	T. Ron/Sheikh Yousef	33°10'55.45 N, 35°37'5.53 E	B			+	+		Ilan 1999, Table 5.1
83	H. ha'Ashan	33°10'49.85 N, 35°35'23.38 E	D	+	+		+		Dayan 1962, 25
84	T. Anafa**	33°10'36.40 N, 35°38'40.46 E	B	+	+	+	+		IAS 11, no. 17
85	T. Na'ama***	33°10'31.97 N, 35°35'42.00 E	B	+	+		+		Dayan 1962, 24
86	Tzomet haGome West	33° 9'56.92 N, 35°34'0.40 E	D			+	+		Ben-Ami 2003, 232–236
87	'Ein Avazim	33° 9'24.03 N, 35°34'16.19 E	D	+	+	+			Ilan 1999, Table 5.1
88	esh-Sheikh Mahmud	33° 9'27.91 N, 35°40'8.88 E	D	+				+	IAS 11, no. 74
89	Wadi Halat el-Mughayir	33° 6'44.99 N, 35°34'2.45 E	D				+		Ben-Ami 2003, 232–236
90	T. Hamol	33° 5'55.62 N, 35°38'12.44 E	D			+	+		Dayan 1962, 26; Ilan 1999, Table 5.1
91	T. Re'emim	33° 5'24.96 N, 35°34'54.25 E	A	+	+	+	+		Dayan 1962, 25
92	Kh. 'Ain et-Tineh	33° 4'39.92 N, 35°38'36.41 E	C			+	+		IAS 15, no. 20
93	'Ein 'Alomim	33° 4'28.55 N, 35°35'9.74 E	D			+	+		Ilan 1999, Table 5.1
94	T. Shahaf/Abalis	33° 3'42.30 N, 35°36'21.92 E	C	+	+	+	+		Dayan 1962, 27; Ilan 1999, Table 5.1
95	Be'er Hasin	33° 2'22.84 N, 35°35'0.60 E	D			+	+		Ilan 1999, Table 5.1
96	Muqabarat Banat-Ya'qub	33° 1'54.96 N, 35°37'47.30 E	D			+	+		Stepansky 1999, 23
97	Nahal Makbram	33° 1'22.38 N, 35°33'26.68 E	C	+				+	IAS 18, no. 16
98	Ayyelet haShahar***	33° 1'20.51 N, 35°34'51.44 E	D			+	+		IAS 18, no. 24; Kletter/Zwickel 2006

Appendix A: Iron Age Sites 241

#	Name	Location	Size	1	2	3	4	5	References
99	T. es-Safa***	33° 1'18.80 N, 35°35'20.33 E	-	+	+	+	+		IAS 18, no. 28
100	T. Mashav Northwest	33° 1'13.79 N, 35°32'9.59 E	C				+		IAS 18, no. 4
101	Hazor*	33° 1'12.52 N, 35°34'7.10 E	A	+	+	+	+		IAS 18, no. 19; Ben-Tor/Ben-Ami/Sandhaus 2012; Ben-Tor et al. 2017; Ben-Tor 2016
102	Druze Caves North	33° 1'11.04 N, 35°33'17.00 E	D		+	+			IAS 18, no. 13
103	T. Mashav	33° 1'3.04 N, 35°32'23.03 E	C			+	+		IAS 18, no. 7
104	Kir'ad el-Baqq'ara South	33° 1'0.76 N, 35°36'18.09 E	-			+	+		IAS 18, no. 32
105	Jaz'ir***	33° 0'57.56 N, 35°34'16.71 E	-		+			+	IAS 18, no. 20
106	Kfar Ya'akov	33° 0'40.94 N, 35°38'2.02 E	D				+		IAS 18, no. 114
107	Nahal Hazor	33° 0'41.75 N, 35°33'43.89 E	C			+			IAS 18, no. 70
108	Metzad 'Ateret**	33° 0'16.67 N, 35°37'38.79 E	D	+		+	+		IAS 18, no. 143
109	Kh. el-Lawziyeh	33° 0'13.97 N, 35°34'49.27 E	-			+	+		IAS 18, no. 138
110	Ard es-Seiyarah	33° 0'0.56 N, 35°37'4.04 E	C	+			+		IAS 18, no. 139
111	Qabba'a	32°59'58.15 N, 35°32'15.12 E	B				+		IAS 18, no. 116
112	H. Arbel Yarden	32°59'44.47 N, 35°36'20.82 E	C	+		+	+		IAS 18, no. 165
113	'Almin	32°59'42.55 N, 35°37'52.10 E	B				+		IAS 18, no. 171
114	Kh. Qatana	32°59'35.09 N, 35°34'26.77 E	C	+		+	+		IAS 18, no. 159
115	'Enot Shuv	32°59'28.34 N, 35°35'48.78 E	C				+		IAS 18, no. 160
116	Kh. el-Bey	32°59'22.78 N, 35°36'2.24 E	C	+		+	+		IAS 18, no. 164
117	T. Ya'af***	32°58'18.96 N, 35°33'31.77 E	B	+	+	+	+		IAS 18, no. 189
118	Rosh Pinna***	32°58'17.56 N, 35°31'59.34 E	B	+		+	+		IAS 18, no. 187; Stepansky 2019
119	T. Ya'af South	32°58'9.21 N, 35°33'37.50 E	C				+		IAS 18, no. 218

#	Name	Location	Size	1	2	3	4	5	References
120	T. Ya'af Southwest	32°58'9.21 N, 35°33'25.95 E	D				+		IAS 18, no. 216
121	Rosh Pinna East	32°58'6.99 N, 35°33'7.84 E	C				+		IAS 18, no. 213
122	E.P. 144	32°57'47.02 N, 35°39'7.44 E	D			+	+		IAS 18/1, no. 72
123	T. Nes East	32°57'35.09 N, 35°33'48.92 E	D					+	IAS 18, no. 242
124	T. Nes***	32°57'31.89 N, 35°33'35.43 E	D				+		IAS 18, no. 241
125	Kh. el-Hammam	32°57'18.19 N, 35°37'24.46 E	C	+			+		IAS 18, no. 266
126	Eliphelet Enclosure	32°57'7.56 N, 35°33'18.01 E	C				+		IAS 18, no. 277
127	H. Sakhar	32°57'3.83 N, 35°36'9.32 E	C	+			+		IAS 18, no. 300
128	Kh. er-Ramliyat	32°55'52.81 N, 35°32'53.15 E	D				+		IAS 36, no. 1–9/4 (unpublished)
129	Kh. et-Tibaq	32°55'52.23 N, 35°33'0.85 E	D				+		IAS 36, no. 1–9/5 (unpublished)
130	Kh. eth-Thaum**	32°55'39.39 N, 35°33'18.77 E	D			+	+?		IAS 36, no. 2–9/1 (unpublished)
131	Kh. Tufah South	32°55'44.51 N, 35°34'44.58 E	-			+			IAS 36, no. 4–9/1 (unpublished)
132	Korazin**	32°54'40.69 N, 35°33'48.40 E	D				+		IAS 36, no. 3–7/1 (unpublished)
133	Nahal Kinnar 'Elyon East	32°54'28.40 N, 35°32'34.39 E	D				+?		IAS 36, no. 1–7/5 (unpublished)

A.3. The Sea of Galilee

#	Name	Location	Size	1	2	3	4	5	References
134	et-Tell/Bethsaida*	32°54'37.59 N, 35°37'50.21 E	A		+	+	+		Epstein/Gutman 1972, 276–277; Arav 2013; idem 2018
135	Mifratz Amnon	32°53'19.75 N, 35°35'31.38 E	D					+	IAS 36, no. 5–4/1 (unpublished)

#	Name	Location	Size	1	2	3	4	5	References
136	Mashra' Seil Musa	32°52'26.50 N, 35°33'34.75 E	D					+	IAS 36, no. 2–3/2 (unpublished)
137	T. Kinrot (Kinnereth)*	32°52'12.26 N, 35°32'22.26 E	A	+?	+	+	+		IAS 36, no. 0–2/1 (unpublished); Münger et al. 2011; Münger 2013
138	Karei Deshe	32°52'10.09 N, 35°32'33.60 E	-			+	+		IAS 36, no. 1–2/5 (unpublished)
139	Karei Deshe Beach	32°52'7.17 N, 35°32'33.09 E	D					+	IAS 36, no. 1–2/2 (unpublished)
140	T. Hodim/el-Hunud	32°51'36.59 N, 35°31'57.20 E	B		+	+	+		IAS 36, no. 0–1/3 (unpublished)
141	T. Hadar*	32°51'1.30 N, 35°38'57.71 E	C	+?	+	+	+		IAS 36/1, no. 89; Kleiman 2019a
142	T. Eqlatiyah	32°48'22.58 N, 35°31'33.07 E	B					?+	Albright 1925, 10
143	T. 'Ein Gev*	32°47'1.24 N, 35°38'14.24 E	B			+	+		IAS 40, no. 68
144	T. Soreg***	32°46'31.40 N, 35°41'7.01 E	D	+	+	+	+		IAS 40, no. 89
145	Har Beriniki	32°46'36.35 N, 35°32'25.61 E	-				+		IAS 39, no. 84
146	H. Menorim***	32°45'20.04 N, 35°32'34.97 E	B	+		+	+		IAS 39, no. 145; Covello-Paran 2010
147	T. 'Ubeidiyah***	32°41'20.03 N, 35°33'42.01 E	B		+	+			Aharoni 1957, 126–127
148	T. Dover***	32°41'0.50 N, 35°37'48.85 E	B		+	+	+		Epstein/Gutman 1972, 292; Golani/Wolff 2018

A.4. The Golan Heights

#	Name	Location	Size	1	2	3	4	5	References
149	H. Sa'ar***	33°14'51.06 N, 35°45'58.25 E	D	+	+	+	+		IAS 8/3, no. 20
150	Banias**	33°14'45.63 N, 35°41'47.13 E	D				+		IAS 8, no. 49

#	Name	Location	Size	1	2	3	4	5	References
151	'Ain Quniyye	33°14'9.42 N, 35°43'50.52 E	D				+		IAS 8, no. 61
152	Mas'ada***	33°14'3.32 N, 35°45'20.09 E	D			+	+		Zwickel 1990a, 351
153	Giv'at 'Az	33°13'31.38 N, 35°40'2.44 E	C				+		IAS 8, no. 77
154	Mitzpe Golani***	33°13'27.81 N, 35°41'27.38 E	C			+	+		IAS 8, no. 79; Zingboym 2008
155	'Ain el-Hamra East	33°10'56.42 N, 35°49'17.47 E	D			+			IAS 11/1, no. 22
156	Wadi Balu'a	33° 9'30.74 N, 35°41'56.94 E	D				+		IAS 11, no. 37
157	esh-Sheikh Muhammad	33° 7'44.33 N, 35°38'51.18 E	D			+			IAS 11, no. 39
158	Summaqa	33° 9'27.09 N, 35°43'37.26 E	D	+		+	+		IAS 11, no. 40
159	'Ayyun Summaqa	33° 9'20.55 N, 35°43'48.80 E	D			+	+		IAS 11, no. 43
160	Sekher Yardinon South	33° 9'14.95 N, 35°40'4.95 E	D	+			+		IAS 11, no. 49
161	Za'arta	33° 9'8.14 N, 35°41'25.95 E	D			+	+		IAS 11, no. 52
162	H. Furan	33° 8'51.02 N, 35°45'1.93 E	C			+	+		IAS 11/1, no. 52
163	Bab el-Hawa***	33° 8'40.85 N, 35°46'38.33 E	D	+	+		+		IAS 11/1, no. 53; Hartal/Segal forthcoming
164	Rawiyeh	33° 7'8.20 N, 35°40'46.71 E	D				+		IAS 11, no. 80
165	'Urfa	33° 6'30.64 N, 35°39'0.87 E	D				+		IAS 15, no. 6
166	el-Bijjeh	33° 6'2.02 N, 35°45'51.02 E	C	+		+	+		IAS 15/1, no. 4
167	Surman	33° 5'57.50 N, 35°50'17.08 E	D	+	+	+	+		IAS 15/1, no. 7
168	H. Hafar	33° 5'39.55 N, 35°41'13.08 E	D				+		IAS 15, no. 12
169	el-Mughayyir	33° 5'13.88 N, 35°43'43.47 E	D			+	+		IAS 15, no. 15
170	Darbashiye	33° 5'13.55 N, 35°39'10.20 E	D	+			+		IAS 15, no. 14
171	Dahar Ahmad	33° 5'9.59 N, 35°47'38.65 E	D					+	IAS 15/1, no. 10
172	Khuweikh Northeast	33° 4'27.24 N, 35°48'9.21 E	D		+		+		IAS 15/1, no. 19
173	Mumsiyyeh Southwest	33° 4'20.47 N, 35°49'6.99 E	B			+			IAS 15/1, no. 20

#	Name	Location	Size	1	2	3	4	5	References
174	Dardara	33° 4'0.28 N, 35°39'13.18 E	D		+	+			IAS 15, no. 24
175	Qal'at et-Tawil	33° 3'38.50 N, 35°48'20.44 E	C	+		+			IAS 15/1, no. 29
176	T. Sheikh Marzuq***	33° 3'10.95 N, 35°42'2.53 E	D		+	+			IAS 15, no. 33
177	'Ain el-'Alaq Pens	33° 3'4.23 N, 35°43'0.30 E	D	+	+	+			IAS 15, no. 34
178	E.P. 712	33° 0'6.16 N, 35°41'3.71 E	D			+			IAS 15, no. 31
179	Dayr Sras	33° 2'45.26 N, 35°40'53.01 E	D	+			+		IAS 15, no. 40
180	Jozieh	33° 2'10.27 N, 35°50'19.31 E	D			+	+		IAS 15/1, no. 44
181	Na'ran	33° 1'46.73 N, 35°41'19.67 E	B				+		IAS 15, no. 53
182	Murtaf'a ed-Durijat	33° 1'44.19 N, 35°38'6.52 E	D			+			Ilan 1999, Table 5.1
183	Wadi el-'Araghrah North	33° 1'23.42 N, 35°43'44.03 E	D				+		IAS 18/1, no. 5
184	er-Ramthaniyye	33° 1'12.44 N, 35°48'19.45 E	D				+		IAS 18/2, no. 8
185	Razan'yye Southwest	33° 1'6.89 N, 35°44'55.21 E	D				+		IAS 18/2, no. 3
186	T. Razan'yye South	33° 1'5.21 N, 35°45'6.76 E	D			+	+		IAS 18/2, no. 2
187	Metzad Nahal Zavitan 'Elyon	33° 0'49.04 N, 35°44'53.18 E	D				+		IAS 18/2, no. 15
188	Razan'yye South	33° 0'24.71 N, 35°44'51.10 E	D				+		IAS 18/2, no. 13
189	Ahmadiyye	33° 0'15.63 N, 35°42'13.10 E	D				+		IAS 18/1, no. 30
190	E.P. 670	33° 0'11.59 N, 35°46'33.10 E	D				+		IAS 18/2, no. 24
191	Fahura Pens***	33° 0'6.16 N, 35°41'3.71 E	D	+		+	+		IAS 18/1, no. 25
192	Ghadir en-Nahas	33° 0'2.10 N, 35°44'24.00 E	D	+		+			IAS 18/1, no. 34
193	Mapal haIrusim	33° 0'2.07 N, 35°44'31.70 E	D			+	+		IAS 18/1, no. 38
194	Qatzrin**	32°59'20.43 N, 35°42'16.64 E	D	+		+			IAS 18/1, no. 44
195	T. Seluqie***	32°58'54.02 N, 35°44'4.33 E	D	+			+		IAS 18/1, no. 59
196	Eshshe	32°58'19.12 N, 35°52'32.43 E	D			+	+		IAS 18/3, no. 8

#	Name	Location	Size	1	2	3	4	5	References
197	Metzad Yonathan/Qasr Tannuriya***	32°57'41.31 N, 35°48'48.83 E	D			+			IAS 18/2, no. 62; Epstein 1976; idem 1984
198	T. el-Faras	32°57'37.11 N, 35°51'57.46 E	D	+				+	IAS 18/3, no. 6
199	en-Nikhele North	32°57'32.49 N, 35°45'32.40 E	C			+			IAS 18/2, no. 73
200	'Ain el-Medaura 'Elyon	32°57'30.41 N, 35°52'35.92 E	D			+	+		IAS 18/3, no. 4
201	'Ain el-Medaura	32°57'30.39 N, 35°52'39.77 E	D		+	+	+		IAS 18/3, no. 3
202	Kh. esh-Sheikh Hussein East	32°57'26.78 N, 35°42'27.55 E	D	+			+		IAS 18/1, no. 88
203	en-Nikhele West	32°57'19.49 N, 35°45'36.17 E	D	+			+		IAS 18/2, no. 71
204	en-Nikhele	32°57'16.37 N, 35°45'43.66 E	D				+		IAS 18/2, no. 72
205	Sahra East	32°57'12.67 N, 35°46'49.28 E	C				+		IAS 18/2, no. 76
206	Tayyiba	32°56'50.87 N, 35°43'17.40 E	D	+			+		IAS 18/1, no. 104
207	Kh. Butmiyye	32°56'48.11 N, 35°52'54.84 E	D			+			IAS 18/3, no. 2
208	Metzad Hiv'ai	32°56'15.12 N, 35°44'43.80 E	D				+		IAS 18/2, no. 99
209	Rasm el-'Abd East	32°56'14.10 N, 35°48'27.06 E	D				+		IAS 18/2, no. 103
210	'Ain el-Qusiba	32°56'6.98 N, 35°43'34.46 E	D	+			+		IAS 18/1, no. 121
211	Shabbe	32°55'55.32 N, 35°44'45.60 E	C	+		+	+		IAS 36/2, no. 1
212	Giv'at Orha***	32°55'52.33 N, 35°51'13.84 E	D			+			IAS 36/3, no. 1
213	es-Salabe	32°55'49.32 N, 35°42'48.17 E	D	+		+			IAS 36/1, no. 11
214	Najil	32°55'38.43 N, 35°47'11.76 E	D			+			IAS 36/2, no. 9
215	es-Salabe Southwest	32°55'10.48 N, 35°42'19.08 E	D	+			+		IAS 36/1, no. 7
216	T. 'Ain el-Hariri	32°54'59.15 N, 35°48'20.78 E	D	+			+		IAS 36/2, no. 42
217	Hanut el-Meydan	32°54'49.13 N, 35°49'18.43 E	D				+		IAS 36/2, no. 59
218	Rujm el-Hiri*	32°54'33.24 N, 35°48'9.06 E	-		+		+		IAS 36/2, no. 56
219	Bab el-Hawa South	32°54'24.69 N, 35°43'43.48 E	D	+		+	+		IAS 36/1, no. 29

Appendix A: Iron Age Sites

#	Name	Location	Size	1	2	3	4	5	References
220	H. Batra	32°54'18.92 N, 35°40'42.59 E	D			+	+		IAS 36/1, no. 38
221	Kh. Farfur North	32°53'36.70 N, 35°47'12.89 E	D				+		IAS 36/2, no. 88
222	H. Zeite	32°53'0.55 N, 35°42'41.44 E	D			+			IAS 36/1, no. 53
223	Qatu' esh-Sheikh 'Ali	32°52'51.51 N, 35°39'40.58 E	D	+			+		IAS 36/1, no. 59
224	Umm el-Qubur	32°52'40.61 N, 35°44'32.88 E	D	+		+	+		IAS 36/1, no. 72
225	el-Qusayyibe	32°52'21.20 N, 35°44'17.38 E	D				+		IAS 36/1, no. 71
226	H. Kanaf	32°52'18.72 N, 35°41'8.88 E	D	+	+	+			IAS 36/1, no. 67
227	Bjuriyye	32°51'51.16 N, 35°47'21.81 E	D	+			+		IAS 36/2, no. 130
228	Kfar 'Akabya	32°51'46.65 N, 35°39'24.86 E	D	+	+	+	+		IAS 36/1, no. 74
229	Buyut Abu Rujm	32°51'45.21 N, 35°45'22.54 E	D				+		IAS 36/2, no. 125
230	T. Shuqayyif	32°51'20.44 N, 35°40'30.11 E	A	+	+	+	+		IAS 36/1, no. 84
231	ed-Dahtamiyye	32°50'53.79 N, 35°43'23.01 E	D	+	+	+			IAS 36/1, no. 99
232	Kh. es-Seybi Southwest	32°50'41.69 N, 35°39'36.07 E	D	+			+		IAS 36/1, no. 90
233	el-Mabara Southwest	32°50'34.67 N, 35°41'54.46 E	D	+			+		IAS 40, no. 2
234	T. edh-Dhahab***	32°50'29.27 N, 35°49'55.08 E	B	+	+?	+	+		IAS 40/1, no. 14; R. Be'eri, personal communication
235	Nahal El-Al 'Elyon East	32°50'26.33 N, 35°46'23.20 E	D					+	IAS 40/1, no. 4
236	el-Fakhuri	32°50'11.69 N, 35°44'7.91 E	C				+		IAS 40, no. 8
237	Nahal El-Al 'Elyon West	32°50'7.66 N, 35°46'0.39 E	D	+		+			IAS 40/1, no. 3
238	Haspin	32°50'28.21 N, 35°47'2.03 E	D	+			+		Tzin/Bron/Kleiman forthcoming
239	T. Abu ez-Zeitun***	32°49'47.60 N, 35°48'7.14 E	D	+		+	+		IAS 40/1, no. 24; Meitlis 1999
240	T. Nov/Nab***	32°49'41.34 N, 35°47'17.12 E	B	+			+		IAS 40/1, no. 23; Weksler-Bdolah 2000

#	Name	Location	Size	1	2	3	4	5	References
241	T. el-Khashash	32°49'36.63 N, 35°40'14.18 E	A		+	+	+		IAS 40, no. 15
242	Kh. el-Hutiya	32°49'31.59 N, 35°41'7.48 E	C	+				+	IAS 40, no. 17
243	Lower Mesil Kharub	32°49'26.50 N, 35°41'54.08 E	D	+	+	+			IAS 40, no. 33
244	Adeise	32°49'26.32 N, 35°42'40.22 E	C	+		+	+		IAS 40, no. 35
245	T. Abu Mudawwar	32°49'22.80 N, 35°43'45.55 E	C	+	+	+			IAS 40, no. 39
246	Nab'a el-Mjahiyye	32°49'16.81 N, 35°41'42.50 E	D	+		+	+		IAS 40, no. 32
247	Adeise South	32°49'16.55 N, 35°42'47.85 E	-				+		IAS 40, no. 38
248	el-Bardawil	32°49'16.12 N, 35°44'31.65 E	C	+	+	+			IAS 40, no. 43
249	'Ain 'Uwenish	32°49'4.25 N, 35°39'50.95 E	D	+			+		IAS 40, no. 25
250	Nab'a et-Tu'eine Enclosure	32°48'47.70 N, 35°41'15.43 E	D		+	+			IAS 40, no. 51
251	Kh. 'Ain et-Taruq	32°48'36.01 N, 35°48'45.10 E	C	+	+	+			IAS 40/1, no. 32
252	Rujm Fiq***	32°47'42.23 N, 35°43'33.43 E	D			+			IAS 40, no. 66
253	'Ayyun Ba'thata North	32°45'58.53 N, 35°42'50.57 E	D				+		IAS 40, no. 109
254	Tzuqey Kavarot	32°45'39.92 N, 35°39'3.79 E	D				+		IAS 40, no. 111
255	E.P. 227	32°45'6.99 N, 35°41'10.40 E	D	+			+		IAS 44, no. 7
256	'Ain Umm el-Adam	32°45'4.12 N, 35°39'30.51 E	D	+			+		IAS 44, no. 4
257	Metzad Metzokey Onn	32°45'0.91 N, 35°39'18.97 E	D	+			+		IAS 44, no. 2
258	Kh. Duwirban	32°44'59.49 N, 35°38'21.34 E	D			+	+		IAS 44, no. 1
259	Tlel	32°44'37.76 N, 35°41'14.08 E	D	+	+	+	+		IAS 44, no. 30
260	'Ayyun Umm el-'Azam	32°44'33.81 N, 35°39'16.75 E	D	+			+		IAS 44, no. 27
261	Sa'ad East	32°44'24.17 N, 35°43'43.80 E	D	+			+		IAS 44, no. 45
262	Sa'ad West	32°44'16.45 N, 35°42'7.74 E	D	+				+	IAS 44, no. 46
263	E.P. 235	32°44'16.45 N, 35°42'7.74 E	D					+	IAS 44, no. 39
264	el-Massiyye West	32°44'8.31 N, 35°42'15.37 E	D	+			+		IAS 44, no. 38

#	Name	Location	Size	1	2	3	4	5	References
265	Maqam Brejaʿ	32°44'8.28 N, 35°40'59.25 E	D	+			+		IAS 44, no. 52
266	Kh. ʿAyyun	32°43'7.13 N, 35°40'4.47 E	D	+		+	+		IAS 44, no. 60
267	ʿAjur Ghazaleh	32°42'56.98 N, 35°41'51.94 E	D				+		IAS 44, no. 69
268	ʿArq el-ʿArbeh	32°42'37.92 N, 35°40'4.32 E	D	+			+		IAS 44, no. 67
269	Metzad en-Nazeryye	32°42'8.99 N, 35°38'43.55 E	D	+	+	+			IAS 44, no. 71
270	en-Nazeryye	32°42'6.16 N, 35°38'17.81 E	D				+		IAS 44, no. 70
271	Mitzpor Negev Kinnerot	32°41'52.75 N, 35°38'47.31 E	D	+	+	+	+		IAS 44, no. 72

A.5. The Nuqra Plain

#	Name	Location	Size	1	2	3	4	5	References
272	Kh. Hatar	33° 1'17.26 N, 36°15'40.68 E	D	+			+?		Rohmer 2020, 86, no. 16
273	T. Qiswa	32°58'20.84 N, 36°13'21.18 E	C	+	+	+	+		Rohmer 2020, 87–99, no. 18
274	T. el-Kutayba North	32°58'12.55 N, 36°10'45.10 E	D	+?	+?	+	+		Rohmer 2020, 359–360, no. 99
275	T. el-ʿAyn	32°55'49.22 N, 36° 9'41.54 E	D				+?		Rohmer 2020, 360, no. 100
276	T. el-Jamus	32°55'28.57 N, 36° 9'11.42 E	D				+?		Rohmer 2020, 360–362, no. 101
277	T. Dilli	32°54'18.44 N, 36° 9'31.55 E	B	+	+		+?		Braemer 1984, 166; Rohmer 2020, 362, no. 102
278	T. Shaqra	32°54'18.32 N, 36°14'23.01 E	C	+?	+?	+?	+?		Rohmer 2020, 114, no. 22
279	T. es-Suhayliyya	32°53'15.52 N, 36° 8'51.06 E	C				+?		Rohmer 2020, 362–363, no. 103
280	Dar el-Qarʿan	32°52'5.18 N, 36°17'19.25 E	D		+?	+?	+		Rohmer 2020, 119, no. 25
281	el-Had	32°51'42.39 N, 36°17'51.96 E	D	+			+		Rohmer 2020, 120, no. 26
282	Kom er-Rumman East	32°51'36.16 N, 36°33'54.16 E	D	+?	+	+?	+		Rohmer 2020, 143–145, no. 38

#	Name	Location	Size	1	2	3	4	5	References
283	T. ed-Dunayba	32°51'3.96 N, 36°13'32.78 E	B	+	+		+		Braemer 1993, 170; Rohmer 2020, 114–118, no. 23
284	Dayr el-Asmar West	32°50'30.69 N, 36°28'0.25 E	C	+		+	+		Rohmer 2020, 127–135, no. 33
285	Sheikh Sa'ad (Qarnayim)**	32°50'14.62 N, 36° 2'8.84 E	A	+	+		+		Braemer 1984, 224; idem 1993, 169; Rohmer 2020, 388–392, no. 108
286	Najran South	32°49'54.81 N, 36°27'2.84 E	D	+			+		Rohmer 2020, 125, no. 32
287	Qarrasa South (Kurussa)***	32°49'51.73 N, 36°24'53.94 E	A	+			+		Rohmer 2020, 123, 190–213, no. 29
288	T. Hamad	32°49'26.21 N, 36° 7'18.84 E	A					+?	Rohmer 2020, 363–365, no. 104
289	T. ed-Dabba***	32°49'35.17 N, 36°34'25.37 E	A	+	+	+?	+		Braemer 1993, 170; Abou Assaf 2005; Rohmer 2020, 222–235, no. 39
290	T. 'Ashtara ('Ashtaroth)*	32°48'15.76 N, 36° 0'56.15 E	A	+	+	+	+		Braemer 1984, 224; idem, 1993, 169; Rohmer 2020, 392–403, no. 109
291	Sahem el-Jawlan***	32°46'54.27 N, 35°56'4.66 E	D		+	+			Fischer 1997
292	T. Saman	32°46'38.13 N, 36° 3'44.86 E	D				+		Rohmer 2020, 365, no. 105
293	Qanawat**	32°45'21.06 N, 36°37'10.51 E	A		+?		+?		Rohmer 2020, 296–304, no. 69
294	T. Kutayba South	32°44'54.63 N, 36°11'54.72 E	C	+	+?	+			Rohmer 2020, 370–372, no. 114
295	T. el-Ash'ari***	32°44'36.58 N, 36° 0'52.40 E	A	+	+		+		Braemer 1984, 224; idem 1993, 169; Rohmer 2020, 382–388, no. 106

Appendix A: Iron Age Sites

#	Name	Location	Size	1	2	3	4	5	References
296	es-Suwayda**	32°42'46.32 N, 36°33'58.27 E	D		+	+	+		Dentzer *et al.* 2010; Rohmer 2020, 339–353, no. 76
297	T. esh-Shihab	32°41'31.82 N, 35°58'6.55 E	A	+	+			+?	Albright 1925, 16–17; Braemer 1984, 224
298	Dar'a (Edrei)**	32°37'1.24 N, 36° 6'3.84 E	A	+	+		+		Braemer 1984, 224; Rohmer 2020, 410–417, no. 120
299	Kom Nebi 'Ira	32°36'38.80 N, 36°35'20.88 E	D	+			+		Braemer 1993, 125, 168; Rohmer 2020, 286, no. 81
300	Tayyiba (Tob)***	32°33'43.84 N, 36°14'43.01 E	A	+	+		+		Braemer 1984, 224; idem 1993, 169
301	Busra esh-Sham (Busruna)**	32°31'20.95 N, 36°28'39.26 E	A	+	+		+		Braemer 1984, 224; Rohmer 2020, 403–410, no. 118

A.6. The Irbid Plateau

#	Name	Location	Size	1	2	3	4	5	References
302	el-Masatib	32°42'49.55 N, 35°55'37.24 E	D				+		Mittmann 1970, 7, no. 4; Zwickel 1990a, 332
303	Kh. el-'Adasiye	32°42'36.44 N, 35°56'0.17 E	D	+		+			Mittmann 1970, 7, no. 3; Zwickel 1990a, 331–332
304	Yubla	32°41'23.81 N, 35°49'43.37 E	D			+?			Mittmann 1970, 22, no. 40
305	Qwayliba (Abila)**	32°40'53.14 N, 35°52'10.80 E	D		+	+	+		Glueck 1951, 125–126; Zwickel 1990a, 331
306	Samar	32°40'35.86 N, 35°47'9.51 E	D		+	+?			Mittmann 1970, 23, no. 43
307	T. Hilya	32°40'20.97 N, 35°53'25.55 E	D	+			+		Mittmann 1970, 20, no. 33; Zwickel 1990a, 330

#	Name	Location	Size	1	2	3	4	5	References
308	Kh. ʻAin Ghazal	32°40'20.97 N, 35°53'25.55 E	D	+		+			Mittmann 1970, 19–20, no. 31; Zwickel 1990a, 331
309	Kh. el-Bayaz	32°40'2.87 N, 35°49'0.59 E	C	+				+	Kamlah 2000, 67–69. no. ZS30
310	Kh. Majid	32°39'24.77 N, 35°56'25.48 E	C	+		+			Mittmann 1970, 8, no. 7; Zwickel 1990a, 325
311	et-Turra	32°38'22.06 N, 35°59'17.61 E	D		+		+		Mittmann 1970, 6–7, no. 1; Zwickel 1990a, 326
312	el-Kom	32°38'17.27 N, 35°54'29.82 E	C		+	+	+		Mittmann 1970, 17, no. 24; Zwickel 1990a, 325
313	Sama	32°38'9.24 N, 35°49'3.66 E	D				+		Mittmann 1970, 27, no. 55; Zwickel 1990a, 323
314	Isʻara	32°37'37.93 N, 35°44'54.09 E	D			+	+		Mittmann 1970, 31–32, no. 67; Zwickel 1990A, 323
315	Kh. el-Qser Fuʻara	32°37'34.26 N, 35°46'29.97 E	C			+			Mittmann 1970, 30–31, no. 64; Zwickel 1990a, 323
316	T. ez-Zaʻfaran	32°37'13.62 N, 35°50'31.50 E	C		+	+	+		Mittmann 1970, 26–27, no. 54; Zwickel 1990a, 322
317	Fuʻara	32°37'5.21 N, 35°45'51.43 E	D			+	+		Mittmann 1970, 30, no. 63; Zwickel 1990a, 322
318	Kh. el-Mughayir East	32°36'48.63 N, 35°57'21.73 E	D			+	+		Mittmann 1970, 8–9, no. 8; Zwickel 1990a, 326; Kamlah 2000, 13–16, no. ZS2
319	T. el-Mughayir***	32°36'28.45 N, 35°56'1.27 E	C	+	+	+	+		Mittmann 1970, 9, no. 10; Zwickel 1990a, 324–325
320	T. el-Muʻallaqa	32°36'16.83 N, 35°55'30.24 E	C	+	+	+	+		Mittmann 1970, 11–13, no. 12;

Appendix A: Iron Age Sites   253

#	Name	Location	Size	1	2	3	4	5	*References*
									Zwickel 1990a, 324; Kamlah 2000, 41–42, no. ZS14
321	Tuqbul	32°36'15.81 N, 35°48'24.53 E	B			+	+		Mittmann 1970, 8–9, no. 62; Zwickel 1990a, 326; Kamlah 2000, 13–16
322	Jabal Abu el-Hussein	32°36'8.49 N, 35°45'31.91 E	D			+	+		Mittmann 1970, 28, no. 68; Zwickel 1990a, 322
323	Kh. Dabulya	32°35'55.87 N, 35°50'0.27 E	D	+	+	+			Mittmann 1970, 28, no. 58; Zwickel 1990a, 322
324	Kh. Umm el-Ghuzlan	32°35'44.91 N, 35°42'31.53 E	C	+	+	+	+		Mittmann 1970, 36–37, no. 81; Zwickel 1990a, 318
325	Kh. es-Samoqa	32°35'40.00 N, 35°48'47.30 E	D		+	+			Mittmann 1970, 29, no. 61; Zwickel 1990a, 321
326	T. es-Subba	32°35'34.15 N, 35°56'50.43 E	D		+	+	+		Zwickel 1990a, 324; Kamlah 2000, 16–19, no. ZS17
327	T. el-Fukhar*	32°35'21.96 N, 35°57'13.11 E	B	+	+	+	+		Mittmann 1970, 13, no. 14; Zwickel 1990a, 324; Strange 2015
328	Kh. Sris	32°35'13.67 N, 35°49'59.98 E	C			+			Mittmann 1970, 28–29, no. 59; Zwickel 1990a, 321
329	Jijjin	32°35'11.43 N, 35°46'29.07 E	D		+	+	+		Mittmann 1970, 33, no. 71; Zwickel 1990a, 321
330	Som	32°35'11.08 N, 35°47'45.76 E	D		+	+	+		Mittmann 1970, 32–33, no. 70; Zwickel 1990a, 321
331	Sal	32°34'4.03 N, 35°54'37.43 E	C		+	+	+		Mittmann 1970, 14–15, no. 18; Zwickel 1990a, 314; Kamlah

#	Name	Location	Size	1	2	3	4	5	References
									2000, 44–53, no. ZS7
332	Kh. el-Bayada	32°33'54.22 N, 35°54'50.77 E	D		+	+	+		Mittmann 1970, 15, no. 19; Zwickel 1990a, 313
333	Ramtha	32°33'39.64 N, 36° 0'31.10 E	A					+?	Zwickel 1990a, 315
334	T. Irbid***	32°33'31.74 N, 35°50'50.63 E	A	+	+	+	+		Zwickel 1990a, 311–312; Kafafi/Abu Dalu 2009
335	Qasr el-Ghul	32°32'44.53 N, 35°49'24.44 E	D					+	Lamprichs 2007, 256–257
336	T. Kufr Yuba	32°32'18.89 N, 35°48'15.29 E	D		+			+	Zwickel 1990a, 310–311; Lamprichs 2007, 254–255
337	el-Ma'tarid Northeast	32°32'3.06 N, 35°57'7.86 E	C				+		Zwickel 1990a, 313; Kamlah 2000, 63–65, no. ZS5
338	el-Ma'tarid Southeast	32°31'53.27 N, 35°57'15.44 E	D			+	+		Zwickel 1990a, 313; Kamlah 2000, 65, ZS4
339	Zaharet Soq'ah	32°31'40.33 N, 35°46'50.73 E	D				+		Glueck 1951, 175–176; Zwickel 1990a, 310; Lamprichs 2007, 253–254
340	T. esh-Sheqaq	32°31'7.80 N, 35°47'5.85 E	D					+	Glueck 1951, 166; Zwickel 1990a, 310; Lamprichs 2007, 252–253
341	T. Beit Yafa	32°30'23.34 N, 35°47'31.15 E	D					+	Glueck 1951, 167–170; Zwickel 1990a, 309; Lamprichs 2007, 250–251
342	T. er-Rumeith*	32°29'50.09 N, 36° 0'48.15 E	C		+		+		Zwickel 1990a, 315; Barako/Lapp 2015
343	T. Johfiyeh*	32°29'35.46 N, 35°49'15.17 E	D	+?	+	+	+		Glueck 1951, 170–172; Lamprichs 2007
344	T. el-Husn***	32°29'26.01 N, 35°52'48.44 E	A	+	+	+	+		Leonard 1987; Zwickel 1990a, 313

#	Name	Location	Size	1	2	3	4	5	References
345	Kh. Umm el-Abar East	32°28'25.62 N, 35°56'58.40 E	C		+?		+?		Mittmann 1970, 124–125, no. 326; Zwickel 1990a, 299
346	Kh. Umm el-Abar West	32°28'25.68 N, 35°56'48.83 E	D	+		+			Mittmann 1970, 124, no. 325; Zwickel 1990a, 299
347	Kh. Kabar	32°25'11.18 N, 35°57'3.04 E	C					+	Leonard 1987, 344, no. 5

Appendix B: Inscriptions and Inscribed Items

#	Site	Reg.	Reading	Context	Description	References
1	T. Abel Beth-Maacah	-	[...]b/n[...] [...]נ\ב[...]	-	Body fragment; the inscription was incised before firing (unpublished)	Panitz-Cohen/Mullins/Bonfil 2015, 51
2	T. Abel Beth-Maacah	-	lbnyw לבניו	-	Complete jar; ink (unpublished)	Yahalom-Mack et al. 2021
3	T. Dan	-	bʻlplṭ בעלפלט	Str. I	Body fragment	Biran 1971, 10; 1994, fig. 218; upper photo; Delavault/Lemaire 1979, 2
4	T. Dan	-	[bʻl/ʼlp]lṭ [בעל\אלפ]לט	Post-Str. I	Body fragment	Biran 1994, fig. 218, lower photo; Renz/Röllig 1995, 337–338
5	T. Dan	L7129 23677/1	zkryw זכריו	Str. II	Stamp impression on a jar handle	Biran 1994, fig. 213; Avigad/Sass 1997, no. 669; Brandl 2009, fig. 4.2, b
6	T. Dan	-	lʻmdyw לעמדיו	Str. II	Stamp impression on a jar handle (unpublished)	Avigad/Sass 1997, no. 692
7	T. Dan	30655	lʻmdyw לעמדיו	Str. II	Stamp impression on a jar handle	Biran 1988, 16, left side; Avigad/Sass 1997, no. 692
8	T. Dan	21175/1	lʻmdyw לעמדיו	Str. II	Stamp impression on a jar handle	Biran 1988, 16, right side; Avigad/Sass 1997, no. 692
9	T. Dan	4705/1	ly[...] [...]לי	Mixed or unknown	Stamp impression on a jar handle (unpublished)	Brandl 2009, 139; n. 17

Appendix B: Inscriptions and Inscribed Items 257

#	Site	Reg.	Reading	Context	Description	References
10	T. Dan	-	ʾ א	Str. IVA or III?	Handle with an alphabetic sign	Greer 2011, 69, fig. 25
11	T. Dan	-	lʾmṣ לאמץ	Str. II	Body fragment	Biran 1971, 9; 1994, fig. 215; Renz/Röllig 1995, 134; Dobbs-Allsopp *et al.* 2005, 147
12	T. Dan	-	lṭb[ḥ]yʾ לטבחיא	-	Bowl	Avigad 1966, 210, pl. 9
13	T. Dan	-	-	Iron Age IIB	Royal inscription (three fragments)	Biran/Naveh 1995, figs. 9–10
14	T. Dan?	-	ʿzʿ עזא	-	Seal	Avigad/Sass 1997, 411, no. 1165
15	T. Hazor	-	[…]lʾrbʿt[…] […]לארבעת[…]	Iron Age IIB?	Jar fragment	Mendel 2011, fig. 1
16	T. Hazor	-	[…]šʿr[…] […]שער[…]	Iron Age IIB?	Jug or jar fragment	Mendel 2011, fig. 2
17	T. Hazor	-	bnʾl בנאל	Iron Age IIB?	Jar fragment; it may belong to a shoulder of a torpedo storage jar	Mendel 2011, fig. 3
18	T. Hazor	B1912/1	[…]yw יו[…]	Str. V	Jar fragment; it may belong to a shoulder of a torpedo storage jar	Yadin *et al.* 1961, pl. CCCLVII, 11; Naveh 1989; Renz/Röllig 1995, 126–127; Dobbs-Allsopp *et al.* 2005, 193
19	T. Hazor	B2241/1 L. 3152	lpdy/h[…] לפדי\ה[…]	Str. V	Body fragment	Yadin *et al.* 1961, pl. CCCLVII, 12; Delavault/Lemaire 1979, 12; Naveh 1989; Dobbs-Allsopp *et al.* 2005, 192
20	T. Hazor	B. 2407/1 L. 3183	[…]spr[…] […]ספר[…]	Str. V	Jug fragment	Yadin *et al.* 1961, pl. CCCLVII, 10; Delavault/Lemaire 1979, 11; Naveh 1989

#	Site	Reg.	Reading	Context	Description	References
21	T. Hazor	B2712/1 L. 324	t šṭrn[…]/š ṭrw ת שטרנ\[...]\ש טרו	Str. VIII or V	Bowl fragment; the inscription was incised before firing	Yadin et al. 1961 pl. CCCLVII, 2; Delavault/Lemaire 1979, 10–11; Naveh 1989
22	T. Hazor	B. 4440 L. 3273	[…]š' zyl[…] [...]שא זיל[...]	Str. IX or VIII	Body fragment; the inscription was incised after firing	Yadin et al. 1961 pl. CCCLVII, 1; Delavault/Lemaire 1979, 10; Naveh 1989
23	T. Hazor	B. 19568 L. 1977	[…]l y[…] [...]ל י[...]	Str. VI	Body fragment	Ben-Tor 2012, fig. 15.5, 3
24	T. Hazor	B. 21064 L. 3129	ly לי	Str. VI or V	Body fragment	Ben-Tor 2012, fig. 15.5, 5
25	T. Hazor	B. 22008 L. 3270	[…]s ס[...]	Str. V	Body fragment	Ben-Tor 2012, fig. 15.5, 2
26	T. Hazor	B. 22312 L. 3320 B. 20451/4 L. 3060	ly/h[…] לי\ה[...]	Str. V	Jar	Ben-Tor 2012, fig. 15.5, 6
27	T. Hazor	B. 22847 L. 3386	[…]š?[…] [...]?ש[...]	Str. V	Body fragment	Ben-Tor 2012, fig. 15.5, 1
28	T. Hazor	B. 41651 L. 7136	[…]lyl לil[...]	Str. IV?	Jar; the piece may belong to a shoulder of a torpedo storage jar	Ben-Tor 2012, fig. 15.5, 4
29	T. Hazor	A105/1	[…]l'y[…] [...]לאי[...]	Str. VIII	Body fragment; the inscription was incised after firing	Yadin et al. 1960, pls. CLXIX, 2; CLXX, 2; Delavault/Lemaire 1979, 7; Dobbs-Allsopp et al. 2005, 186
30	T. Hazor	A150/4	[l]yrb'[m/l] bn 'lm[lk] ל[י]רבע[ם\ל] בן אלמ[נ]ל[ך?]	Str. V	Jar fragment; it may belong to a shoulder of a torpedo storage jar	Yadin et al. 1960, pls. CLXIX, 6; CLXX, 6; Delavault/Lemaire 1979, 9–10; Dobbs-Allsopp et al. 2005, 188–189

Appendix B: Inscriptions and Inscribed Items   259

#	Site	Reg.	Reading	Context	Description	References
31	T. Hazor	A189/6	[...]'w'[...] [...]אוא[...]	Str. VIII	Body fragment	Yadin et al. 1960, pls. CLXIX, 1; CLXX, 1; Delavault/Lemaire 1979, 6–7; Dobbs-Allsopp et al. 2005, 185
32	T. Hazor	A382/1	bt z[...] בת ז[...]	Str. VIII	Jar; inscription was incised after firing	Yadin et al. 1960, pls. CLXIX, 3; CLXX, 3; Delavault/Lemaire 1979, 7–8; Dobbs-Allsopp et al. 2005, 186–187; Sass 2005, 85
33	T. Hazor	A1693/3	[...]tt'[...] [...]תתא[...]	Str. VIII	Body fragment; inscription was incised after firing	Yadin et al. 1960, pls. CLXIX, 4; CLXX, 4; Delavault/Lemaire 1979, 8; Dobbs-Allsopp et al. 2005, 187
34	T. Hazor	B2423/1	mz, [...]yḥḥ, qdš מז, [...]יהח, קדש	Str. V	Complete bowl	Yadin et al. 1961, pl. CCCLVII, 4, 6; Naveh 1961; Renz/Röllig 1995, 127–128; Dobbs-Allsopp et al. 2005, 190–191
35	T. Hazor	B489/1	ldlyw לדליו	Str. V	Body fragment; inscription was (probably) incised before firing	Yadin et al. 1960, pls. CLXXII; Renz/Röllig 1995, 125; Dobbs-Allsopp et al. 2005, 190
36	T. Hazor	A76/4	lmkbrm/dm למכברם\למכבדם	Str. VI	Jar fragment; inscription was incised before firing	Yadin et al. 1960, pls. CLXIX, 5; CLXX, 5; Delavault/Lemaire 1979, 8–9; Dobbs-Allsopp et al. 2005, 187–188
37	T. Hazor	B190/1	lpqḥ smdr לפקח סמדר	Str. V	Jar fragment; inscription was incised after firing	Yadin et al. 1960, pls. XCV, 4; CLXXI; Renz/Röllig 1995, 124; Dobbs-Allsopp et al. 2005, 189–190

#	Site	Reg.	Reading	Context	Description	References
38	T. Hazor	B4851	gḫ[…] […]חג	Str. VI	Bowl fragment	Yadin et al. 1961, pls. CCCLVII, 3; CCCLVIII, 3; Delavault/Lemaire 1979, 11; Naveh 1989
39	T. Hazor	A2088/1	Unclear reading	Str. VI or V	Bowl fragment	Yadin et al. 1961, pls. CCCLVII, 7; CCCLVIII, 7; Delavault/Lemaire 1979, 11; Naveh 1989
40	T. Hazor	A3008/2	Unclear reading	Str. V	Bowl fragment	Yadin et al. 1961, pl. CCCLVII, 8; Naveh 1989; Renz/Röllig 1995, 125–126
41	T. Hazor	A2092/1	ḥ ח	Str. V	Bowl fragment	Yadin et al. 1961, pl. CCCLVII, 9; Naveh 1989; Renz/Röllig 1995, 126
42	T. Hazor	L201/4	[…]l[…] […]ל[…]	Str. V	Bowl fragment	Garfinkel 1997, III.43, 4
43	T. Hazor	L439	[…]kšt[…]? ?[…]כשת[…]	Str. VII	Bowl fragment	Garfinkel 1997, figs. III.33, 15; III.55
44	T. Hazor	A4101/1	ʾ א	Str. VI	Bowl fragment with an alphabetic sign	Yadin et al. 1961, pls. CLXXXII, 7; CCCXLIX, 7
45	T. Hazor	B2017/1	š ש	Str. VI	Bowl fragment with an alphabetic sign	Yadin et al. 1961, pls. CCXX, 34; CCCLIX
46	T. Kinrot	1690/1	nʿnnr[…] […]נעננ	-	Body fragment	Fritz 1990, pl. 101, 1; Renz/Röllig 1995, 65
47	T. Kinrot	1587/1	ʾ א	Str. IV	Jar handle with an alphabetic sign	Fritz 1990, pl. 104, 9
48	T. Kinrot	2500/1	[…]ʾg[…] […]גא[…]	Str. IA	Body fragment	Fritz 1990, pl. 101, 3; Renz/Röllig 1995, 226–227
49	T. Kinrot	2506/1	[…]ḥ?[…]? […]?ח[…]	Str. IA	Body fragment; the two signs located to the left of the ḥ are	Fritz 1990, pl. 101, 2; Renz/Röllig 1995, 226

Appendix B: Inscriptions and Inscribed Items 261

#	Site	Reg.	Reading	Context	Description	References
					probably not alphabetic (numbers?)	
50	T. Kinrot	2530/1	kd hš'r כד השער	Str. IA	Jug	Fritz 1990, pl. 100, 2; Renz/Röllig 1995, 225
51	T. Kinrot	2391/1	l'plṭ אלפלט	Str. I	Almost complete jug	Fritz 1990, pl. 100, 1; Renz/Röllig 1995, 132–133
52	et-Tell/Bethsaida	9210	zkryw זכריו	Str. V	Jar handle	Avigad/Sass 1997, no. 669; Brandl 2009, fig. 4.1
53	et-Tell/Bethsaida	-	'qb' עקבא	Str. II	Body fragment	Arav 1995, fig. 11
54	et-Tell/Bethsaida	-	lšm לשם	Str. V	Complete jug	Arav 2009, figs. 1.107, a; 1.108; Savage 2009, fig. 3.2
55	et-Tell/Bethsaida	-	mky מכי	-	Body fragment	Arav 1999, fig. 36; Dobbs-Allsopp *et al.* 2005, 137
56	T. Hadar	2022/1	šd'l.nz'' שדאל נזאא	Str. III?	Jar fragment; inscription was incised after firing	Kleiman 2019a, 161–163; pl. 100
57	T. 'Ein Gev	-	lšky' לשקיא	Str. MIII	Complete jar	Mazar *et al.* 1964, fig. 8, 1
58	T. 'Ein Gev	-	[…]'rt[…] [...]ארת[...]	-	Bowl fragment; inscription was probably incised after firing	Kleiman 2019, 397
59	T. er-Rumeith	Handle 522	' א	-	Jar handle with an alphabetic sign; incised before firing	Lapp/Cooper 2015, fig. 11.5
60	T. er-Rumeith	Handle 521	s ס	-	Jar handle with an alphabetic sign; incised before firing	Lapp/Cooper 2015, fig. 11.4

Appendix C: Short-Lived Radiocarbon Samples

#	Site/Str.	Period	Reg. No.	Material	Uncalibrated	68.2%	95.4%	References
1	T. Abel K-2	Iron Age IIA?	--- Fill	Olive pit	2729±19	898–833 BCE	911–821 BCE	Yahalom-Mack *et al.* 2021, 6, n. 6
2	T. Dan V	Early Iron Age I	L. 3024 Floor	Olive pits	2930±50	1210–1053 BCE	1283–940 BCE	Ilan 1999, Table 3.12; Kaniewski *et al.* 2017, Table S4
3	T. Hazor XII/XI	Late Iron Age I?	L. 8254 Pit	Olive pits	2996±18	1268–1205 BCE	1283–1130 BCE	Sharon *et al.* 2007, Tables 7–8
4	T. Hazor Xa	Late Iron Age IIA	B. 3784 L. 8579 Floor	Olive pits	2632±27	813–792 BCE	831–776 BCE	Sharon *et al.* 2007, Tables 7–8
5	T. Hazor IXa	Late Iron Age IIA	B. 3785 L. 8087 Floor	Olive pits	2692±21	894–809 BCE	900–806 BCE	Sharon *et al.* 2007, Tables 7–8
6	T. Hazor Xb	Late Iron Age IIA	B. 3786 L. 8595 Floor	Olive pits	2650±25	822–796 BCE	895–788 BCE	Sharon *et al.* 2007, Tables 7–8
7	T. Kinneret VI	Late Iron Age I	B. 5071	Olive pit	---	1120–995 BCE	-	Fritz 1999, 112–114; Fritz/Münger 2002, 12
8	et-Tell/Bethsaida VI	Late Iron Age I?	B. 4281/1 Granary Destruction layer	Grain seeds	2815±17	997–931 BCE	1013–913 BCE	Sharon *et al.* 2007, Tables 7–8
9	et-Tell/Bethsaida VI	Late Iron Age I?	VIRI	Grain seeds	2820±3.3	1003–933 BCE	1008–927 BCE	Scott *et al.* 2007, Table 5

#	Site/Str.	Period	Reg. No.	Material	Uncalibrated	68.2%	95.4%	References
10	et-Tell/Bethsaida VI	Late Iron Age I?	Granary Destruction layer	Wheat seeds	2780±30	983–854 BCE	1007–835 BCE	Arav et al. 2014, 6
11	et-Tell/Bethsaida VI	Iron Age IIA	R 3320 Destruction layer	Barley	2550±25	793–596 BCE	799–566 BCE	Arav/Boaretto 2009, Table 10.1
12	et-Tell/Bethsaida VI/V	Iron Age IIA?	B. 12656 Fill	Grain seeds	2710±30	898–816 BCE	912–807 BCE	Arav et al. 2016, 17–18
13	T. Hadar IV	Late Iron Age I	B. 3795/1 L. 334 Destruction layer	Grain seeds	2791±52	1009–846 BCE	1107–817 BCE	Sharon et al. 2007, Tables 7–8
14	T. Hadar IV	Late Iron Age I	B. 4291/1 L. 334 Destruction layer	Grain seeds	2856±30	1105–935 BCE	1119–926 BCE	Sharon et al. 2007, Tables 7–8
15	T. Hadar IV	Late Iron Age I	VIRI L. 334 Destruction layer	Grain seeds	2836±3.3	1012–938 BCE	1044–930 BCE	Scott et al. 2007, Table 5
16	T. 'Ein Gev KIV	Late Iron Age I	B. 91395 Destruction	Leguminosae	2800±40	1006–906 BCE	1051–832 BCE	Sugimoto 2015a, n. 2
17	T. 'Ein Gev KIV	Late Iron Age I	B. 91395 Destruction	Leguminosae	2800±30	996–913 BCE	1044–841 BCE	Sugimoto 2015a, n. 2
18	T. 'Ashtara	Iron Age I?	Destruction layer?	Grape seeds	2885±35	1120–1010 BCE	1203–934 BCE	Vogel/Waterbolk 1972, 53
19	T. Irbid	Iron Age I?	001.53.8.6 Destruction layer	Grain seeds	3040±40	1385–1227 BCE	1414–1133 BCE	Ambers/Matthews/Bowman 1989, 28

Note: All the calibrated dates, excluding the sample from Tel Kinrot, are according to IntCal 20 (Reimer et al. 2020).

Bibliography*

ABD EL-KADER, D. (1931): Les fouilles de Tsil et de Tell-el-Asch'ari, *Revue Archéologique Syrienne* I–V, 69–70.
– (1949): Un orthostate du temple de Hadad à Damas, *Syria* 26, 191–195.
ABOU ASSAF, A. (1968): Tell-'Aschtara in Südsyrian. Erste Kampagne 1966, *Annales Archéologiques Arabes Syriennes* 18, 103–122.
– (1969): Tell Aschtara. 2. Kampagne 1967, *Annales Archéologiques Arabes Syriennes* 19, 101–108.
– (1974): Ein Mittelbronzezeitliches Grab in aṭ-Ṭaiybih und die Gleichsetzung von aṭ-Ṭaiybih mit Tub-ja, *Baghdader Mitteilungen* 7, 13–20.
– (2005): Dibbet Brekeh, des Nabatéens aux Cananéens, in: M. AL-MAQDISSI et al. (eds.), *Hauran V: La Syrie du Sud du Néolithique à l'Antiquité Tardive Vol. II* (Bibliothèque archéologique et historique 202), Beirut, 33–49.
ABOUSAMRA, G. (2019): Biblical Ṣoba: A Location Attempt, in: J. DUŠEK/J. MYNÁŘOVÁ (eds.), *Aramaean Borders: Defining Aramaean Territories in the 10th–8th Centuries B.C.E.* (CHANE 101), Leiden/Boston, 231–244.
AHARONI, Y. (1953): The Land of 'Amqi, *IEJ* 3, 153–161.
– (1957): *The Settlement of the Israelite Tribes in the Upper Galilee*, Jerusalem [Hebrew].
– (1979): *The Land of the Bible: A Historical Geography*, London.
AHARONI, Y./AMIRAN, R. (1958): A New Scheme for the Sub-Division of the Iron Age in Palestine, *IEJ* 8, 171–184.
AḤITUV, S./MAZAR, A. (2013): The Inscriptions from Tel Rehov and Their Contribution to the Study of Script and Writing during the Iron Age IIA, *Maarav* 20, 205–246.
– (2014): The Inscriptions from Tel Rehov and their Contribution to the Study of Script and Writing during Iron Age IIA, in: E. ESHEL/Y. LEVIN (eds.), *"See, I Will Bring a Scroll Recounting What Befell Me" (Ps 40:8): Epigraphy and Daily Life from the Bible to the Talmud Dedicated to the Memory of Professor Hanan Eshel* (Journal of Ancient Judaism Supplement 12), Göttingen, 39–68.
AHLSTRÖM, G. (1985): The Cult Room at 'En Gev, *TA* 12, 93–95.
AHRENS, A. (2010): The Egyptian Objects from Tell Hizzin in the Beqa'a Valley (Lebanon): An Archaeological and Historical Reassessment, *AeL* 25, 201–222.
AKKERMANS, P.M.M.G./SCHWARTZ, G.M. (2003): *The Archaeology of Syria: From Complex Hunter-gatherers to Early Urban Societies (c. 16,000–300 BC)*, Cambridge.
AL-BASHAIREH, K./AL-MUHEISEN, Z. (2011): Subsistence Strategies and Palaeodiet of Tell al-Husn, Northern Jordan: Nitrogen and Carbon Stable Isotope Evidence and Radiocarbon Dates, *Journal of Archaeological Science* 38, 2606–2612.
ALBRIGHT, W.F. (1925): Bronze Age Mounds of Northern Palestine and the Hauran: The Spring Trip of the School in Jerusalem, *BASOR* 19, 5–19.
– (1929): New Israelite and Pre-Israelite Sites: The Spring Trip of 1929, *BASOR* 35, 1–14.
– (1956): The Biblical Tribe of Massa' and Some Congeners, in: R. CIASCA (ed.), *Studi Orientalistici in Onore di Giorgio Levi Della Vida* (Pubblicazioni dell'Istituto per l'Oriente 52), Rome, 1–14.

---

* All the abbreviations of journal and series names follow the *Society of Biblical Literature Handbook of Style*, second edition (Atlanta, 2014).

ALBRIGHT, W.F./ROWE, A. (1928): A Royal Stele of the New Empire from Galilee, *Journal of Egyptian Archaeology* 14, 281–287.

ALEXANDRE, Y. (1995): The 'Hippo' Jar and Other Storage Jars at Hurvat Rosh Zayit, *TA* 22, 77–88.

– (2002): A Fluted Bronze Bowl with a Canaanite-Early Phoenician Inscription from Kefar Veradim, in: Z. GAL (ed.), *Eretz Zaphon: Studies in Galilean Archaeology*, Jerusalem, 65–74.

– (2019): Rosh Pinna, *HA-ESI* 131 [online publication].

AL-MUHAMMAD, Q. (2015): Tell al-Ashaari in Hauran throughout the Bronze Age: The 2010 Excavation Results, in: J.A. MASSIH/S. NISHIYAMA (eds.), *Archaeological Explorations in Syria 2000–2011: Proceedings of ISCACH-Beirut 2015*, Oxford, 91–99.

AMADASI GUZZO, M.G. (2014): Tell Afis in the Iron Age: The Aramaic Inscriptions, *NEA* 77, 54–57.

– (2019): What Do We Know about the Borders and Exchanges between Aram and Phoenicia in the 9th–8th Centuries B.C.E. in Anatolia and Syria?, in: J. DUŠEK/J. MYNÁŘOVÁ (eds.), *Aramaean Borders: Defining Aramaean Territories in the 10th–8th Centuries B.C.E.* (CHANE 101), Leiden/Boston, 149–171.

AMBERS, J./MATTHEWS, K./BOWMAN, S. (1989): British Museum Radiocarbon Measurements XXI, *Radiocarbon* 31, 15–32.

AMIRAN, R. (1969): *Ancient Pottery of the Holy Land: From its Beginnings in the Neolithic Period to the End of the Iron Age*, Jerusalem.

ARAV, R. (1992): Golan, in: N.L. FREEDMAN (ed.), *ABD* (Volume 2), New York, 1057–1058.

– (1995): Tzer and the Fortified Cities of Naphtali, in: R. ARAV/R.A. FREUND (eds.), *Bethsaida: A City by the North Shore of the Sea of Galilee 1*, Kirksville, 193–201.

– (1999): Bethsaida – A Preliminary Report, 1994–1996, in: R. ARAV/R.A. FREUND (eds.), *Bethsaida: A City by the North Shore of the Sea of Galilee 2*, Kirksville, 3–114.

– (2004a): Towards a Comprehensive History of Geshur, in: R. ARAV/R.A. FREUND (eds.), *Bethsaida: A City by the North Shore of the Sea of Galilee 3*, Kirksville, 1–48.

– (2004b): Field Report on the 2004 Excavation Season. https://bethsaidaarchaeologyorg.files.wordpress.com/2017/01/bethsaida-2004-field-report.pdf [online publication].

– (2009a): Final Report on Area A, Stratum V, in: R. ARAV/R.A. FREUND (eds.), *Bethsaida: A City by the North Shore of the Sea of Galilee 4*, Kirksville 4, 1–222.

– (2009b): A Chronicle of a Pre-known Destruction. Analysis of the Stages of the Conquest and Destruction of the City of Bethsaida by Tiglath-Pileser III (732–734 BCE), *ErIsr* 20, 328–338 [Hebrew with English summary].

– (2013): Geshur: The Southernmost Aramean Kingdom, in: A. BERLEJUNG/M.P. STRECK (eds.), *Arameans, Chaldeans, and Arabs in Babylonia and Palestine in the First Millennium B.C.* (Leipziger altorientalistische Studien 3), Wiesbaden, 1–29.

– (2015): The Fortified Cities of the Ṣiddim (Josh 19:35) Again: Rejoinder to N. Na'aman. *BN* 166, 3–9.

– (2018): Bethsaida: The Capital City of the Kingdom of Geshur, in: Z.I. FARBER/WRIGHT, J.L. (eds.), *Archaeology and History of Eighth-Century Judah* (ANE Monographs 23), Atlanta, 79–98.

– (2020): Thirty Years to the Excavations of Beth Saida, The Capital of the Forgotten Kingdom the Land of Geshur, *Qadmoniot* 160, 96–105 [Hebrew with English summary].

ARAV, R./BERNETT, M. (2000): The bīt ḫilāni at Bethsaida: Its Place in Aramaean/Neo-Hittite and Israelite Palace Architecture in the Iron Age II, *IEJ* 50, 47–81.

ARAV, R./BOARETTO, E. (2009): Radiocarbon Dating of the City Gate, in: R. ARAV/R.A. FREUND (eds.), *Bethsaida: A City by the North Shore of the Sea of Galilee 4*, Kirksville 4, 200–203.

ARAV, R. et al. (2014): Field Report on the 2016 Excavation Season. https://bethsaidaarchaeologyorg.files.wordpress.com/2017/01/bethsaida-2014-field-report.pdf [online publication].

– (2016): Field Report on the 2016 Excavation Season. https://bethsaidaarchaeologyorg.files.wordpress.com/2017/01/bethsaida-2016-field-report.pdf [online publication].

ARIE, E. (2006): The Iron Age I Pottery: Levels K-5 and K-4 and an Intra-Site Spatial Analysis of the Pottery from Stratum VIA, in: I. FINKELSTEIN/D. USSISHKIN/B. HALPERN (eds.), *Megiddo IV: The 1998–2002 Seasons* (SMNIA 24), Tel Aviv, 191–298.
- (2008): Reconsidering the Iron Age II Strata at Tel Dan: Archaeological and Historical Implications, *TA* 35, 6–64.
- (2011): *"In the Land of the Valley": Settlement, Social and Cultural Processes in the Jezreel Valley from the End of the Late Bronze Age to the Formation of the Monarchy* (PhD diss., Tel Aviv University), Tel Aviv [Hebrew with English summary].
- (2013a): The Iron IIA Pottery, in: I. FINKELSTEIN/D. USSISHKIN/E.H CLINE (eds.), *Megiddo V: The 2004–2008 Seasons* (SMNIA 31), Tel Aviv, 668–828.
- (2013b): The Late Bronze III and Iron I Pottery: Levels K-6, M-6, M-5, M-4 and H-9., in: I. FINKELSTEIN/D. USSISHKIN/E.H CLINE (eds.), *Megiddo V: The 2004–2008 Seasons* (SMNIA 31), Tel Aviv, 475–667.
- (2017): The Omride Annexation of the Beth-Shean Valley, in: O. LIPSCHITS/Y. GADOT/M.J. ADAMS (eds.), *Rethinking Israel: Studies in the History and Archaeology of Ancient Israel in Honor of Israel Finkelstein*, Winona Lake, 1–18.

ARO, S. (2016): Der Basaltlöwe von Sheikh Sa'ad und die Neuassyrische Provinz Qarnina, *Mitteilungen der Deutschen Orient-Gesellschaft zu Berlin* 148, 143–164.

ASTER, S.Z./FAUST, A. (2018): *The Southern Levant under Assyrian Domination*, Winona Lake.

AVIGAD, N. (1966): An Inscribed Bowl from Dan, *IEJ* 100, 42–44.

AVIGAD. N./SASS, B. (1997): *Corpus of West Semitic Stamp Seals*, Jerusalem.

AVSHALOM-GORNI, D./GETZOV, N. (2001): Tell el-Wawiyat – 1999, *HA-ESI* 113, 1*–3*.
- (2003): Tell el-Wawiyat – 2001, *HA-ESI* 115, 1*–2*.

AZNAR, C. (2005): *Exchange Networks in the Southern Levant during the Iron Age II: A Study of Pottery Origin and Distribution* (PhD diss., Harvard University), Cambridge.

BALLARD, R.D. et al. (2002): Iron Age Shipwrecks in Deep Water off Ashkelon, Israel, *AJA* 106, 151–168.

BARAKO, T.J. (2015a): The Setting and Identification, in: T.J. BARAKO/N.L. LAPP (eds.), *Tell er-Rumeith: The Excavations of Paul W. Lapp, 1962 and 1967* (AASOR 22), Boston, 3–8.
- (2015b): Summary and Conclusions, in: T.J. BARAKO/N.L. LAPP (eds.), *Tell er-Rumeith: The Excavations of Paul W. Lapp, 1962 and 1967* (AASOR 22), Boston, 189–195.
- (2015c): The Iron Age Pottery, in: T.J. BARAKO/N.L. LAPP (eds.), *Tell er-Rumeith: The Excavations of Paul W. Lapp, 1962 and 1967* (AASOR 22), Boston, 71–187.

BARAKO, T.J./N.L. LAPP (2015): *Tell er-Rumeith: The Excavations of Paul W. Lapp, 1962 and 1967* (AASOR 22), Boston.

BARAMKI, D.C. (1961): Preliminary Report on the Excavations at Tell el-Ghassil, *Bulletin du Musée de Beyrouth* XVI, 9–97.
- (1964): Second Preliminary Report on the Excavations at Tell el-Ghassil, *Bulletin du Musée de Beyrouth* XVII, 47–101.
- (1966): Third Preliminary Report on the Excavations at Tell el-Ghassil, *Bulletin du Musée de Beyrouth* XIX, 29–48.

BARKAY, G. et al. (1974): Archaeological Survey in the Northern Bashan (Preliminary Report), *IEJ* 24, 173–184.

BASTERT, K./HOCKMANN, D. (2008): Tell Johfiyeh Die Keramik des Tiefschnitts (eine Quantitative Analyse), *UF* 40, 65–127.

BAUCKHAM, R. (2015): Gergesa is Tel Hadar, Not Kursi, *RA* 122, 268–283.

BECHAR, S. (2017): The Middle and Late Bronze Age Pottery, in: A. BEN-TOR et al. (eds.), *Hazor VII: The 1990–2012 Excavations: The Bronze Age*, Jerusalem, 199–467.

BEN-AMI, D. (2001): The Iron Age I at Tel Hazor in Light of the Renewed Excavations, *IEJ* 51, 148–170.

- (2003): The *Galilee and the Hula Valley during the Early Iron Age: The Characteristics of the Material Culture in Northeastern Israel in View of the Recent Excavations at Hazor* (PhD diss., Hebrew University of Jerusalem), Jerusalem [Hebrew with English summary].
BEN-AMI, D. (2013): Hazor at the Beginning of the Iron Age, *NEA* 76, 101–104.
BEN-DOR EVIAN, S. (2011): Shishak's Karnak Relief – More than Just Name-Rings, in: S. BAR/D. KAHN/J.J. SHIRLEY (eds.), *Canaan and Israel: History, Imperialism, Ideology and Literature* (CHANE 52), Leiden/Boston, 11–22.
BEN-DOV, R. (2011): *Dan III: The Late Bronze Age*, Jerusalem.
BEN-SHLOMO (2019): Chemical and Petrographic Analysis of Aegean/Philistine Pottery from Tel Dan, in: D. ILAN (ed.), *Dan IV: The Iron Age I Settlement. The Avraham Biran Excavations (1966–1999)*, Jerusalem, 415–418.
BEN-SHLOMO, D./SHAI, I./MAEIR, A.M. (2004): Late Philistine Decorated Ware ("Ashdod Ware"): Typology, Chronology, and Production Centers, *BASOR* 335, 1–35.
BEN-TOR, A. (1993): Tel Hazor – 1991, *HA-ESI* 108, 10–12 [Hebrew].
- (2000): Hazor and the Chronology of Northern Israel: A Reply to Israel Finkelstein, *BASOR* 317, 9–15.
- (2003): Old Canaan and New Israel, *ErIsr* 27, 50–54 [Hebrew with English summary].
- (2012): Varia, in: BEN-TOR, A./BEN-AMI, D./SANDHAUS, D. (eds.), *Hazor VI: The 1990–2009 Excavations. The Iron Age*, Jerusalem, 578–585.
- (2016): *Hazor: Canaanite Metropolis, Israelite City*, Jerusalem.
- (2020): Building 7050 at the Acropolis of Late Bronze Hazor: A Palace After All, *TA* 47, 173–192.
BEN-TOR, A./BEN-AMI, D. (1998): Hazor and the Archaeology of the Tenth Century B.C.E., *IEJ* 48, 1–37.
BEN-TOR, A./M.-T. RUBIATO (1999): Did the Israelites Destroy the Canaanite City? *BAR* 25, 22–29.
BEN-TOR, A./ZARZECKI-PELEG, A. (2015): Iron Age IIA–B: Northern Valleys and Upper Galilee, in: S. GITIN (ed.), *The Ancient Pottery of Israel and Its Neighbors: From the Iron Age through the Hellenistic Period*, Jerusalem, 135–188.
BEN-TOR, A./ZUCKERMAN, S. (2007): Hazor at the End of the Late Bronze Age: Back to Basics, *BASOR* 350, 1–6.
BEN-TOR, A./BEN-AMI, D./SANDHAUS, D. (2012): *Hazor VI: The 1990–2009 Excavations. The Iron Age*, Jerusalem.
BEN-TOR, A./COHEN-WEINBERGER, A./WEEDEN, M. (2017): A Cooking-pot from Hazor with Neo-Hittite (Luwian) Seal Impressions, in: O. LIPSCHITS/Y. GADOT/M.J. ADAMS (eds.), *Rethinking Israel: Studies in the History and Archaeology of Ancient Israel in Honor of Israel Finkelstein*, Winona Lake, 29–45.
BEN-TOR, A. et al. (2017): *Hazor VII: The 1990–2012 Excavations. The Late Bronze Age*, Jerusalem.
BEN-YOSEF, E. (2016): Back to Solomon's Era: Results of the First Excavations at "Slaves' Hill" (Site 34, Timna, Israel), *BASOR* 376, 169–198.
BECK, P./KOCHAVI, M. (1986): A Dated Assemblage of the Late 13th Century B.C.E. from the Egyptian Residency at Aphek, *TA* 12, 29–42.
BENZ, B.C. (2019): The Destruction of Hazor: Israelite History and the Construction of History in Israel, *JSOT* 44, 262–78.
BERGER, U. (2013): Tel Yaʻaf (South-East), *HA-ESI* 127 [online publication].
BERLEJUNG, A. (2009): Twisting Traditions: Programmatic Absence-Theology for the Northern Kingdom in 1 Kgs 12:26–33* (The "Sin of Jeroboam"), *JNSL* 35, 1–42.
- (2012): Assyrians in the West: Assyrianization, Colonialism, Indifference or Development Policy?, in: M. NISSINEN (ed.), *Congress Volume Helsinki 2010* (VTSup 148), Leiden/Boston, 21–59.
- (2014): Outlook: Aramaeans Outside of Syria; Palestine, in: H. NIEHR (ed.), *The Aramaeans in Ancient Syria* (HdO 106), Leiden/Boston, 339–365.
- (2019): Identity Performances in Multilinguistic Contexts: The Cases of Yariḥ-ʻezer from Amman and Ikausu/Achish from Ekron, *WO* 49, 252–287.

BERNETT, M./KEEL, O. (1998): *Mond, Stier und Kult am Stadttor: Die Stele von Betsaida (et-Tell)* (OBO 161), Fribourg/Göttingen.

BETANCOURT, P.P. (1977): *The Aeolic Style in Architecture: A Survey of Its Development in Palestine, the Halikarnassos Peninsula, and Greece, 1000–500 B.C.*, Princeton.

BIRAN, A. (1971): Laish-Dan — Secrets of a Canaanite City and an Israelite City, *Qadmoniot* 13, 2–11 [Hebrew with English summary].

– (1982): The Temenos at Dan, *ErIsr* 16, 15–43 [Hebrew with English summary].

– (1988): A Mace-Head and the Office of Amadiyo at Dan, *Qadmoniot* 81–82, 11–17 [Hebrew with English summary].

– (1993): Dan, in: E. STERN (ed.), *NEAEHL*, Volume 1, 323–332.

– (1994): *Biblical Dan*, Jerusalem.

– (1996): High Places at the Gates of Dan? *ErIsr* 25, 55–58.

– (1999a): The Ḥuṣṣot of Dan, *ErIsr* 26, 25–29 [Hebrew with English summary].

– (1999b): Two Bronze Plaques and the Ḥuṣṣot of Dan, *IEJ* 49, 43–54.

– (2002): A Chronicle of the Excavations 1993–1999, in: A. BIRAN/R. BEN-DOV (eds.), *Dan II: A Chronicle of the Excavations and the Late Bronze Age "Mycenaean" Tomb*, Jerusalem, 5–32.

BIRAN, A./NAVEH, J. (1993): An Aramaic Stela Fragment from Tel Dan, *IEJ* 43, 81–98.

– (1995): The Tel Dan Inscription: A New Fragment, *IEJ* 45, 1–18.

BLOCH-SMITH, E. (1992): *Judahite Burial Practices and Beliefs about the Dead* (JSOTSup 123), Sheffield.

BLOMQUIST, H.T. (1999): *Gates and Gods: Cults in the City Gates of Iron Age Palestine. An Investigation of the Archaeological and Biblical Sources* (OTS 46), Stockholm.

BLUM, E. (2016): The Relations between Aram and Israel in the 9th and 8th Centuries BCE: The Textual Evidence, in: O. SERGI/M. OEMING/I. DE HULSTER (eds.), *In Search of Aram and Israel: Politics, Culture and Identity* (ORA 20), Tübingen, 37–56.

BOARETTO, E. (2022): Radiocarbon Results, in: I. FINKELSTEIN/M.A.S. MARTIN (eds.), *Megiddo VI: The 2010–2014 Seasons* (Monograph Series of the Institute of Archaeology of Tel Aviv University), Tel Aviv.

BONATZ, D. (2002): Preliminary Remarks on an Archaeological Survey in the Anti-Lebanon, *BAAL* 6, 283–307.

– (2019): The Myth of Aramean Culture, in: A. BERLEJUNG/A.M. MAEIR (eds.), *Researches on Israel and Aram: Autonomy, Interdependence and Related Issues. Proceedings of the First Annual RIAB Center Conference, Leipzig, June 2016* (ORA 34), Tübingen, 159–177.

– (2020): Tell Ushayer, *ACOR: Archaeology in Jordan* 2, 32–34.

BONFIL, R./ZARZECKI-PELEG, A. (2007): The Palace in the Upper City of Hazor as an Expression of a Syrian Architectural Paradigm, *BASOR* 348, 25–47.

BÖRKER-KLÄHN, J. (1982): *Altvorderasiatische Bildstelen und vergleichbare Felsreliefs* (BaF 4), Mainz.

BOSSERT, H.T. (1951): *Altsyrien: Kunst und Handwerk in Cypern, Syrien, Paläistina, Transjordanien und Arabien von den Aufängen bis zum völligen Aufgehen in der griechisch-römischen Kultur*, Tübingen.

BOUZEK, J. (2019): Hrozný's Excavations, 1924–1925: Sheikh Sa'ad, Tell Erfad, in: R.I. KIM//J. MYNÁŘOVÁ/P. PAVÚK (eds.), *Hrozný and Hittite: The First Hundred Years* (CHANE 107), Leiden/Boston, 32–43.

BRAEMER, F. (1984): Prospections archéologiques dans le Ḥawrān (Syrie), *Syria* 61, 219–250.

– (1993): Prospections archéologiques dans le Hawran (Syrie) III, *Syria* 70, 117–170.

– (2002): Le rempart de Bosra au IIe millénaire avant notre ère, *Syria* 79, 65–74.

BRAEMER, F./IBAÑEZ, J.J./SHAARANI, W. (2011): Qarassa (Mohafazat de Suweida), Campagne 2009, *Chronique Archéologique en Syrie* 4, 31–42.

BRANDL, B. (1984): A Proto-Aeolic Capital from Gezer, *IEJ* 34, 173–176.

– (2009): An Israelite Administrative Jar Handle Impression from Bethsaida (et-Tell), in: R. ARAV/R.A. FREUND (eds.), *Bethsaida: A City by the North Shore of the Sea of Galilee 4*, Kirksville, 136–146.

BRAUN, E. (2001): Iron Age II Burials and Archaeological Investigations at Ḥorbat Menorim, *Atiqot* 42, 171–182.

– (2015): Two Seasons of Rescue and Exploratory Excavations at Horbat 'Avot, Upper Galilee, *Atiqot* 83, 1–66.

BREASTED, J.H. (1929): Forward, in: C.S. FISHER (ed.), *The Excavation of Armageddon* (OIP 4), Chicago, vii–xiii.

BRON, F./LEMAIRE, A. (1989): Les inscriptions araméennes de Hazaël, *RA* 83, 35–44.

BROSHI, M./FINKELSTEIN, I. (1992): The Population of Palestine in Iron Age II, *BASOR* 287, 47–60.

BRYCE, T. (2012): *The World of the Neo-Hittite Kingdoms: A Political and Military History*, Oxford.

BUNIMOVITZ, S. (1994): The Problem of Human Resources in Late Bronze Age Palestine and its Socioeconomic Implications, *UF* 26, 1–20.

BUNIMOVITZ, S./LEDERMAN, Z. (2001): The Iron Age Fortifications of Tel Beth Shemesh: A 1990–2000 Perspective, *IEJ* 121–147.

– (2009): The Archaeology of Border Communities: Renewed Excavations at Tel Beth-Shemesh. Part 1: The Iron Age, *NEA* 72, 114–142.

BURNS, R. (2019): *Damascus: A History* (Second Edition), London/New York.

BUTLER, H.C./NORRIS, F.A./STOEVER, E.R. (1930): *Syria: Publications of the Princeton University Archaeological Expeditions to Syria in 1904–5 and 1909. Division I: Geography and Itinerary*, Leiden.

CAHILL, J.M. (2006): The Excavations at Tell el Hammah: A Prelude to Amihai Mazar's Beth-Shean Valley Regional Project, in: A.M. MAEIR/P.M. MIROSCHEDJI (eds.), *"I Will Speak the Riddles of Ancient Times": Archaeological and Historical Studies in Honor of Amihai Mazar*, Winona Lake, 429–460.

CANTRELL, D.O./FINKELSTEIN, I. (2006): A Kingdom for a Horse: The Megiddo Stables and Eighth Century Israel, in: I. FINKELSTEIN/D. USSISHKIN/B. HALPERN (eds.), *Megiddo IV: The 1998–2002 Seasons* (SMNIA 24), Tel Aviv, 643–665.

CHARVÁT, P. (2015): The Archaeological Investigation by Bedřich Hrozný at Sheikh Sa'ad in Syria, in: Š. VELHARTICKÁ (ed.), *Bedřich Hrozný and 100 Years of Hittitology*, Prague, 150–160.

CHAMBON, A. (1984): *Tell el-Far'ah I: L'Âge du Fer* ("Mémoire" 31), Paris.

CLINE, E.H. (2014): *1177 B.C.: The Year Civilization Collapsed*, Princeton.

COHEN-WEINBERGER, A./PANITZ-COHEN, N. (2014): The Black Juglets, in: Y. GARFINKEL/S. GANOR/M.G. HASEL (eds.), *Khirbet Qeiyafa, Vol. 2: Excavation Report 2009–2013. Stratigraphy and Architecture (Areas B, C, D, E)*, Jerusalem, 403–414.

COLDSTREAM, N. (2003): Some Aegean Reactions to the Chronological Debate in the Southern Levant, *TA* 30, 247–258.

– (1998): The First Exchange between Euboeans and Phoenicians: Who Took the Initiative?, in: S. GITIN/A. MAZAR/E. STERN (eds.), *Mediterranean Peoples in Transition, Thirteenth to Early Tenth Centuries BCE: In Honor of Professor Trude Dothan*, Jerusalem, 353–360.

CONTENAU, G. (1924): L'institut français d'archéologie et d'art musulmans de Damas, *Syria* 5, 203–211.

COPELAND, L./WESCOMBE, P.J. (1966): *Inventory of Stone-Age Sites in Lebanon: Part Two. North, South and East-Central Lebanon*, Beirut.

COVELLO-PARAN, K. (2010): Settlement Remains from the Bronze and Iron Ages at Ḥorbat Menorim (el-Manara), Lower Galilee, *Atiqot* 63, 1–14.

– (2012): The Iron Age Occupation at Qiryat Shemona (S), Stratum IV, in: Y. GADOT/A. YASUR-LANDAU (eds.), *Qiryat Shemona (S): Fort and Village in the Hula Valley* (Salvage Excavation Reports 7), Tel Aviv, 88–119.

CRANE, H.R./GRIFFIN, J.B. (1972): University of Michigan Radiocarbon Dates XV, *Radiocarbon* 14, 195–222.

DAJANI, R.W. (1964): Iron Age Tombs from Irbed, *ADAJ* 8–9, 99–101.

– (1966): Four Iron Age Tombs from Irbed, *ADAJ* 11, 88–101.

DAR, S. (1998): *The History of the Hermon: Settlement and Cult Sites of the Ituraeans*, Tel Aviv [Hebrew with English summary].

DALLEY, S. (1990): Yahweh in Hamath in the 8th Century BC: Cuneiform Material and Historical Deductions, *VT* 60, 21–32.

DAVIAU, M.P.M. (2001): Family Religion: Evidence for the Paraphernalia of the Domestic Cult, in: M.P.M. DAVIAU/J.W. WEVERS/M. WEIGL (eds.), *The World of the Aramaeans II: Studies in History and Archaeology in Honour of Paul-Eugène Dion* (JSOTSup 325), Sheffield, 199–229.

DAVID, A./MULLINS, R.A./PANITZ-COHEN, N. (2016): A Mnḫprr' from Tel Abel Beth Maacha, *Journal of Ancient Egyptian Interconnections* 9, 1–13.

DAVIS, A.R. (2013): *Tel Dan in Its Northern Cultic Context*, Atlanta.

DAY, J. (1992): Ashtaroth, in: N.L. FREEDMAN (ed.), *ABD* (Volume 1), New York, 491.

DAYAN, Y. (1962): *An Archaeological Survey in the Hula Valley*, Kibbutz Dan [Hebrew].

DELAVAULT, B./LEMAIRE, A. (1979): Les inscriptions phéniciennes de Palestine, *Rivista di Studi Fenici* 5, 1–39.

DENTZER, J.-M. *et al.* (2010): Formation et développement des villes en Syrie du Sud de l'époque hellénistique à l'époque byzantine: les exemples de Bosra, Suweida, Shahba, in: M. AL-MAQDISSI/F. BRAEMER/J.-M. DENTZER (eds.), *Hauran V: La Syrie du Sud du Néolithique à l'Antiquité tardive. Recherches récentes. Actes du colloque de Damas 2007 Vol. I* (Bibliothèque archéologique et historique 191), Beirut, 139–169.

DEVER, W.G. (1986): Abel-Beth-Ma'acah: Northern Gateway of Ancient Israel, in: L.T. GERATY/L.G. HERR (eds.), *The Archaeology of Jordan and Other Studies: Presented to Siegfried H. Horn*, Berrien Springs, 207–223.

– (2003): *Who Were the Early Israelites and Where Did They Come From?* Grand Rapids/Cambridge.

DEVER, W.G./HARRISON, A. (2017): Pottery of the Bronze and Iron Ages, in: A.M. BERLIN/S.C. HERBERT (eds.), *Tel Anafa II, iii*, Ann Arbor, 265–327.

DIJKSTRA, N. (2018): The Stele of Ramesses II from Sheikh Sa'ad, Syria (The Stone of Job): Rediscovered and Reconsidered, *UF* 49, 71–93.

DOBBS-ALLSOPP, F.W. *et al.* (2005): *Hebrew Inscriptions: Texts from the Biblical Period of the Monarchy with Concordance*, New Haven.

DOTHAN, M. (1975): Aphek on the Israel-Aram Border and Aphek on the Amorite Border, *ErIsr* 12, 63–65.

DOTHAN, T. (1982): *The Philistines and Their Material Culture*, Jerusalem.

DOUMET-SERHAL, C. (1996): *Les Fouilles de Tell el-Ghassil de 1972 à 1974: Étude du Matériel*, Beirut.

DUŠEK, J./MYNÁŘOVÁ, J. (2019): *Aramaean Borders: Defining Aramaean Territories in the 10th–8th Centuries B.C.E.* (CHANE 101), Leiden/Boston.

ECHT, R. (1984): *Kamid el-Loz 5: Die Stratigraphie* (Saarbrücker Beiträge zur Altertumskunde 34), Bonn.

EDWARDS, P.C. *et al.* (1990): Preliminary Report on the University of Sydney's Tenth Season of Excavations at Pella (Tabaqat Fahl) in 1988, *ADAJ* 34, 57–93.

EITAM, D. (1979): Olive Presses of the Israelite Period, *TA* 6, 3–4.

– (1983): "And Oil Out of the Flinty Rock", *Qadmoniot* 61, 23–27 [Hebrew with English summary].

EPH'AL, I. (1971): URU Ša-za-e-na = URU Sa-za-na, *IEJ* 21, 155–157.

– (1982): *The Ancient Arabs: Nomads on the Borders of the Fertile Crescent, 9th–5th Centuries B.C.*, Jerusalem.

EPH'AL, I./NAVEH, J. (1989): Hazael's Booty Inscriptions, *IEJ* 39, 192–200.

EPSTEIN, C. (1970): An Iron Age Lion's Head from the Golan, *Qadmoniot* 12, 134–135 [Hebrew with English summary].
- (1976): Mezad Tannuriya, *HA-ESI* 84, 5–6 [Hebrew].
- (1982): A Correction Concerning the Statue of a Lion from Kh. Mishrafawi, *Qadmoniot* 60, 126 [Hebrew with English summary].
- (1984): Mezad Tannuriya, *HA-ESI* 84, 5–6 [Hebrew].
- (1993): The Cities of the Land of Garu-Geshur Mentioned in EA 256 Reconsidered, in: M. HELTZER/A. SEGAL/D. KAUFMAN (eds.), *Studies in Archaeology and History of Ancient Israel in Honour of Moshe Dothan*, Haifa, 83–90.

EPSTEIN, C./GUTMAN, S. (1972): The Golan, in: M. KOCHAVI (ed.), *Judaea, Samaria and the Golan: Archaeological Survey 1967–1968*, Jerusalem [Hebrew].

ESHEL, E. et al. (in press): Two Iron Age Alphabetic Inscriptions from Tell es-Safi/Gath, Israel, *BASOR*.

FANTALKIN, A. (2001): Low Chronology and Greek Protogeometric and Geometric Pottery in the Southern Levant, *Levant* 33, 117–125.
- (2008): The Appearance of Rock-Cut Bench Tombs in Iron Age Judah as a Reflection of State Formation, in: A. FANTALKIN/A. YASUR-LANDAU (eds.), *Bene Israel: Studies in the Archaeology of Israel and the Levant during the Bronze and Iron Ages in Honour of Israel Finkelstein* (CHANE 31), Leiden/Boston, 17–44.

FANTALKIN, A./FINKELSTEIN, I. (2006): The Sheshonq I Campaign and the 8th Century BCE Earthquake—More on the Archaeology and History of the South in the Iron I–IIA, *TA* 33, 18–42.
- (2017): The Date of Abandonment and Territorial Affiliation of Khirbet Qeiyafa: An Update, *TA* 44, 53–60.

FANTALKIN, A./FINKELSTEIN, I./PIASETZKY, E. (2015): Late Helladic to Middle Geometric Aegean and Contemporary Cypriot Chronologies: A Radiocarbon View from the Levant, *BASOR* 373, 25–48.

FANTALKIN, A./KLEIMAN, A./MOMMSEN, H. (2022): The Greek Pottery from Area Q, in: I. FINKELSTEIN/M.A.S. MARTIN (eds.), *Megiddo VI: The 2010–2014 Seasons* (SMNIA 39), Tel Aviv: 1055–1065.

FANTALKIN, A. et al. (2020): Aegean Pottery in Iron IIA Megiddo: Typological, Chronological and Archaeometric Aspects, *Mediterranean Archaeology and Archaeometry* 20, 135–147.

FAßBECK, G. (2008): A Decorated Chalice from Tell el-ʿOrēme/Kinneret, *ZDPV* 124, 15–37.

FAUST, A. (2006): *Israel's Ethnogenesis: Settlement, Interaction, Expansion and Resistance* (Approaches to Anthropological Archaeology), London/Oakville.
- (2012): *The Archaeology of Israelite Society in Iron Age II*, Winona Lake.
- (2015): Settlement, Economy, and Demography under Assyrian Rule in the West: The Territories of the Former Kingdom of Israel as a Test Case, *JAOS* 135, 765-789.
- (2020): Between the Highland Polity and Philistia: The United Monarchy and the Resettlement of the Shephelah in the Iron Age IIA, with a Special Focus on Tel ʿEton and Khirbet Qeiyafa, *BASOR* 383, 115–136.
- (2021): *The Neo-Assyrian Empire in the Southwest: Imperial Domination and Its Consequences*, Oxford.

FAUST, A./BUNIMOVITZ, S. (2003): The Four Room House: Embodying Iron Age Israelite Society, *NEA* 66, 22–31.

FAUST, A./SAPIR, Y. (2018): The "Governor's Residency at Tel ʿEton, the United Monarchy, and the Impact of the Old-House Effect on Large-Scale Archaeological Reconstructions, *Radiocarbon* 60, 801–820.

FAUST, A. et al. (2017): The Birth, Life and Death of an Iron Age House at Tel ʿEton, Israel, *Levant* 49, 136–173.

FINKELSTEIN, I. (1988): *The Archaeology of the Israelite Settlement*, Jerusalem.
- (1995): The Date of the Settlement of the Philistines in Canaan, *TA* 22, 213–239.

- (1996): The Archaeology of the United Monarchy: An Alternative View, *Levant* 28, 177–187.
- (1999a): State Formation in Israel and Judah: A Contrast in Context, a Contrast in Trajectory, *NEA* 62, 35–52.
- (1999b): Hazor and the North in the Iron Age: A Low Chronology Perspective, *BASOR* 314, 55–70.
- (2000a): Hazor XII–XI with an Addendum on BEN-TOR's Dating of Hazor X–VII, *TA* 27, 231–247.
- (2000b): Omride Architecture, *ZDPV* 116, 114–138.
- (2002): The Campaign of Shoshenq I to Palestine: A Guide to the 10th Century BCE Polity, *ZDPV* 118, 109–135.
- (2003): City-States and States: Polity Dynamics in the 10th–9th Centuries B.C.E., in: W.G. DEVER/S. GITIN (eds.), *Symbiosis, Symbolism and the Power of the Past: Canaan, Ancient Israel, and their Neighbors*, Winona Lake, 75–83.
- (2005): Hazor at the End of the Late Bronze Age, *UF* 37, 341–349.
- (2009): Destructions. Megiddo as a Case Study, in: J.D. SCHLOEN (ed.), *Exploring the Longue Durée: Essays in Honor of Lawrence E. Stager*, Winona Lake, 113–126.
- (2010a): A Great United Monarchy? Archaeological and Historical Perspectives, in: R.G. KRATZ/H. SPIECKERMANN (eds.), *One God, One Cult, One Nation: Archaeological and Biblical Perspectives* (BZW 405), Berlin/New York, 3–28.
- (2010b): Kadesh Barnea: A Reevaluation of Its Archaeology and History, *TA* 37, 111–125.
- (2011a): Jerusalem in the Iron Age: Archaeology and Text; Reality and Myth, in: K. GALOR/G. AVNI (eds.), *The Jerusalem Perspective: 150 Years of Archaeological Research in the Holy City*, Winona Lake, 189–201.
- (2011b): Observations on the Layout of Iron Age Samaria, *TA* 38, 194–207.
- (2011c): Stages in the Territorial Expansion of the Northern Kingdom, *VT* 61, 227–242.
- (2012): Comments on the Date of Late-Monarchic Judahite Seal Impressions, *TA* 39, 203–211.
- (2013): *The Forgotten Kingdom: The Archaeology and History of Northern Israel* (Ancient Near Eastern Monographs 5), Atlanta.
- (2014a): Settlement Patterns and Territorial Polity in the Transjordanian Highlands in the Late Bronze Age, *UF* 45, 143–159.
- (2014b): The Archaeology of Tell el-Kheleifeh and the History of Ezion-geber/Elath, *Semitica* 56, 105–136.
- (2016a): Israel and Aram: Reflections on their Border, in: O. SERGI/M. OEMING/I. DE HULSTER (eds.), *In Search of Aram and Israel: Politics, Culture and Identity* (ORA 20), Tübingen, 17–36.
- (2016b): Does Rehob of the Beth Shean Valley appear in the Bible? *BN* 169, 3–9.
- (2017): What the Biblical Authors Knew about Canaan before and in the Early Days of the Hebrew Kingdoms, *UF* 48, 173–198.
- (2019): Jerusalem and the Benjamin Plateau in the Early Phases of the Iron Age: A Different Scenario, *ZDPV* 134, 190–195.
- (2020): Iron Age Chronology and Biblical History Rejoinders: The Late Bronze/Iron age Transition, Tel 'Eton and Lachish, *PEQ* 152, 82–93.

FINKELSTEIN, I./KLEIMAN, A. (2019): The Archaeology of the Days of Baasha? *RB* 126, 277–296.

FINKELSTEIN, I./NA'AMAN, N. (2005): Shechem of the Amarna Period and the Rise of the Northern Kingdom of Israel, *IEJ* 55, 172–193.

FINKELSTEIN, I./PIASETZKY, E. (2005): 14C Results from Megiddo, Tel Dor, Tel Rehov and Tel Hadar: Where do they Lead Us?, in: T.E. LEVY/T. HIGHAM (eds.), *The Bible and Radiocarbon Dating: Archaeology, Texts, and Science*, London/Oakville, 294–301.

- (2007a): Radiocarbon Dating and the Late-Iron I in Northern Canaan: A New Proposal, *UF* 39, 247–260.
- (2007b): Radiocarbon, Iron IIa Destructions and the Israel-Aram Damascus Conflicts in the 9th Century BCE, *UF* 39, 261–276.
- (2009): Radiocarbon-Dated Destruction Layers: A Skeleton for Iron Age Chronology in the Levant, *OJA* 28, 255–274.

– (2011): The Iron Age Chronology Debate: Is the Gap Narrowing? *NEA* 74, 50–54.
FINKELSTEIN, I./SASS, B. (2013): The West Semitic Alphabetic Inscriptions, Late Bronze II to Iron IIA: Archeological Context, Distribution and Chronology, *HeBAI* 2, 149–220.
FINKELSTEIN, I/SCHMID, K. (2017): *Jeroboam's Israel*, *HeBAI* 6, 259–261.
FINKELSTEIN, I./SILBERMAN, N.A. (2002): *The Bible Unearthed: Archaeology's New Vision of Ancient Israel and the Origin of Its Sacred Texts*, New York.
FINKELSTEIN, I./SINGER-AVITZ, L. (2009): Reevaluating Bethel, *ZDPV* 125, 33–48.
FINKELSTEIN, I./KOCH, I./LIPSCHITS, O. (2012): The Biblical Gilead. Observations on Identifications, Geographic Divisions and Territorial History, *UF* 43, 131–159.
FINKELSTEIN, I./LIPSCHITS, O./SERGI, O. (2013): Tell er-Rumeith in Northern Jordan: Some Archaeological and Historical Observations, *Semitica* 55, 7–23.
FINKELSTEIN, I./D. USSISHKIN/E.H. CLINE (2013): *Megiddo V: The 2004–2008 Seasons* (SMNIA 31), Tel Aviv.
FINKELSTEIN, I./ZIMHONI, O./KAFRI, A. (2000): The Iron Age Pottery Assemblages from Areas F, K and H and their Stratigraphic and Chronological Implications, in: I. FINKELSTEIN/D. USSISHKIN/B. HALPERN (eds.), *Megiddo III: The 1992–1996 Seasons* (SMNIA 18), Tel Aviv, 244–324.
FINKELSTEIN, I. et al. (2017): New Evidence on the Late Bronze-Iron I Transition at Megiddo: Implications for the End of the Egyptian Rule and the Appearance of Philistine Pottery, *AeL* 27, 261–280.
– (2022): *Megiddo VI: The 2010–2014 Seasons* (SMNIA 41), Tel Aviv.
FISCHER, P.M. (1997): *A Late Bronze to Early Iron Age Tomb at Saḥem, Jordan* (ADPV 21), Wiesbaden.
– (1998): A Late Bronze to Early Iron Age Tomb at Sahem, Jordan, *NEA* 61, 255.
– (2013): *Tell Abu al-Kharaz in the Jordan Valley* (Contributions to the Chronology of the Eastern Mediterranean XXXIV), Vienna.
FISCHER, P.M./KEEL, O. (1995): The Saḥem Tomb: The Scarabs, *ZDPV* 111, 135–150.
FISCHER, P.M./BÜRGE, T./AL-SHALABI, M. (2015): The "Ivory Tomb" at Tell Irbid, Jordan: Intercultural Relations at the End of the Late Bronze Age and the Beginning of the Iron Age, *BASOR* 374, 209–232.
FISCHER-GENZ, B./EHRIG, H. (2005): First Results of the Archaeological Survey Project in the Territory of Ancient Heliopolis-Baalbek, *Bulletin d'archéologie et d'architecture libanaises* 9, 135–138.
FRANKEL, R. et al. (2001): *Settlement Dynamics and Regional Diversity in Ancient Upper Galilee* (IAA Reports 14), Jerusalem.
FRANKLIN, N. (2004): Samaria: From the Bedrock to the Omride Palace, *Levant* 36, 189–202.
– (2006): Revealing Stratum V at Megiddo, *BASOR* 342, 95–111.
– (2011): From Megiddo to Tamassos and Back. Putting the "Proto-Ionic Capital" in Its Place, in: I. FINKELSTEIN/N. NA'AMAN (eds.), *The Fire Signals of Lachish: Studies in the Archaeology and History of Israel in the Late Bronze Age, Iron Age, and Persian Period in Honor of David Ussishkin*, Winona Lake, 129–140.
FREIKMAN, M. (2012): A Near Eastern Megalithic Monument in Context, *eTopoi* 3, 143–147.
FREIKMAN, M./PORAT, N. (2017): Rujm el-Hiri: The Monument in the Landscape, *TA* 44, 14–39.
FREVEL, C. (2018a): *Geschichte Israels* (second edition), Stuttgart.
– (2018b): Was Aram an Empire? A Kind of a Shibboleth-Question, *Semitica* 60, 397–426.
– (2019a): State Formation in the Southern Levant – The Case of the Arameans and the Role of Hazael's Expansion, in: A. BERLEJUNG/A.M. MAEIR (eds.), *Researches on Israel and Aram: Autonomy, Interdependence and Related Issues. Proceedings of the First Annual RIAB Center Conference, Leipzig, June 2016* (ORA 34), Tübingen, 347–372.
– (2019b): Wicked Usurpers and the Doom of Samaria. Further Views on the Angle of 2 Kings 15–17, in: S. HASEGAWA/C. LEVIN/K. RADNER (eds.), *The Last Days of the Kingdom of Israel* (BZAW 511), Berlin/Boston, 303–334.
FRITZ, V. (1990): *Kinneret: Ergebnisse der Ausgrabungen auf dem Tell el-'Orēme am See Gennesaret 1982–1985* (ADPV 15), Wiesbaden.

- (1999): Kinnereth, Excavations at Tell el-'Oreimeh (Tel Kinrot): Preliminary Report on the 1994–1997 Seasons, *TA* 26, 92–115.
FRITZ, V./MÜNGER, M. (2002): Vorbericht über die zweite Phase der Ausgrabungen in Kinneret (Tell el-'Orēme) am See Gennesaret, 1994–1999, *ZDPV* 118, 2–32.
GADOT, Y. (2009): Iron Age (Strata X11–X6), in: Y. GADOT/E. YADIN (eds.), *Aphek-Antipatris II: The Remains on the Acropolis. The Moshe Kochavi and Pirhiya Beck Excavations* (SMNIA 27), Tel Aviv, 88–108.
- (2017): The Iron I in the Samaria Highlands: A Nomad Settlement Wave or Urban Expansion?, in: O. LIPSCHITS/Y. GADOT/M.J. ADAMS (eds.), *Rethinking Israel: Studies in the History and Archaeology of Ancient Israel in Honor of Israel Finkelstein*, Winona Lake, 103–114.
GADOT, Y./UZIEL, J. (2017): The Monumentality of Iron Age Jerusalem Prior to the 8th Century BCE, *TA* 44, 123–140.
GADOT, Y./YASUR-LANDAU, A. (2012): *Qiryat Shemona (S): Fort and Village in the Hula Valley* (Salvage Excavation Reports 7), Tel Aviv.
GAL, Z. (2009): The Lower Galilee between Tiglath Pileser III and the Beginning of the Persian Period, *ErIsr* 29, 77–81 [Hebrew with English summary].
GAL, Z./ALEXANDRE, Y. (2000): *Horvat Rosh Zayit: An Iron Age Storage Fort and Village* (IAA Reports 8), Jerusalem.
GALIL, G. (1998): Ashtaroth in the Amarna Period, in: S. ISRE'EL/I. SINGER/R. ZADOK (eds.), *Past Links: Studies in the Languages and Cultures of the Ancient Near East* (IOS 18), Winona Lake, 373–386.
- (2001): A Re-Arrangement of the Fragments of the Tel Dan Inscription and the Relations Between Israel and Aram, *PEQ* 133, 16–21.
- (2014): A Concise History of Palistin/Patin/Unqi/'mq in the 11th–9th Centuries BC, *Semitica* 56, 75–104.
GALLING, K. (1953): Archäologisch-historische Ergebnisse einer Reise in Syrien und Liban im Spätherbst 1952, *ZDPV* 69, 181–187.
GARFINKEL, Y. (1997): Area L, in: A. BEN-TOR/R. BONFIL (eds.), *Hazor V: An Account of the Fifth Season of Excavations, 1968*, Jerusalem, 177–294.
GARFINKEL, Y./KREIMERMAN, I./ZILBERG, P. (2016): *Debating Khirbet Qeiyafa: A Fortified City in Judah from the Time of King David*, Jerusalem.
GARFINKEL, Y. et al. (2015): The 'Išba'al Inscription from Khirbet Qeiyafa, *BASOR* 373, 217–233.
- (2019): Lachish Fortifications and State Formation in the Biblical Kingdom of Judah in Light of Radiometric Dating, *Radiocarbon* 61, 695–712.
GEORGIADOU, A. (2014): Productions et styles régionaux dans l'artisanat céramique de Chypre à l'époque géométrique (XIe-VIIIe s. av. J.-C.), *Bulletin de Correspondance Hellénique* 138, 361–385.
GENZ, H. (2006): Middle Bronze Age Pottery from Baalbek, in: M. VAN ESS (ed.), *Baalbek/Heliopolis: Results of Archaeological and Architectural Research 2002–2005* (Bulletin d'Archéologie et d'Architecture Libanaise Hors Série IV), Beirut, 127–149.
GENZ, H./SADER, H. (2008): Tell Hizzin: Digging Up New Material from an Old Excavation, *Bulletin d'archéologie et d'architecture libanaises* 12, 183–201.
GEVA, H. (2014): Jerusalem's Population in Antiquity: A Minimalist View, *TA* 41, 131–160.
GEVA, S. (1984): The Settlement Pattern of Hazor Stratum XII, *ErIsr* 17, 158–161 [Hebrew with English summary].
GHANTOUS, H. (2013): *The Elisha-Hazael Paradigm and the Kingdom of Israel: The Politics of God in Ancient Syria-Palestine*, Durham.
GILBOA, A. (1999): The Dynamics of Phoenician Bichrome Pottery: A View from Tel Dor, *BASOR* 316, 1–22.
- (2001): *Southern Phoenicia during Iron Age I–IIA in the Light of the Tel Dor Excavations: The Evidence of Pottery* (PhD diss., the Hebrew University of Jerusalem), Jerusalem.

– (2005): Sea Peoples and Phoenicians along the Southern Phoenician Coast: A Reconciliation: An Interpretation of Šikila (SKL) Material Culture, *BASOR* 337, 47–78.
– (2015): Iron Age I–II Cypriot Imports and Local Imitations, in: S. GITIN (ed.), *The Ancient Pottery of Israel and Its Neighbors: From the Iron Age through the Hellenistic Period*, Jerusalem, 483–508.
– (2018): The Iron Age Pottery of Phases 10–5: Sequence, Contexts, Typology, Cultural Affinities and Chronology, in: A. GILBOA et al. (eds.), *Excavations at Dor, Final Report: Volume IIA. Area G, the Late Bronze and Iron Ages: Pottery, Artifacts, Ecofacts and Other Studies* (Qedem Reports 11), Jerusalem, 97–172.
– (forthcoming): The Southern Levantine Roots of the Phoenician Mercantile Phenomenon, *BASOR*.
GILBOA, A./SHARON, I. (2003): An Archaeological Contribution to the Early Iron Age Chronological Debate: Alternative Chronologies for Phoenicia and Their Effects on the Levant, Cyprus, and Greece, *BASOR* 332, 7–80.
GILBOA, A./SHARON, I./BLOCH-SMITH, E. (2015): Capital of Solomon's Fourth District? Israelite Dor, *Levant* 47, 51–74.
GILBOA, A. et al. (2018): *Excavations at Dor, Final Report: Volume IIA. Area G, the Late Bronze and Iron Ages: Synthesis, Architecture and Stratigraphy* (Qedem Reports 11), Jerusalem.
GILIBERT, A. (2011): *Syro-Hittite Monumental Art and the Archaeology of Performance: The Stone Reliefs at Carchemish and Zincirli in the Earlier First Millennium BCE* (Berlin Studies of the Ancient World 2), Berlin.
GITIN, S. (2015): *The Ancient Pottery of Israel and Its Neighbors: From the Iron Age through the Hellenistic Period*, Jerusalem.
GIVEON, R. (1965): Two Egyptian Documents Concerning Bashan from the Time of Ramses II, *Rivista degli Studi Orientali* 40, 197–202.
GLUECK, N. (1943): Ramoth-Gilead, *BASOR* 92, 10–16.
– (1951): *Explorations in Eastern Palestine IV* (AASOR 25–28), New Haven.
GOLANI, A./WOLFF, S.R. (2018): The Late Bronze I and Iron Age I Remains at Tel Dover in the Jordan Valley, Israel, in: B. HOREJS et al. (eds.), *Proceedings of the 10th International Congress on the Archaeology of the Ancient Near East, 25–29 April 2016, Vienna*, Wiesbaden, 511–519.
GOLDING-MEIR, R. (2015): The Material Culture of the North-Western Negev at the End of Iron Age I and Iron Age IIA. A Case Study in the Sites Tel Sera, Qubur el-Walaydah and Tell el-Farʻah South (MA thesis, Ben-Gurion University of the Negev), Beersheba [Hebrew with English summary].
GOLUB, M. (2014): The Distribution of Personal Names in the Land of Israel and Transjordan during the Iron II Period, *JAOS* 134, 621–642.
GOREN, Y./FINKELSTEIN, I./NA'AMAN, N. (2004): *Inscribed in Clay: Provenance Study of the Amarna Tablets and Other Near Eastern Texts* (SMNIA 23), Tel Aviv.
GRAYSON, A.K. (1996): *Assyrian Rulers of the Early First Millennium BC II (858–745 BC)* (RIMA 3), Toronto.
GREENBERG, R. et al. (2012): Tel Bet Yerah: Hub of the Early Bronze Age Levant, *NEA* 75, 88–107.
GREENFIELD, J.C. (1976): The Aramean God Rammān/Rimmōn, *IEJ* 26, 195–198.
GREER, J.S. (2011): *Dinner at Dan: A Biblical and Archaeological Exploration of Sacred Feasting at Iron Age II Tel Dan* (PhD diss., The Pennsylvania State University), Pennsylvania.
– (2017): The Cult at Dan: Aramean or Israelite?, in: A. BERLEJUNG/A.M. MAEIR/A. SCHÜLE (eds.), *Wandering Arameans: Arameans Outside Syria. Textual and Archaeological Perspectives* (Leipziger altorientalistische Studien 5), Wiesbaden, 3–18.
GUÉRIN, V.M. (1987) [1880]: *Geographical, Historical, and Archaeological Description of the Land of Israel: Volume 7. The Galilee*, Jerusalem [Hebrew, translated by H. Ben-Amram].
GUR-ARIEH, S./MAEIR, A.M. (2020): The Excavations in Area C, in: A.M. MAEIR/J. UZIEL (eds.), *Tell es-Safi/Gath II: Excavations and Studies* (ÄAT 105), Münster, 117–188.
HACHLILI, R. (2013): *Ancient Synagogues – Archaeology and Art: New Discoveries and Current Research* (HdO 105), Leiden/Boston.

HACHMANN, R. (1983): *Frühe Phöniker im Libanon: 20 Jahre deutsche Ausgrabungen in Kāmid el-Lōz*, Mainz.

HAFTHORSSON, S. (2006): *A Passing Power: An Examination of the Sources for the History of Aram-Damascus in the Second Half of the Ninth Century B.C.* (CBOTS 54), Stockholm.

HALPERN, B. (1994): The Stela from Dan: Epigraphic and Historical Considerations, *BASOR* 296, 63–80.

HALBERTSMA, D.J.H./ROUTLEDGE, R. (2021): Between Rocks and 'High Places': On Religious Architecture in the Iron Age Southern Levant, *Religions* 12, DOI: 10.3390/rel12090740.

HANBURY-TENISON, J.W. et al. (1984): Wadi Arab Survey, *ADAJ* 28, 305–385.

HARRISON, T.P. (2004): *Megiddo 3: Final Report of the Stratum VI Excavations* (OIP 127), Chicago.

– (2009): "The Land of Medeba" and Early Iron Age Madaba, in: P. BIENKOWSKI (ed.), *Studies on Iron Age Moab and Neighbouring Areas in Honour of Michèle Daviau* (Ancient Near Eastern Studies 29), Leuven/Paris/Walpole.

HARTAL, M. (1989): *The Northern Golan: The Archaeological Survey as a Source for the History of the Region*, Qasrin.

– (2009a): Rosh Pinna, *HA-ESI* 121 [online publication].

– (2009b): Bab al-Hawa, *HA-ESI* 121 [online publication].

– (2013): Tel Ya'af, *HA-ESI* 125 [online publication].

– (2014): Archaeological Survey as a Source for the History of the Golan, *Qadmoniot* 148, 80–89.

HARTAL, M./SEGAL, O. (forthcoming): *The Excavations at Bab el-Hawa, Northern Golan: The Iron Age Strata*.

HARUSH, O. (2014): *Regional, Chronological, Typological and Technological Aspects of 'Hippo' Jars from North Israel in the Iron Age IIA* (MA thesis, the Hebrew University of Jerusalem), Jerusalem.

HASEGAWA, S. (2012): *Aram and Israel during the Jehuite Dynasty* (BZAW 434), Berlin.

– (2014): The Conquests of Hazael in 2 Kings 13: 22 in the Antiochian Text, *JBL* 133, 61–76.

– (2019): 'En Gev in the Iron Age II: Material Culture and Political History, in: A. BERLEJUNG/A.M. MAEIR (eds.), *Researches on Israel and Aram: Autonomy, Interdependence and Related Issues. Proceedings of the First Annual RIAB Center Conference, Leipzig, June 2016* (ORA 34), Tübingen, 212–231.

HASEGAWA, S./PAZ, I. (2009): Tel 'En Gev, *HA-ESI* 121 [online publication].

HASEGAWA, S./LEVIN, C./RADNER, K. (2019): *The Last Days of the Kingdom of Israel* (BZAW 511), Berlin/Boston.

HÄSER, J./SOENNECKEN, K./VIEWEGER, D. (2016): Tall Zirā'a in northwest Jordan between Aram and Israel, in: O. SERGI/M. OEMING/I. DE HULSTER (eds.), *In Search of Aram and Israel: Politics, Culture and Identity* (ORA 20), Tübingen, 121–137.

HAWKINS, J.D. (2000): *Corpus of Hieroglyphic Luwian Inscriptions 1: Inscriptions of the Iron Age* (Studies in Indo-European Language and Culture N.S. 8.1), Berlin.

– (2011): The Inscriptions of the Aleppo Temple, *AnSt* 61, 35–54.

– (2016): Hamath in the Iron Age: The Inscriptions, in: D. PARAYRE (ed.), *Le fleuve rebelle: Géographie historique du moyen Oronte d'Ebla à l'époque médiévale. Actes du colloque international tenu les 13 et 14 décembre 2012 à Nanterre (MAE) et à Paris (INHA)* (Syria Supplément IV), Beirut.

HEGENEUER, S./VAN DER HEYDEN, S. (2019): Perceiving Monumentality, in: F. BUCCELLATI et al. (eds.), *Size Matters: Understanding Monumentality Across Ancient Civilizations* (Histoire 146), Bielefeld, 65–89.

HEINZ, M. (2010): *Kamid el-Loz: Intermediary between Cultures. More than 10 Years of Archaeological Research in Kamid el-Loz (1997–2007)* (Bulletin d'Archéologie et d'Architecture Libanaise Hors-série 7), Beirut.

– (2016): *Kamid el-Loz 4000 Years and More of Rural and Urban Life in the Lebanese Beqa'a Plain*, Beirut.

HEINZ, M. et al. (2004): Kamid el-Loz in the Beqa'a Plain/Lebanon: Excavations in 2001, 2002 and 2004, *Bulletin d'archéologie et d'architecture libanaises* 8, 83–117.

– (2006): Note on the 2005 Season at Kamid el-Loz - From the Romans to the Late Bronze Age, *Bulletin d'archéologie et d'architecture libanaises* 10, 85–96.
– (2010): Kamid el-Loz: Report on the Excavations in 2008 and 2009, *Bulletin d'archéologie et d'architecture libanaises* 14, 103–129.
HERBERT, S. (1992): Anafa, Tel, in: E. STERN (ed.), *NEAEHL* (Volume 1), Jerusalem, 58–61.
HERR, L.G. (2013): Review of Tell es-Safi/Gath I: The 1996–2005 Seasons by Aren M. Maeir, *BASOR* 370, 240–242.
HERR, L.G./NAJJAR, M. (2001): The Iron Age, in: B. MACDONALD/R. ADAMS/P. BIENKOWSKI (eds.), *The Archaeology of Jordan* (Levantine Archaeology 1), Sheffield, 323–345.
– (2008): The Iron Age, in: R.B. ADAMS (ed.), *Jordan: An Archaeological Reader*, London, 311–334.
HERZOG, Z./SINGER-AVITZ, L. (2004): Redefining the Centre: The Emergence of State in Judah, *TA* 31, 209–244.
– (2006): Sub-Dividing the Iron Age IIA in Northern Israel: A Suggested Solution to the Chronological Debate, *TA* 33, 163–195.
HERMANN, V.R. (2019): Manipulation of Memory in the Iron Age Syro-Hittite Kingdoms, *Semitica* 61, 399–439.
HINDAWI, A.-N. (2006): *The Archaeology of the Northern Jordanian Plateau During the Iron Age ca. Late 13th–6th Centuries BC. Tell Ya'amoun as a Key Site* (PhD diss., Albert-Ludwigs-Universität zu Freiburg), Freiburg.
HOLLADAY, J.S. (1990): Red Slip, Burnish, and the Solomonic Gateway at Gezer, *BASOR* 277–278, 23–70.
HOMSHER, R.S./KLEIMAN, A. (2022): Area Q: Levels Q-6 to Q-1, in: I. FINKELSTEIN/M.A.S. MARTIN (eds.), *Megiddo VI: The 2010–2014 Seasons* (SMNIA 39), Tel Aviv, 119–150.
ILAN, D. (1999): *Northeastern Israel in the Iron Age I: Cultural, Socioeconomic and Political Perspectives* (PhD diss., Tel Aviv University), Tel Aviv.
– (2008): The Socioeconomic Implications of Grain Storage in Early Iron Age Canaan: The Case of Tel Dan, in: A. FANTALKIN/A. YASUR-LANDAU (eds.), *Bene Israel: Studies in the Archaeology of Israel and the Levant during the Bronze and Iron Ages in Honour of Israel Finkelstein* (CHANE 31), Leiden/Boston, 87–104.
– (2011): Household Gleanings from Iron I Tel Dan, in: A. YASUR-LANDAU/J.R. EBELING/L.B. MAZOW (eds.), *Household Archaeology in Ancient Israel and Beyond* (CHANE 50), Leiden/London, 133–154.
– (2019a): *Dan IV: The Iron Age I Settlement. The Avraham Biran Excavations (1966–1999)*, Jerusalem.
– (2019b): Iron Age II et-Tell/Bethsaida and Dan: A Tale of Two Gates, in: F. STRICKERT/R.A. FREUND, (eds.), *A Festschrift in Honor of Rami Arav: "And They Come to Bethsaida..."*, Cambridge, 112–132.
ILAN, D./GREER, J.S. (2021): A Pilgrimage to Iron Age II Tel Dan, *Advances in Ancient, Biblical, and Near Eastern Research* 1, 143–190.
IRVINE, S.A. (1994): The Southern Border of Syria Reconstructed, *Catholic Biblical Quarterly* 56, 21–41.
ISSERLIN, B.S. (1961): Israelite Art during the Period of the Monarchy, in: C. ROTH (ed.), *Jewish Art: An Illustrated History*, Tel Aviv, 75–118.
JI, C.C.-H. (1997): A Note on the Iron Age Four-room House in Palestine, *Orientalia* 66, 387–413.
JOFFE, A.H. (2002): The Rise of Secondary States in Iron Age Levant, *JESHO* 45, 425–467.
JOUDAH, A.H. (1987): *Revolt in Palestine in the Eighteenth Century: The Era of Shaykh Zahir al-'Umar* (Munaqashat: Gorgias Studies in the Modern Middle East 2), Piscataway.
JOUKOWSKY, M.S. (1972): *The Pottery of Tell el-Ghassil in the Beqa'a: A Comparative Study and Analysis of the Iron Age and Bronze Age Wares* (MA thesis, American University of Beirut), Beirut.
KAFAFI, Z. (2014): Tell Irbid Tomb (Excavated in 1968), in: Z. KAFAFI/M. MARAQTEN (eds.), *A Pioneer of Arabia: Studies in the Archaeology and Epigraphy of the Levant and the Arabian Peninsula*

in Honor of Moawiyah Ibrahim (Studies on the Archaeology of Palestine and Transjordan 10), Rome, 108–145.

KAFAFI, Z./ABU DALU, R. (2009): Tell Irbid during the Late Bronze and Iron Ages, *UF* 40, 453–470.

KAHN, D. (2007): The Kingdom of Arpad (Bit Agusi) and 'All Aram': International Relations in Northern Syria in the Ninth and Eighth Centuries BCE, *ANES* 44, 66–89.

KAMLAH, J. (1993): Tell el-Fuḫḫār (Zarqu?) und die Pflanzenhaltende Göttin in Palästina Ergebnisse des Zeraqōn – Surveys 1989, *ZDPV* 109, 101–127.

– (2000): *Der Zeraqon-Survey 1989–1994 mit Beitragen zur Methodik und Geschichtlichen Auswertung Archäologischer Oberflächenuntersuchungen in Palästina* (ADPV 27), Wiesbaden.

KANIEWSKI, D.E. et al. (2010): Late Second–Early First Millennium BC Abrupt Climate Changes in Coastal Syria and their Possible Significance for the History of the Eastern Mediterranean, *Quaternary Research* 74, 207–215.

– (2017): Climate Change and Water Management in the Biblical City of Dan, *Science Advances* 3, 1–8.

KATZ, H. (2020): Settlement Processes in the Meiron Ridges during the Iron Age I, *BASOR* 383, 1–18.

– (2021): Mount Adir: An Iron I Polity in the Upper Galilee? *TA* 48, 171–198.

KATZ, H./FAUST, A. (2014): The Chronology of the Iron Age IIA in Judah in the Light of Tel 'Eton Tomb C3 and Other Assemblages, *BASOR* 371, 103–127.

KILLEBREW, A.E. (2001): The Collared Pithos in Context: A Typological, Technological, and Functional Reassessment, in: S.R. WOLFF (ed.), *Studies in the Archaeology of Israel and Neighboring Lands in Memory of Douglas L. Esse* (SAOC 59), Chicago, 377–398.

KISLEV, M.E. (2015): Infested Stored Crops in the Iron Age I Granary at Tel Hadar, *Israel Journal of Plant Sciences* 62, 86–97.

KLEIMAN, A. (2015): A Late Iron IIA Destruction Layer at Aphek in the Sharon Plain, *TA* 42, 177–232.

– (2016): The Damascene Subjugation of the Southern Levant as a Gradual Process (ca. 842–800 BCE), in: O. SERGI/M. OEMING/I. DE HULSTER (eds.), *In Search of Aram and Israel: Politics, Culture and Identity* (ORA 20), Tübingen, 57–76.

– (2017): A North Israelite Royal Administrative System and its Impact on Late-Monarchic Judah, *HeBAI* 6, 354–371.

– (2018): Comments on the Archaeology and History of the Tell el-Farʿah North (Biblical Tirzah) in the Iron IIA, *Semitica* 60, 85–104.

– (2019a): *The Archaeology of Borderlands between Israel and Aram in the Iron I–II (ca. 1150–750 BCE)* (PhD diss., Tel Aviv University), Tel Aviv.

– (2019b): Invisible Kingdoms? Settlement Oscillations in the Northern Jordan Valley and State Formation in Southwestern Syria, in: A. BERLEJUNG/A.M. MAEIR (eds.), *Researches on Israel and Aram: Autonomy, Interdependence and Related Issues. Proceedings of the First Annual RIAB Center Conference, Leipzig, June 2016* (ORA 34), Tübingen, 293–311.

– (2021): Two Cultural Biography of Two Volute Capitals at Iron Age Hazor, *PEQ*, DOI: 10.1080/00310328.2021.1951987.

– (2022a): The Iron II Pottery from Area Q, in: I. FINKELSTEIN/M.A.S. MARTIN (eds.), *Megiddo VI: The 2010–2014 Seasons* (SMNIA 39), Tel Aviv, 894–1054.

– (2022b): Living on the Ruins: The Case of Stratum XII/XI at Hazor, in: A. BERLEJUNG/A.M. MAEIR/T.M. OSHIMA (eds.), *Writing and Re-Writing History by Destruction: Proceedings of the Annual Minerva Center RIAB Conference, Leipzig, 2018* (ORA 45), Tübingen: 27–38.

– (forthcoming): Beyond Hazor: Urban Durability, Political Instability and Collective Memory in the Northern Jordan Valley at the Turn of the Second Millennium BCE, in: I. KOCH/O. LIPSCHITS/ O. SERGI (eds.), *From Nomadism to Monarchy? Revisiting the Early Iron Age Southern Levant* (Mosaics: Studies on Ancient Israel), Tel Aviv, 101–118.

KLEIMAN, A./DUNSETH, Z.C. (2022): Area W: Sounding in the Northeastern Sector of the Mound, in: I. FINKELSTEIN/M.A.S. MARTIN (eds.), *Megiddo VI: The 2010–2014 Seasons* (SMNIA 39), Tel Aviv, 166–179.

KLEIMAN, A./FINKELSTEIN, I. (2018): The Date of Building 338 at Megiddo: Eppur Si Muove!, *IEJ* 68, 50–55.

KLEIMAN, A./KAPLAN, A./FINKELSTEIN, I. (2016): Building 338 at Megiddo: New Evidence from the Field, *IEJ* 66, 161–176.

KLEIMAN, A. et al. (2017): Cult Activity at Megiddo in the Iron Age: New Evidence and a Long-Term Perspective, *ZDPV* 133, 24–52.

– (2019): The Date and Origin of Black-on-Red Ware: The View from Megiddo, *AJA* 123, 531–555.

KLEIMAN, S. (2021): Potters in Transition: Ceramic Traditions and Innovations in the Shephelah at the Dawn of the Iron Age, *AF* 48, 233–249.

KLEIMAN, S./KLEIMAN, A./BEN-YOSEF, E. (2017): Metalworkers' Material Culture in the Early Iron Age Levant: The Ceramic Assemblage from Site 34 (Slaves' Hill) in the Timna Valley, *TA* 44, 232–264.

KLETTER, R. (1999): Pots and Polities: Material Remains of Late Iron Age Judah in Relation to Its Political Borders, *BASOR* 314, 19–54.

– (2006): Can a Proto-Israelite Please Stand Up? Notes on the Ethnicity of Iron Age Israel and Judah, in A.M. Maeir and P. de Miroschedji (eds.), *'I Will Speak the Riddles of Ancient Times': Archaeological and Historical Studies in Honor of Amihai Mazar on the Occasion of his Sixtieth Birthday*, Winona Lake, 573–586

– (2015): Shrine Models and Volute Capitals, in: R. KLETTER/I. ZIFFER/W. ZWICKEL (eds.), *Yavneh II: The 'Temple Hill' Repository Pit* (OBO 36), Fribourg/Göttingen, 55–64.

– (2016): Water from a Rock: Archaeology, Ideology, and the Bible, *SJOT* 30, 161–184.

KLETTER, R./ZWICKEL, W. (2006): The Assyrian Building of 'Ayyelet ha-Šaḥar, *ZDPV* 122, 151–186.

KNAPP, B.A. (2021): *Migration Myths and the End of the Bronze Age in the Eastern Mediterranean*, Cambridge.

KNAUF, E.A. (1992): The Cultural Impact of Secondary State Formation: The Cases of the Edomites and Moabites, in: P. BIENKOWSKI (ed.), *Early Edom and Moab: The Beginning of the Iron Age in Southern Jordan* (Sheffield Archaeological Monographs 7), Oxford, 47–54.

– (2001): The Mists of Ramathalon, or: How Ramoth Gilead Disappeared from the Archaeological Record, *BN* 110, 33–36.

KOCH, I. (2012): The Geopolitical Situation in the Judean Lowland during the Iron Age I–IIa (1150–800 BCE), *Cathedra* 143, 45–64 [Hebrew].

– (2020): Southern Levantine Temples during the Iron Age II: Towards a Multivocal Narrative, *Ancient Judaism* 8, 325-344.

– (2021): *Colonial Encounters in Southwest Canaan during the Late Bronze Age and the Early Iron Age* (CHANE 119), Leiden/Boston.

KOCHAVI, M. (1989): The Land of Geshur Project: Regional Archaeology of the Southern Golan (1987–1988 Seasons), *IEJ* 39, 1–17.

– (1993): Soreg, Tel, in: E. STERN (ed.), *NEAEHL* (Volume 4), Jerusalem, 1410.

– (1996): The Land of Geshur: History of a Region in the Biblical Period, *ErIsr* 25, 184–201 [Hebrew with English summary].

– (1998): The Eleventh Century BCE Tripartite Pillar Building at Tel Hadar, in: S. GITIN/A. MAZAR/E. STERN (eds.), *Mediterranean Peoples in Transition, Thirteenth to Early Tenth Centuries BCE: In Honor of Professor Trude Dothan*, Jerusalem, 468–478.

KOPCKE. G. (2002): 1000 B.C.E.? 900 B.C.E.? A Greek Vase from Lake Galilee, in: E. EHRENBERG (ed.), *Leaving no Stones Unturned: Essays on the Ancient Near East and Egypt in Honor of Donald P. Hansen*, Winona Lake, 109–117.

KREIMERMAN, I. (2017): A Typology of Destruction Layers. The Late Bronze Age Southern Levant as a Case Study, in: *Crisis to Collapse: The Archaeology of Social Breakdown*, ed. Tim Cunningham and Jan Driessen (Aegis 11), Leuven 173–203.

KROPP, A./MOHAMMAD, Q. (2006): Dion of the Decapolis. Tell al-Ash'ari in Southern Syria in the Light of Ancient Documents and Recent Discoveries, *Levant* 38, 125–144.

KULEMANN-OSSEN, S. (2010): The Pottery of the East-Slope: Areas II-e-5/II-e-6 and II-e-7, in: M. HEINZ (ed.), *Kamid el-Loz: Intermediary between Cultures. More than 10 Years of Archaeological Research in Kamid el-Loz (1997 to 2007)* (Bulletin d'Archéologie et d'Architecture Libanaise Hors-Serie VII), Beirut, 61–72.

LAGARCE, B. (2010): Une stèle ramesside à Meydaa (région de Damas) et la présence égyptienne en Upé, *Syria* 87, 53–68.

LAMON, R.S./SHIPTON, G.M. (1939): *Megiddo I: Seasons of 1925–34, Strata I–V* (OIP 42), Chicago

LAMPRICHS, R. (2002): Tell Johfiyeh and its Surrounding: A Look into the Future of some Small Iron Age Sites in Northern Jordan, in: Z. SA'AD (ed.), *Proceedings of the 7th International Forum UNESCO-University on Heritage Conference 2002, Irbid*, Irbid.

– (2007): *Tell Johfiyeh: Ein Archäologischer Fundplatz und seine Umgebung in Nordjordanien* (AOAT 334), Münster.

LANGGUT, D./FINKELSTEIN, I./LITT, T. (2013): Climate and the Late Bronze Collapse: New Evidence from the Southern Levant, *TA* 40, 149–175.

LAPP, N.L. (1992): Rumeith, Tell er-, in: E. STERN (ed.), *NEAEHL* (Volume 4), Jerusalem, 1291–1293.

LAPP, N.L./COOPER, K.B. (2015): Stamped and Marked Handles, in: T.J. BARAKO/N.L. LAPP (eds.), *Tell er-Rumeith: The Excavations of Paul W. Lapp, 1962 and 1967* (AASOR 22), Boston, 321–322.

LAPP, P. (1963): Tell er-Rumeith, *RB* 70, 406–411.

– (1968): Tell er-Rumeith, *RB* 75, 98–105.

– (1975): *The Tale of the Tell: Archaeological Studies*, Pittsburg, 111–119.

LEE, S./BRONK RAMSEY, C./MAZAR, A. (2013): Iron Age Chronology in Israel: Results from Modeling with a Trapezoidal Bayesian Framework, *Radiocarbon* 55, 731–740.

LEHMANN, G. (1996): *Untersuchungen zur Späten Eisenzeit in Syrien und Libanon: Stratigraphie und Keramikformen zwischen ca. 720 bis 300 v. Chr.* (Archäologische Studien zur Kultur und Geschichte des Alten Orients 5), Münster.

– (2002): *Bibliographie der Archäologischen Fundstellen und Surveys in Syrien und Libanon* (Orientabteilung, Orient-Archäologie 9), Rahden.

– (2004): Reconstructing the Social Landscape of Early Israel: Rural Marriage Alliances in the Central Hill Country, *TA* 31, 141–193.

– (2019): Hazael in the South, in: A. BERLEJUNG/A.M. MAEIR (eds.), *Researches on Israel and Aram: Autonomy, Interdependence and Related Issues. Proceedings of the First Annual RIAB Center Conference, Leipzig, June 2016* (ORA 34), Tübingen, 277–292.

LEHMANN, G./KILLEBREW, A.E. (2010): Palace 6000 at Megiddo in Context: Iron Age Central Hall Tetra-Partite Residencies and the "Bīt-Ḫilāni" Building Tradition in the Levant, *BASOR* 359, 13–33.

LEHMANN, G./NIEMANN, H.M. (2014): When Did the Shephelah Become Judahite? *TA* 41, 77–94.

LEHMANN, G./VARONER, O. (2018): Early Iron Age Tombs in Northern Israel Revisited, *TA* 45, 235–272.

LEMAIRE, A. (1991): Hazaël de Damas, roi d'Aram, in: D. CHARPIN/F. JOANNES (eds.), *Marchands, diplomats et empereurs: Études sur la civilisation mésopotamienne offertes à Paul Garelli*, Paris, 91–108.

– (1998): The Tel Dan Stela as a Piece of Royal Historiography, *JSOT* 81, 3–14.

– (2019): The Boundary between the Aramaean Kingdom of Damascus and the Kingdom of Israel, in: J. DUŠEK/J. MYNÁŘOVÁ (eds.), *Aramaean Borders: Defining Aramaean Territories in the 10th–8th Centuries B.C.E.* (CHANE 101), Leiden/Boston, 245–266.

LEMOS, I.S. (2002): *The Protogeometric Aegean: The Archaeology of the Late Eleventh and Tenth Centuries BC*, Oxford.

LENZEN, C.J. (1986): Tall Irbid Bait Ras, AfO 33, 164–166.
LENZEN, C.J./KNAUF, E.A. (1987): *Notes on Syrian Place Names in Egyptian Sources*, Göttingen.
LENZEN, C.J./GORDON, R.L./MCQUITTY, A.M. (1985): Excavations at Tell Irbid and Beit Ras, 1985, *ADAJ* 29, 151–159.
LEONARD, A. (1987): Tell Jarash - Tell el-Husn Highway Survey, *ADAJ* 31, 343–390.
LEVY, E. (2017): A Note on the Geographical Distribution of New Kingdom Egyptian Inscriptions from the Levant, *Journal of Ancient Egyptian Interconnections* 14, 14–21.
LEVY, S./EDELSTEIN, G. (1972): Cinq années de fouilles a Tel 'Amal (Nir David), *RB* 79, 325–367.
LEVY, T.E./NAJJAR, M./BEN-YOSEF, E. (2014): *New Insights into the Iron Age Archaeology of Edom, Southern Jordan (Surveys, Excavations, and Research from the University of California, San Diego–Department of Antiquities of Jordan, Edom Lowlands Regional Archaeology Project [ELRAP])*, Los Angeles.
LIPIŃSKI, E. (1977): An Assyro-Israelite Alliance in 842/841 BCE? *Proceedings of the Sixth World Congress of Jewish Studies* 1, 273–278.
– (2000): *The Aramaeans: Their Ancient History, Culture, Religion* (OLA 100), Leuven/Paris.
LIPSCHITS, O. (2011): The Origin and Date of the Volute Capitals from the Levant, in: I. FINKELSTEIN/N. NA'AMAN (eds.), *The Fire Signals of Lachish: Studies in the Archaeology and History of Israel in the Late Bronze Age, Iron Age, and Persian Period in Honor of David Ussishkin*, Winona Lake, 203–225.
LIPSCHITS, O./SERGI, O./KOCH, I. (2010): Royal Judahite Jar Handles: Reconsidering the Chronology of the lmlk Stamp Impressions, *TA* 37, 3–32.
MA'OZ, U.Z. (1986): Golan Heights in Antiquity: A Geographical-History Research, Qasrin [Hebrew].
– (1992): Geshur, in: N.L. FREEDMAN (ed.), *ABD* (Volume 2), New York, 996.
MAEIR, A.M. (2004): The Historical Background and Dating of Amos VI 2: An Archaeological Perspective from Tell eṣ-Ṣâfî/Gath, *VT* 54, 319–334.
– (2012): Tell es-Safi/Gath Archaeological Project 1996–2010: Introduction, Overview and Synopsis of Results, in: A.M. MAEIR (ed.), *Tell eṣ-Ṣāfī/Gath I: The 1996–2005 Seasons, Part 1. Text* (ÄAT 69), Wiesbaden, 1–88.
– (2017): Can Material Evidence of Aramean Influences and Presence in Iron Age Judah and Israel be Found?, in: A. BERLEJUNG/A.M. MAEIR/A. SCHÜLE (eds.), *Wandering Arameans: Arameans Outside Syria. Textual and Archaeological Perspectives* (LAS 5), Wiesbaden, 53–67.
– (2019): Philistine and Israelite Identities: Some Comparative Thoughts, *WO* 49, 151–160.
– (2020): Introduction and Overview, in: A.M. MAEIR/J. UZIEL (eds.), *Tell es-Safi/Gath II: Excavations and Studies* (ÄAT 105), Münster, 3–52.
– (2021): On Defining Israel: Or, Let's do the Kulturkreislehre Again! *HeBAI* 10, 106–148.
MAEIR, A.M./ESHEL, E. (2014): Four Short Alphabetic Inscriptions from Iron Age IIa Tell es-Safi/Gath and their Contribution for the Development of Literacy in Iron Age Philistia and Environs, in: E. ESHEL/Y. LEVIN (eds.), *"See, I Will Bring a Scroll Recounting What Befell Me" (Ps 40:8): Epigraphy and Daily Life from the Bible to the Talmud Dedicated to the Memory of Professor Hanan Eshel* (Journal of Ancient Judaism Supplement 12), Göttingen, 69–88, 205–210.
MAEIR, A.M./GUR-ARIEH, S. (2011): Comparative aspects of the Aramean Siege System at Tell es-Sāfi/Gath, in: I. FINKELSTEIN/N. NA'AMAN (eds.), *The Fire Signals of Lachish: Studies on the Archaeology and History of Israel in the Late Bronze Age, Iron Age and Persian Period in Honor of David Ussishkin*, Winona Lake, 113–128.
MAEIR, A.M./SHAI, I. (2016): Reassessing the Character of the Judahite Kingdom: Archaeological Evidence for Non-Centralized, Kinship-Based Components, in: S. GANOR et al. (eds.), *From Shaar Hagolan to Shaaraim: Essays in Honor of Prof. Yosef Garfinkel*, Jerusalem, 323–340.
MAEIR, A.M./FANTALKIN, A./ZUKERMAN, A. (2009): The Earliest Greek Import in the Iron Age Levant: New Evidence from Tell es-Safi/Gath, Israel, *Ancient West and East* 8, 57–80.
MAEIR, A.M. et al. (2008): A Late Iron Age I/Early Iron Age II Old Canaanite Inscription from Tell eṣ-Ṣâfî/Gath, Israel: Paleography, Dating, and Historical-Cultural Significance, *BASOR* 351, 39–71.

MALENA, S. (2020): Influential Inscriptions Resituating Scribal Activity during the Iron I–IIA Transition, in: M, LEUCHTER (ed.), Scribes and Scribalism, London, 13–27.
MARE, W.H. (1993): Abila of the Decapolis Excavations, *Syria* 70, 208–214.
MARFOE, L. (1979a): *Between Qadesh and Kumidi: A History of Frontier Settlement and Land Use in the Biqa', Lebanon* (PhD diss., University of Chicago), Chicago.
– (1979b): The Integrative Transformation: Patterns of Sociopolitical Organization in Southern Syria, *BASOR* 234, 1–42.
– (1995): *Kāmid el-Lōz 13: The Prehistoric and Early Historic Context of the Site* (Saarbrücker Beiträge zur Altertumskunde 41), Bonn.
– (1998): *Kāmid el-Lōz 14: Settlement History of the Biqa up to the Iron Age* (Saarbrücker Beiträge zur Altertumskunde 53), Bonn.
MARTIN, M.A.S. (2013): The Late Bronze IIB Pottery from Levels K-8 and K-7, in: I. FINKELSTEIN/D. USSISHKIN/E.H. CLINE (eds.), *Megiddo V: The 2004–2008 Seasons* (SMNIA 31), Tel Aviv, 343–457.
– (2017): The Provenance of Philistine Pottery in Northern Canaan, with a Focus on the Jezreel Valley, *TA* 44, 193–231.
MASTER, D.M. (2001): State Formation Theory and the Kingdom of Ancient Israel, *JNES* 60, 117–131.
– (2014): Economy and Exchange in the Iron Age Kingdoms of the Southern Levant, *BASOR* 372, 81–97.
MASTER, D.M. et al. (2005): *Dothan I: Remains from the Tell (1953–1964)*, Winona Lake.
MAZAR, A. (1985): *Excavations at Tell Qasile (Part Two)* (Qedem 20), Jerusalem.
– (1990): *Archaeology of the Land of the Bible 10,000–586 B.C.E.*, New York.
– (1998): On the Appearance of Red Slip in the Iron Age I Period in Israel, in: S. GITIN/A. MAZAR/E. STERN (eds.), *Mediterranean Peoples in Transition, Thirteenth to Early Tenth Centuries BCE: In Honor of Professor Trude Dothan*, Jerusalem, 368–378.
– (2005): The Debate over the Chronology of the Iron Age in the Southern Levant. Its History, the Current Situation, and a Suggested Resolution, in: T.E. LEVY/T. HIGHAM (eds.), *The Bible and Radiocarbon Dating: Archaeology, Texts, and Science*, London/Oakville, 15–30.
– (2006a): The Iron Age II Pottery from Areas S and P, in: A. MAZAR (ed.), *Excavations at Tel Beth-Shean 1989–1996. Volume I: From the Late Bronze Age IIB to the Medieval Period*, Jerusalem, 313–384.
– (2006b): Iron Age Inscriptions and Amulets, in: A. MAZAR (ed.), *Excavations at Tel Beth-Shean 1989–1996. Volume I: From the Late Bronze Age IIB to the Medieval Period*, Jerusalem, 505–513.
– (2009a): Introduction and Overview, in: N. PANITZ-COHEN/A. MAZAR (eds.), *Excavations at Tel Beth-Shean 1989–1996. Volume III: The 13th–11th Century BCE Strata in Areas N and S*, Jerusalem, 1–32.
– (2009b): The Iron Age Dwellings at Tell Qasile, in: J.D. SCHLOEN (ed.), *Exploring the Longue Durée: Essays in Honor of Lawrence E. Stager*, Winona Lake, 319–336.
– (2011): The Iron Age Chronology Debate: Is the Gap Narrowing? Another Viewpoint, *NEA* 74, 105–111.
– (2014): Archaeology and the Bible: Reflections on Historical Memory in the Deuteronomistic History, in: C.M. MAIER (eds.), *Congress Volume Munich 2013*, Leiden/Boston, 347–369.
– (2015): Iron Age: Northern Coastal Plain, Galilee, Samaria, Jezreel Valley, Judah, and the Negev, in: S. GITIN (ed.), *The Ancient Pottery of Israel and Its Neighbors: From the Iron Age through the Hellenistic Period*, Jerusalem, 5–70.
– (2016): Culture, Identity and Politics Relating to Tel Reḥov in the 10th–9th Centuries BCE, in: O. SERGI/M. OEMING/I. DE HULSTER (eds.), *In Search of Aram and Israel: Politics, Culture and Identity* (ORA 20), Tübingen, 89–119.
– (2020a): Jerusalem in the 10th Cent. B.C.E.: A Response, *ZDPV* 136, 139–151.

- (2020b): The Tel Reḥov Excavations: Overview and Synthesis, in: A. MAZAR/N. PANITZ-COHEN (eds.), *Tel Reḥov: A Bronze and Iron Age City in the Beth-Shean Valley, Volume I* (Qedem 59), Jerusalem, 69–140.
- (2021): The Beth Shean Valley and its Vicinity in the 10th Century BCE, *Jerusalem Journal of Archaeology* 1, 241–271.

MAZAR, A./BRONK RAMSEY, C. (2008): 14C Dates and the Iron Age Chronology of Israel: A Response, *Radiocarbon* 50, 159–180.

MAZAR, A./KOUROU, N. (2019): Greece and the Levant in the 10th–9th Centuries BC: A View from Tel Rehov, *Opuscula* 12, 369–392.

MAZAR, A./PANITZ-COHEN, N. (2020): *Tel Reḥov, A Bronze and Iron Age City in the Beth-Shean Valley, Volume I. Introductions, Synthesis and Excavations on the Upper Mound* (Qedem 59), Jerusalem.

MAZAR, A. et al. (2005): Ladder of Time at Tel Reḥov: Stratigraphy, Archaeological Context, Pottery and Radiocarbon Dates, in: T.E. LEVY/T. HIGHAM (eds.), *The Bible and Radiocarbon Dating: Archaeology, Text and Science, London*, 193–255.

MAZAR, B. (1961): Geshur and Maacah, *JBL* 80, 16–28.

- (1962): The Aramean Empire and Its Relations with Israel, *BA* 25, 97–120.

MAZAR, B. et al. (1964): Ein Gev: Excavations in 1961, *IEJ* 14, 1–49.

MAZZONI, S. (2014): The Aramean States During the Iron Age II–III Periods, in: A.E. KILLEBREW/M. STEINER (eds.), *The Oxford Handbook of the Archaeology of the Levant: c. 8000–332 BCE*, Oxford, 683–705.

MCGOVERN, P.E./STRANGE, J. (2015): The Pottery from the 1990–93 Excavation and the Later Pottery from 2002, in: J. STRANGE (ed.), *Tall al-Fukhar: Result of Excavations in 1990–93 and 2002* (Proceedings of the Danish Institute in Damascus 9), Aarhus, 240–328.

MEITLIS, Y. (1999): The Central and Southern Golan in the Iron Age, *Journal of Eretz-Israel Matters* 3–4, 11–39 [Hebrew].

MENDEL, A. (2011): Three Incised Potsherds from Yadin's Excavations at Hazor, *ErIsr* 30, 328–332.

MESHEL, Z. (2012): *Kuntillet 'Ajrud (Ḥorvat Teman): An Iron Age II Religious Site on the Judah-Sinai Border*, Jerusalem.

MEYNERSEN, M. (2015): "Im Archäologischen Zukunftsland": Bedřich Hrozný und die Späthellenistisch-Kaiserzeitlichen Bildwerke aus Sheikh Sa'ad in Südsyrien, in: Š. VELHARTICKÁ (ed.), *Bedřich Hrozný and 100 Years of Hittitology*, Prague, 162–180.

MILLEK, J.M. (2020): *Exchange, Destruction, and a Transitioning Society* (Ressourcenkulturen 9), Tübingen.

MILLER, J.M. (1966): The Elisha Cycle and the Accounts of the Omride Wars, *JBL* 85, 441–454.

MILSON, D. (1991): On the Chronology and Design of "Ahab's Citadel" at Hazor, *ZDPV* 107, 39–47.

MITTMANN, S. (1970): *Beiträge zur Siedlungs- und Territorialgeschichte des Nördlichen Ostjordanlandes* (ADPV 2), Wiesbaden.

MIYAZAKI. S./PAZ, Y. (2005): Tel 'En Gev - 2003, *HA-ESI* 117 [online publication].

MIZRACHI, Y. et al. (1996): The 1988–1991 Excavations at Rogem Hiri, *IEJ* 46, 169–175.

MONTERO FENOLLOS, J.-L./CARAMELO, F. (2021): Nouvelles recherches archéologiques sur l'âge du Fer IIA à Tell el-Far'a, Palestine, *Cuadernos de Prehistoria y Arqueología de la Universidad Autónoma de Madrid* 47, 11–30.

MULLINS, R.A. (1992): Ijon, in: N.L. FREEDMAN (ed.), *ABD* (Volume 3), New York, 387–388.

MÜNGER, S. (2013): Early Iron Age Kinneret – Early Aramaean or Just Late Canaanite? Remarks on the Material Culture of a Border Site in Northern Palestine at the Turn of an Era, in: A. BERLEJUNG/M.P. STRECK (eds.), *Arameans, Chaldeans, and Arabs in Babylonia and Palestine in the First Millennium B.C.* (Leipziger altorientalistische Studien 3), Wiesbaden, 149–182.

- (2017): Khirbet Qeiyafa – A View from Tel Kinrot in the Eastern Lower Galilee, in: S. SCHROER/S. MÜNGER (eds.), *Khirbet Qeiyafa in the Shephelah: Papers Presented at a Colloquium of the Swiss*

Society for Ancient Near Eastern Studies Held at the University of Bern, September 6, 2014 (OBO 282), Fribourg/Göttingen, 113–136.

MÜNGER, S./ZANGENBERG, J./PAKKALA, J. (2011): Kinnereth–an Urban Center at the Crossroads: Excavations on Iron IB Tel Kinrot at the Lake of Galilee, *NEA* 74, 68–90.

NA'AMAN, N. (1975): *The Political Disposition and Historical Development of Eretz-Israel According to the Amarna Letters* (PhD diss., Tel Aviv University), Tel Aviv [Hebrew with English summary].
- (1977): Yeno'am, *TA* 4, 168–177.
- (1988): Biryawaza of Damascus and the Date of the Kāmid el Lōz 'Apiru Letters, *UF* 20, 179–193
- (1991): Forced Participation in Alliances in the Course of the Assyrian Campaigns to the West, in: M. COGAN/I. EPH'AL (eds.), *"Ah, Assyria...": Studies in Assyrian History and Ancient Near Eastern Historiography Presented to Hayim Tadmor* (ScrHier 33), Jerusalem, 80–98.
- (1992): Israel, Edom and Egypt in the 10th Century B.C.E., *TA* 19, 71–93.
- (1994): The 'Conquest of Canaan' in the Book of Joshua and in History, in: I. FINKELSTEIN/N. NA'AMAN (eds.), *From Nomadism to Monarchy: Archaeological and Historical Aspects of Early Israel, Jerusalem*, 218–281.
- (1995a): Hazael of 'Amqi and Hadadezer of Beth-rehob, *UF* 27, 381– 394.
- (1995b): Rezin of Damascus and the Land of Gilead, *ZDPV* 111, 195–117.
- (1997): Historical and Literary Notes on the Excavation of Tel Jezreel, *TA* 24, 122–128.
- (1998): Shishak's Campaign to Palestine as Reflected by the Epigraphic, Biblical and Archaeological Evidence, *Zion* 3, 247–276 [Hebrew].
- (1999): Lebo-Hamath, Ṣūbat-Hamath and the Northern Boundary of the Land of Canaan, *UF* 31, 417–441.
- (2000): Three Notes on the Aramaic Inscription from Tel Dan, *IEJ* 50, 92–104.
- (2002a): *The Past that Shaped the Present: The Formation of the Biblical Historiography at the end of the First Temple Period* (Yeriot 3), Jerusalem [Hebrew].
- (2002b): In Search of Reality behind the Account of David's Wars with Israel's Neighbours, *IEJ* 52, 200–224.
- (2007): The Northern Kingdom in the Late Tenth–Ninth Centuries BCE, in: H.G.H. WILLIAMSON (ed.), *Understanding the History of Ancient Israel* (Proceedings of the British Academy 143), Oxford/New York, 399–418.
- (2010a): Khirbet Qeiyafa in Context, *UF* 42, 497–526.
- (2010b): Does Archaeology Really Deserve the Status of A 'High Court' in Biblical and Historical Research?, in: G. BECKING/L.L. GRABBE (eds.), *Between Evidence and Ideology* (OtSt 59), Leiden/Boston, 163–183.
- (2011): Hazor in the Fourteenth–Thirteenth Centuries BCE in the Light of Historical and Archaeological Research, *ErIsr* 30, 333–341 [Hebrew with English summary].
- (2012): The Kingdom of Geshur in History and Memory, *SJOT* 26, 88–101.
- (2013): The Kingdom of Judah in the 9th Century BCE: Text Analysis versus Archaeological Research, *TA* 40, 247–276.
- (2014): The Fortified Cities of the Siddim (Joshua 19:35), *BN* 160, 59–76.
- (2016a): Memories of Canaan in the Old Testament, *UF* 47, 129–146.
- (2016b): Tel Dor and Iron Age IIA Chronology, *BASOR* 376, 1–5
- (2016c): The lmlk Seal Impressions Reconsidered, *TA* 43, 111–125.
- (2017a): Was Khirbet Qeiyafa a Judahite City? The Case Against It, *JHS* 17, 1–40.
- (2017b): Memories of Monarchical Israel's in the Narratives, *HeBAI* 6, 308–328.
- (2019): Samaria and Judah in an Early 8th-Century Assyrian Wine List, *TA* 46, 12–20.

NAM, R.S. (2012): Power Relations in the Samaria Ostraca, *PEQ* 144, 155–163.

NAVEH, J. (1989): The Epigraphic Finds from Areas A and B, in: Y. YADIN *et al.* (eds.), *Hazor III–IV: An Account of the Third and Fourth Seasons of Excavation, 1957–1958 (Text)*, Jerusalem, 346–347.

NIEHR, H. (2011): König Hazael von Damaskus im Licht Neuer Funde und Interpretationen, in: E. GASS/H.J. STIPP (eds.), *"Ich Werde Meinen Bund mit Euch Niemals Brechen!" (Ri 2,1): Festschrift Für Walter Groß Zum 70. Geburtstag* (Herders Biblische Studien 62), Freiburg, 339–356.
– (2014): *The Aramaeans in Ancient Syria* (HdO 106), Leiden/Boston.
– (2019): The Relations between the Kingdoms of Hamath and Israel (10th to 8th Centuries BCE), in: A. BERLEJUNG/A.M. MAEIR (eds.), *Researches on Israel and Aram: Autonomy, Interdependence and Related Issues. Proceedings of the First Annual RIAB Center Conference, Leipzig, June 2016* (ORA 34), Tübingen, 373–394.
NIEMANN, H.M. (1997): The Socio-Political Shadow Cast by the Biblical Solomon, in: L.K. HANDY (ed.), *The Age of Solomon: Scholarship at the Turn of the Millennium*, Leiden/New York/Köln.
– (2008): A New Look at the Samaria Ostraca: The King-Clan Relationship, *TA* 249–266.
– (2017): Comments and Questions about the Interpretation of Khirbet Qeiyafa: Talking with Yosef Garfinkel, *ZABR* 23, 245–262.
NISSINEN, M./MÜNGER, S. (2009): "Down the River...": A Shrine Model from Tel Kinrot in Its Context, in: E. KAPTIJN/L.P. PETIT (eds.), *A Timeless Vale: Archaeological and Related Essays on the Jordan Valley in Honour of Gerrit van der Kooij on the Occasion of His Sixty-Eighth Birthday* (Archaeological Studies Leiden University 19), Leiden, 129–144.
NÚÑEZ, F.J. (2009): A Snapshot of the Phoenician Ceramic Sequence: The Neck-Ridge Jug from Tell el-Ghassil at the AUB Museum, *Berytus* 51–52, 47–70.
ODED, B. (1971): Darb el-Hawarneh: An Ancient Route, *ErIsr* 10, 191–97 [Hebrew with English summary].
ONN, A. (1988): Tell el-Wawiyat, *HA-ESI* 92, 1–2 [Hebrew].
ONN, A. et al. (1995): Tell el-Wawiyat (Tel Tannim) – 1993, *HA-ESI* 103, 8–10 [Hebrew].
ORNAN, T. (2001): The Bull and its Two Masters: Moon and Storm Deities in Relation to the Bull in Ancient Near Eastern Art, *IEJ* 51, 1–26.
– (2006): The Lady and the Bull: Remarks on the Bronze Plaque from Tel Dan, in: Y. AMIT et al. (eds.), *Essays on Ancient Israel in Its Near Eastern Context: A Tribute to Nadav Na'aman*, Winona Lake, 297–312.
ORTHMANN, W. (1971): *Untersuchungen zur späthethitischen Kunst* (Saarbrücker Beitragen zur Altertunskunde 8), Bonn.
OSBORNE, J.F. (2011): *Spatial Analysis and Political Authority in the Iron Age Kingdom of Patina, Turkey* (PhD diss., Harvard University), Cambridge.
– (2014a): Monuments and Monumentality, in: J.F. OSBORNE (ed.), *Approaching Monumentality in Archaeology*, New York, 1–19.
– (2014b): Settlement Planning and Urban Symbology in Syro-Anatolian Cities, *CAJ* 24, 195–214.
– (2021): *The Syro-Anatolian City-States. An Iron Age Culture*, Oxford.
OTTOSSON, M. (1993): Tell el-Fukhar in Northern Jordan. The First Season 1990, Syria 70, 214–218.
– (2015): 1990–93 – Area B, in: J. STRANGE (ed.), *Tall al-Fukhar: Results from Excavations in 1990–93 and 2002* (Proceedings of the Danish Institute in Damascus 9), Gylling, 15–27.
PAKKALA, J. (2010): What Do We Know about Geshur? *SJOT* 24, 155–173.
– (2013): The Methodological Hazards in Reconstructing the So-called Kingdom of Geshur, *SJOT* 27, 226–246.
PANITZ-COHEN, N. (2009): The Local Canaanite Pottery, in: N. PANITZ-COHEN/A. MAZAR (eds.), *Excavations at Tel Beth-Shean 1989–1996: Volume III. The 13th–11th Century BCE Strata in Areas N and S*, Jerusalem, 195–433.
– (2016): The Ceramic Assemblage, in: I. Ziffer (ed.), *It is a Land of Honey: Discoveries from Tel Rehov. The Early Days of the Israelite Monarchy*, Tel Aviv, 46–48.
– (2022): An Iron Age IIA Phoenician Bichrome Jar from Tel Abel Beth Maacah, in: U. DAVIDOVICH/N. YAHALOM-MACK/S. MATSKEVICH (eds.), *Material, Method, and Meaning: Papers in Eastern Mediterranean Archaeology in Honor of Ilan Sharon*, Münster, 223–240.

PANITZ-COHEN, N./MULLINS, R.A. (2016): Aram-Maacah? Aramaeans and Israelites on the Border: Excavations at Tell Abil al-Qameḥ (Abel Beth Maacah) in Northern Israel, in: O. SERGI/M. OEMING/I. DE HULSTER (eds.), *In Search of Aram and Israel: Politics, Culture and Identity* (ORA 20), Tübingen, 139–167.

PANITZ-COHEN, N./MULLINS, R.A./BONFIL, R. (2013): Northern Exposure: Launching Excavations at Tell Abil el-Qameḥ (Abel Beth Maacah), *Strata* 31, 27–42.

– (2015): Second Preliminary Report of the Excavations at Tell Abil el-Qameḥ (Abel Beth Maacah), *Strata* 33, 35–59.

PARKER, B.J. (2006): Towards an Understanding of Borderland Processes, *American Antiquity* 71, 77–100.

PAZ, I. et al. (2010): Excavations at Tel Rekhesh, *IEJ* 60, 22–40.

PAZ, S. (2007): *Drums, Women, and Goddesses: Drumming and Gender in Iron Age II Israel* (OBO 232), Fribourg/Göttingen.

PFOH, E. (2008): Dealing with Tribes and States in Ancient Palestine, *SJOT* 22, 86–113.

– (2009): Some Remarks on Patronage in Syria-Palestine During the Late Bronze Age, *JESHO* 52, 363–381.

PIOSKE, D. (2019): The "High Court" of Ancient Israel's Past: Archaeology, Texts, and the Question of Priority, *JHS* 19, 1–25.

PITARD, W.T. (1987): *Ancient Damascus: A Historical Study of the Syrian City-State from the Earliest Times until its Fall to the Assyrians in 732 B.C.E.*, Winona Lake.

PORTER, J.L. (1885): *Five Years in Damascus*, London.

PRATICO, G.D. (1985): Nelson Glueck's 1938-1940 Excavations at Tell el-Kheleifeh: A Reappraisal, *BASOR* 259, 1–32.

PRITCHARD, J.B. (1988): *Sarepta IV: The Objects from Area II, X. The University Museum of the University of Pennsylvania. Excavations at Sarafand, Lebanon*, Beirut.

PUCCI, M. (2019): *Excavations in the Plain of Antioch III: Stratigraphy, Pottery, and Small Finds from Chatal Höyük in the Amuq Plain* (OIP 143), Chicago.

RAINEY, A.F. (2015): *The El-Amarna Correspondence: A New Edition of the Cuneiform Letters from the Site of El-Amarna Based on Collations of All Extant Tablets* (HdO 110), Leiden/Boston.

RAPUANO, Y. (2001): Tel Dover, *HA-ESI* 113, 19*-21*.

RAST, W.E. (1978): *Taanach I. Studies in the Iron Age Pottery*, Cambridge.

REIMER, P.J. et al. (2020): The IntCal20 Northern Hemisphere Radiocarbon Age Calibration Curve (0–55 cal kBP), *Radiocarbon* 62, 725–757

RENZ, J./RÖLLIG, W. (1995): *Handbuch der Althebräischen Epigraphik: Die Althebräischen Inschriften, Vol. 1, Part 1: Text und Kommentar*, Darmstadt.

RICHELLE, M. (2010): Les conquêtes de Hazaël selon la recension lucianique en 4 Règnes 13,22, *BN* 146, 19–25.

RIIS, P.J. (1948): *Les cimetières à cremation* (Hama: Fouilles et recherches 1931–1938 II 3), Copenhagen.

RIIS, P.J./BUHL, M-L. (1990): *Les objets de la periode dite Syro-Hittite (Age du Fer)* (Hama. Fouilles et recherches, 1931–1938 II 2), Copenhagen.

ROHMER, J. (2020): *Hauran VI: D'Aram à Rome. La Syrie du Sud de l'âge du Fer à l'annexion romaine (xiie siècle av. J.-C. - ier siècle apr. J.-C.)*, Beirut.

RÖLLIG, W. (1988): Die Aramäische Inschrift für Haza'el und ihr Duplikat, in: H. KYRIELEIS/W. RÖLLIG (eds.), *Ein Altorientalischer Pferdeschmuck aus dem Heraion von Samos* (Mitteilungen des Deutchen Archäologischen Instituts, Athenische Abteilung 103), Athens, 62–75.

ROLLSTON, C.A. (2006): Scribal Education in Ancient Israel: The Old Hebrew Epigraphic Evidence, *BASOR* 344, 47–74.

– (2008): The Phoenician Script of the Tel Zayit Abecedary and Putative Evidence or Israelite Literacy, in: R.E. TAPPY/P.K. Jr. MCCARTER (eds.), *Literate Culture and Tenth-Century Canaan: The Tel Zayit Abecedary in Context*, Winona Lake.

ROUTLEDGE, B. (1997): Learning to Love the King: Urbanism and the State in Iron Age Moab, in: W.E. AUFRECT/N.A. MIRAU/S. GAULEY (eds.), *Urbanism in Antiquity: From Mesopotamia to Crete* (JSOTSup 244), Sheffield, 130–144.
– (2004): *Moab in the Iron Age: Hegemony, Polity, Archaeology*, Philadelphia.
ROUTLEDGE, B. et al. (2014): A Late Iron Age I Ceramic Assemblage from Central Jordan: Integrating Form, Technology and Distribution, in: E. VAN DER STEEN/J. BOERTIEN/N. MULDER-HYMANS (eds.), *Exploring the Narrative: Jerusalem and Jordan in the Bronze and Iron Ages*, London/New York, 82–107.
ROWAN, Y.M./KERSEL, M.M./HILL, A. (2018): Galilee Prehistory Project: Excavations at Tel Nes (Tell es-Sanjak), *Oriental Institute Annual Report* 17–18, 71–79.
SADER, H. (1987): *Les États Araméens de Syrie: Depuis leur Fondation jusqu'à leur Transformation en Provinces Assyriennes* (Beiruter Texte und Studien 36), Wiesbaden.
– (2014a): History, in: H. NIEHR (ed.), *The Aramaeans in Ancient Syria* (HdO 106), Leiden/Boston, 1–36.
– (2014b): The Northern Levant During the Iron Age I Period, in: A.E. KILLEBREW/M. STEINER (eds.), *The Oxford Handbook of the Archaeology of the Levant: c. 8000–332 BCE*, Oxford, 607–623.
– (2019): *The History and Archaeology of Phoenicia* (ABS 25), Atlanta.
SADER, H./VAN ESS, M. (1998): Looking for Pre-Hellenistic Baalbek, in: H. SADER/T. SCHEFFLER/A. NEUWIRTH (eds.), *Baalbek: Image and Monument 1898–1998* (Beiruter Texte und Studien 69), Beirut, 247–268.
SAPIR-HEN, L./BEN-YOSEF, E. (2013): The Introduction of Domestic Camels to the Southern Levant: Evidence from the Aravah Valley, *TA* 40, 277–285.
SASS, B. (2005): *The Alphabet at the Turn of the Millennium. The West Semitic Alphabet ca. 1150–850 BCE; The Antiquity of the Arabian, Greek and Phrygian Alphabets* (Tel Aviv University, Institute of Archaeology, Occasional Publications 4), Tel Aviv.
– (2010): Four Notes on Taita King of Palistin with an Excursus on King Solomon's Empire, *TA* 37, 169–174.
– (2016): Aram and Israel during the 10th–9th centuries BCE, or Iron Age IIA: The Alphabet, in: O. SERGI/M. OEMING/I. DE HULSTER (eds.), *In Search of Aram and Israel: Politics, Culture and Identity* (ORA 20), Tübingen, 199–227.
– (2017): The Emergence of Monumental West Semitic Alphabetic Writing, with an Emphasis on Byblos, *Semitica* 59, 109–141.
SASS, B./FINKELSTEIN, I. (2016): The Swan-Song of Proto-Canaanite in the Ninth Century BCE in Light of an Alphabetic Inscription from Megiddo, *Semitica et Classica* 9, 19–42.
– (2021): The Exceptional Concentration of Inscriptions at Iron IIA Gath and Rehob and the Nature of the Alphabet in the Ninth Century BCE, in: T. RÖMER/H. GONZALEZ/L. MARTI (eds.), *Oral et écrit dans le Proche-Orient ancien: les processus de rédaction et d'édition. Actes du colloque organisé par le Collège de France, Paris, les 26 et 27 mai 2015* (OBO 291), Leuven, 127–173.
SAUER, J.A. (1986): Transjordan in the Bronze and Iron Ages: A Critique of Glueck's Synthesis, *BASOR* 263, 1–26.
SAVAGE, C. (2009): The Leshem Inscription, in: R. ARAV/R.A. FREUND (eds.), *Bethsaida: A City by the North Shore of the Sea of Galilee 4*, Kirksville, 125–135.
SCHÄFER-LICHTENBERGER, C. (2001): Hazor - A City State between the Major Powers, *SJOT* 15, 104–22.
SCHIPPER, B.U. (2012): Egypt and Israel: The Ways of Cultural Contacts in the Late Bronze Age and Iron Age (20th – 26th Dynasty), *Journal of Egyptian Interconnections* 4, 30–47.
– (2018): *Geschichte Israels in der Antike*, München.
SCHLOEN, J.D. (2001): *The House of the Father as Fact and Symbol: Patrimonialism in Ugarit and the Ancient Near East* (Studies in the Archaeology and History of the Levant 2), Winona Lake.
SCHNIEDEWIND, W.M. (1996): Tel Dan Stela: New Light on Aramaic and Jehu's Revolt, *BASOR* 302, 75–90.

SCHREIBER, N. (2003): *The Cypro-Phoenician Pottery of the Iron Age* (CHANE 13), Leiden/Boston.
SCHROER, S. (2018): *Die Ikonographie Palästinas: Eine Religionsgeschichte in Bildern. Die Eisenzeit bis zum Beginn der Achämenidischen Herrschaft* (Israels und der Alte Orient 4), Göttingen.
SCHUMACHER, G. (1888): *The Jaulan: Surveyed for the German Society for the Exploration of the Holy Land*, London.
– (1889): Across the Jordan: An Exploration and Survey of Part of Hauran and Jaulan, London.
– (1891): Der Hiobstein, Sachrat Eijub, im Hauran, *ZDPV* 14, 142–147.
– (1914): Unsere Arbeiten im Ostjordanlande, *ZDPV* 37, 260–266.
SCHWARTZ, G.M. (1989): The Origins of the Aramaeans in Syria and Northern Mesopotamia, in: O.M.C. HAEX/H.H. CURVES/P.M.M.G. AKKERMANS (eds.), *To the Euphrates and Beyond: Archaeological Studies in Honour of M.N. van Loon*, Rotterdam, 275–291.
SCOTT, E.M. *et al.* (2007): A Report on Phase 1 of the 5th International Radiocarbon Intercomparison (VIRI), *Radiocarbon* 49, 409–426.
SEEDEN, H. (1986): Bronze Age Village Occupation at Busra: AUB Excavations on the Northwest Tell 1983–84, *Berytus* 34, 11–81.
– (1988): Busra 1983–84: Second Archaeological Report, Damaszener Mitteilungen 3, 387–411.
SERGI, O. (2013): Judah's Expansion in Historical Context, *TA* 40, 226–246.
– (2016): The Gilead between Aram and Israel: Political Borders, Cultural Interaction and the Question of Jacob and Israelite Identity, in: O. SERGI/M. OEMING/I. DE HULSTER (eds.), *In Search of Aram and Israel: Politics, Culture and Identity* (ORA 20), Tübingen, 333–354.
– (2015): The Emergence of Judah between Jerusalem and Benjamin, *New Studies in the Archaeology of Jerusalem and its Environs* 9, 50–73 [Hebrew with English summary].
– (2017): The Emergence of Judah as a Political Entity between Jerusalem and Benjamin, *ZDPV* 133, 1–23.
– (2019): Israelite Identity and the Formation of the Israelite Polities in the Iron I–IIA Central Canaanite Highlands, *WO* 49, 206–235.
SERGI, O./DE HULSTER, I. (2016): Some Historical and Methodological Considerations Regarding the Question of Political, Social and Cultural Interaction between Aram and Israel in the Early Iron Age, in: O. SERGI/M. OEMING/I. DE HULSTER (eds.), *In Search of Aram and Israel: Politics, Culture and Identity* (ORA 20), Tübingen, 1–14.
SERGI, O./GADOT, Y. (2017): Omride Palatial Architecture as Symbol in Action: Between State Formation, Obliteration, and Heritage, *JNES* 76, 103–111.
SERGI, O./KLEIMAN, A. (2018): The Kingdom of Geshur and the Expansion of Aram-Damascus into the Northern Jordan Valley: Archaeological and Historical Perspectives, *BASOR* 379, 1–18.
SEYRIG, H. (1931): Travaux archéologiques en Syrie. Tsil et Tell el-al-Asch'ari, *AA* 3–4, 589–590.
– (1959): Antiquites syriennes: Nr. 69. Deux reliquaires, *Syria* 36, 43–48.
SHAI, I./MAEIR, A.M. (2012): The Late Iron IIA Pottery Assemblage from Stratum A3, in: A.M. MAEIR (ed.), *Tell eṣ-Ṣāfi/Gath I: The 1996–2005 Seasons, Part 1. Text* (ÄAT 69), Wiesbaden, 313–363.
– (2018): Reassessing the Character of the Judahite Centralized Kingdom: An Updated Archaeological View, *In the Highlands' Depth* 8, 29–45 [Hebrew with English summary].
SHARON, I./ZARZECKI-PELEG, A. (2006): Podium Structures with Lateral Access: Authority Ploys in Royal Architecture in the Iron Age Levant, in: S. GITIN/J.E. WRIGHT/J.P. DESSEL (eds.), *Confronting the Past: Archaeological and Historical Essays on Ancient Israel in Honor of William G. Dever*, Winona Lake, 145–167.
SHARON, I. *et al.* (2007): Report on the First Stage of the Iron Age Dating Project in Israel: Supporting a Low Chronology, *Radiocarbon* 49, 1–46.
SHILOH, Y. (1973): The Four-Room House-The Israelite Type House? *ErIsr* 11, 277–285.
– (1979): The Proto-Aeolic Capital and Israelite Ashlar Masonry (Qedem 11), Jerusalem.
SHILOH, Y./HOROWITZ, A. (1975): Ashlar Quarries of the Iron Age in the Hill Country of Israel, *BASOR* 217, 37–48.

SHOCHAT, H. (2017): *A Cultural Change at Dor in the Iron Age II: The Annexation of Dor to the Kingdom of Israel – Stratigraphical and Typological Analysis of the Findings from Area D2* (MA thesis, Haifa University), Haifa.
SHOCHAT, H./GILBOA, A. (2019): Elusive Destructions: Reconsidering the Hazor Iron Age II Sequence and its Chronological and Historical Implications, *Levant* 363–386.
SHOVAL, S./BECK, P./YADIN, E. (2006): The Ceramic Technology Used in the Manufacture of Iron Age Pottery from Galilee, in: M. MAGGETTI/B. MESSIGA (eds.), *Geomaterials in Cultural Heritage*, London, 101–117.
SHUSTER, R. (2009): Petrographic Analysis of a Hippo Jar from the Storage Room of the Stratum V City Gate, in: R. ARAV/R.A. FREUND (eds.), *Bethsaida: A City by the North Shore of the Sea of Galilee 4*, Kirksville, 123–124.
SIDDAL, L.R (2013): *The Reign of Adad-nīrārī III: An Historical and Ideological Analysis of An Assyrian King and His Times* (CM 45), Leiden/Boston.
SINGER-AVITZ, L. (1989): Iron Age Pottery (Strata XIV–XII), in: Z. HERZOG/G. RAPP/O. NEGBI (eds.), *Excavations at Tel Michal, Israel*, Minneapolis, 76–87.
– (2014): The Pottery of Megiddo Strata III–II and a Proposed Subdivision of the Iron IIC Period in Northern Israel, *BASOR* 372, 123–145.
– (2016): Khirbet Qeiyafa: Late Iron Age I in Spite of It All — Once Again, *IEJ* 66, 232–244.
– (2018): The Iron IIB Pottery: On Typological Differences between the Regions of Judah and Israel, in: I. SHAI et al. (eds.), *Tell it in Gath: Studies in the History and Archaeology of Israel Essays in Honor of Aren M. Maeir on the Occasion of his Sixtieth Birthday* (ÄAT 90), Münster, 663–679.
SLAYTON, J.C. (1992): Bashan, in: N.L. FREEDMAN (ed.), *ABD* (Volume 1), New York, 623–624.
SMITH, G.A. (1901): Notes of a Journey through Hauran, with Inscriptions Found by the Way, *PEQ* 33, 340–361.
SMITH, R.H. (1992): Baalbek, in: N.L. FREEDMAN (ed.), *ABD* (Volume 1), New York, 556.
STAGER, L.E. (1985): The Archaeology of the Family in Ancient Israel, *BASOR* 260, 1–35.
– (2003): The Patrimonial Kingdom of Solomon, in: W.G. DEVER/S. GITIN (eds.), *Symbiosis, Symbolism, and the Power of the Past*, Winona Lake, 63–74.
STAGER, L.E./WOLFF, S.R. (1981): Production and Commerce in Temple Courtyards: An Olive Press in the Sacred Precinct at Tel Dan, *BASOR* 243, 95–102.
STEPANSKY, Y. (1999): *The Periphery of Hazor during the Bronze Age, the Iron Age and the Persian Period: A Regional-Archaeological Study* (MA thesis, Tel Aviv University), Tel Aviv.
– (2005): Tel Abel Bet Ma'akha, *HA-ESI* 117 [online publication].
– (2008a): Rosh Pinna, *HA-ESI* 120 [online publication].
– (2008b): Between Hazor and the Kinnereth: The Korazim Plateau in the Biblical Period, in: S. BAR (ed.), *In the Hill-Country, and in the Shephelah, and in the Arabah (Joshua 12, 8): Studies and Researches Presented to Adam Zertal in the Thirtieth Anniversary of the Manasseh Hill-Country Survey*, Jerusalem, 271–289 [Hebrew with English summary].
– (2014): Between Ayelet and Kinneret: The Archaeological Survey of the Korazim Plateau and North of Lake Kinneret, *Qadmoniot* 148, 102–109 [Hebrew with English summary].
– (2019): Settlement Remains from the Iron Age, Hellenistic, Roman-Byzantine and Early Islamic Periods on the Ancient Tell of Rosh Pinna (Ja'una), *Atiqot* 96, 1–57.
– (forthcoming): *Archaeological Survey of Israel: Map of Kfar Nahum Map (36)*, Jerusalem.
STEPANSKY, Y./SEGAL, D./CARMI, I. (1996): The 1993 Sounding at Tel Sasa: Excavation Report and Radiometric Dating, *Atiqot* 28, 63–76.
STEINER, R.C. (2009): On the Rise and Fall of Canaanite Religion at Baalbek: A Tale of Five Toponyms, *JBL* 128, 507–525.
STERN, E. (1993): *NEAEHL*, Jerusalem.
STRANGE, J. (2015): *Tall al-Fukhar: Results from Excavations in 1990–93 and 2002* (Proceedings of the Danish Institute in Damascus 9), Gylling.
STUBBINGS, F.H. (1951): *Mycenaean Pottery from the Levant*, Cambridge.

SUGIMOTO, D.T. (1999): Iron Age Potteries from Tel En-Gev, Israel: Seasons 1990–1992, *Orient* 34, 1–21.
- (2015a): Stratigraphy of Tel 'En Gev, Israel: Correlation among Three Archaeological Missions, *PEQ* 147, 195–219.
- (2015b): History and Nature of Iron Age Cities in the Northeastern Sea of Galilee Region: A Preliminary Overview, *Orient* 50, 91–108.

TADMOR, H. (1962): The Southern Border of Aram, *IEJ* 12, 114–122.

TADMOR, H./YAMADA, S. (2011): *The Royal Inscriptions of Tiglath-Pileser III (744–727 BC) and Shalmaneser V (726–722 BCE), Kings of Assyria*, Winona Lake.

TAPPY, R. (1992): *The Archaeology of Israelite Samaria: Early Iron Age through the Ninth Century B.C.E. Volume I* (HSS 44), Atlanta.

TARAQJI, A. (1999): Nouvelles Découvertes sur les Relations avec l'Égypte à Tel Sakka et à Keswé, dans la Région de Damas, *Bulletin de la Société française d'égyptologie* 144, 27–43.
- (2015): Tell Sakka, Fouilles Syriennes dans la Région de Damas, in: P. PFÄLZNER/M. AL-MAQDISSI (eds.), *Qatna and the Networks of Bronze Age Globalism: Proceedings of an International Conference in Stuttgart and Tübingen in October 2009*, Wiesbaden, 101–109.
- (2016): Tell Sakka, in: Y. KANJOU/A. TSUNEKI (eds.), *A History of Syria in One Hundred Sites*, Oxford, 167–170.

TENU, A. (2015): Funerary Practices and Society at the Late Bronze-Iron Age Transition. A View from Tell Shiukh Fawqani and Tell an-Nasriyah (Syria), in: K.A. YENER (ed.), *Across the Border: Late Bronze-Iron Age Relations between Syria and Anatolia* (ANESSup 42), Leuven/Paris/Walpole, 423–447.

THAREANI, Y. (2016a): Enemy at the Gates? The Archaeological Visibility of the Aramaeans at Dan, in: O. SERGI/M. OEMING/I. DE HULSTER (eds.), *In Search of Aram and Israel: Politics, Culture and Identity* (ORA 20), Tübingen, 169–197.
- (2016b): Imperializing the Province: A Residence of a Neo-Assyrian City Governor at Tel Dan, *Levant* 48, 254–283.
- (2018): *Revenge of the Conquered: Paths of Resistance in the Assyrian City of Dan, Semitica* 60, 473–492.
- (2019a): Changing Allegiances in Disputed Borderlands: Dan's Political Status on the Eve of the Aramaean Invasion, *PEQ* 151, 184–201.
- (2019b): Archaeology of an Imagined Community: Tel Dan in the Iron Age IIa, in: A. BERLEJUNG/A.M. MAEIR (eds.), *Researches on Israel and Aram: Autonomy, Interdependence and Related Issues. Proceedings of the First Annual RIAB Center Conference, Leipzig, June 2016* (ORA 34), Tübingen, 264–276.
- (2019c): From Expelled Refugee to Imperial Envoy: Assyria's Deportation Policy in Light of the Archaeological Evidence from Tel Dan, *Journal of Anthropological Archaeology* 54, 218–234.

THOMAS, Z. (2021): On the Archaeology of the 10th Century BCE Israel and the Idea of the 'State', *PEQ*, DOI: 10.1080/00310328.2021.1886488.

THOMPSON, H.O. (1992): Argob, in: N.L. FREEDMAN (ed.), *ABD* (Volume 1), New York, 376.

THOMSEN, I./ZWICKEL, W. (2011): Was Kinneret Destroyed by an Earthquake? *NEA* 74, 76.

THUREAU-DANGIN, F./DUNAND, M. (1936): *Til-Barsip*, Paris.

THUREAU-DANGIN, F. et al. (1931): *Arslan Tash*, Paris.

TOFFOLO, M.B. et al. (2014): Absolute Chronology of Megiddo, Israel, in the Late Bronze and Iron Ages: High-Resolution Radiocarbon Dating, *Radiocarbon* 56, 221–244.

TRIGGER, B. (1990): Monumental Architecture: A Thermodynamic Explanation of Symbolic Behaviour, *World Archaeology* 22, 119–32.

TYNJÄ, T. (2017): *From the Field to the Publication: The Retrieval and Presentation of Pottery – A Case study from Early Iron Age Tel Kinrot, Israel* (PhD diss., University of Helsinki), Helsinki.

TZIN, B./BRON, H./KLEIMAN, A. (forthcoming): Ḥaspin: A Fortified Complex from the Middle Bronze and Iron Ages in the Southern Golan Heights, *Michmanim*.

USSISHKIN, D. (1967): Observations on Some Monuments from Carchemish, *JNES* 26, 87–92.
- (1970): On the Original Position of Two Proto-Ionic Capitals at Megiddo, *IEJ* 20, 213–215.
- (1989): Schumacher's Shrine in Building 338 at Megiddo, *IEJ* 39, 149–172.
- (1990): Notes on Megiddo, Gezer, Ashdod, and Tel Batash in the Tenth to Ninth Centuries B.C, *BASOR* 277–278, 71–91.
- (2004): A Synopsis of the Stratigraphical, Chronological and Historical Issues, in: USSISHKIN, D. *The Renewed Archaeological Excavations at Lachish (1973–1994)* (SMNIA 22), Tel Aviv, 50–122.
- (2007): On the So-called Aramaean 'Siege Trench' in Tell eṣ-Ṣafi, Ancient Gath, *IEJ* 59, 137–157.
- (2011): The Dating of the lmlk Storage Jars and Its Implications: Rejoinder to Lipschits, Sergi and Koch, *TA* 38, 220–240.
- (2017): The Date of Building 338 at Megiddo: A Rejoinder, *IEJ* 67, 50–60.
- (2018): The Date of Building 338 at Megiddo: Additional Comments, *IEJ* 68, 232–236.

USSISHKIN, D./WOODHEAD, J. (1997): Excavations at Tel Jezreel 1994–1996: Third Preliminary Report, *TA* 24, 6–72

UZIEL, J./GADOT, Y. (2010): The 'Cup-and-Saucer' Vessel: Function, Chronology, Distribution and Symbolism, *IEJ* 60, 41–57.

UZIEL, J./SHAI, I./CASSUTO, D. (2014): The Ups and Downs of Settlement Patterns: Why Sites Fluctuate, in: J. SPENCER/R.A. MULLINS/A. BRODY (eds.), *Material Culture Matters: Essays on the Archaeology of the Southern Levant in Honor of Seymour Gitin*, Winona Lake, 295–308.

VAN DER OSTEN, H.H. (1956): *Svenska Syrien Expeditionen 1952–1953: Die Grabung von Tell es-Salihiyeh (Skrifter Utgivna av Svenska Institutet* I Athen 4°, 4), Lund.

VANDERHOOFT, D.S. (2017): The Final Phase of the Common "Proto-Semitic" Alphabet in the Southern Levant. A Rejoinder to Sass and Finkelstein, in: O. LIPSCHITS/Y. GADOT/M.J. ADAMS (eds.), *Rethinking Israel: Studies in the History and Archaeology of Ancient Israel in Honor of Israel Finkelstein*, Winona Lake, 441–450.

VANVALKENBURGH, P./OSBORNE, J.F. (2013): Home Turf: Archaeology, Territoriality, and Politics, *Archaeological Papers of the American Anthropological Association* 22, 1–27.

VIEWEGER, D./HÄSER, J. (2017): *Tall Zirāʿa: Gadara Region Project 2001–2011. Final Report 1*, Jerusalem/Amman/Wuppertal.

VOGEL, J.C./WATERBOLK, H.T. (1972): Groningen Radiocarbon Dates X, *Radiocarbon* 14, 6–10.

WAGNER-DURAND, E. (2020): Kamed el-Loz during the Early Centuries of the Iron Age, *Archaeology and History of Lebanon* 52–53, 73–101.

WALDBAUM, J.C. (2015): Iron Age I–II: Greek Imports, in: S. GITIN (ed.), *The Ancient Pottery of Israel and Its Neighbors: From the Iron Age through the Hellenistic Period*, Jerusalem, 509–531.

WAMPLER, J.C. (1947): *Tell en-Naṣbeh II: The Pottery*, Berkeley/New Haven.

WARD, W.A./JOUKOWSKY, M.S. (1992): *The Crisis Years: The 12th Century B.C. From Beyond the Danube to the Tigris*, Dubuque.

WATZINGER, C. (1929): *Tell el-Mutesellim II: Die Funde*, Leipzig.

WEEDEN, M. (2013): After the Hittites: The Kingdoms of Karkamish and Palistin in Northern Syria, *Bulletin of the Institute of Classical Studies* 56, 1–20.

WEINSTEIN, J.M. (1981): The Egyptian Empire in Palestine: A Reassessment, *BASOR* 241, 1–28.
- (1984): Radiocarbon Dating in the Southern Levant, *Radiocarbon* 26, 297–366.

WEKSLER-BDOLAH, S. (2000): An Archaeological Excavation at Tel Nov, *Atiqot* 39, 13*-26*.

WIGHTMAN, G.J. (1984): Building 434 and Other Public Buildings in the Northeastern Sector of Megiddo, *TA* 11, 132–145.
- (1990): The Myth of Solomon, *BASOR* 277–278, 5–22.

WILDE, E.M./FISCHER, P.M. (2013): Radiocarbon Dates from Tell Abu Kharaz, in: P.M. FISCHER (ed.), *Tell Abu al-Kharaz in the Jordan Valley* (Contributions to the Chronology of the Eastern Mediterranean XXXIV), Vienna, 457–461.

WIMMER, S.J. (2002): A New Stela of Ramesses II in Jordan in the Context of Egyptian Royal Stelae in the Levant. *Unpublished Lecture at ICAANE 3 in Paris*.

WIMMER, S.J./JANAYDEH, K. (2011): Eine Mondgottstele aus "eṭ-Ṭurra"/Jordanien, *ZDPV* 127, 135–141.
WINN, S.M.M./YAKAR, J. (1984): The 1982 Excavations at Tel Kinrot: The Early Bronze Age Settlement, *TA* 11, 20–47.
WINTER, I.J. (1981): Is There a South Syrian Style of Ivory Carving in the Early First Millennium B.C.? *Iraq* 43, 101–130.
WORKMAN, V. et al. (2020): An Iron IIA Iron and Bronze Workshop in the Lower City of Tell es-Safi/Gath, *TA* 47, 208–236.
YADIN, E./KOCHAVI, M. (2008): Hadar, Tel, in: E. STERN (ed.), *NEAEHL* (Volume 5), Jerusalem, 1756–1757.
YADIN, Y. (1970): Megiddo of the Kings of Israel, *BA* 33, 65–96.
– (1959a): Excavations at Hazor, 1958: Preliminary Communiqué, *IEJ* 9, 74–88.
– (1959b): The Fourth Season of Excavations at Hazor, *BA* 22, 1–20.
– (1972): *Hazor: The Head of All Those Kingdoms*, London.
YADIN, Y. et al. (1958): *Hazor I: An Account of the First Season of Excavations, 1955*, Jerusalem.
– (1960): *Hazor II: An Account of the Second Season of Excavations, 1956*, Jerusalem.
– (1961): *Hazor III–IV: An Account of the Third and Fourth Seasons of Excavations, 1957–1958 (Plates)*, Jerusalem.
– (1989): *Hazor III–IV: An Account of the Third and Fourth Seasons of Excavation, 1957–1958 (Text)*, Jerusalem.
YAHALOM-MACK, N./PANITZ-COHEN, N./MULLINS, R.A. (2018): From a Fortified Canaanite City-State to "a City and a Mother" in Israel: Five Seasons of Excavation at Tel Abel Beth Maacah, *NEA* 81, 145–156.
– (2019): An Iron Age I Cultic Context at Tel Abel Beth-Maacah, in: A. BERLEJUNG/A.M. MAEIR (eds.), *Researches on Israel and Aram: Autonomy, Interdependence and Related Issues. Proceedings of the First Annual RIAB Center Conference, Leipzig, June 2016* (ORA 34), Tübingen, 233–250.
YAHALOM-MACK, N. et al. (2014): Metalworking at Hazor: A Long-Term Perspective, *OJA* 33, 19–45.
– (2017): Metalworking at Megiddo during the Late Bronze and Iron Ages, *JNES* 76, 53–74.
– (2021): The Iron Age IIA 'Benyaw Inscription' on a Jar from Tel Abel Beth Maacah, *PEQ*, DOI: 10.1080/00310328.2021.1975070.
YAMADA, S. (2000): *The Construction of the Assyrian Empire: A Historical Study of the Inscriptions of Shalmaneser III (859–824 BC) Relating to His Campaigns to the West* (CHANE 3), Leiden/Boston.
YASUR-LANDAU, A. (2012a): A Mace/Scepter Head from Tomb 1136, in: Y. GADOT/A. YASUR-LANDAU (eds.), *Qiryat Shemona (S): Fort and Village in the Hula Valley* (Salvage Excavation Reports 7), Tel Aviv, 202–204.
– (2012b): Near East: Iron Age Civilizations in the Southern Levant, in: N.A. SILBERMAN (ed.), *The Oxford Companion to Archaeology* (second edition), Oxford, 467–473.
YOUNGER, K.L. (2016): *A Political History of the Arameans: From Their Origins to the End of their Polities* (ABS 13), Atlanta.
– (2020a): The God 'El of Ramesses II's Stela from Sheikh S'ad (the "Job Stone"), in: R.E. AVERBECK/K.L. YOUNGER (eds.), *"An Excellent Fortress for His Armies, a Refuge for the People": Egyptological, Archaeological, and Biblical Studies in Honor of James K. Hoffmeier*, Winona Lake, 407–421.
– (2020b): Reflections on Hazael's Empire in Light of Recent Study in the Biblical and Ancient Near Eastern Texts, in: I. KALIMI (ed.), *Writing and Rewriting History in Ancient Israel and Near Eastern Cultures*, Wiesbaden, 79–102.
ZARZECKI-PELEG, A. (1997): Hazor, Jokneam and Megiddo in the Tenth Century B.C.E., *TA* 24, 258–288.

ZARZECKI-PELEG, A./COHEN-ANIDJAR, S./BEN-TOR. A. (2005): Pottery Analysis, in: A. BEN-TOR/A. ZARZECKI-PELEG/S. COHEN-ANIDJAR (eds.), *Yoqne'am II: The Iron Age and the Persian Period. Final Report of the Archaeological Excavations (1977–1988)* (Qedem Reports 6), Jerusalem, 233–344.
– (2016): *Yadin's Expedition to Megiddo: Final Report of the Archaeological Excavations (1960, 1966, 1967 and 1971/2 Seasons)* (Qedem 56), Jerusalem.
ZEVIT, Z. (1991): Yahweh Worship and Worshippers in 8th-Century Syria, *VT* 41, 363–366.
ZINGBOYM, O. (2008): Mizpe Golani, *HA-ESI* 120 [online publication].
– (2010): Shuqayif, Survey, *HA-ESI* 122 [online publication].
ZUCKERMAN, S. (2003): *The Kingdom of Hazor in the Late Bronze Age: Chronological and Regional Aspects of the Material Culture of Hazor and its Settlement* (PhD diss., the Hebrew University of Jerusalem), Jerusalem.
– (2007): Anatomy of a Destruction: Crisis Architecture, Termination Rituals and the Fall of Canaanite Hazor, *Journal of Mediterranean Archaeology* 20, 3–32.
– (2010): "The City, its Gods Will Return There…": Towards an Alternative Interpretation of Hazor's Acropolis in the Late Bronze Age, *JNES* 69, 163–178.
– (2011): Ruin Cults at Iron Age I Hazor, in: I. FINKELSTEIN/N. NA'AMAN (eds.), *The Fire Signals of Lachish: Studies in the Archaeology and History of Israel in the Late Bronze Age, Iron Age, and Persian Period in Honor of David Ussishkin*, Winona Lake, 387–394.
ZUKERMAN, A. (2019): Notes on the Philistine, Aegean and Cypriot-style Decorated Pottery, in: D. ILAN (ed.), *Dan IV: The Iron Age I Settlement. The Avraham Biran Excavations (1966–1999)*, Jerusalem, 351–367.
ZWICKEL, W. (1990a): *Eisenzeitliche Ortslagen im Ostjordanland* (TAVO 81), Wiesbaden.
– (1990b): *Räucherkult und Räuchergeräte: Exegetische und Archäologische Studien zum Räucheropfer im Alten Testament* (OBO 97), Fribourg/Göttingen.
– (2017): *Settlement History around the Sea of Galilee from the Neolithic to the Persian Period* (ÄAT 86), Münster.
– (2019): Borders between Aram-Damascus and Israel: A Historical Investigation, in: J. DUŠEK/J. MYNÁŘOVÁ (eds.), *Aramaean Borders: Defining Aramaean Territories in the 10th–8th Centuries B.C.E.* (CHANE 101), Leiden/Boston, 267–335.

Index of References

Biblical Texts

Genesis
10:23	216
14:5	101

Numbers
21:33	96

Deuteronomy
1:4	101
3:1	96; 108
3:4	96

Joshua
9:10	101
11	4
11:10	39
11:10–13	206
12:4	101
13:11–12	96
13:12	101
13:13	4
13:26	73; 127
19:35	67
19:36	57
21:27	101

Judges
11:3	100; 108
18	4
18:25	19
18:27	11

2 Samuel
3:3	7; 63; 216
8	229
8:3	6
8:3–10	229
8:8	29
8:10	229
9:4–5	73; 127
10:6	19; 100; 108
10:8	19; 100; 108
10:17	110
13:37–38	63; 216
14:32	63; 216
15:8	63; 216
17:18–19	224
17:27	127
20	7
20:14–22	39; 42

1 Kings
4:13	116
4:14	96
9:15	4; 7
11:23–24	7
12:26–33	7
12:29	39
14:25	211
15:20	7–8; 32–33; 42
15:21	214
15:27	214
16:9	214
16:23–24	214
19:16	214
22	8

2 Kings
9	8; 199
9:2	214
9:14	214
9:20	214
12:18	9; 213
12:19	214
13:3	9
13:14–19	11; 218
13:17	72; 87
13:22	9; 214

13:25	218	*Ezekiel*	
14:11–13	15	47:17–18	9
14:23–24	218		
14:25	4; 9; 11; 22; 219	*Hosea*	
15:10	219	1:4	8
15:14	219	10:14	119; 128
15:16	219		
15:25	219	*Amos*	
15:29	4; 8; 33; 42; 220	1:3	9; 11
15:30	219	4:1	82; 96
15:36	10	6:2	9
16:1–6	10	6:13	73; 98; 127; 218
22	128	6:14	22
		6:13–14	9–11
Isaiah			
7:1	10	*1 Chronicles*	
22:10	218	18:8	29
		18:10	229
Jeremiah			
41:7–8	224–225	*2 Chronicles*	
		16:4	33
		22:7	214

Amarna Letters

EA 174	34
EA 175	23; 34
EA 176	34
EA 179	29
EA 197	101; 108–109
EA 205	100; 108
EA 256	88–89; 94–95; 101; 107; 118; 206; 209; 216

Index of Ancient Names and Places

'Adasiye, Khirbet el- 251
'Ajur Ghazaleh 249
'Aked, 'Ein 240
'Alaq Pens, 'Ain el- 24
'Alaq, Tell el- 237; 245
'Almin 241
'Alomim, 'Ein 240
'Aqaibi 35; 238
'Arq el-'Arbeh 249
'Ashtara, Tell (see also 'Ashtaroth) 89; 97; 101–107; 109–113; 118; 143; 150; 167; 184; 187; 190; 205; 207; 210; 221–222; 250
'Ashtaroth (see also 'Ashtara, Tell) 82; 94; 96; 101; 107; 109; 206–207; 209; 220; 232; 250
'Ayn, Tell el- 249
'Ayyun Ba'thata North 248
'Ayyun Summaqa 244
'Ayyun Umm el-'Azam 248
'Ayyun, Kh. 11; 19; 20; 33; 35; 39; 42; 94; 221; 236; 244; 248–249
'Ayyun, Tell el- 33; 236
'Ein Gev, Tell 64; 69; 72; 74–78; 80–81; 89; 104; 139–141; 143; 150; 156; 162; 168–169; 177; 191–192; 194; 196; 200; 208; 210; 218–219; 226; 228; 232; 243; 261; 263
'Eitun, Tel 5; 139
'Enot Shuv 241
'Ubeidiyah 77; 243
'Urfa 244
'Uwenish, 'Ain 248

Abel Beth-Maacah, Tel 7; 39–42; 53; 58–59; 168–169; 192; 196–198; 208–210; 220; 222–223; 225; 228–229; 239
Abel Shittim 10
Abu ez-Zeitun, Tell 86–87; 90; 92–93; 247
Abu Kharaz, Tell 196; 222
Abu Mudawwar 84; 94
Adad-Idri / Ezer 29
Adad-Nirari III 9; 232
Adeise 248
Adeise South 248

Adra, 114–115
Afis, Tell 9; 85; 213; 230
Ahab 46 (see also Omride Dynasty)
Ahaziah 8
Ahla, 'Ain 236
Ahmadiyye 245
Amenhotep II 67; 198
Anafa, Tel 49; 169; 240
Anti-Lebanon Mountains 19–20; 36–38
Aphek, Tel 15; 51; 72; 87; 213–214
Arad, Tel 213; 215
Aram-Damascus 2–3; 6–11; 15; 19; 22; 57; 98; 114; 116; 123–125; 128; 148; 174–175; 179; 182; 193; 201; 205; 212–213; 216–222; 226–227; 230–232 (see also Damascus)
Arbel Yarden, Horvat 241
Ard es-Seiyarah 241
Ash'ari, Tell el- 87; 97; 106–107; 109–111; 113; 181–182; 205; 228; 250
Avazim, 'Ein 240
Ayyelet haShahar 222

Baalbek 20; 22; 25; 35; 236–237
Baasha 32
Bab el-Hawa 84–85; 89–91; 93; 169; 205; 244; 246
Balata, Tell (see also Shechem) 207
Banias 243
Bardawil, el- 248
Barr Elyas, Tell 20, 29; 33–34; 208; 219; 238
Barum, Tel 239
Basha, 'Ain el- 237
Bashan (see also Hauran) 82; 96; 101
Batra 247
Bayada, Khirbet el- 254
Bayaz, Khirbet el- 252
Be'er Hasin 240
Beit Ahu 239
Beit Yafa 254
Bellan, Tell el- 21
Ben-Hadad I 8; 32; 218

Ben-Hadad II 199
Beth-Rehob 6; 19; 199; 208
Beth-Shean, Tel 8; 11; 49; 64; 160; 170; 192; 200; 211; 213–214; 216; 221; 227
Bey, Khirbet el- 241
Bijjeh, el- 244
Bir Dhakwa 21; 238
Bjuriyye 94; 247
Burna 214
Busaybis 236
Busra 11; 97–98; 109–111; 113; 207; 251
Busra esh-Sham 11; 109; 251
Butmiyye 246
Buyut Abu Rujm 247

Chtaura / Jedithe 238
Coastal Plain 15; 213

Dabba, Tell ed- 8; 97; 100; 110–111; 113; 250
Dabulya 127; 253
Dahar Ahmad 244
Dahtamiyye, ed- 247
Dalhamiya 33; 34; 208; 219; 238
Damascus 2–3; 6–12; 15; 20; 22; 32; 36–38; 57; 96; 98; 101; 114–116; 123–125; 128; 148; 174; 175; 178–179; 182; 193; 198–199; 201; 205; 212–213; 216–222; 227; 230–232 (see also Aram-Damascus)
Dan, Tel 4; 8–11; 15–16; 24–25; 31; 39–40; 42–48; 52–53; 58–59; 62; 71; 77; 84; 135; 137; 144–146; 148–151; 153; 155–156; 158–160; 162; 164–165; 167–169; 171; 173–177; 179; 182; 191–201; 205; 208–210; 212–213; 215; 218–222; 225–232; 235; 239; 256–257; 263
Danabu 8; 98; 100; 118
Dar el-Qar'an 249
Dar, ed- 33–34; 238
Dar'a 97–99; 108–110; 112; 251 (see also Edrei)
Darbashiye 244
Dardara 245
David 4–7; 10; 29; 173; 209
Dayr el-Asmar West 190; 250
Dayr Sras 245
Dayr Zanun 21; 29; 33–38; 208; 219; 238
Dhahab, edh- 89
Dibbin, Tell (see also Ijon) 21; 32–33; 35–38; 239
Dilli, Tell 249
Dor, Tel 12–13; 15; 210; 217; 230

Dothan, Tel 15; 53; 193; 196; 213; 215–216
Dover, Tel 73–74; 78–81; 184–187; 190; 243
Druze Caves North 241
Dunayba, ed- 8; 97–98; 100; 118; 250
Duris, Tell 237
Duwirban 248

E.P. 144 242
E.P. 227 248
E.P. 235 248
E.P. 670 245
E.P. 712 245
Edrei 108; 251 (see also Dar'a)
Eliphelet Enclosure 242
Eqlatiyah, Tell 243
Eshshe 245
et-Tell / Bethsaida 64–67; 69; 78–81; 86–87; 104; 135; 137–139; 148; 151; 153; 160; 168–169; 181–182; 191–198; 210; 216–219; 222; 226; 228; 232
et-Turra 118; 127–128; 182; 198; 207; 228; 252

Fahura Pens 245
Fakhuri, el- 94; 247
Far'ah North, Tell el- (see also Tirzah) 54; 139; 142; 213–214
Faras, Tell el- 246
Farfur North, Khirbet 247
Fawqa 'Ain el- 238
Fu'ara 252
Fukhar, Tell el- 94; 107; 116–119; 127–131; 143; 167; 169; 206; 253
Furan, Horvat 244

Galilee 3; 11; 39–40; 64; 77; 160; 190; 213; 221; 223
Gath (see also es-Safi, Tell) 3; 10; 15; 213–214; 224; 229; 235
Geshur 3; 7; 10; 63–65; 70; 74; 216–217; 232
Ghadir en-Nahas 245
Ghassil, Tell el- 19–20; 24–29; 31; 33–38; 150; 159; 165; 169; 206; 208; 210; 228; 231; 237
Ghazal, 'Ain 128; 252
Ghazza, Tell 35; 238
Giv'at 'Az 244
Giv'at haShoket 239
Giv'at Orha 246
Giv'at Shhomit 240
Goded, Tel 214

Golan Heights 2; 4; 11; 39–40; 58; 64; 70–71; 77; 82–97; 109; 127; 169–170; 181–182; 192; 206; 209; 212; 216; 223–226; 228; 235; 243

ha'Ashan, Horvat 240
Had, el- 237; 249
Hadad-Ramman 114
Hadar, Tel 13; 24–25; 31; 48; 64–66; 69–73; 76–81; 86–87; 89; 104; 120–121; 139–143; 145–150; 153; 156; 158–162; 164–165; 168–172; 188; 191–192; 194; 196–198; 205; 208–210; 217–219; 224–226; 228; 231–232; 243; 261; 263
Hadat, Tell el- 237
Hadyan 9
Hafar, Horvat 244
Hama Citadel (see also Hamath) 9; 230
Hamad, Tell 250
Hamath (see also Hama Citadel) 19; 22; 155; 182; 229
Hammam, Tell el- 10; 242
Hamol, Tell 240
Hamra East 'Ain el- 244
Hanut el-Meydan 246
Haql el-Bayda 236
Haql el-Jami', Tell 236
Har Beriniki 243
Hariri 'Ain el- 94; 246
Harshum, Tell 114–115
Hasas, Tell 239
Hashabu (see also Hashbe, Tell) 19; 25; 34; 237
Hashbe, Tell (see also Hashabu) 19; 25; 33–34; 237
Hasi (see also Hizzin, Tell) 19; 23; 34; 206; 237; 240
Haspin 88; 181–182; 228; 235; 247
Hatar, Khirbet 249
Hauran (see also Bashan) 8; 98; 109
Hawsh es-Safiya, Tell 237
Hazael 6–7; 9; 39; 124; 180; 199; 201; 212–215; 217; 232
Hazor, Tel 4; 6; 10; 13–16; 39–40; 43; 47–56; 58–62; 67; 71; 77; 82; 85; 89; 125; 136–146; 148–151; 153–158; 160; 162; 164–170; 172–177; 182–183; 189–194; 196–198; 200; 205–209; 212–232; 235; 241; 257–260; 262
Hebike 8
Hilya, Tel 251

Hirmil Old Town Center, el- 236
Hirmil Wadi el-Jawz, el- 236
Hizzin (see also Hasi) 19–20; 23–25; 31; 33–35; 150; 169; 183; 185–186; 205; 237
Hodim, Tel 243
Hula Valley 2; 4; 7; 10–11; 39–62; 89; 150; 152; 167–168; 172; 177; 182; 192; 195; 201; 206; 208–209; 212–213; 215; 220–227; 229–231; 235; 239
Husn, Tell el- 21; 116–117; 120; 125–131; 236; 254
Hutiya, Khirbet el- 248

Ijon (see also Dibbin, Tell) 32; 35; 220; 239
Irbid Plateau 2; 8; 11; 16; 73; 116–131; 150–152; 166–168; 170; 192; 198; 206–207; 209; 212; 219–220; 222–224; 228; 231–232; 235; 251
Irbid, Tell 8; 11; 16; 73; 116–122; 124–131; 150–153; 158; 166–170; 182–184; 187–188; 192; 198; 205–207; 209; 212; 219–220; 222–224; 228; 231–232; 235; 251; 254; 263
Is'ara 128; 252
Israel / Northern Kingdom 4; 6–8; 10; 33; 54; 57; 124; 128; 139; 141; 160; 161; 173–176; 182; 191–193; 199–201; 205–207; 209; 211–214; 217–222; 225–227; 229–232; 235

Jabal Abu el-Hussein 253
Jabal ed-Druz 8; 97; 181–182
Jamus, Tell el- 249
Jaz'ir 229; 241
Jehoahaz 9; 214
Jehoash 214
Jehu 8–9; 199; 214
Jeroboam I 8; 200
Jeroboam II 7; 9–10; 22; 124; 201; 217–219; 221; 229
Jerusalem 3; 5–6; 14; 39; 42; 49
Jezreel, Tel 14; 54; 196; 216
Jezreel Valley 7; 11; 13–15; 49; 149; 152; 154; 161; 171–173; 183; 191; 193; 199; 208; 210; 212; 214; 230
Jijjin 127; 253
Jisr, Tell el- 35; 238
Jita, Tell 34; 237
Johfiyeh, Tell 125; 127–128; 150–151; 221; 254
Joram 8; 229

Jordan River 8; 10; 60–62; 64; 79–81; 94; 130–131; 153
Jordan Valley 10; 64; 116; 153; 213; 226
Jozieh 245
Judean Shephelah 14–15; 78; 192; 209; 213; 219; 221–222; 231

Kabar, Khirbet 255
Kadesh Barnea, Tel 214
Kamid el-Loz, Tell (see also Kumidi) 20; 24; 29–37; 144; 146; 149–150; 165; 169; 192; 205; 207–210; 225–226; 239
Kanaf, Horvat 86; 247
Karei Deshe 77; 243
Karei Deshe Beach 243
Karmita, Tell 238
Katlit, Tell 239
Kefrein, Tell el- 10
Kfar 'Akabya 86; 247
Kfar Ya'akov 241
Khanzira 'Ain el- 238
Khashash, Tell el- 170; 248
Kheleifeh, Tell 220
Khuweikh Northeast 244
Kinnereth (see also Kinrot, Tel) 208–209; 231
Kinrot, Tel (see also Kinnereth) 13; 53; 58; 63–65; 67–69; 71; 77–81; 139–141; 143; 145–150; 153; 156; 158; 162; 165; 167; 169; 171; 183; 185–186; 190–191; 196–198; 205; 208; 210; 212; 221–223; 225–226; 231; 243; 260–261; 263
Kir'ad el-Baqq'ara South 183; 189; 241
Kiryat Shmona South 49; 169; 183; 185–186; 190; 240
Kom er-Rumman East 249
Kom Nebi 'Ira 251
Kom, el- 252
Korazin 242
Kufr Yuba, Tell 254
Kumidi (see also Kamid el-Loz, Tell) 19; 30; 206; 224; 239
Kurussa (see also Qarrasa South) 98; 250
Kutayba North, Tell el- 249
Kutayba South, Tell 250

Labwa (see also Qasr Labwa, Tell) 20–22; 33; 35; 219; 236
Labwa North 236
Labwa South, Tell 236
Lachish, Tel 12; 16; 213; 215; 222
Lawziyeh, Khirbet el- 183; 189; 241

Lebanese Beqaa 2; 9; 11; 16; 19–38; 150; 168; 192; 206–209; 211–212; 219; 222–223; 229; 235–236
Lebanon Mountains 19–20, 36–38
Lower Mesil Kharub 248

Ma'tarid Northeast, el- 254
Ma'tarid Southeast, el- 254
Mabara Southwest, el- 247
Mahada, el- 238
Majdalun, Tell 237
Majdub / Ayyub, Tell el- 238
Majid, Khirbet 252
Malah es-Sarrar (see also Malaha) 8
Malaha (see also Malah es-Sarrar) 8
Mamzie, Khirbet 239
Mapal haIrusim 245
Maqam Breja' 249
Maqna, Tell 237
Marah el-Wazza 236
Marj 'Ayyun 11; 19–20; 35; 39; 42; 221
Mas'ada 84; 244
Mas'ud, Tell 237
Masatib, el- 251
Mashav Northwest, Tel 183
Mashav, Tel 183; 241
Mashra' Seil Musa 243
Massiyye, el- West 248
Mathani, Tell el- 236
Medaura 'Ain el- 246
Medaura 'Elyon 'Ain el- 246
Megiddo, Tel 6–7; 12–15; 43; 46; 48; 51; 53–54; 69; 125; 137; 140; 149; 165; 167–168; 170–171; 173; 176–177; 192; 196; 207; 209–211; 213–217; 220–221; 229–230
Menorim, Horvat 77; 184; 186; 243
Merneptah 107; 198; 207
Metzad 'Ateret 241
Metzad en-Nazeryye 249
Metzad Hiv'ai 246
Metzad Metzokey Onn 248
Metzad Nahal Zavitan 'Elyon 245
Metzad Yonathan / Qasr Tannuriya 85; 246
Mezudat Honin, Horvat 239
Mifratz Amnon 242
Mitzpe Golani 84; 90; 205; 244
Mitzpor Negev Kinnerot 249
Mu'allaqa, Tell el- 252
Mughayir East, Khirbet el- 252; 128; 170
Mughayir, Khirbet el- 252; 127–128; 170; 240
Mughayyir, el- 244

Mujedda, Tell el- 8
Mumsiyyeh Southwest 244
Muqabarat Banat-Ya'qub 240
Murtaf'a ed-Durijat 245

Na'ama, Tel 240
Na'ran 245
Nab' Litani, Tell 237
Nab'a el-Mjahiyye 248
Nab'a et-Tu'eine Enclosure 248
Nab' el-Fa'ur, Tell 238
Naba', Tell en- 236
Nahal El-Al 'Elyon East 247
Nahal El-Al 'Elyon West 247
Nahal Hazor 241
Nahal Kinnar 'Elyon East 242
Nahal Makbram 240
Nahal Misgav 239
Nahr el-Litani 20; 33–34; 36–38
Najil 246
Najran South 250
Nazeryye, en- 249
Nes East, Tel 242
Nes, Tel 57; 59; 242
Nikhele North, en- 246
Nikhele West, en- 246
Nikhele, en- 246
Nimshi 8; 214
Nimshide Dynasty, 8 (see also Jehu)
Nov, Tel 85; 87–90; 93–95; 205; 247
Nuqra Plain 2; 8; 11; 86–87; 89; 95–115; 150; 166; 182; 192; 198; 206–207; 209; 211–212; 222–224; 228–229; 235; 249

Omri 46 (see also Omride Dynasty)
Omride Dynasty 7–8; 46; 54; 124; 173–174
Orontes River 20; 33; 34; 36–38

Pekah 33
Pella 216; 221
Philistia / Philistine Coast 167; 213
Phoenicia / Phoenician Coast 13–14; 24–25; 31; 34; 140; 168; 174; 189; 191; 194; 198; 225; 227; 229–231

Qabb Elyas, Tell 238
Qabba'a 241
Qal'at et-Tawil 245
Qalil, Tel 240
Qanawat 250
Qarnayim (see also Sheikh Sa'ad) 98; 250

Qarqur, Tell 9
Qarrasa South (see also Kurussa) 98; 110; 250
Qasile, Tell 13
Qasr el-Ghul 254
Qasr Labwa, Tell (see also Labwa) 21; 33; 35–38; 219; 236
Qata'an, Tell 239
Qatana, Khirbet 241
Qatu' esh-Sheikh 'Ali 247
Qatzrin 245
Qeiyafa, Khirbet 5
Qiswa, Tell 249
Qser Fu'ara, Khirbet el- 252
Quniyye, 'Ain 244
Qusayyibe, el- 247
Qusiba 'Ain el- 246
Qwayliba / Abila 118; 251

Rahib, Tell er- 238
Ramesses II 50; 99; 118; 127–128; 198–199; 207
Ramliyat, Khirbet er- 242
Ramtha 108; 123; 128; 245; 254
Ramthaniyye, er- 245
Ras Baalbek 236
Rasm el-'Abd East 246
Rawiyeh 244
Rayyaq, Tell 237
Razan'yye South 245
Razan'yye Southwest 245
Re'emim, Tel 240
Rehov, Tel 12; 14–15; 54; 125; 165; 168; 171; 196; 200; 213–216; 221; 227; 230
Rekhesh, Tel 68; 77; 211
Rezin 7; 10; 124; 220–221
Riha Station 237
Ron, Tel / Sheikh Yousef 240
Rosh Pinna 41; 56–59; 61–62; 150; 213; 216; 241–242
Rosh Pinna East 242
Rosh Zayit, Horvat 192; 196; 213; 215–216; 220–221
Rujm el-Hiri 85; 91; 93; 246
Rujm Fiq 248
Rumeith, Tell er- 116–117; 122–124; 128; 150–151; 166; 168–169; 191–192; 196; 205; 212; 215–216; 219–221; 225; 231; 254
Ruqqad River 8; 95; 97

Sa'ad East 248
Sa'ad West 248

Sa'ar, Horvat 82; 84; 243
Sa'uda 'Ain es- 237
Safa, Tell es- 183; 188–190; 241
Safi, Tell es- (see also Gath) 10; 15; 171; 213–214; 229
Sakhar, Horvat 242
Sahem el-Jawlan 107; 150; 190
Sahra East 246
Sakka, Tell 114–115
Sal 253
Salabe Southwest, es- 246
Salabe, es- 246
Salahiyah, Tell es- 114; 177–178; 182
Sama 252
Saman, Tell 250
Samar 251
Samaria 2–3; 5–7; 9; 11; 54; 100; 114; 137; 142; 148; 172–173; 176; 182; 193–194; 196; 200–201; 207; 213–214; 217; 220–221; 229; 232
Samaria Highlands 6; 9; 11; 142; 148; 182; 194; 195; 201; 207; 213–214; 217; 229; 231
Samoqa, Khirbet es- 253
Sanbariyeh, Khirbet 239
Satiya South, Tell 35; 238
Saufar, 'Ain 237
Sea of Galilee 2; 10–11; 63–84; 86–87; 89–90; 104; 150; 169; 176; 181–182; 195; 198; 206; 208–209; 212; 215–219; 222–228; 231–232; 235; 242
Sekher Yardinon South 244
Seluqie, Tell 94; 245
Sera', Tel 213
Seti I 107; 118; 198–199; 207
Seybi Southwest, Khirbet es- 247
Sha't, 'Ain 237
Shabbe 246
Shahaf, Tell / Abalis 240
Shalmaneser III 8; 11; 118; 128
Shaqra, Tell 249
Sharif, 'Ain 19; 33; 34; 237
Shechem (see also Balata, Tell) 5–6; 214
Sheikh Hussein East, Khirbet esh- 246
Sheikh Mahmud, esh- 240
Sheikh Marzuq, Tell 245
Sheikh Muhammad, esh- 246
Sheikh Sa'ad (see also Qarnayim) 87; 97–99; 109–113; 177–180; 198; 205; 207; 222; 250
Sheqaq, Tell esh- 254
Shihab, Tell esh- 97; 107–109; 118; 198; 207; 251 (see also Yeno'am)

Shishak / Shoshenq I 198; 209; 211; 213
Shkitan, 'Ein 239
Shuqayyif, Tell 77; 83–84; 86–87; 89; 91–94; 247
Siret ed-Diyab 35; 239
Sirhan, Tell es- 33; 208; 219; 238
Solomon 4–7; 53; 124; 173
Som 253
Soreg, Tel 72; 162; 183–186; 243
Sris, Khirbet 253
Subba, Tell es- 118; 127; 170; 253
Sugha, Tell 21; 236
Suhayliyya, Tell es- 249
Sultan East, Tell el- 114–115
Sultan West, Tell el- 114–115
Summaqa 244
Surman 244
Suwayda, es- 110; 148; 251

T'albaya, Tell 238
Ta'nayil, Tell 238
Tahunat et-Tabgha 239
Tannim North, Tel 239
Tannim, Tel 48; 58–59; 224–225; 239–240
Taruq 'Ain et- 88; 89; 94; 248
Tayinat, Tell 230
Tayyiba (in the Golan Heights) 246
Tayyiba (in the Nuqra Plain) (see also Tob) 100; 108–109; 111; 113; 251
Thaum Khirbet eth- 242
Thutmose III 67; 101
Tibaq, Khirbet et- 242
Tiglath-Pileser III 8; 10; 33; 56; 59; 67; 69; 98; 124; 219–220
Tineh 'Ain et- 240
Tirzah (see also Far'ah North, Tell el-) 213–214
Tlel 248
Tob (see also Tayyiba) 100; 108; 251
Tufah South, Khirbet 242
Tuqbul 128; 253
Tzomet haGome West 240
Tzuqey Kavarot 248

Umm el-Abar East, Khirbet 127; 255
Umm el-Abar West, Khirbet 255
Umm el-Adam, 'Ain 94; 248
Umm el-Ghuzlan, Khirbet 253
Umm el-Qubur 247

Wadi Balu'a 244

Wadi el-'Araghrah North
Wadi Halat el-Mughayir 240

Ya'af South, Tel 57; 241
Ya'af Southwest, Tel 242
Ya'af, Tel 241
Yarmouk River 97; 101; 117; 127; 181; 206
Yeno'am 107; 199; 208 (see also Shihab, Tell esh-)
Yoqne'am, Tel 7; 13; 211; 213; 215–216; 221
Yubla 251

Za'arta 244
Za'faran, Tell ez- 127; 252
Zaharet Soq'ah 254
Zayit, Tel 192; 213–214; 216; 221
Zeite, Horvat 247
Zeitun, Tell ez- 33; 86–87; 90; 239; 249

Index of Modern Authors

Abd el-Kader, D. 107; 178–179
Abou Assaf, A. 100–105; 108; 150; 167; 169; 184; 187; 210; 221
Abousamra, G. 21
Abu Dalu, R.120; 254
Aharoni, Y. 23; 55; 107; 208; 243
Aḥituv, S. 192; 227
Ahlström, G. 74
Ahrens, A. 23
Akkermans, P.M.M.G. 103; 106
Al-Bashaireh, K. 127
Albright, W.F. 65; 67; 78; 97–99; 101; 106–108; 120; 198; 216; 243; 251
Alexandre, Y. 57; 160; 192; 216; 221
al-Muhammad, Q. 106
al-Muheisen, Z. 127
Amadasi Guzzo, M.G. 201; 213; 227
Ambers, J. 122; 263
Amiran, R. 13–14; 55; 157
Arav, R. 122; 197; 263
Arie, E. 3; 7–8; 10; 13–16; 31; 39; 45–47; 56; 69; 77; 144–145
Aro, S. 99; 178–179
Aster, S.Z. 2
Avigad, N. 151; 179; 192; 197; 256–257; 261
Avshalom-Gorni, D. 48
Aznar, C. 225

Ballard, R.D. 194
Barako, T.J. 117; 123–125; 128; 151–152; 166; 168–169; 216; 222; 254
Baramki, D.C. 26–28; 169
Barkay, G. 97
Bastert, K. 126; 151
Bauckham, R. 70
Bechar, S. 51; 53; 155
Beck, P. 51; 70; 153; 159; 164
Ben-Ami, D. 4; 15; 40; 48–49; 51–54; 72; 135; 137; 141–143; 145–146; 150–158; 160; 162; 164–165; 168–171; 175; 177; 216; 218–219; 221; 224; 227; 240–241
Ben-Dor Evian, S. 211

Ben-Dov, R. 43
Ben-Shlomo, D. 14; 167; 168
Ben-Tor, A. 4; 7; 10; 13; 15; 39; 49–54; 135; 137; 141–143; 145–146; 150–158; 160; 162; 164–165; 168–171; 174–175; 177; 189; 207; 216; 218–221; 224; 227; 230; 235; 241; 258
Ben-Yosef, E. 1; 13; 103;
Benz, B.C. 51
Berger, U. 57; 154
Berlejung, A. 2; 6–8; 227; 230
Bernett, M. 135–136; 139; 148; 180–182
Betancourt, P.P. 174
Biran, A. 43–47; 135–137; 145; 148; 161; 174; 177; 195; 197; 199–200; 213; 218; 256–257
Bloch-Smith, E. 13; 190; 217
Blomquist, H.T. 200
Blum, E. 199; 213
Boaretto, E. 12; 14–15; 54; 263
Bonatz, D. 2; 20; 127
Bonfil, R. 42; 50; 135; 169; 192; 230; 256
Börker-Klähn, J. 175; 178–179
Bossert, H.T. 178–179
Bouzek, J. 99
Bowman, S. 122
Braemer, F. 8; 97–100; 107–109; 116; 235; 249–251
Brandl, B. 176; 180; 194; 256; 261
Braun, E. 184; 186; 211
Breasted, J.H. 198
Bron, F. 213
Bron, H. 88; 181–182; 247
Bronk Ramsey, C. 12; 14–15
Broshi, M. 222–224
Bryce, T. 1
Buhl, M-L. 159
Bunimovitz, S. 15; 58; 138; 141; 222
Bürge, T. 120; 184; 188
Burns, R. 114
Butler, H.C. 8

Cahill, J.M. 211; 216
Cantrell, D.O. 139; 177; 217
Caramelo, F. 54; 214
Carmi, I. 211
Cassuto, D. 78
Chambon, A. 142
Charvát, P. 99
Cline, E.H. 1; 5; 12
Cohen-Anidjar, S. 13; 151; 153; 155; 164; 169; 170; 216; 221
Cohen-Weinberger, A. 120; 155
Coldstream, N. 71; 168
Contenau, G. 99; 178–179
Cooper, K.B. 8; 192; 261
Copeland, L. 20–23; 25–26; 29; 32
Covello-Paran, K. 49; 169; 183; 185; 243
Crane, H.R. 124

Dajani, R.W. 120–121; 151; 158; 169–170; 184; 188;
Dalley, S. 229
Dar, S. 84
Daviau, M.P.M. 165
David, A. 42
Davis, A.R. 46–47; 137
Day, J. 74; 101
Dayan, Y. 40; 49; 56; 239–240
de Hulster, I. 1; 3; 11
Delavault, B. 191–192; 195; 227; 256–258
Dentzer, J.M. 109; 251
Dever, W.G. 4; 42; 49; 169
Dijkstra, N. 99
Dobbs-Allsopp, F.W. 191–192; 227; 257–259; 261
Dothan, M. 87
Dothan, T. 53
Doumet-Serhal, C. 26
Dunand, M. 179
Dunseth, Z.C. 198
Dušek, J. 11

Echt, R. 30; 144
Edelstein, G. 158; 188; 216
Edwards, P.C. 216; 221
Ehrig, H. 20
Eitam, D. 217
Eph'al, I. 29
Epstein, C. 65; 70; 82; 84–88; 94; 242–243; 246
Eshel, E. 192

Fantalkin, A. 5; 12; 14; 168–171; 183; 221;
Faßbeck, G. 163
Faust, A. 2–3; 5; 14; 135; 138–139; 141; 183; 221–222
Finkelstein, I. 1; 3; 5–16; 21; 23; 26; 28; 33; 39; 43; 46–47; 50–54; 56; 59; 71; 73; 76; 82; 97; 101; 108–110; 114; 116; 120; 123–125; 127–128; 137–139; 143; 149; 155; 158; 161; 168; 173–174; 177; 191–192; 200; 207–215; 217–218; 220; 222–224; 227; 230; 235
Fischer, P.M. 107; 120; 150; 156; 184; 188; 190; 210; 221; 250
Fischer-Genz, B. 20
Frankel, R. 40; 223
Franklin, N. 6; 46; 173; 214
Freikman, M. 86
Frevel, C. 2; 6; 9; 39; 199; 213–214; 216–217; 219–220
Fritz, V. 67–69; 141; 143; 150; 153; 156; 158; 162; 165; 169; 197; 208; 210; 221–223; 260–262

Gadot, Y. 5–6; 135; 164; 173; 223–224; 240
Gal, Z. 160; 192; 216; 221
Galil, G. 118; 199; 208
Galling, K. 179
Garfinkel, Y. 5; 15; 54; 192; 260
Genz, H. 20; 22–25; 150; 167–169; 183; 185; 237
Georgiadou, A. 28; 120
Getzov, N. 48
Geva, H. 222
Geva, S. 53
Ghantous, H. 6; 9–10; 47; 199; 213
Gilboa, A. 12–14; 28; 31; 54–56; 120; 155; 167–168; 175; 217; 230
Gilibert, A. 177; 182; 230
Gitin, S. 229
Giveon, R. 99
Glueck, N. 117–118; 122; 125; 127; 220; 235; 251; 254
Golani, A. 73–74; 84; 90; 184; 186; 205; 243; 244
Golding-Meir, R. 214
Golub, M. 195
Goren, Y. 21; 23; 26; 43; 82; 101; 108–109; 120; 127; 194
Grayson, A.K. 8–9
Greenberg, R. 63
Greenfield, J.C. 114

Greer, J.S. 47–48; 192; 200; 257
Griffin, J.B. 124
Guérin, V.M. 65; 67; 70
Gur-Arieh, S. 213
Gutman, S. 65; 70; 82; 84–88

Hachlili, R. 87
Hachmann, R. 30
Hafthorsson, S. 6–7; 9; 98–99; 118; 199; 213
Halbertsma, D.J.H. 228
Halpern, B. 199
Hanbury-Tenison, J.W. 116
Harrison, A. 49; 169
Harrison, T.P. 176; 198; 209
Hartal, M. 57; 82; 84–85; 89; 169; 221
Harush, O. 160
Hasegawa, S. 6–10; 47; 74–75; 98; 141; 177; 213; 218–219
Häser, J. 116–117; 210
Hawkins, J.D. 155; 208
Hegeneuer, S. 173
Heinz, M. 19; 30–31; 144; 150; 169; 192; 239
Herbert, S. 49
Hermann, V.R. 173
Herr, L.G. 10; 116
Herzog, Z. 5; 14–15; 50; 54; 56; 77
Hill, A. 58
Hindawi, A.-N. 116
Hockmann, D. 126; 151
Holladay, J.S. 170
Homsher, R.S. 12; 14; 177
Horowitz, A. 174

Ilan, D. 4; 40; 43; 45–49; 53; 58; 67; 144–145; 150; 153; 156; 158; 161–162; 164–169; 200; 210; 217; 224–225; 239–240; 245; 262
Irvine, S.A. 220
Isserlin, B.S. 179

Janaydeh, K. 118; 182
Ji, C.C.-H. 141; 143
Joffe, A.H. 3
Joudah, A.H. 3
Joukowsky, M.S. 1; 5; 26–29; 150; 168–169; 210

Kafafi, Z. 120; 150; 188; 254
Kafri, A. 28; 155; 158; 215
Kahn, D. 213
Kamlah, J. 94; 117–118; 127–128; 170; 235–236; 252–254

Kaniewski, D.E. 110; 262
Kaplan, A. 46; 137
Katz, H. 11; 14
Kersel, M.M. 58
Killebrew, A.E. 43; 137; 139; 161
Kislev, M.E. 71
Kleiman, A. 3; 7; 10; 12–15; 28; 46; 50; 54–56; 63; 65–67; 70–72; 77; 88; 120; 137; 139; 141; 145–171; 176–177; 181–182; 188; 192–194; 197; 200–201; 208–211; 213–218; 221–228; 235; 243; 247; 261
Kleiman, S. 13; 54; 56; 176; 200–201; 218; 222
Kletter, R. 4; 11; 141; 174; 222; 240
Knapp, B.A. 1; 5
Knauf, E.A. 3; 119; 123
Koch, I. 5; 10; 73; 116; 127; 192; 198; 228
Kochavi, M. 4; 10; 51; 70–74; 139; 177; 184; 186; 208; 216
Kopcke. G. 71; 168
Kourou, N. 171
Kreimerman, I. 209
Kropp, A. 106–107
Kulemann-Ossen, S. 31

Lagarce, B. 199
Lamon, R.S. 46; 177
Lamprichs, R. 117; 126; 151; 170; 221; 254
Lapp, N.L. 117; 124; 123; 128; 192; 254; 261
Lapp, P. 123
Lederman, Z. 5; 15
Lee, S. 12; 15
Lehmann, G. 5; 10; 14; 21–23; 26; 28; 43; 98; 101; 103; 115; 137; 139; 154; 183; 185–186; 190; 214; 235
Lemaire, A. 4; 6–8; 98; 127; 191–192; 195; 199; 213; 227; 256
Lemos, I.S. 168
Lenzen, C.J. 119–122
Leonard, A. 117; 126–127; 254–255
Levin, C. 219
Levy, E. 198
Levy, S. 158; 216
Levy, T.E. 1
Lipiński, E. 1; 6–8; 10; 19; 25; 29; 34; 98; 108; 118; 213–214; 216; 229
Lipschits, O. 10; 73; 116; 123–125; 127–128; 173–174; 176; 192; 218

Ma'oz, U.Z. 88; 94

Index of Modern Authors

Maeir, A.M. 2–3; 5; 10; 14–15; 63; 171; 192; 213–214; 219
Malena, S. 191
Mare, W.H. 118
Marfoe, L. 3; 19–23; 25–26; 29–32; 150; 210; 235–239
Martin, M.A.S. 153; 156; 167
Master, D.M. 3; 216
Matthews, K. 122
Mazar, A. 5; 8; 12–15; 54; 141; 151; 153; 155; 157; 164–165; 170–171; 174; 192; 200; 209; 214; 216–217; 221; 227; 235
Mazar, B. 4; 9–10; 74–78; 141; 150; 162; 169; 176; 261
Mazzoni, S. 9
Mcgovern, P.E. 119
Meitlis, Y. 87; 88; 247
Mendel, A. 192; 194; 197; 257
Meynersen, M. 99
Millek, J.M. 1; 51
Milson, D. 138
Mittmann, S. 117–119; 128; 235; 251–255
Miyazaki, S. 74
Mizrachi, Y. 85–86
Mohammad, Q. 106–107
Mommsen, H. 169
Montero Fenollos, J.-L. 54; 214
Mullins, R.A. 32; 42–43; 53; 169; 239; 256
Münger, S. 13; 67–69; 145–146; 150; 159; 165; 171; 183; 185–186; 209; 230; 243; 262
Mynářová, J. 11

Na'aman, N. 1; 5–10; 14–15; 19; 21–23; 25–26; 43; 46–47; 50–51; 63; 65; 82; 89; 94–95; 101; 107–110; 120; 127; 192; 199; 206; 211–213; 216–217; 220; 229
Najjar, M. 1; 116
Nam, R.S. 3
Naveh, J. 195; 197; 199; 213; 227; 257–260
Niehr, H. 6; 9; 229–230
Niemann, H.M. 3; 5; 14; 214
Nissinen, M. 165
Norris, F.A. 8
Núñez, F.J. 29

Oded, B. 208
Onn, A. 48; 248
Ornan, T. 145; 180–181
Orthmann, W. 177; 179; 182
Osborne, J.F. 1; 3; 11; 153; 164; 173; 230
Ottosson, M. 118–119; 143

Pakkala, J. 10; 13; 67–68; 82; 94; 118; 127; 146; 209; 216–217
Panitz-Cohen, N. 12; 42–43; 53; 120; 168–169; 192; 211; 216; 220–221; 229; 239; 256
Parker, B.J. 11
Paz, I. 74–75; 141; 211
Paz, S. 120
Paz, Y. 74
Pfoh, E. 1; 3
Piasetzky, E. 12–16; 71; 168; 209–210; 218
Pioske, D. 6
Pitard, W.T. 6; 9–10; 114; 213
Porat, N. 86
Porter, J.L. 178
Pratico, G.D. 220
Pritchard, J.B. 194
Pucci, M. 159; 164; 171

Radner, K. 219
Rainey, A.F. 9; 19; 23; 34; 94; 206
Rapuano, Y. 73
Rast, W.E. 216; 221
Reimer, P.J. 263
Renz, J. 191–192; 256–257; 259–261
Richelle, M. 214; 218
Riis, P.J. 159; 189
Rohmer, J. 8; 97–101; 105–109; 116; 143; 148; 150; 166; 182; 221; 223; 230; 235; 249–251
Röllig, W. 191–192; 213; 256–257; 259–261
Rollston, C.A. 191–193
Routledge, B. 3; 13; 135; 228
Rowan, Y.M. 58
Rowe, A. 67; 78; 198
Rubiato, M.-T. 51

Sader, H. 2; 8; 11; 14; 19–20; 22–29; 34; 99; 109; 150; 167–169; 183; 185; 229–230; 237;
Sandhaus, D. 4; 15; 49; 51–54; 135; 137; 141–143; 145–146; 150–158; 160; 162; 164–165; 168–171; 175; 177; 189; 216; 218–219; 221; 224; 227; 241
Sapir, Y. 5; 103; 139
Sapir-Hen, L. 103
Sass, B. 14; 179–180; 191–192; 195; 197; 199; 201; 208; 227; 256–257; 259; 261
Sauer, J.A. 116; 120; 235
Savage, C. 197; 261
Schäfer-Lichtenberger, C. 51
Schipper, B.U. 198; 211; 229

Schloen, J.D. 3
Schmid, K. 9
Schniedewind, W.M. 199
Schreiber, N. 14; 168
Schroer, S. 175; 179
Schumacher, G. 82; 98–99; 104; 106; 109; 137; 198
Schwartz, G.M. 5; 103; 106
Scott, E.M. 71; 168; 210; 262–263
Seeden, H. 109
Segal, D. 211
Segal, O. 84–85; 169; 211; 244
Sergi, O. 1; 3; 5–8; 10–11; 14; 50; 56; 63; 66; 71; 123–125; 128; 135; 173; 192; 200; 208; 216–218; 226; 235
Seyrig, H. 107
Shai, I. 3; 5; 14–15; 78; 219
Sharon, I. 13; 15; 28; 43; 46; 51; 66; 71; 120; 137–139; 168; 210–217; 262–263
Shiloh, Y. 138; 141; 143; 173–174; 176
Shipton, G.M. 46; 177
Shochat, H. 14–15; 54–56; 155; 175
Shoval, S. 77; 153; 159–160; 164
Shuster, R. 160
Siddall, L.R. 9
Silberman, N.A. 5
Singer-Avitz, L. 5; 8; 14–15; 28; 50; 54; 56; 69; 77; 120; 158; 164; 221
Slayton, J.C. 96
Smith, G.A. 118; 198
Smith, R.H. 22
Soennecken, K. 117
Stager, L.E. 3; 45; 141; 222
Steiner, R.C. 22
Stepansky, Y. 40; 42; 56–58; 64; 150; 183; 189; 208; 211; 216; 223; 236; 240–241
Stern, E. 12–13
Stoever, E.R. 8
Strange, J. 117–119; 167; 169; 253
Stubbings, F.H. 106
Sugimoto, D.T. 47; 63; 74–76; 141; 150; 156; 162; 170; 177; 210; 263

Tadmor, H. 10; 98; 101; 220–221
Tappy, R. 6
Taraqji, A. 114–115; 199
Tenu, A. 189; 229
Thareani, Y. 3–4; 10; 16; 43; 47–48; 160; 174; 176–177; 200; 220–222; 230; 235
Thomas, Z. 3
Thompson, H.O. 96

Thomsen, I. 209
Thureau-Dangin, F. 177; 179
Toffolo, M.B. 12–13; 15; 211; 216
Trigger, B. 174
Tynjä, T. 53; 68–69; 150; 153; 156; 158; 162; 165; 167; 169; 210
Tzin, B. 88; 181–182; 247

Ussishkin, D. 12; 14; 137; 176; 179; 192; 211; 213
Uziel, J. 5; 78; 164

Van der Heyden, S. 173
Van der Osten, H.H. 115
Van Ess, M. 19–20; 22–23; 25–26; 29; 34
Vanderhooft, D.S. 192
Vanvalkenburgh, P. 3
Varoner, O. 184–196; 190
Vieweger, D. 116–117; 210
Vogel, J.C. 104; 207; 210; 263

Wagner-Durand, E. 30; 34
Waldbaum, J.C. 168
Wampler, J.C. 164
Ward, W.A. 1; 5; 46
Waterbolk, H.T. 104; 207; 210
Watzinger, C. 209
Weeden, M. 1; 154–155; 208
Weinstein, J.M. 99; 107; 124
Weksler-Bdolah, S. 87; 88; 170; 247
Wescombe, P.J. 20–23; 25–26; 29; 32
Wightman, G.J. 5; 198
Wilde, E.M. 210
Wimmer, S.J. 99; 118; 182; 198
Winn, S.M.M. 67; 185
Winter, I.J. 74; 175; 178–179
Wolff, S.R. 45; 73–74; 184; 186; 243
Woodhead, J. 14
Workman, V. 229

Yadin, E. 70–71; 153; 159; 164; 198
Yadin, Y. 39; 49; 51–55; 135–138; 141–146; 148; 150; 153; 156; 158; 171; 174–175; 177; 192; 194; 197; 206; 218–219; 227
Yahalom-Mack, N. 7; 42 43; 138; 145–146; 192; 197; 220; 228–230; 239; 256; 262
Yakar, J. 67; 185
Yamada, S. 8; 10; 98; 101; 199; 213; 220–221
Yasur-Landau, A. 185; 209; 240
Younger, K.L. 1; 6–9; 19; 21; 47; 73; 98–99; 101; 103; 114–115; 208; 212–213; 216; 218

Zangenberg, J. 13; 68; 146; 209
Zarzecki-Peleg, A. 13; 43; 46; 50; 135; 137–138; 151; 153; 155; 164; 169–170; 198; 211; 216; 221; 230
Zevit, Z. 229
Zimhoni, O. 28; 155; 158; 215
Zingboym, O. 84; 86; 244
Zuckerman, S. 40; 49–51; 167; 230
Zukerman, A. 167; 169; 171
Zwickel, W. 6–8; 10; 63; 88; 94; 96; 115; 118; 165; 200; 209; 219; 222; 235; 240; 244; 251–255

Oriental Religions in Antiquity

Egypt, Israel, Ancient Near East

Edited by
Angelika Berlejung (Leipzig)
Nils P. Heeßel (Marburg)
Joachim Friedrich Quack (Heidelberg)

Advisory Board
Uri Gabbay (Jerusalem)
Michael Blömer (Aarhus)
Christopher Rollston (Washington, D.C.)
Rita Lucarelli (Berkeley)

The series, founded in 2009, shows that interdisciplinary collaboration and individual research in the fields of Old Testament/Palestine studies, Assyriology and Egyptology, have experienced a considerable revival in the last decades. The aim of this series is to create a forum for the issues pertaining to the history of religion in these fields by encouraging scholars to share their findings and by creating a space for innovative developments and approaches. With its specialized individual studies, its more diversified volumes of essays plus its conference volumes on individual subjects on the history of religion, it is ORA's goal to trigger discussions in the appropriate disciplines.

ISSN: 1869-0513
Suggested citation: ORA

All published volumes at *www.mohrsiebeck.com/ora*

Mohr Siebeck
www.mohrsiebeck.com